The Birth of the Irish Free State 1921-1923

ATLANTIC
OCEAN

**NORTHERN
IRELAND**

Londonderry
LONDONDERRY

DONEGAL

Larne
ANTRIM

Bangor

TYRONE

Belfast

Dungannon

Lisburn

FERMANAGH

ARMAGH

DOWN

Sligo

LEITRIM

MONAGHAN

SLIGO

Newry

CAVAN

Dundalk

MAYO

ROSCOMMON

LONGFORD

LOUTH

MEATH

Drogheda

IRISH
SEA

WESTMEATH

GALWAY

Athlone

DUBLIN

Galway

OFFALY

KILDARE

Dublin

Kingstown

WICKLOW

LEIX

Wicklow

**IRISH
FREE
STATE**

CLARE

CARLOW

Kilkenny

Limerick

TIPPERARY

KILKENNY

LIMERICK

WEXFORD

Clonmel

Kilmallock

Wexford

Tralee

Waterford

WATERFORD

KERRY

CORK

Cork

Queenstown

Beal na mBlath

ST. GEORGE'S
CHANNEL

0   20   40

MILES

IRELAND IN 1922

SHOWING THE

TWENTY-SIX COUNTIES OF THE IRISH FREE STATE AND

THE SIX COUNTIES OF NORTHERN IRELAND

JOSEPH M. CURRAN

The Birth of the Irish Free State 1921-1923

The University of Alabama Press
University, Alabama

SECOND PRINTING 1981

Library of Congress Cataloging in Publication Data

Curran, Joseph Maroney, 1932–
  The birth of the Irish Free State, 1921–1923.

  Bibliography: p.
  Includes index.
  1. Ireland—History—1910–1921. 2. Ireland—
History—Civil War, 1922–1923. I. Title.
DA960.C87   941.5082'2   79-4088
ISBN 0-8173-0013-9

Contents

Preface

More than half a century has passed since Ireland won freedom at the cost of partition and civil war. During that time, much has been written about the revolution of 1916–1923, because of its historic importance and enduring popular appeal. Not surprisingly, most of this attention has centered on the struggle with Great Britain rather than its immediate aftermath, when issues seem to lose clarity and drama turns to tragedy. Yet what happened in the revolution's final phase, from 1921 to 1923, has largely determined the course of Irish history and Anglo-Irish relations over the past fifty years.

In this book, I have tried to write a comprehensive and balanced account of that period, analyzing in detail both the background and the impact of the Treaty of 1921. If my work provides a fuller understanding of the conflicting forces that created—and almost destroyed—the Irish Free State, I will have succeeded in the task I set myself as a historian.

Acknowledgments

Credit for this book, although not blame for any of its shortcomings, must be shared with many people, some of whose contributions deserve explicit recognition. Grants from the Faculty Research Committee of Le Moyne College greatly facilitated my work. I also should like to thank for their assistance the staffs of the Public Record Office (London), the Beaverbrook Library (London), the Special Collections Division of the University of Birmingham Library, the Archives of University College, Dublin, and, most of all, the National Library of Ireland. Almost all the Irishmen whom I interviewed about the events described in this volume are now dead, but the history that they made, they brought to life for me, and I can only hope that I have been able to transmit some of that vitality to the reader. The late Charles Loch Mowat, my mentor in graduate school at the University of Chicago, first aroused my interest in Irish history, and I will be grateful always for his inspiration. Professor Kevin B. Nowlan of University College, Dublin helped me to obtain access to the rich collection of General Richard Mulcahy's papers. Professor Thomas E. Hachey of Marquette University read my manuscript and made several useful suggestions. Mrs. Joyce Bell did a superb job typing it. Over many years, Alf MacLochlainn, Director of the National Library of Ireland, has proved himself the best of friends as well as the most helpful of guides. Finally, I am most deeply indebted to Professor Lawrence J. McCaffrey of Loyola University, Chicago. Like many others in the field of Irish studies, I have benefited immensely from his encouragement and advice. If this book has a patron, it is surely he.

JOSEPH M. CURRAN
Syracuse, New York

For permission to quote from various documents, the following acknowledgments are due:

The Controller of H. M. Stationery Office for extracts from Crown-copyright material in the Public Record Office, London (Records of the Cabinet Office).

The Keeper of State Papers for extracts from documents relating to the Anglo-Irish Treaty negotiations of 1921 in the State Paper Office, Dublin Castle (Dail Eireann files, DE 2/304).

The First Beaverbrook Foundation for extracts from the Lloyd George papers.

The Sub-Librarian, Special Collections Division, University of Birmingham Library for extracts from the Austen Chamberlain papers.

To the memory of my mother

Margaret Maroney Curran

and of my father,

John William Curran,

For their Faith, Hope, and Love

Chapter 1
The Seedbed of
Revolution: 1890-1914

Notwithstanding popular hopes and politicians' promises during World War I, victory in "the war to end war," did not usher in a golden age for Great Britain. The collapse of the postwar boom in 1920 left tens of thousands of workers to survive on the dole. In continental Europe, the situation was even worse, while overseas, much of the Empire seethed with unrest. On top of everything else there was Ireland. Trouble in Ireland was nothing new, but by 1921 it was worse than at any time in living memory. Although an armed rising had been quickly crushed in 1916, a Republican government, supported by a guerrilla army, had arisen from the ashes of defeat, confronting Britain with a new version of an age-old problem that seemed to defy solution.

The roots of the "Irish Question" can be found as far back as the twelfth century, when England began the conquest of its neighbor, but the legislative union between the two countries in 1801 put the problem in its modern context, both clarifying and aggravating it. From its inception, Irish nationalists opposed the Union. Extremists sought to undo it by force, but the constitutional methods of Daniel O'Connell and his successors proved more popular and effective in asserting Ireland's claims. Pioneering new tactics of political agitation, O'Connell used them to win Catholic Emancipation in 1829, the nationalists' first major victory. Building on the foundations laid by O'Connell, Charles Stewart Parnell rallied the support of Irish-Americans, land-hungry peasants, and an ambitious middle class to create a highly disciplined party, which secured substantial concessions from Britain in the 1880s. The success of Parnell's campaign for an Irish Parliament seemed assured when Gladstone committed the Liberal Party to Home Rule for Ireland. However, Liberal dissidents joined Conservative Unionists to defeat Home Rule in 1886, and Parnell's fall from power four years later (the result of a divorce scandal) ended any hope of its enactment for a generation. In the two decades following 1886, Unionist governments did their best to bury Home Rule by combining coercion with various reforms, notably a series of measures which facilitated tenants' purchase of their farms.

By the time they left office at the end of 1905, the Unionists appeared to have achieved their aim, for Ireland seemed quiet and reasonably content. Yet, as was so often the case with Ireland, appearances were deceiving. Since the Union, alienation and oppression had given Irish nationalism a life of its own, independent of the grievances which had created it. British reforms came too late to extirpate this nationalism, and new ideas that nourished it boded ill for the Union.

In the barren years following Parnell's fall, many young people turned away from politics, and some of them found an outlet for their energy and idealism in the promotion of native culture. In 1893, scholars founded the Gaelic League to revive the moribund Irish language, and it soon became the spearhead of the Irish-Ireland movement, whose dedicated members scorned the prevailing materialism and cultural conformity which they dubbed "West Britonism." Complementing the work of the Gaelic League was a literary renaissance, which found its inspiration in ancient Celtic legends as well as contemporary Irish life. While both the literary and the linguistic movements were nonpolitical, their retelling of heroic myths and idealization of the Gael helped plant the seeds of revolution in Ireland's "four green fields."

A radical faction of Irish labor expressed a different kind of protest in the early years of the twentieth century. Unskilled and unorganized, the majority of Irish workers suffered from high unemployment, low wages, and some of the worst housing conditions in Europe. Two dynamic leaders, James Larkin and James Connolly, set out to change this. In 1909 Larkin founded the Irish Transport and General Workers' Union, which grew rapidly as it fought to secure social justice for an exploited proletariat. A strike against the Dublin Tramway Company in 1913 was countered by a lockout of union members and sympathizers in the city. After a bitter five-month dispute reduced them to abject poverty, the workers returned to their jobs. Although the transport union was not destroyed, it had suffered a major defeat, and so had the labor movement.

The struggle against capitalism played an important part in the growth of aggressive nationalism. Many Irish strikers felt that their defeat was caused by withdrawal of support by British trade unions, and this conviction intensified their hostility to Britain. Larkin's principal lieutenant, James Connolly, was now certain that there could be no social revolution in Ireland until armed revolt freed the country from British rule, which he regarded as the main bulwark of Irish capitalism. Organization of the Irish Citizen Army in October 1913 reflected increasing labor militancy. The ICA, a small force established to protect strikers from police brutality, was not representative of Ireland's predominantly moderate labor force, but its profession of separatist as well as socialist ideals made it part of the advanced nationalist movement. Connolly was the ICA's moving spirit, and when Larkin went to the United States in October 1914 to raise funds, he was left in charge of both the union and the army.[1]

The most important political organization in the advanced nationalist movement was Arthur Griffith's Sinn Fein. Born in Dublin in 1871, Griffith was a printer and journalist who expounded his ideas for winning national freedom in a series of newspapers he published and edited between 1898 and 1916. In November 1905 Griffith promulgated his program of national self-reliance, calling it *Sinn Fein* (We Ourselves), and by 1908, several nationalist groups had formed an organization with that name which embodied Griffith's ideas. Sinn Fein called for aggressive but nonviolent action to obtain Ireland's liberation. Irish MPs were to abandon Westminster and establish a national assembly, which would create an Irish executive, civil service, and system of arbitration courts, as well as reform education, promote native culture, and develop the economy. National initiative and determination would force Britain to recognize Ireland's independence, and once this was done, tariff protection would foster industrialization.

Although personally a separatist, that is, a republican, Griffith's goal was not an Irish Republic. Instead he sought a dual monarchy, similar to that of Austria-Hungary, demanding the return of the legislative independence enjoyed by Ireland before the Union of 1801. Although this compromise was designed to win the support of Irish Unionists and Home Rulers, Republicans persuaded Griffith to make it Sinn Fein's minimum demand, with the clear understanding that its achievement would not prejudice separatist claims. Whatever his views on Ireland's ultimate constitutional status, Griffith firmly opposed armed revolt to win freedom, on the grounds that Britain could easily crush any insurrection. For him, passive resistance, coupled with active support of a native government, was the only viable alternative to sterile parliamentarianism and futile uprisings.

Despite Griffith's imaginative program and forceful propaganda, Sinn Fein was never a serious rival to the Home Rule Party before the First World War. Griffith had no desire to be a political leader, and his blunt words and dictatorial manner alienated many potential supporters. More important, his program did not appeal to Irish farmers or businessmen, who were heavily dependent on the British market, or to most workers, who opposed Griffith's strong commitment to capitalism. Even political developments worked against Sinn Fein, as events before the First World War brought a dramatic revival in the fortunes of the Irish Parliamentary Party. Sinn Fein's importance lay chiefly in serving as a school of advanced nationalist ideas for politically conscious members of the Irish-Ireland movement.[2]

The militant nationalism stimulated by the Gaelic revival and Sinn Fein was eventually translated into armed rebellion by leaders of the Irish Republican Brotherhood. Founded in Dublin and New York in 1858 by veterans of an abortive uprising a decade before, the IRB was a secret

society dedicated to the overthrow of British rule. Members were popularly known as Fenians (ancient Irish warriors), the name originally
given the American branch, and it was this organization that gave the
movement real significance. Access to a large and growing Irish-
American community enabled the Fenian Brotherhood and its successor, the Clan na Gael, to supply fellow militants at home with funds and
to exploit the Irish Question in Anglo-American relations.

After the collapse of an attempted insurrection in 1867 the IRB was
reorganized, and in its 1873 constitution pledged that it would not make
war without the Irish people's approval. In the meantime, the IRB
would support every movement for independence that was consistent
with preservation of its own integrity. However, this more moderate
approach did not abate opposition from the Roman Catholic hierarchy,
which condemned both the character and the aims of Fenianism.

Despite some reservations, the Clan na Gael supported Parnell, but the
IRB's Supreme Council did not, and inaction left the Brotherhood
moribund by the turn of the century. Soon afterward, however, energetic young separatists set out to revitalize the organization with the aid
of a veteran Fenian, Tom Clarke, and the powerful head of the Clan na
Gael, John Devoy. Their successful struggle for control was accompanied by an intensive recruiting and propaganda campaign. Many of
the society's carefully chosen 2,000 members were placed in key positions in various Irish-Ireland organizations, where they worked to further separatist aims.[3]

When British political strife revived the issue of Home Rule, it precipitated a constitutional crisis which threatened to end in civil war. After
Gladstone's retirement in 1894, the Liberals soft-pedaled Home Rule,
and the question played no part in their sweeping electoral victory in
1906. But four years later, a parliamentary deadlock over the powers of
the House of Lords necessitated two general elections, and the Liberal
government sought Irish support. John Redmond, the Irish Parliamentary Party's leader, agreed to give it in return for assurance that
the Liberals would limit the Lords' veto power and enact Home Rule if
the Liberal Party were returned to office. When a heavy loss of seats
made the government dependent on Irish votes for survival, Home Rule
seemed certain.

In 1911, Prime Minister Asquith secured passage of the Parliament
Act, which sharply curtailed the powers of the upper house. Early the
next year, he introduced a Home Rule Bill conferring very limited powers of self-government on Ireland. Under the terms of the Parliament
Act, this bill would become law in two years, despite its inevitable rejection by the Unionist-controlled House of Lords. With the resources of
parliamentary opposition fast running out, the Unionists resorted to
unconstitutional methods to defeat Home Rule, contending these tactics

were justified because of the bill's alleged pernicious character, especially its threat to Protestant loyalists in the province of Ulster.

Until the early seventeenth century, Ulster was the last stronghold of Gaelic Ireland, but after the defeat and flight of the northern province's rebel chieftains, the Crown confiscated their lands and colonized them with Scots and English settlers. In the struggle between Parliament and the Stuart kings, Ulster's Protestant colonists generally supported Parliament while Irish Catholics favored the Crown. The culmination of this constitutional conflict in Ireland came with the defeat of James II's Catholic forces by William of Orange in 1690 (the Battle of the Boyne). The symbolic importance of this victory was underlined a century later when Irish Protestants founded the Orange Order to help perpetuate their ascendancy over the Catholic majority.

In the eighteenth century, discrimination by the Anglican establishment led many Ulster Presbyterians to emigrate to America, where they played an important role in overthrowing British rule. Similarly inspired by republican and egalitarian ideals, some of their coreligionists at home rose in rebellion against Britain in 1798. However, continuing conflict with Catholics over land and religion kept most Ulster Presbyterians loyal to the government during this crisis. The rebellion was thus largely confined to the south and west, and the excesses committed by oppressed Catholic peasants sharpened sectarian fears and hatreds.

Whatever resentment was felt in Ulster at the Union of 1801 was dispelled by rapid economic development in the century that followed. Shipbuilding, engineering, and textile manufacture made the city of Belfast a great industrial center, with close ties to Britain. At the same time, removal of the political and religious grievances of Presbyterians and other Dissenters enabled Protestants to form a united front against the growing threat of Catholic nationalism. Convinced that Catholics were an ignorant and superstitious rabble, ruled by priests and demagogues, Ulster Unionists insisted that Home Rule meant Rome Rule and financial ruin for them. The small but influential minority of Protestant landlords and businessmen in southern Ireland felt the same way and joined their northern coreligionists in voicing determined opposition to an Irish Parliament.

British Unionists were as strongly opposed to Home Rule as their Irish counterparts and employed a wide range of arguments against it. On the one hand, they maintained that Irish nationalism was an artificial creation; only English rule had given Ireland political unity, and its people were much more English than Celtic in language and culture. At the same time, they claimed that the Irish were racially inferior, priest ridden, incapable of self-government, and animated only by hostility toward Britain. Home Rule was therefore not only unjustifiable but unworkable. Moreover, its enactment would encourage the Irish to press for complete separation and would stimulate agitation by other subject peoples in the Empire, threatening both British security and imperial unity.

In their fight against Home Rule, British Unionists exploited the issue of Ulster because the idea of protecting its large loyalist population had much more popular appeal than support of the small and privileged minority in the rest of Ireland. Furthermore, they believed that Home Rule could not succeed without Belfast's wealth and industry, a conviction shared by nationalist leaders. However, as their opposition to Home Rule was largely motivated by British fears and interests, most Conservatives did not seek special treatment for Ulster since such an arrangement would deprive them of their strongest argument against Home Rule.[4]

As soon as the Liberals made clear their intention to enact Home Rule, Ulster Unionists took action. Under the flamboyant leadership of Sir Edward Carson, a highly successful barrister and Irish MP, they held a series of mass meetings in the autumn of 1911, pledging to resist Home Rule to the death. To lend weight to these protests, loyalists also organized a militia, the Ulster Volunteer Force, in 1912.

Where Carson led, Andrew Bonar Law, the newly elected leader of the Conservative Party, was quick to follow. A dour businessman turned politician, Law was of Ulster descent and unshakably committed to its cause. In July 1912 he publicly declared that if an attempt were made to force Home Rule on Ulster, "I can imagine no length of resistance to which Ulster can go in which I should not be prepared to support them, and in which, in my belief, they would not be supported by the overwhelming majority of the British people."[5]

Prime Minister Asquith could not believe that such threats were meant seriously, and initially regarded the whole opposition campaign as a gigantic bluff. But continued defiance soon made it appear that the Unionists were not bluffing. And if they were not, the government and its nationalist allies could trigger civil war by enacting Home Rule.

Neither side gave way in the two years which followed introduction of the Home Rule Bill, and tension mounted dangerously. In November 1913, nationalists organized their own militia, the Irish Volunteers, to support Redmond's demand for a united Ireland. Although the public initiative for formation of this body came from a moderate nationalist, Professor Eoin MacNeill, the IRB was the real moving force. Its Supreme Council realized the value of an open military organization to promote independence, and used moderates to create one in order to minimize the risk of British interference. MacNeill became head of the Irish Volunteers, but the IRB exerted a large measure of control by placing its own men in key positions in the new force. Once the organization demonstrated its popularity, Redmond endorsed it, and by September 1914 the Irish Volunteers numbered about 200,000 men, twice the size of the rival force in Ulster.

As the political situation deteriorated, the government sought an escape from its predicament, and excluding Ulster from Home Rule seemed the only way out. In the fall of 1913 Asquith explored this possibility with Law. Unsure that the Conservatives could win a general election on the issue of Home Rule, Law was willing to accept exclusion for Ulster, and so was Carson. Redmond reluctantly agreed to consider the idea, but negotiations soon bogged down on questions of the area and duration of exclusion.

Ulster's argument for exclusion was its Protestant majority—but the province contained a very large Catholic minority. In fact, Catholics constituted a majority in five of Ulster's nine counties. Their majority was overwhelming in Donegal, Cavan, and Monaghan, and small but indisputable in Fermanagh and Tyrone. Protestants outnumbered Catholics by substantial margins in Antrim, Down, Armagh, and Londonderry; their stronghold was the city of Belfast, 75 percent of whose inhabitants were Protestants.[6]

The suggestion of partition was not a solution to the Irish problem in 1913–14 but only an indication of its difficulty. Even if party leaders had been able to work out a compromise on this basis, there was no guarantee their followers would accept it. As it turned out, however, the leaders were unable to come to terms. Bonar Law and Carson refused to settle for anything less than permanent exclusion for the six counties of northeast Ulster, an area they considered had both a safe Unionist majority and economic viability. Restricted by Redmond, Asquith could offer only exclusion by county option, which would probably be permanent but would give the unionists only four counties. Fermanagh and Tyrone, the two counties of contention, were the subject of long and futile discussion by the principals.

In the summer of 1914, negotiations broke down, and the United Kingdom seemed on the verge of civil war. Under the terms of the Parliament Act, the Home Rule Bill was due to become law very soon, but the government had lost control of the situation. The Unionist-dominated officer corps had demonstrated that the British army could not be relied on to impose Home Rule on Ulster, and the Irish Volunteers had followed Ulster's example and engaged in gunrunning to arm themselves for a showdown. Some sort of violent confrontation seemed inevitable, when the outbreak of war in Europe thrust the Irish Question into the background.

A general closing of ranks followed Britain's entry into the war. Unionists at once pledged support of the war effort, and the Ulster Volunteers were enrolled as a division of the British army. Convinced of the justice of Britain's fight against German autocracy and militarism, and eager to ensure enactment of Home Rule, Redmond also proclaimed his unconditional support of the Allied cause. When he called on the Irish Volunteers to join the British army in September 1914, however, he precipitated a split in the organization. The great majority of its members followed Redmond and joined his National Volunteers, but some 13,000 advanced nationalists remained in the Irish Volunteers, declaring their only allegiance was to Ireland.

Redmond's loyalty to Britain brought no real gains for either his country or his party. Over Unionist protests, the Home Rule Bill was made law, but Parliament suspended its operation for the duration of the war, and Asquith pledged that Ulster would not be coerced. Despite their success in delaying Home Rule, the Unionists were no better off than Redmond. As both Carson and Law realized, some form of Home Rule was now inevitable. The Unionists had safeguarded Ulster, but this was not their real purpose, and Ulster's very victory spelled their defeat. Furthermore, Unionist tactics in the Home Rule controversy had helped arouse a militant nationalism that would alter Anglo-Irish relations in a way neither they nor John Redmond dreamed of in 1914.

Chapter 2
Ireland Transformed:
1914-1918

Although the war caused some economic dislocation in Ireland, this was largely overshadowed by the prosperity it induced. People were generally indifferent or hostile toward the small separatist minority and, deferring to Redmond's judgment, the government did little to suppress subversive activities. Separatists openly denounced Britain's dishonesty and selfish war aims, while both the Irish Volunteers and the Citizen Army frequently staged parades and maneuvers. Among advanced nationalists, however, there were sharp differences of opinion on policy. Moderate leaders, such as Griffith and MacNeill, felt that the Volunteers should fight only if the British tried to suppress them or impose military conscription on Ireland. But militants, such as Connolly, called for insurrection without preconditions, arguing that the opportunity presented by Britain's involvement in the war must not be wasted.

In September 1914 a meeting of IRB leaders with Griffith, Connolly, and other advanced nationalists upheld the extremist view. An insurrection was to be staged and independence declared before the war ended, in order to ensure Ireland's representation at the peace conference. In the months that followed, Tom Clarke and Sean MacDermott, an energetic IRB organizer, made plans for a rebellion. These plans were to be carried out by the Irish Volunteers, directed by IRB agents within their ranks, the most important of whom was P. H. Pearse.

Patrick Henry Pearse was a poet, educator, and fervent cultural nationalist who became politically active during the Home Rule controversy and moved rapidly to an extremist position. One of the founders of the Irish Volunteers, he soon became a member of the IRB. When the Volunteers split, Pearse became director of organization for the militant minority. He cherished a vision of a free and Gaelic Ireland and was willing, even eager, to sacrifice his life for this end. His dedicated separatism, as well as his key military position, led Clarke and MacDermott to include him in their conspiracy.

Pearse became head of the IRB's Military Council, which was set up in 1915 to draw detailed plans for an insurrection. This body eventually included all seven men who signed the 1916 Proclamation of the Irish Republic. The fact that four of the seven held important positions in the Volunteers seemed to ensure the Military Council's control of that force.

While the conspirators' original plans apparently called for a Dublin rising in September 1915, the prospect of military aid from Germany led them to postpone the date and expand their plans to include the provinces. Connolly's impatience for action threatened to upset the conspirators' timetable; so he was brought into their confidence in January 1916 and agreed to join them. The rising was to begin on Easter Sunday, April 23, 1916. On that day the rebel forces were to be mobilized, with units in the south and west supplied with German arms landed in Kerry.

Any chance of military success was lost before the insurrection began by faulty communications, divided counsels, and plain bad luck. A few weeks prior to the revolt, the date for the arms landing was changed. By the time this information reached Germany, the arms ship had sailed and could not be notified. No one met the ship when it arrived off Kerry on April 20, and the next day it was captured by the British but scuttled by its crew. Sir Roger Casement, a distinguished former British consular officer and recent convert to separatism, was captured by police in Kerry the same day, having come from Germany by submarine to prevent an insurrection he was sure would fail without more military aid. Loss of the German arms ended the possibility of a large-scale uprising, while interception of the arms ship and the capture of Casement alerted authorities in Dublin to the fact that a rising was imminent.

Divisions within the Volunteers' Executive proved disastrous for the conspirators. Eoin MacNeill, the chief of staff, and some other members of the Executive opposed offensive action because they held it was bound to fail and was therefore unjustifiable. Consequently, the Military Council did not inform them of its plans. When MacNeill belatedly learned of the conspiracy on April 20, he was outraged at the deception and heated discussions ensued between him and some of the extremist leaders. At first, MacNeill vacillated, but in the end he canceled the Sunday mobilization orders (the signal for the rising), convinced it would be a futile gesture that would only inflict unnecessary suffering on the people.

Up to this point the conspirators had enjoyed the advantages of secrecy; now they discovered its drawbacks. The Military Council had tried to determine policy for the IRB and the Volunteers without disclosing its plans to those whose support was vital for success. Although angry at MacNeill's action and upset by the loss of the expected arms shipment, Council members nevertheless decided unanimously, on Sunday morning, to proceed with the insurrection in Dublin. They would strike the next day with as many Volunteers as could be mobilized on short notice. The rebel leaders knew there was no hope for military victory, but they agreed that an armed protest was necessary to reawaken the national spirit and inspire the people to demand real freedom. The conspirators had only one advantage: surprise. Believing that MacNeill's cancellation order removed any immediate danger, the authorities deferred the arrest of leading subversives.[1]

On Easter Sunday the conspirators dispatched orders to the Dublin Volunteer battalions. About 800 men turned out the next morning, including the Citizen Army contingent. An equal number joined the insurgents during the fighting, so that roughly 1,600 men took part in the insurrection—about half the full strength of the Dublin Brigade. According to plan, the rebel forces seized positions guarding the main approaches to the city center. A static defense ensured defeat, but insurgent leaders felt this strategy would impress public opinion more than a series of scattered skirmishes.

Around noon the rebels moved into action, in the midst of carefree citizens enjoying the quarterly bank holiday. A strong contingent occupied the General Post Office in O'Connell (then Sackville) Street, which was to serve as rebel headquarters. Shortly afterward, Pearse read the Proclamation of the Irish Republic to a surprised but indifferent crowd gathered in front of the Post Office (see appendix I).

There were 5,500 British troops in or near Dublin and 21,000 soldiers and 9,500 armed police in the whole country. Martial law was quickly declared, the Dublin garrison was reinforced to 12,000 troops by week's end, and artillery was used to reduce the rebels' fortified positions. Resistance was stubborn and there was heavy fighting, especially in Commandant Eamon de Valera's area around Mount Street Bridge, but superior resources soon began to tell, as the rebel commands were isolated and driven from their outlying posts. On Friday the Volunteers evacuated the burning Post Office, and on Saturday afternoon Pearse, the commander of the insurgent forces, surrendered unconditionally. His surrender order was communicated to other rebel units throughout the city, and their resistance ended the next day.

Although the Military Council had tried to alert Volunteers outside Dublin, there was little action elsewhere. Contradictory orders, the arms shortage, and the absence of detailed plans made the insurrection almost exclusively a Dublin affair (something its leaders may have intended all along). The most notable action outside the city was in north County Dublin, where a group of Volunteers attacked a police barracks and ambushed a relief column (anticipating the guerrilla tactics employed in later stages of the struggle for independence).

The rising produced over 3,000 casualties. About 60 rebels were killed and more than 100 were wounded. The British lost 132 men killed (116 soldiers and 16 police) and 397 wounded. More than 300 civilians were killed and perhaps as many as 2,000 wounded.[2]

Ireland was shocked by the Easter Rising. Viewing them as allies of Germany, whose lunatic action would only further delay Home Rule, most Irishmen were hostile to the insurgents. Dubliners were outraged at the death and destruction caused by the rising. Although some citizens were sympathetic to the defeated rebels, the dominant mood was expressed by the jeers and cold silence which greeted the prisoners as they were marched through the city's streets.[3]

Redmond was quick to condemn what he called "the German plot," and Ireland's leading nationalist newspapers, as well as many of its public bodies, echoed his sentiments. Irish Unionists denounced the rising as treason and called for stern measures to root out sedition. The rebels' ideal of a Gaelic and republican Ireland was as repugnant to loyalists as the insurrection itself, and the whole, desperate enterprise widened the gap between Unionist and nationalist.[4]

The Catholic hierarchy was much less outspoken in its condemnation than might have been expected, given its past pronouncements on violence. Only seven bishops emphatically denounced the rebellion, while one condemned it hesitantly. Twenty-two bishops said nothing publicly, and Bishop O'Dwyer of Limerick made what amounted to a defense of the rebels. The bishops' reserved reaction was largely due to growing dissatisfaction with Redmond's policy and anger at British treatment of the insurgents. Many priests, especially young ones, were openly sympathetic to the separatist movement, but their attitude, like that of their superiors, was determined less by the rising itself than by the events which followed it.[5]

John Dillon, Redmond's chief lieutenant, who had been in Dublin during the insurrection, sensed the danger of harsh reprisals. On April 30 he warned Redmond that large-scale executions could have a disastrous effect. "*So far* feeling of the population in Dublin is *against* the Sinn Feiners. But a reaction might very easily be created."[6] Redmond urged leniency, but it came too late to prevent what Dillon feared.

On April 27 the government sent General Sir John Maxwell to stamp out the revolt. When the fighting ended, the authorities rounded up 3,500 actual and suspected rebels. About 1,500 were released after investigation. Over 1,800 untried prisoners were interned in Britain, but almost 1,300 of them were discharged after inquiry. Most of the 170 prisoners who were tried and convicted by court-martial were soon transferred to English jails, but a different fate awaited the others.[7]

Between May 2 and 12, fourteen insurgents were tried for treason by court-martial, found guilty, and shot—singly or in small groups. The executed included the seven signatories of the Republican proclamation, six senior officers, and Patrick Pearse's brother, William. Another rebel was executed in Cork, and Casement's hanging in London on August 3, after his conviction for treason, brought the total number of executions to sixteen.

The shootings produced a wave of Irish protest. In the House of Commons, Dillon defended the rebels as brave and honorable men, warned the government that it was washing out the constitutionalists' life work "in a sea of blood," and demanded an "absolute stop" to the executions.[8] Redmond had already impressed on Asquith that wholesale executions would destroy constitutional nationalism, and other Home Rulers told the prime minister the same thing. Increasing pressure eventually had an effect, and ninety-seven death sentences were commuted. But fifteen men had been shot.[9]

The government's reaction to rebellion in wartime was not unreasonable, but it ignored the lessons of Irish history and initiated a decisive shift in Irish opinion. After the first executions, Sean MacDermott (who was soon to die) told Griffith triumphantly: "Now I know we were right." If there had been no executions, MacDermott said, the people would have turned against them; now the people would support their protest.[10] This is what Pearse meant when he told his court-martial: "We seem to have lost, [but] we have not lost. To refuse to fight would have been to lose, to fight is to win [;] we have kept faith with the past, and handed a tradition to the future."[11] Execution transformed the rebel leaders into martyrs for Irish freedom, ensuring their popular canonization.

The changed Irish attitude manifested itself in many ways. Mourning badges and rebel flags were widely displayed. There were popular demonstrations at masses for the dead leaders, and many public bodies passed resolutions of sympathy for the rebels. People sang ballads about the rising, and photographs of its leaders appeared in shop windows. Now the crowds shouted cheers and blessings (instead of catcalls) to prisoners bound for British jails and pressed small gifts on them.[12]

In June, General Maxwell admitted that Redmond's power was slipping as his followers lost faith in constitutional methods. It was becoming increasingly difficult, he said, to distinguish between a Home Ruler and a Republican. In short, Irish nationalism was becoming dangerously militant.[13] Ireland's greatest poet confirmed Maxwell's judgment. In September 1916 a deeply moved William Butler Yeats wrote that out of the rising and the executions: "A terrible beauty is born."

To appease Irish as well as American opinion, the latter angered at both the British blockade of Germany and the Irish executions, the Cabinet agreed to explore a Home Rule settlement. Asquith assigned this task to David Lloyd George, the government's most energetic and resourceful minister.[14] However, even his talents could not overcome Unionist opposition to Home Rule or resolve differences over partition, and the abortive negotiations further discredited Redmond.[15]

As the summer of 1916 passed, Ireland was gradually returned to civil administration, and most of the internees were sent home. In November, Maxwell was recalled to England, and the next month Lloyd George became prime minister in response to demands for more vigorous prosecution of the war. Shortly before Christmas, the new prime minister ordered the release of the remaining internees as a good-will gesture. This left only about 150 rebel prisoners in British hands.

As they had received news from home while in custody, the liberated patriots were probably not too surprised at the public's changed attitude toward them; but some of them may have been puzzled to find that the insurrection was popularly known as the Sinn Fein Rebellion. However, the reason for this misnomer is easy to understand. While not committed to a republic, Sinn Fein was a political party well known for its militant nationalism, and the authorities, the press, and the people used "Sinn Fein" as a convenient shorthand description for anyone or anything that savored of disaffection during the war. Hence the popular identification of the movement with the rising, despite the fact that Griffith had played no part in either its planning or execution. Upon his release by the British, Griffith found this alleged association had given him an eager audience who knew little about Sinn Fein except that it offered an alternative to Redmond's bankrupt policy.

The newly freed internees lost no time in exploiting public sympathy. British camps and jails were excellent schools for the propagation of revolutionary ideas. At Frongoch, the main internment camp in North Wales, hundreds of advanced nationalists studied, argued, agitated, and planned, emerging from confinement as a revolutionary elite.[16] In the early months of 1917, while Griffith ground out his Sinn Fein propaganda, zealous Republicans began reorganization of the IRB and the Volunteers. In February the revolutionary movement won its first election victory, when Count Plunkett, the father of one of the executed leaders, defeated the Home Rule candidate in a parliamentary by-election. Plunkett ran as an Independent, but he had strong support from advanced nationalists and he beat his opponent almost two to one. Soon afterward, he announced that he would not take his seat at Westminster, but would remain in Ireland to work for national independence.[17]

In April 1917 a National Council was set up to coordinate the work of advanced nationalist groups. The convention that established it declared that Ireland was a separate nation, demanded Irish representation at the eventual European peace conference, and bound affiliated organizations to use every means in their power to attain complete national freedom. The National Council at once entered the political arena, nominating an imprisoned rebel, Joseph McGuinness, in another parliamentary by-election. The issues of the Republic, Home Rule, and partition were hotly debated in a tumultuous campaign. Despite an all-out effort by the Redmondites, McGuinness won a narrow victory. His supporters celebrated with meetings, processions, bonfires, and widespread display of the orange, white, and green Republican flag.[18]

Britain responded to Ireland's resurgent nationalism with fitful attempts at suppression, but something more positive was needed to placate American opinion. Although the United States had entered the war against Germany in April 1917, the British government felt it must make another effort to resolve the Irish Question to ensure the wholehearted cooperation of its new ally.

In May 1917 Lloyd George offered Redmond immediate Home Rule, with a provision for what amounted to permanent exclusion for the six counties of northeast Ulster. As an alternative, the prime minister proposed something already suggested by Redmond himself: a convention, representative of all major Irish interests, to work out a scheme of self-government—coupled with the prime minister's assurance that Britain would implement any plan that won substantial agreement in the convention. Hoping to restore his party's standing, Redmond accepted the convention proposal, unaware that Lloyd George had privately promised Carson that Ulster's rights would not be compromised. To improve the atmosphere for the convention, Lloyd George released the remaining Irish prisoners in June. Ignoring this gesture, Sinn Fein refused to take part in a "sham" conference, designed to delude Ireland and America. Organized labor (outside Ulster) also refused to participate, and the ninety-odd members who met in late July represented only Unionists, Home Rulers, and the Catholic bishops.[19]

The Irish Convention met off and on until April 1918 but failed to reach substantial agreement on anything. Ulster Unionists insisted on exclusion from Home Rule, while Redmond lost the support of some of his followers in his efforts to conciliate the southern Unionists. The convention's final report recommended something between Home Rule and Dominion status for a united Ireland. Ulster Unionists dissented from this fragile compromise, and the British government ignored it. Still, the convention was significant, and not only because its failure aided Sinn Fein and confirmed Ulster's exclusionist demand. The convention appeased American opinion at a critical stage of the war; it also demonstrated that the more realistic southern Unionists were finally beginning to come to terms with Irish nationalism.[20] And it showed that the Home Rule Party was shifting its goal toward greater national independence. For Redmond himself, the convention proved a final tragedy. Unable to win the agreement of various nationalists for his proposals, he retired from the conference in January 1918 and died in March of complications following an operation for gallstones. John Dillon succeeded him as head of the Home Rule Party.[21]

In retrospect, the most important development in Irish politics in 1917 was not the abortive convention but the emergence of Eamon de Valera as leader of the advanced nationalist movement. The senior surviving officer of the Easter Rising, de Valera had demonstrated a marked capacity for leadership during the fighting and in his ensuing imprisonment. News of his courage and ability led to his nomination as Sinn Fein's candidate in an east Clare by-election while he was still in jail.

Released under the amnesty of June 1917, de Valera waged a vigorous campaign in Clare, leaving no doubt of his commitment to the Republic and rejection of partition. He beat the Home Rule candidate by a vote of 5,000 to 2,000. The magnitude of this victory enhanced his claim to leadership and struck a serious blow to the convention even before it met.

Before the Easter Rising, de Valera was scarcely known outside advanced nationalist circles. He was born in New York City of a Spanish father and an Irish mother in 1882. His father died when Eamon was only two years old, and his mother sent him to be raised by her family on their farm near Bruree in County Limerick, where he grew up with strong nationalist convictions. In 1904 he took a degree in mathematics from the Royal (afterward the National) University and settled into a career as a schoolteacher. An active member of the Gaelic League, de Valera became a charter member of the Irish Volunteers, and for a brief period was enrolled in the IRB. His command offered the most effective resistance to British troops during Easter Week, and a court-martial condemned him to death. The intervention of the American consul, occasioned by an appeal from de Valera's wife, may have led the authorities to commute this sentence to life imprisonment. Although de Valera never claimed American citizenship, he had been born in the United States, and the British were eager to avoid trouble with America. It is possible, however, that de Valera's life was spared simply because the government decided to stop the executions.[22]

Although de Valera had no political experience, he seemed an ideal candidate for national leadership in 1917. No one could question his separatist credentials or personal heroism, and he had no enemies. Always courteous and approachable, he had an air of dignity and authority that set him apart from his fellows and made them look to him for decisions. His speeches were usually long, involved, and repetitious, but he delivered them with an impassioned sincerity that rarely failed to move his audience. Finally, and most important, de Valera appealed to extreme as well as moderate factions of the revolutionary movement. He had fought in 1916, but admitted he had thought the insurrection was a mistake. He revered the dead leaders, but would tolerate no disrespect toward MacNeill and the others who had refused to join them in armed revolt. He stood by the demand for a republic, but in prison he had seemed to prefer Dominion status as a more realistic objective for Ireland, and afterward never tired of telling his followers that he was "not a doctrinaire Republican."[23] This balanced approach enabled de Valera to bridge the gap between moderates and extremists in Sinn Fein. The situation seemed made for him; whether *he* was made for the situation, only time would tell.

A month after de Valera's victory in east Clare, Sinn Fein won another

by-election in Kilkenny. The new MP was William T. Cosgrave, a
member of the Dublin Corporation as well as a veteran of the rising. Like
de Valera, he had been condemned to death and reprieved. Combining
an easygoing manner with sharp wit and determination, Cosgrave also
was destined to play a leading role in Ireland's future.

Although the government was eager to suppress separatism, it did not
want to provoke trouble while the Irish Convention was in session; consequently, the authorities did not interfere with the national Sinn Fein
conference which met in October 1917. Some 1,700 delegates from
1,200 Sinn Fein clubs attended the party's tenth annual Ard Fheis on
October 25–26. Leaders had already spent much time trying to define
their movement's program in some way which would preserve its fragile
unity. Moderates, headed by Griffith, opposed committing Sinn Fein to
an all-out struggle for a republic, arguing that the advance to complete
independence should be gradual and nonviolent so as to maximize
popular support and chances for success. On the other hand, militant
separatists such as Cathal Brugha, a fiery veteran of the rising, demanded commitment to an Irish republic and refused to rule out the use
of force in their pursuit of freedom. While spokesmen for the Volunteers wanted popular support for the independence movement, they
were less concerned than the moderates about public opinion. Given
their outlook, it is not surprising that many Republicans resented being
called Sinn Feiners and wanted to make a clean break with Griffith's
organization. Yet such a split would be disastrous for their cause. It
would mean the loss of considerable support and of a name and organization that were strongly identified in the public mind with the struggle
for national liberation. Moreover, as the extremists themselves admitted,
the tactics advocated by Griffith could play an important part in that
struggle.

De Valera was well aware of the dangers of division, and he labored
successfully to draft a statement of purpose acceptable to both factions.
This formula, which became the preamble of the new Sinn Fein constitution, declared:

> Sinn Fein aims at securing the international recognition of Ireland as an
> independent Irish Republic.
>
> Having achieved that status the Irish people may by Referendum freely
> choose their own form of Government.

The preamble also stated that Sinn Fein, "in the name of the Sovereign
Irish people," would

(a)   Deny the right and oppose the will of the British Parliament and
      British Crown or any other foreign government to legislate for
      Ireland;

(b)   Make use of any and every means available to render impotent
       the power of England to hold Ireland in subjection by military
       force or otherwise.

The new declaration was clearly a victory for the extremists. Sinn Fein
was now committed to a republic and would use whatever means were
necessary to secure it. If the Irish people endorsed this program, well
and good; but they were to decide Ireland's form of government only
after the republic was firmly established. Griffith thought this arrangement unwise, but he could not argue with the dead men whose executions had given Sinn Fein mass support, and in the end he gave way. The
Ard Fheis approved de Valera's formula unanimously, and the danger
of an open split was averted.

In another gesture designed to promote unity, Griffith declined to
stand for reelection as president of Sinn Fein. Instead he endorsed de
Valera, who was elected unopposed when Count Plunkett also withdrew
as a candidate. While the new president professed adherence to the
separatist ideal, he left the door open for possible compromise by declaring: "We are not doctrinaire Republicans."[24]

Extremists and moderates were elected to the new party executive.
The IRB tried hard to influence these elections but had little success. De
Valera and Brugha left the secret society after the insurrection, maintaining that the struggle for independence should now be carried on in
the open. But others, including a dynamic young Corkman, Michael
Collins, believed the IRB still had an important role to play, and they
worked diligently to extend its power.[25]

The day after the Sinn Fein Ard Fheis, the Irish Volunteers met in
secret session. The delegates elected de Valera president of the Volunteers and Brugha became chief of staff. Three IRB members, including
Collins, were also elected to the executive. Although some men served
on the governing bodies of both organizations, the Volunteers remained
independent of Sinn Fein. Strangely, neither the 1917 convention nor
their new constitution committed the Volunteers to a republic, although
this was clearly their ultimate aim.[26]

In the spring of 1918 the British army needed men desperately to halt
Ludendorff's sledgehammer offensives in France. Anxious generals and
Unionists pressed the government to extend conscription to Ireland,
where, it was alleged, up to 150,000 men were available for military
service because of the wartime ban on emigration and the decline in
recruiting. Although such a step seemed likely to precipitate an explosion, the Cabinet hoped to defuse the issue by coupling it with Home
Rule. In seeking parliamentary authority to impose conscription on Ireland if necessary, Lloyd George declared that the government intended
to enact Home Rule as soon as possible and to conduct an intensive
recruiting campaign in Ireland.

The prime minister's ploy failed, however, and the threat of conscription touched off a storm of protest. Even before the Conscription Bill was passed, John Dillon led the Irish Party out of the House of Commons and returned to Ireland to help organize resistance. On April 18 nationalist leaders attended an anticonscription meeting sponsored by Dublin's lord mayor. At this gathering de Valera established his primacy, because of Sinn Fein's growing strength and his own skill and tenacity. He won acceptance of a pledge which bound all who took it to resist conscription by the most effective means at their disposal. An indignant Catholic hierarchy readily agreed that parish priests should administer the pledge to their congregations, and this was done the following Sunday. On April 23 Irish trade unions protested conscription with a one-day general strike, which was highly successful everywhere outside Belfast.

Field Marshal Lord French's appointment as viceroy indicated that the government was prepared to deal sternly with nationalist opposition. This was confirmed when the authorities rounded up and deported most Sinn Fein leaders in May, alleging (on flimsy evidence) that they were involved in treasonable communication with Germany. Dublin Castle followed these arrests with a new round of repressive measures, and the authorities tried energetically to root out disaffection during the summer. Heavy-handed methods produced a superficial calm, which would have been shattered by any attempt to impose conscription. Griffith's victory in a parliamentary by-election, while he was held in an English jail, showed the popularity of Sinn Fein's outspoken stand against conscription. This fact was further demonstrated by the rush of recruits to the Volunteers, whose numbers exceeded 100,000 by war's end. Volunteer leaders did their best to arm and drill these recruits, making clear they would fight if the British tried to draft Irishmen.

The Volunteers were not put to the test in 1918. Despite the failure of its recruiting campaign, the government did not extend conscription to Ireland. The United States strongly opposed the idea, and the rapid increase of American troops in France during the summer weakened the argument for it. Furthermore, the government gave up trying to draft a Home Rule bill, having found it impossible to deal with such a controversial issue in wartime. However, the principal reason for the government's inaction was undoubtedly the solid front of nationalist opposition led by Sinn Fein.[27]

When the war ended, in November 1918, Lloyd George and his colleagues decided to continue their wartime coalition to deal more effectively with the problems of peace. In December's general election the coalition scored a smashing victory over a divided opposition. Led by "the man who won the war" and supported by the Conservative Party, the government was in a strong position to settle the Irish Question. Experience had taught Conservative leaders the futility of opposing

Home Rule, and many of their new followers in the House of Commons lacked a firm commitment to unionism. The party's changed attitude was reflected in the government's election pledge to grant Ireland self-government, ruling out only secession from the Empire and coercion of the six counties of northeast Ulster.[28]

Although Sinn Fein was committed to abstention from Parliament, the party was eager to show its popular support. Thanks to the government's round-up of prominent Sinn Feiners the previous May, the party machinery was in the hands of militant separatists, who ruthlessly excluded moderates and made a list of candidates that was overwhelmingly Republican.[29]

While Sinn Fein encountered some serious difficulties in its campaign, these were far outweighed by the advantages Sinn Fein enjoyed. The authorities censored its manifestoes, arrested its director of elections, and held half its candidates in jail. But this repression probably convinced many voters that Sinn Fein was, as it claimed, the authentic representative of national aspirations, while the aggressive tactics of the party's agents helped offset official efforts at intimidation. In contrast to the Home Rule Party, Sinn Fein was confident, well organized, and well financed. Also, it enjoyed considerable support from the Catholic clergy, many of whom were fed up with the Parliamentary Party. The decision of the fledgling Irish Labor Party not to contest the election was another important gain for the Republicans. Although Labor was dissatisfied with Sinn Fein's conservative social outlook, it decided to stand down to allow a clear, popular expression on the issue of national self-determination. Sinn Fein pressure, internal division, and political caution played a part in this decision, but so did patriotism. By all odds, however, Sinn Fein reaped its biggest advantage from the 1918 electoral reform act, which enfranchised every man over twenty-one and most women over thirty, thereby nearly tripling the Irish electorate. The new voters were very often young or poor and not bound by traditional loyalties; many of them would eagerly support a new party which challenged the political *status quo*.[30]

British censors deleted about one-quarter of Sinn Fein's election manifesto, including its pledge to use any available means to overthrow British rule. But voters were told that Sinn Fein proposed to establish a republic by withdrawing Irish MPs from Westminster, setting up a national government, and appealing to the European peace conference for recognition of Ireland's independence. Sinn Fein also condemned the idea of partition, but in some Ulster constituencies the loyalist vote was too large to be overcome. In others, however, agreement with Home Rulers could secure a nationalist victory. Consequently, the two nationalist parties arranged not to compete in eight northern constituencies, each party taking four for itself.[31]

When the election results were announced in late December, it was clear that Sinn Fein had won a great victory, capturing 73 of 105 Irish seats in the House of Commons. The Home Rulers retained only six seats, four of them through prior agreement with Sinn Fein. The magnitude of this defeat destroyed the Home Rule Party outside northeast Ulster. As expected, southern Unionists did very poorly, winning only three seats. On the other hand, Ulster Unionists gained several seats, after waging a hard campaign, and tightened their hold on the six counties.

Voting statistics, coupled with charges that Sinn Feiners were guilty of widespread intimidation and fraud, have led to suggestions that Sinn Fein's electoral triumph was exaggerated. Thirty-one percent of registered voters in contested constituencies did not vote in the 1918 election, and Sinn Fein won only 47 percent of the votes cast, compared to a combined total of 52 percent for its opponents.[32] However, these statistics are deceptive. For one thing, they do not show Sinn Fein's strength in the twenty-six constituencies where its candidates were returned unopposed. If contests had been held for these seats, Sinn Fein's share of the total vote would have been much larger than it was. Even without these votes, it is obvious that Sinn Fein was the overwhelming choice of the electorate outside northeast Ulster. In twenty-six of Ireland's thirty-two counties, the party won 47 percent of the total registered vote in contested constituencies and 65 percent of the votes actually cast. Sinn Fein's victory was just as genuine as that of the coalition in Britain, which won two-thirds of the seats in the House of Commons, with only 47.6 percent of the popular vote, in an election in which 41 percent of the electorate did not vote.[33] As for illegal practices, the government and its agents went to great lengths to defeat Sinn Fein, and Sinn Fein was probably no more guilty of unfair tactics than its opponents. Perhaps even less so.

When the necessary qualifications have been made, the fact remains that Sinn Fein scored a very impressive victory in its first general election. In less than three years, a political splinter group had become the largest party in Ireland, overthrowing the party that had dominated Irish politics for almost forty years and forcing Ulster Unionists into an all-out effort to secure their political defenses.

Why the voters chose Sinn Fein is much less clear than that they did so. One of the party's leaders remarked after the election: "The people have voted Sinn Fein. What we have to do now is to explain to them what Sinn Fein is."[34] This was more truth than jest. Sinn Fein had snowballed into a national movement, and enthusiasm tended to overpower reason among its new supporters. Most Sinn Fein voters probably had no real understanding of its program. Although they endorsed the demand for national self-determination, it is very doubtful that they were convinced

Republicans or grasped the full significance of the party's Republican commitment. After all, even party members had reservations or were confused on this score. Moreover, Sinn Fein could not fairly claim that it had won a mandate for armed conflict with Britain, because this question had not been put squarely before the voters.

In the final analysis, the election results were more a vote against Britain and the Home Rule Party than a vote for Sinn Fein. A greatly enlarged nationalist electorate was reacting angrily to the 1916 executions, coercion, and threats of conscription and partition. It was also protesting the caution and timidity of the Home Rulers, who had broken too many promises and become so involved in politics at Westminster that they had lost touch with their followers and neglected the powerful forces stirring at home.

Dillon had seen the danger of supporting Britain during the war and the growing Sinn Fein threat. He had tried to stake out a more radical position for his party by denouncing conscription and demanding Dominion status in the election. But Dillon was too late; most Irish voters were turning toward the rising sun of Sinn Fein, which had stood up to the British government and done more than any other group to prevent conscription. It should be given a chance to do what the Old Party had clearly failed to do: secure self-government for a united Ireland. With British help, the Irish Parliamentary Party had been digging its grave for years, and in December 1918 it was finally buried.[35]

Chapter 3
The Struggle for
Independence: 1919-1920

On January 21, 1919, the twenty-seven Sinn Fein MPs who were not confined in British jails met publicly in Dublin to establish the Irish Republic. Cathal Brugha was elected speaker of Dail Eireann (Assembly of Ireland), and a brief provisional Constitution was adopted. Next, a Declaration of Independence was read; it ratified the establishment of the Republic proclaimed in 1916, recognized Dail Eireann as the sovereign national authority, demanded British evacuation, and appealed to all free nations for recognition and support of Irish independence. Without discussion or dissent, the Dail adopted this declaration. It then appointed a delegation to the Paris peace conference and passed a resolution repeating the appeal for international recognition and asking admission to the conference.[1]

The final business of the Republican Parliament's historic first meeting was consideration of a Democratic Program, based on the principles of social justice set forth in the 1916 Republican Proclamation. Asserting the nation's sovereignty over all its resources and wealth, the program decreed the subordination of private property to public need and proclaimed the new government's duty to secure social welfare and promote national economic development. Although the Dail approved the Democratic Program unanimously, this endorsement was more a maneuver to win labor's support than a commitment to radical economic reform. With the exception of James Connolly and a few disciples, the leaders of the Irish revolution were much more concerned about expelling the British than attacking the evils of capitalism.[2]

In confirming the demand for a Republic, the extremists in Sinn Fein kept faith with their ideal, but they probably acted unwisely. Circumstances had changed drastically since the Republic was first proclaimed in 1916. Germany had been defeated; and however sympathetic they were to Irish aspirations, neither the United States nor other victor nations could afford to quarrel with Britain over such an issue. Sinn Fein should simply have called for national self-determination, leaving open the question of relations with Britain. Such a demand would have won substantial support in Britain and the Dominions and left ample room for eventual compromise. But as Cathal Brugha made plain, militant Republicans were not interested in practical considerations: "Deputies,

you understand from what is asserted in this Declaration that we are now
done with England. Let the world know it and those who are concerned
bear it in mind. For come what may now, whether it be death itself, the
great deed is done."[3]

After meeting only two hours on January 21, the Dail adjourned. In
private session the next day, it elected Brugha acting president until de
Valera was released from prison.[4] Dublin Castle took note of the Dail's
proceedings, but did nothing to interfere. Preoccupied with peacemaking, the British government marked time in Ireland.

On the same day that Dail Eireann established the Republic, Volunteers staged an ambush at Soloheadbeg, County Tipperary, killing two
policemen and opening a guerrilla war against the Crown forces. To
understand that struggle and the Volunteers' role in it, certain facts must
be made clear.

Maintenance of order in Ireland was the task of the Royal Irish Constabulary, an armed and barrack-quartered force whose jurisdiction covered the whole country outside Dublin, which had its own, unarmed
police force. Although the highest positions in the RIC were generally
held by Protestants, its rank and file were largely Catholic, and their
primary function was to provide their superiors with reliable information about local affairs. In 1919 RIC was a much less formidable force
than it had been a generation earlier. The government's political vacillation during the previous decade had hurt police morale and efficiency,
the force was about 1,000 men under its authorized strength of 10,000,
and its military training was obsolete. Nevertheless, the RIC was Britain's
first line of defense, and if the Volunteers could cripple it, Dublin Castle
would lose its main source of intelligence.[5]

The decision to take the offensive against the police was made by local
Volunteer commanders, although GHQ endorsed their action and did
what it could to support and coordinate their operations. By striking at
the enemy, these officers had hoped to prevent the disintegration of
their forces once the war's end removed the threat of conscription. At
the same time, such action helped build effective fighting units,
obstructed efforts to suppress separatist activities, and, most important,
helped focus public attention on Ireland's struggle for independence.
The Volunteers adopted guerrilla tactics because this was the only way
they could hope to survive and to demoralize an enemy with vastly
superior military resources. Understandably, this resort to ambush and
assassination shocked many people. Like other Sinn Fein moderates,
Griffith feared such tactics would only hurt Ireland's cause, but he loyally concealed his misgivings to maintain a united front against Britain.
The same was true of most other Irishmen; however much they might
disapprove of Volunteer terrorism, they would not betray their fellow
countrymen, fighting an alien authority whose terrorism was far more

indiscriminate. This patriotism was reinforced by fear of the harsh penalties meted out to informers by the Volunteers. Thus the guerrillas possessed the decisive advantage of popular support, which ensured them vital intelligence while denying it to their adversaries.[6]

In August 1919, Dail Eireann approved a motion by Brugha to have the Volunteers formally swear allegiance to the Republic and the Dail. Griffith and other deputies felt this step would establish the Dail's authority over the army, although Brugha's primary aim was to destroy the IRB's power within the Volunteers. Local units took the oath during 1920, and the Volunteers became officially known as the Irish Republican Army. But although the oath weakened the IRB's influence, it made no real change in the Volunteers' status. In practice, they remained an autonomous organization, whose loyalty to the Dail was secondary to their loyalty to the army and the Republic.[7] From the time of Soloheadbeg until the truce of July 1921, the IRA set the pace in the struggle for independence, leaving the politicians and the people to keep up as best they could.

In February 1919, de Valera escaped from Lincoln jail, and soon afterward the British released the other "German plot" prisoners (who had been held since May 1918). De Valera had decided he would go to the United States as soon as he regained his freedom. Sinn Fein had been unable to win a hearing at the Paris peace conference, and he hoped a personal appeal to the American people would win their support for the cause of Irish independence. In de Valera's view, such support was essential to raise money for the Republic and to secure its official recognition by the United States. Before he left for America, the Dail unanimously elected de Valera its president, and he formed a Cabinet that included moderates and extremists. Its most important members were Griffith, minister for home affairs and acting president during de Valera's absence; Collins, minister for finance; Brugha, minister for defense; and Cosgrave, minister for local government.[8]

Arriving in the United States in June, de Valera made a triumphal progress across the country, rallying widespread support from Irish-Americans and other anti-British groups. At the same time, efforts to win sympathy for the Irish cause were also under way in Britain. In March 1919, Sinn Fein supporters organized the Irish Self-Determination League in England and Wales, and a similar association was set up in Scotland. The ISDL eventually formed 300 branches, and its propaganda and fund-raising activities made it an invaluable ally of Sinn Fein.[9]

At home, the Dail boldly asserted its authority. In June it authorized the creation of a consular service and a commission to take stock of Ireland's industries and resources. It also ordered establishment of a national civil service, arbitration courts, and a land bank to help tenants purchase their holdings. In April the Dail declared the issue of an internal loan of £250,000 to finance the government and develop the economy. Despite British obstruction, Collins raised £358,000 from the sale of Republican bonds in 1919-20. An American loan of $25 million was authorized in August and raised over $5 million in 1920–21.[10] On April 10, 1919, the Dail struck a serious blow at the police when it called on the people to ostracize members of the RIC. The resulting social boycott increased resignations and reduced the number of recruits for a force already short of men. More important, Dublin Castle's sources of information rapidly dried up as the police were isolated.[11]

Like the Dail, the Volunteers grew more active in the summer of 1919. In August they mounted a series of arms raids on police barracks, thereby beginning a siege which soon led the RIC to evacuate its smaller and more remote posts. In September, Cork Volunteers attacked British soldiers in Fermoy and made off with their rifles, leaving one soldier dead and three wounded. When the coroner's jury failed to return a verdict of murder against the assailants, troops from the local garrison wrecked the jurymen's shops, with no interference from the authorities.[12] This sequence of events was repeated with increasing frequency during the next two years.

Dublin Castle sought to stem the rising tide of rebellion with more repression. Dail Eireann was declared an illegal organization in September. Two months later, Sinn Fein, the Volunteers, and other separatist groups were banned throughout the country. The authorities also did their best to break up seditious meetings, suppress subversive publications, and lock up suspected rebels. But nothing seemed to work. The Dail continued to meet in secret, and the new *Irish Bulletin* ground out highly effective separatist propaganda. About 1,500 political offenses were reported during the latter half of 1919, including eighteen murders and seventy-seven armed attacks. In December, an assassination attempt on the viceroy, Lord French, pointed the way to bloodier times in 1920.[13]

The deterioration of the Irish situation was due largely to the British government's refusal to face political realities. As so often in the past, imagination, insight, and even common sense deserted the Crown's ministers when they dealt with Irish affairs. None of the Conservative ministers in the coalition had any real understanding of Irish nationalism. Belated recognition that some measure of autonomy could no longer be denied led them to approve Home Rule grudgingly, but only on condition that northeast Ulster be excluded from nationalist rule. Opposed to Sinn Fein's separatist demand and its terrorist tactics, Conservative leaders tried to ignore them as long as possible, and then tried to suppress them. While generally less belligerent than their Tory colleagues, Liberal ministers also held that Britain could not tolerate an

Irish Republic and that restoration of law and order must precede any political settlement.

Perhaps the most stubborn political foe of the rebels was the Liberal prime minister, Lloyd George. Although he had once championed the rights of his fellow Welshmen and the Boers, Lloyd George's opposition to Irish separatism was not out of character. He had never sought independence for Wales, only local autonomy within a federated United Kingdom. And he was not the enemy of the British Empire during the Boer War but of finance capitalism. Lloyd George was never a fervent advocate of Irish Home Rule, and he was one of the first Liberals to suggest separate treatment for Ulster. Since then, his wartime leadership had made the prime minister a convinced believer in power politics. He was more autocratic than before the war and more inclined to overrate the efficacy of force in resolving political problems. He had never really trusted Irishmen's capacity to govern themselves. He was disillusioned by their behavior during the war, and he strongly opposed any concessions to Irish nationalism that were likely to endanger Britain's security or the Empire's integrity. Sinn Fein's resort to force made Lloyd George even more determined to crush the Republican movement.

While it is true that Lloyd George's mishandling of Irish affairs from 1919 to 1921 was partly the result of political circumstances, this does not sensibly diminish his responsibility for a disastrous policy. He was heavily dependent on Conservative support, but the Tories needed Lloyd George almost as much as he needed them. His political skill and towering reputation enabled him to dominate Conservative colleagues and thereby exercise considerable influence over the party, however opposed to him some of its members might be. Had he urged conciliation, things could scarcely have gone as badly as they did, but he chose to take a hard line, preferring the counsel of those who shared his prejudices to the sensible advice offered by others. With this attitude, it is not surprising that a prime minister, preoccupied with other pressing problems, failed to give Ireland the attention it deserved. In the final analysis, Lloyd George's reliance on coercion was primarily the outgrowth of his willful ignorance and misunderstanding.

Given the attitude prevailing among its members, it is not surprising that the Cabinet's Irish policy from 1919 to 1921 was made and implemented without serious consideration of political ends or military means. Late in 1919, the government announced plans to enact a new Home Rule Bill. But this measure marked no advance beyond that of 1914 and was mainly intended to safeguard Ulster and pacify foreign opinion. Mistakenly assuming that a moderate majority could be found to implement Home Rule in nationalist Ireland if terrorism were suppressed, the government decided to isolate and crush the gunmen as the

Home Rule Bill made its way through Parliament. But this policy was bound to fail, not only because Home Rule was outdated, but also because the government lacked the means to destroy the IRA without alienating the Irish people—and the British as well. This muddled and self-defeating approach meant that the Cabinet would sanction stern measures, yet deny the means to implement them effectively. At the same time, it refused to revise its ideas on a political settlement or negotiate with the Irish people's elected leaders, whom British ministers dubbed a "murder gang." Inevitably, this course of action made a bad situation worse.[14]

In the autumn of 1919 the Cabinet appointed a committee to draft a scheme for Home Rule. In its report of November 1919 the Irish Committee recommended Home Rule for both Ulster and the rest of Ireland on equal terms. Inclusion of Ulster in an Irish parliament with minority safeguards was rejected because this would probably involve coercion and because safeguards were judged unworkable and undemocratic. The committee also rejected exclusion by plebiscite because this would create almost insuperable administrative problems for the excluded area, deepen and harden religious and political divisions, and impede eventual attainment of national unity more than any British-imposed settlement could do. Conferring Home Rule on both parts of Ireland would not involve coercion of Ulster, and by leaving the question of unity to be settled by the two Irish governments, it would demonstrate to Ireland, the Dominions, and the United States the sincerity of Britain's commitment to Irish self-government. The committee proposed that all nine counties of Ulster be included in the projected northern substate on grounds of administrative convenience and maintenance of something approaching an even balance between Catholics and Protestants in its population. To promote unity, which was not only desirable in itself but essential to secure moderate nationalist support for the new proposals, the committee recommended establishment of a Council of Ireland, composed of members of both Irish parliaments. The committee's report emphasized that the British government must withdraw from control of Irish domestic affairs altogether, so that Britain could not be accused of ruling nationalist majorities against their will or of giving support to Ulster in its refusal to unite with the rest of Ireland.[15]

Although the Cabinet felt these recommendations would arouse little enthusiasm and much opposition in Ireland, it approved them in principle and instructed the committee to work out the details. The need to improve relations with the United States and the Dominions ruled out inaction or delay.[16]

Initially, the aspect of the proposed settlement that most engaged the Cabinet's attention was the area to be included in Northern Ireland. Ministers generally felt that the government's ultimate aim was a united

Ireland, but this had to be achieved with maximum support and without offending Ulster's Protestants. With this in mind, the Cabinet provisionally approved a nine-county substate, but left the question open to further consideration. When the Cabinet learned that Ulster Unionist leaders wanted a substate that included only the six northeastern counties, so as to avoid governing three counties with large nationalist majorities, ministerial opinion changed. A six-county solution seemed to offer a greater chance of general acceptance and success than the one previously endorsed. Final Cabinet approval was given in February 1920, and Ulster Unionists were assured a safe majority in a substate which would be two-thirds Protestant.[17]

The question of finance was another important feature of Home Rule. Some ministers favored giving both Irish parliaments outright control of income tax, as well as customs and excise, or at least providing that this control be transferred if and when Ireland were unified. They believed that such a concession would show Britain's generous concern for Irish autonomy and rally support for Home Rule.[18] The prime minister adamantly opposed this idea, however, arguing that granting fiscal autonomy would break up the unity of the United Kingdom and that Sinn Fein would use it to secure complete separation. Only if there were no other way to obtain peace could such an important concession be made. The government must not barter away a great inheritance in a moment of despair to get "peace in our time, O Lord!"[19] Lloyd George had his way, and the only financial plum in his "good and generous" bill was the Treasury's gift of land-purchase payments to the two Irish governments.

Its financial limitations were a good indication of the character of the Government of Ireland Bill. Britain was to retain permanent control not only of customs and excise but of all matters involving the Crown, foreign affairs, defense, and external trade. Westminster would control income tax and the Post Office until Ireland was unified and would control the police for three years after Home Rule went into operation. To help safeguard minorities, the senates in the north and the south were to be chosen by small groups of voters, while both houses of commons would be elected by proportional representation. Irish representation at Westminster would continue, though on a much reduced basis. Almost the only hopeful note in the bill was its provision for a Council of Ireland representing both Irish parliaments. This body was to have power over railways, fisheries, and contagious animal diseases, and additional powers might be transferred to it by agreement of the two legislatures. By mutual accord, north and south might also establish an all-Ireland parliament, which would assume the powers given the two local legislatures, those given the Council of Ireland, and those reserved to Britain pending unification.[20] The prime minister outlined the Home Rule Bill to Parliament in December 1919; it was formally introduced in

February 1920 and, after much debate, became law on December 23, 1920.

Not surprisingly, the Home Rule Bill received almost no support in Ireland. Moderate nationalists as well as Sinn Feiners denounced partition and restrictions on Irish autonomy, while most southern Unionists felt betrayed. Ulster Unionists were also generally unhappy with a measure that conceded Home Rule to nationalist Ireland, gave the nationalists three of Ulster's counties, and conferred on the remaining six a parliament that loyalists had not sought. Despite these objections, Ulster Unionists decided not to oppose the bill. It excluded most of Ulster from nationalist rule and ensured a safe Unionist majority in the excluded area. Furthermore, if northern loyalists did not accept the bill, they risked being abandoned by their Conservative allies, who had lost most of their prewar enthusiasm for Ulster once Home Rule became inevitable.[21]

However ambivalent their original attitude, Ulster Unionists soon came to appreciate how much they gained from the Government of Ireland Act. Direct control of local affairs provided the most effective guarantee of Unionist supremacy in northeast Ulster and continued exclusion from an Irish state. Existence of a Unionist-dominated local parliament made it difficult for the British government to prevent discrimination against the Catholic minority in northern Ireland, and even more difficult to end partition by agreement with southern nationalists, however advantageous this might be for Britain. Once Ulster got Home Rule, its position became "unassailable."[22]

The government's Liberal and Labor critics not only denounced partition but demanded a more generous approach to the whole question of Home Rule. While there was general agreement that Britain could not tolerate an Irish republic, the idea that Ireland should be given Dominion status was gaining widespread support. In June 1919 the Irish Dominion League was formed, and its proposal of self-government with adequate minority safeguards appealed to moderate nationalists and some influential southern Unionists. By the end of 1920 the British Trades Union Congress and the Labor Party had endorsed this idea, and so had Asquith and other leaders of the Liberal opposition. General Macready, the military commander in Ireland, and Tom Jones, deputy secretary to the Cabinet, were among those who privately advised Lloyd George to offer Sinn Fein Dominion status, while some Conservative ministers urged the grant of fiscal autonomy to both parts of Ireland.[23]

However, the government categorically rejected proposals for Dominion status in 1919–20. In December 1919 the Cabinet agreed that "Dominion Home Rule had never been contemplated" for Ireland. Early in 1920, Bonar Law ruled out Dominion status on the grounds that Sinn Fein would use the freedom it conferred to secede from the Empire and establish a republic in southern Ireland. In October, Lloyd George asserted that the Irish could not be trusted with control of their own armed forces; that is, an Irish Dominion would be too great a menace to Britain and Ulster. Government spokesmen argued convincingly that it would be no use imposing restrictions on Ireland's freedom in a Dominion settlement because they would be incompatible with the practical independence enjoyed by other Dominions.[24]

While the British argued about the suitability of various forms of Home Rule, Sinn Fein pressed its drive for full independence. In the local-government elections of 1920, the party did very well, despite British introduction of proportional representation to encourage minority interests. Municipal elections in January gave Sinn Fein control of 10 of 12 cities and boroughs. With Home Rulers in power in Derry City, only the Belfast Corporation remained in Unionist hands. Sinn Fein also won a majority of seats on 72 of 127 municipal corporations and urban councils, and with Home Rule support controlled 26 others. In the rural elections in June, Sinn Fein captured all but four county councils (Antrim, Down, Armagh, and Derry remained Unionist) and won control of the great majority of rural councils and poor-law boards. While many seats were uncontested in these elections, a good-size vote, independent of Sinn Fein and Unionism, was recorded, and the results may be taken as a fair indication of the state of Irish political opinion.[25]

Local-government bodies controlled by Sinn Fein soon repudiated the authority of Dublin Castle and declared allegiance to Dail Eireann. By the end of 1920, almost all of them were acting under the supervision of Cosgrave's Ministry of Local Government. Outside Dublin, the British were unable to end this defiance of their authority. Cutting off Treasury grants-in-aid to rebellious public bodies forced curtailment of services, but local government continued to operate under Republican auspices.[26]

The British government lost another round when Sinn Fein supplanted its judicial authority outside northeast Ulster. Rural agitation early in 1920 caused landholders to turn to newly created Republican arbitration courts. The initial success of these bodies led to establishment of a national system of civil and criminal courts in August. The IRA enforced the edicts of the Republican courts, and they attracted business from all classes; judges were Irish, law and procedure English, and decisions usually just. Even Unionists soon ignored the heavily guarded but empty British courts. Embarrassed by this development, the British tried to suppress the Sinn Fein tribunals, but they were only partially successful. Driven underground by raids and arrests, some courts still managed to meet secretly and carry on business. To Britain's chagrin, Griffith's program of national initiative and self-reliance was proving much more than an idle theory.[27]

Military developments caused the British even more discomfort in 1920. Attacks on the RIC provoked a number of reprisals in Cork and Tipperary. Dublin Castle ordered more arrests and raids, and in February instituted a curfew in Dublin. Curfew was later extended to other cities and towns, but it punished the people more than it obstructed rebel activities. On April 3 the Volunteers burned over 300 evacuated police barracks and almost 100 income-tax offices, hampering tax collection and preventing reoccupation of many villages by the RIC. Such an operation showed that the rebels could mount large-scale actions without betraying advance warning.[28]

Captured rebels caused almost as much trouble as those at liberty. Prisoners in Dublin's Mountjoy jail staged a ten-day hunger strike in April to compel prisoner-of-war treatment or release. Their protest won widespread support and the government capitulated, releasing the prisoners unconditionally. Other hunger strikes met with similar success, until the government decided it must take a firm line. Once this was made clear and hunger strikers began to die, Sinn Fein ordered the tactic abandoned.[29]

In May, Irish railwaymen added to Britain's problems when they refused to transport troops, police, or munitions. Although they eventually had to surrender, the railway workers' strike lasted seven months, hindering efforts to crush the IRA and providing an impressive display of labor's support for Sinn Fein.[30]

By far the most crucial part of the Anglo-Irish struggle, however, was the secret war waged by rival intelligence services. Spies and informers had frustrated every previous attempt at revolt in Ireland, and another defeat was certain if Sinn Fein failed to checkmate British intelligence. Success in this vital area owed something to British mistakes but much more to the work of Michael Collins.

Born in west Cork in October 1890, Collins was raised in that region's strongly nationalist tradition and became a boyhood admirer of the Fenians and Arthur Griffith. In 1906 he went to London to work as a junior clerk in the Post Office. For ten years he lived in the metropolis, holding a succession of clerical jobs and becoming active in various Irish organizations, including the London branch of the IRB, which he joined in 1909. Collins returned to Dublin in January 1916 to take part in the coming insurrection and to escape conscription in Britain. As a staff captain at rebel headquarters, he played a creditable if minor part in the fighting.

After the rising, Collins was interned at Frongoch, where he and like-minded separatists began reorganization of the IRB, which had been broken up by executions and arrests.[31] His ability and energy quickly won the bluff, burly Corkman a position of leadership among the younger and more militant internees, but his forceful, domineering manner annoyed some prisoners, who sneered: "Collins thinks he's a big fellow."[32] Before long, Collins' achievements turned this gibe into a tribute, and he became widely and affectionately known among his countrymen as the "Big Fellow."

Returning to Ireland in December 1916, Collins became secretary to the National Aid Association, a relief organization for victims of the rising. He made many valuable contacts in this job and made good use of them in the work of rebuilding the IRB and the Volunteers. When the Supreme Council was reconstituted in the autumn of 1917, Collins became a member, serving first as secretary and later as president.[33] Largely through IRB influence, he was elected to both the Volunteer and Sinn Fein executives in October 1917. He also became director of organization and adjutant general of the Volunteers, and in 1919 director of intelligence.

It was in this last job that Collins made his greatest contribution to the revolutionary movement. He created a highly effective network of agents in Dublin and kept in close touch with Volunteer units throughout the country and with Sinn Fein agents in Britain. His contacts were legion—postal clerks, waiters, maids, porters, barmen, bootblacks, telephone operators, dockers, seamen, and members of the social elite; even Dublin Castle detectives worked for Collins. From an army of unpaid agents he received a constant stream of information, which his well-ordered mind assembled, evaluated, and acted upon. But Collins knew that it was not enough to know British plans if the British also knew his; so he dealt with detectives, spies, and informers as occasion dictated—by stratagems, threats, or death. To carry out dangerous assignments, he formed an elite unit, "the Squad," from men of the Dublin Brigade. By 1920, Collins' intelligence system functioned smoothly and efficiently. He acquired a reputation as a man who got things done, and in return for his aid and encouragement active IRA officers gave Collins their trust and information and led hard-hitting attacks on the enemy.

Although he was mainly involved in military affairs, Collins was also active in other areas. As head of the IRB, he sought to use the Brotherhood's influence to encourage and coordinate revolutionary operations. As minister of finance, he raised and disbursed the money essential for these operations, allocating funds where they were most needed. Finally, for a brief period at the end of 1920, Collins was acting president of the Republic and played a leading role in abortive truce negotiations at that time.

The British recognized Collins' importance and did their utmost to capture him, but they never succeeded. He had encounters with Crown forces but always managed to bluff his way through. Many people knew him by sight, but they were either friends or they learned to look the other way when he passed. Day after day he cycled through Dublin on his rounds, and night after night he kept his business appointments in bars and hotels. Although members of the Squad sometimes hovered nearby, Collins usually traveled alone.[34] He believed it best to go his way as inconspicuously as possible, affecting no elaborate precautions or disguise. Burdened by too much work to be cautious in his movements, he realized that a crowd is the most effective cover for a wanted man. Somehow, his luck and nerves held up, and his work got done.

While Collins was never the legendary figure that foreign journalists made him out to be, he was much more than just a clever gunman. Few people knew it during his lifetime, but Collins was an extremely complex person. Most associates knew him simply as quick thinking and hard working, alternating between moods of boisterous good humor and ferocious anger, lamenting all the hours "wasted" in sleep. He had another side, but it was rarely seen because of his tremendous self-discipline. Behind the tough facade, Collins was sensitive and idealistic. A man of almost feminine compassion, he was increasingly oppressed by constant strain and the knowledge that his decisions had sent comrades to their death. Occasionally, his optimism and buoyant spirits deserted him, and he lapsed into moods of black despair, to be revived only by his indomitable will and faith in a free Ireland. Acutely aware that his humanity could prove fatal, Collins sought to repress his deeper feelings, thereby intensifying the strain on his nerves. Close friends knew of Collins' inner warmth and idealism, and it was these traits as much as his awesome efficiency and energy that inspired their devotion and enabled them to put up with his brusque behavior and frequent rages.[35]

Collins' relations with other revolutionary leaders powerfully influenced events from 1917 to 1922. His association with active IRA officers was friendly and productive. Most separatist politicians also liked and admired Collins, but he made some enemies because of his IRB activities, blunt manner, and interference in others' areas of authority.[36] Within the Republican Cabinet, Cathal Brugha and Austin Stack hated him. Brugha, as minister of defense, strongly opposed Collins' efforts to control the Volunteers through the IRB and resented the attention given him by the press. Others realized that Collins shunned, rather than sought, publicity and that his influence in the IRA was the result of hard work rather than sensational journalism or IRB connections. Brugha was convinced, however, that Collins was trying to undermine his authority over the army, partly by claiming credit for the military achievements of others. This enraged Brugha, largely because he felt it dishonored the Republican cause but probably also because he was jealous of Collins' power and fame. Brugha's enmity was a real danger to Collins and to rebel unity. Although Brugha had no executive ability, he was Collins' military superior and was widely admired in the IRA for his courage and dedication. He could therefore undermine Collins' effectiveness by trying to discredit him. Brugha made no secret of his mistrust and contempt for Griffith's moderation, and he attacked de Valera himself when he believed that the president might compromise the Republican ideal. But Collins was the main object of his hostility.

Brugha gained an ally in 1920 when Austin Stack replaced acting President Griffith as minister for home affairs. Until this time, Collins and Stack had been close friends, and Stack owed his inclusion in the Cabinet partly to Collins' high opinion of his ability. In this case, however, Collins was mistaken; Stack could run hunger strikes but not an important government department. The fact that his health had been undermined and his disposition soured by prison hardships only made matters worse. The impatient and forthright Collins lost no time in pointing out Stack's deficiencies, telling him his department was "a bloody joke." Characteristically, Collins quickly forgot these outbursts, but Stack did not. He nursed his resentment, until it grew into a hatred as fierce as Brugha's. It made no difference that Collins bore no malice toward either man. He knew they hated him and could be counted upon to oppose almost anything he said or did.[37]

Surprisingly, there was no real friction between Collins and Griffith during the Anglo-Irish war. They had clashed frequently over policy from 1917 to 1919, and Griffith continued to harbor misgivings about the Republican commitment and terrorist tactics; however, he stood loyally behind the IRA. This attitude suited Collins; he and Griffith worked together throughout the war and learned mutual respect.[38]

Collins' relationship with de Valera was more ambiguous. The two men respected each other but they never became close. De Valera was polite and considerate but always reserved, and his deliberation over even the smallest matters puzzled and sometimes annoyed Collins. He tried to dissuade de Valera from going to America, and when de Valera returned, Collins was both amused and disturbed by his ignorance of the military situation and less inclined to accept his views on other matters. Probably the main cause of the coolness between them was the IRB, which de Valera regarded as a threat to the government's authority. Despite their differences, there was nothing like an open breach between them. De Valera valued Collins' ability and loyalty, and Collins respected de Valera's integrity and tact. The essence of their relationship might best be described as mutual but guarded admiration.[39]

By the spring of 1920, events had convinced the British government that new men and measures were necessary to stamp out rebellion in Ireland. Reorganization of the Irish Executive was given first priority. The separatist challenge and British vacillation had left Dublin Castle's administration in a state of near collapse, out of touch with all but Unionist opinion and unable to control the Crown forces.[40]

In April, Sir Hamar Greenwood, a coalition Liberal, was appointed chief secretary for Ireland. A Canadian by birth, Greenwood was cheerful, bluff, and outspoken, with a reputation as a "strong man" from his army service during the European war. He did not lack physical courage, but he was not the man to govern Ireland. He knew nothing of the country, and his attempts to justify coercion were marked by evasions, exaggeration, and outright lies. Instead of discrediting Sinn Fein and the government's critics, Greenwood ended by discrediting the government.[41]

Sir John Anderson was Greenwood's ranking subordinate and the most important man in the new regime. Appointed senior undersecretary in May, he served as resident head of the Castle administration, restoring efficiency to its creaking machinery and demonstrating the ability which led to a highly distinguished career in Whitehall. Alfred W. "Andy" Cope was named assistant undersecretary in the summer of 1920. A former customs detective with an aversion to orthodox administrative methods, Cope was really Lloyd George's special agent, charged with informally exploring avenues of settlement with Sinn Fein.[42]

Control of the police was entrusted to Major General H. H. Tudor in May 1920, and Colonel Sir Ormonde Winter was sent to Dublin as Tudor's deputy to reorganize the intelligence system. His job was to coordinate police and military intelligence, reopen channels of information from spies and informers, and set up a secret service. Since police intelligence had virtually collapsed, Winter had to rely heavily on military aid in his efforts to defeat Collins.[43] General Sir Nevil Macready was named general officer commanding-in-chief in Ireland in late March. He had no sympathy for either Sinn Feiners or Ulster Unionists, having served in Ulster during the prewar crisis. Indeed, his unhappy experience in Ireland made Macready reluctant to return there, but he accepted command of the military garrison out of loyalty to his old chief, Lord French, now viceroy.[44]

Although the conflict in Ireland was becoming nasty in 1920, the British government was unwilling to admit that a state of war existed. Such an admission would have conferred belligerent status on the rebels and acknowledged that resistance was not confined to a small band of terrorists. This fact, together with a shortage of troops and lack of public support, ruled out martial law and left the police to play the main role in suppressing rebellion.[45] To prepare the RIC for its formidable task, units were concentrated in heavily fortified barracks in the larger towns. The government also decided to equip the constabulary with wireless and signal equipment, automatic weapons, and motor vehicles for extended patrols. To bring the depleted force up to strength, recruiting was opened in Britain early in 1920.[46]

The initial appeal for 1,500 men was very successful, and by the time recruiting ended, two years later, there were 5,200 British members of the RIC (plus another 1,450 in its Auxiliary Division). Many more had volunteered, but were rejected or discharged as undesirable. Recruits got ten shillings a day and maintenance, but neither this nor interest in police work explains the press of volunteers, because many police vacancies in Britain, with equal pay and little risk, went unfilled in 1920.[47]

In March 1920 the first recruits arrived from Britain. Since there was a shortage of RIC uniforms, the new men were dressed in army khaki with black belts and RIC caps. Almost at once they were dubbed "Black and Tans" (after a famous pack of Limerick foxhounds) and the name stuck, even after they received regular police uniforms, because their accents and behavior usually distinguished them from Irish members of the RIC.

In July the government created the Auxiliary Division of the RIC. The Auxiliary cadets (or "Auxies"), an elite unit of 1,500 ex-officers, were paid twice as much as regular police and eventually outfitted in dark blue uniforms with dark green caps. Their fifteen companies were commanded by an excitable Anglo-Irishman, Brigadier Frank P. Crozier, under General Tudor's overall authority. The Auxies, however, were largely a law unto themselves, with even less discipline than the Tans.

Despite their notorious reputation, the RIC's British recruits were not a collection of criminals and psychotics, although examples of both could be found in their ranks. They were mostly veterans who wanted the excitement of military life without its discipline or boredom, and the government deserves much of the blame for their misconduct because it gave them a job they could not do. The Tans and Auxies were useless as police because they lacked proper experience and training. Furthermore, they knew nothing about the Irish people or the areas in which they were stationed, and they did not benefit from association with embittered regulars in the RIC. On the other hand, the Tans and Auxies were almost useless as soldiers because they had no experience of guerrilla warfare and no training in counterinsurgency tactics. Nor were they subject to military discipline; bad conduct usually meant only discharge, and this did not matter to men uninterested in police careers.

In trying to carry out a task for which they were hopelessly unfit, the recruits and regulars of the RIC only made things worse. Their casualties were minimal but they were under constant strain. Crown forces were exposed to attack whenever they left their barracks, and all but the largest of these barracks might be assaulted at any time. When the rebels staged a raid or an ambush, it was hard to kill or capture them. The IRA generally chose the time and place for a fight, broke off action if seriously threatened, and melted away into crowded Dublin streets or the lonely hills of Cork. Goaded into rage by the unseen enemy, the police struck back at the civil population, whom they blamed for shielding the

IRA. Roaring into a town or village in the middle of the night, drunken police tore up and down the streets in their lorries, yelling and shooting, frequently looting pubs and shops, and setting fire to homes, stores, and Sinn Fein clubs. Sometimes they killed people, adding charges of murder to those of assault, arson, and robbery. Reprisals provoked by IRA attacks caused more attacks, and these in turn brought more reprisals in a mounting spiral of violence.

Police anger was natural enough under the circumstances, but, quite apart from this, it was difficult to punish their outrages. Policemen could not be court-martialed, yet it was hardly fair to turn them over to Irish juries, which convicted servants of the Crown as routinely as they acquitted Sinn Feiners. Fines and dismissal of offenders were common, but this was not adequate punishment for some police crimes. The authorities compounded the problem by their reluctance to admit that crimes had been committed. This attitude may have prevented a complete breakdown of police discipline and morale, but it further antagonized the Irish people and raised storms of protest when the facts were made known.[48]

To assist the Crown forces and control indiscipline, Parliament passed the Restoration of Order Act in August 1920. It empowered military courts to try and condemn civilians to death if they were convicted of specified seditious offenses. However, military courts were hampered by dependence on unreliable witnesses and by defendants' right of appeal to regular courts. General Macready was well aware of these limitations, but he was willing to use any legal weapon that would help curb "unauthorized reprisals," which he felt would destroy military and police discipline if allowed to continue. By the end of 1920, Macready felt compelled to press for martial law, not because he believed it would resolve the Irish problem but because it was distinctly preferable to undisciplined terrorism.[49]

The government's chief military adviser was much more critical of its policy than Macready, but also more confident of the success of drastic measures. Field Marshal Sir Henry Wilson, chief of the Imperial General Staff, was a fanatic Unionist who opposed any concessions to Irish nationalism. In July 1920 he told Winston Churchill, the secretary of state for war, that existing policy was suicidal; the government must take strong measures or retire. However, Wilson warned that the government must convince the British people that strong measures were necessary or coercion was bound to fail. In September, he denounced police reprisals to Lloyd George and Bonar Law, declaring that they would lead to ruin. The government must govern, and if some men should be murdered, the government should murder them. Lloyd George reacted angrily to this suggestion, asserting that no government could take responsibility for such action. Yet the Cabinet was disturbed at the effects of unauthorized reprisals; it tried to curb them, and ministerial concern mounted as indiscipline grew worse.[50]

In December 1920, drunken Auxies set fires in the center of Cork City which destroyed several million pounds' worth of property. The prime minister took this occasion to impress upon Greenwood and Tudor the need for tighter police discipline, prevention of embarrassing incidents, and investigation and punishment of misconduct. He was especially concerned about the effect of such outrages on American opinion.[51]

In January 1921, the government instituted a policy of official reprisals against property, but it failed to halt excesses by Crown forces. At the end of February, the prime minister protested to Greenwood that misbehavior must be stopped at once. It seriously weakened the Irish Executive and its continuance would completely alienate an already unhappy public and force surrender to rebellion.[52] But while ministers privately acknowledged that police misconduct was a serious problem, they minimized the problem in public, even denying that it existed. When government critics proved that outrages had occurred, government spokesmen tried to blame the IRA and, failing this, claimed that police indiscipline was the result of intolerable provocation. Apologists also argued that, however regrettable reprisals might be, they helped crush rebellion. To one of its critics, the Cabinet's position seemed to be: "There is no such thing as reprisals, but they have done a great deal of good."[53]

By any sane reckoning, the government's policy was disastrous. Its Home Rule Bill had no nationalist support, and its competition in crime with the rebels was the worst sort of folly. Reports of police outrages by Sinn Fein, courageous British journalists, and independent commissions of inquiry turned domestic and world opinion against the government. By the end of 1920 the actions of the police were clearly hurting the Crown more than they did the rebels.

But however forceful the denunciations of the Black and Tans, more than propaganda was needed to defeat them. To meet the challenge, the IRA formed "flying columns," small units that were capable of ambushing large patrols and undertaking other offensive operations. These columns, based in concealed camps, spent most of their time on the move, seeking favorable conditions to engage the enemy. Although the IRA numbered over 70,000 men by mid-1921, its active service units probably numbered only about 5,000, not more than 3,000 of whom served in flying columns. Available arms and ammunition determined the strength of fighting units, and the IRA never had more than about 3,300 rifles, most of them obtained from the enemy.[54]

Flying columns were most active in the southwest, particularly in County Cork. On November 28, 1920, a column of thirty-six men, led by Tom Barry, a daring young veteran of the British army, ambushed a motorized patrol of eighteen Auxies near Kilmichael in west Cork and killed all but one of them, with a loss of only three Volunteers. In March 1921, Barry commanded a column of over 100 men in a series of attacks against four converging forces of more than 1,000 soldiers and Auxies at Crossbarry, near Bandon. He broke through the closing ring with a loss of only three killed and four wounded. The British lost thirty-nine killed and forty-seven wounded, as well as a large quantity of rifles and ammunition and several lorries.[55]

While the IRA and the Crown forces shot it out in the south, the intelligence duel in Dublin entered a more critical and deadly phase. Colonel Winter did his best to construct an effective espionage network, but reliable spies and informers were hard to come by and police and military intelligence efforts were never fully coordinated.[56] However, one operation posed a serious threat to Collins. A group of secret-service officers was sent to Ireland to break up his intelligence system, and perhaps to kill him as well. For some months, Collins gathered information about these agents, and when he was satisfied of their identity and purpose, he struck. On Sunday morning, November 21, 1920, the Squad and other picked Volunteers shot fourteen men to death and wounded several others. These shootings apparently wiped out most of the important secret-service operatives in Dublin and drove other intelligence personnel to seek refuge inside the Castle, ending their usefulness as spies.[57]

The second act of "Bloody Sunday" took place that afternoon at Dublin's Croke Park, where thousands had gathered for a football match. Castle authorities planned to search the crowd in hope of capturing some IRA gunmen. A party of Auxies arrived at the park and, almost immediately, shots were fired. Who fired them is uncertain, but once the Auxies heard the shots, they began firing into the crowd. The shooting lasted several minutes, as the panic-stricken spectators tried to escape. When it ended, twelve people were dead and sixty injured. In the public mind, this outrage overshadowed the morning's assassinations. While it may not have been a reprisal for the killings, it was triggered by the anger and nervous strain the assassinations produced among the Crown forces, and it *seemed* like a reprisal to the public, intensifying hostility to British rule.[58]

Bloody Sunday and the Kilmichael ambush marked the beginning of the final and most savage phase of the Anglo-Irish war, whose tragedy was heightened by the deaths of Terence McSwiney and Kevin Barry. MacSwiney, the imprisoned lord mayor of Cork, died on October 25 after a hunger strike of seventy-four days. A week later, Kevin Barry, an eighteen-year-old medical student, was hanged for his part in a Dublin ambush. Despite public demands for clemency in both cases, the government stood firm, creating two more heroic martyrs and further impeding efforts to pacify Ireland.[59]

Strange as it may seem, mounting violence did not prevent the Irish people from living generally normal lives. Hostilities were largely confined to a small area of the country, with relatively few people actively involved. Except during the strike in the latter half of 1920, trains continued to run without interference and most main roads were open. Newspapers appeared regularly, business was carried on more or less as usual, and public houses did a flourishing trade, although a number were robbed or wrecked by the Tans. Curfew made theatergoing and formal dances impossible, but the cinema and tea dances proved popular replacements. Most important, the Irishman's traditional love of sport was gratified. Football matches were still held up and down the country, and race meetings continued through a tacit agreement to abstain from violence at the tracks. At the races, gunmen rubbed elbows with soldiers and police while people in pubs and restaurants in Dublin and Cork discussed the latest sporting event, sometimes to the accompaniment of shots or explosions in the street outside. The Irish people devoutly wished for an end to violence, but while it lasted, they adapted.[60]

The attitude of the Catholic hierarchy offers a good example of moderate men caught in an agonizing dilemma. The bishops refused to recognize the Republican government, and only one of their number, Dr. Fogarty of Killaloe, could accurately be labeled a Sinn Fein supporter. On the other hand, Dr. Cohalan of Cork was the only bishop to condemn the IRA unequivocally. When episcopal condemnations were issued, they usually condemned both sides. And though bishops warned their priests against defending the IRA, little if any disciplinary action was taken against clergy or laity who took part in the struggle against Britain. The hierarchy's attitude left Sinn Fein and Dublin Castle alike dissatisfied, but the bishops could hardly have acted otherwise. They were the defenders of morality and legitimate authority, but it was difficult to decide what was moral and what was legitimate during a revolution. Whatever protests the bishops' political caution evoked, it entailed the least risk to their spiritual authority and so served the Church's primary interest.[61]

Violence in Ulster during 1920 threatened to supplant rebellion as the main problem in Ireland. In May and June, Protestant mobs attacked the Catholic quarter in Derry City, and four days of rioting in July left nineteen persons dead and more than fifty wounded. In Belfast, trouble erupted on July 21. Catholics had replaced many Protestants in the shipyards during the war, and the sudden collapse of the postwar boom in 1920 left shipbuilding a depressed industry. Protestant workers had their own remedy for job competition and suspected political disloyalty: they drove 5,000 Catholic workers out of the yards. The fighting that began on July 21 set off an orgy of riot and destruction that convulsed Belfast repeatedly during the next two years.

In the initial violence, Orange mobs attacked Catholic homes, shops, pubs, convents, churches, and hostels, leaving seven dead and about 200 wounded. Disorder spread quickly to neighboring towns where Catholics were burned out of their homes and forced to flee to refugee centers in Belfast. Order was restored on July 25 but the respite was short, and by September sixty-two civilians had been killed in Belfast. When the carnival of violence ended in June 1922, it was estimated that 428 people had been killed and 1,766 wounded, most of them Catholics. Almost 9,000 Catholics had been driven from their employment, and about 23,000 had been expelled from their homes.[62]

British ministers were alarmed by these disturbances and by the pessimistic assessment of the Ulster Unionist leader, Sir James Craig, who claimed that loyalists were losing faith in the government's determination to protect them and were threatening to resort to arms to protect themselves. To help put matters right, Craig asked for what amounted to a separate administration for the six counties in anticipation of passage of the Government of Ireland Bill. The British gave Craig part of what he asked for by agreeing to appointment of an assistant under-secretary for the northeast and to organization of a force of special constables to help maintain order.[63]

Nationalists contributed to the troubles in Ulster by their obvious failure to understand the loyalist mentality. Even when it was defensive, IRA activity in the northeast encouraged more attacks on the Catholic minority and widened the division between north and south. The Belfast boycott was the crowning blunder of Sinn Fein's Ulster policy. A boycott of Belfast goods began in the west of Ireland during the summer of 1920 as a reaction to the imposition of loyalty tests on Catholics who sought employment in the city. The IRA enforced this boycott, and it spread to Dublin. In August, its supporters urged the Dail to sanction the boycott, but several deputies strongly opposed this. Griffith, while warning against practically declaring war on a part of Ireland, admitted that action was called for to aid Ulster nationalists. The Dail outlawed loyalty tests and, as they remained in force, appointed a director of the boycott. In January 1921 the Cabinet took full responsibility for the boycott and later extended its application to other Unionist towns in the northeast. Some parts of the south and west applied it to the entire six counties. The boycott became increasingly effective, but it hurt Ulster Catholics more than Protestants. Moreover, it constituted tacit recognition of partition before it was formally enacted. Admittedly, there was little hope of winning unity by conciliation, but coercion only made matters worse.[64]

During the autumn of 1920 there were several abortive attempts at Anglo-Irish peacemaking. The most important of these came in December, owing to the intercession of Archbishop Clune of Australia. While in London after a visit to his native Ireland, Clune met Lloyd

George and pressed for a truce and negotiations with Sinn Fein. When the prime minister expressed interest in the idea, Clune returned to Dublin, saw Griffith and Collins, and helped draft a truce formula, which he presented to Lloyd George. However, unofficial overtures had convinced the prime minister that Sinn Fein was anxious for peace, and he was reluctant to make concessions.

On December 9 the British Cabinet approved the imposition of martial law in Cork, Kerry, Limerick, and Tipperary. At the same time, it stated Britain's terms for peace: no coercion of northeast Ulster, no secession from the United Kingdom, and effective guarantees for British security. Moreover, an end to violence and surrender of arms by the rebels were made essential conditions for a truce. Griffith and Collins rejected the truce terms as a demand for capitulation and broke off the talks. Clune reported to Lloyd George that there would be no truce so long as the Cabinet insisted on arms surrender. On December 24 the Cabinet discussed the question and decided to adhere to its demand. It also agreed to elicit the views of senior officials in Ireland on whether to postpone further approaches to Sinn Fein until the Home Rule Act had been put into operation.[65]

On December 29 Lloyd George, Bonar Law, and Churchill conferred with Greenwood, Anderson, Wilson, Macready, Tudor, and Generals Boyd and Strickland, the military commanders of the Dublin and Cork areas. Macready expressed optimism about the military situation and asked that martial law be extended to four more counties in the south. Tudor was also optimistic. The police were in much better shape than during the previous spring; they could now move about freely and were almost out of danger, except for ambushes.

The prime minister wondered whether the police could be controlled if a truce were made. Tudor thought so, but Lloyd George appeared dubious and pressed for measures to end police misconduct. Questioned about the risks of a truce without the surrender of rebel arms, Macready replied that if this were judged politically desirable, it would cause no great problem, but he warned that if the military stopped raids and arrests, its intelligence machinery would suffer, placing the army at a disadvantage if the struggle were resumed. Anderson, Tudor, and Boyd expressed similar fears and opposed a truce. So did Bonar Law, who argued that a truce might discourage the troops and intensify Sinn Fein propaganda. Wilson declared that a truce would be "absolutely fatal."

Lloyd George inquired how long it would take to smash the rebels without a truce. Could Sinn Fein interfere with a Home Rule election in February or March? Macready answered that Collins would enforce a general boycott of the election at pistol point. Lloyd George commented sharply that this did not say much for the success of the government's policy. Macready countered by declaring that imposition of martial law throughout Ireland would break the rebels. Strickland, Boyd, and Tudor maintained that a valid election could be held in four months if there were no truce, while Wilson thought that countrywide martial law would bring decisive results in six months.[66]

On December 30 the Cabinet agreed to extend martial law to Kilkenny, Clare, Wexford, and Waterford, and to put the Government of Ireland Act into operation as soon as possible. Archbishop Clune was dismissed with thanks early in January. A week later, he publicly blamed the failure of the truce negotiations on the government's demand for arms surrender. Further desultory peace efforts in the early months of 1921 served only to keep communication open between the two sides.[67]

Although 1920 closed with no end of the war in sight, Ireland received one Christmas present. President de Valera returned from his eighteen-month mission to the United States and resumed control of the Republican government.

De Valera had been warmly received in the United States, but his work had been hampered from the start by the antagonism of two powerful Irish-American leaders, John Devoy and Judge Daniel Cohalan, the former an aged Fenian, the latter a New York Democratic Party chieftain. Together, the two men controlled the Clan na Gael, although the real power rested with Cohalan, who wielded decisive influence over his deaf and querulous associate. Through their most powerful front organization, the Friends of Irish Freedom, Cohalan and Devoy directed propaganda and fund raising before de Valera's arrival. Jealous of their power, they strongly opposed the Irish president's proposal to float a loan that would be under the Dail's control, and the bond drive's success only alienated them further.

The trouble went much deeper than this, however. Cohalan believed that Germany's defeat had ruined any chance for an Irish republic; he therefore favored an appeal for Irish national self-determination rather than for recognition of the Republic. The judge was also intent on using the Irish issue to help prevent American membership in the League of Nations. He and his allies wanted America to remain free of foreign entanglements and prepare for a war with Britain which would win the United States world supremacy. While sympathetic to the Irish cause, Cohalan and his followers were also chauvinistic, and their insistence on controlling Irish agitation in America was motivated primarily by their devotion to what they saw as American national interests.

De Valera, of course, saw things differently. He wanted agitation in America to further Irish aims. He had no interest in fomenting discord between the United States and Britain once Ireland won its freedom, and he believed that the League of Nations was a hopeful experiment in the cause of world peace which all nations should support.

The quarrel with the Clan leaders was brought to a head by publication of de Valera's "Cuban Statement" in February 1920. Seeking to allay British fears about an independent Ireland, the Sinn Fein leader declared that Ireland was prepared to accept the status of permanent neutrality, which might be guaranteed by treaty. In outlining this idea, de Valera used the analogy of the 1903 treaty between the United States and Cuba, which provided that Cuba would not enter into arrangements with foreign powers directed against the United States.[68]

Although de Valera had no thought of making Ireland a British satellite (as Cuba was an American satellite), Devoy and Cohalan tried to make it appear otherwise. Seizing on the Irish president's hint of compromise, they attacked him for surrendering Ireland's demand for complete independence. De Valera fought back vigorously, informing the Dublin Cabinet that his suggestion was designed simply to promote peace negotiations and alleging that Cohalan and Devoy had attacked him only because they wanted to discredit him and make him their puppet. The Cabinet loyally accepted this explanation and so did the IRB, which severed its connection with the Clan in October 1920. However, Joseph McGarrity and other supporters of de Valera excluded the Devoy-Cohalan faction from a reorganized Clan, and the Supreme Council eventually recognized this body.[69]

But while de Valera's counterattack was fairly successful, the Irish-American community remained deeply divided and was unable to exert much influence in the national election of 1920. However, even had there been no split it is doubtful that either the Democrats or the Republicans in the United States would have done more than endorse Ireland's right to self-determination; few, if any, American politicians were willing to risk war with Britain for the sake of a phantom republic. And when the victorious Republicans interpreted their triumph at the polls as a mandate for isolationism, it was clear that Ireland could expect no favors from the new administration. To rally his supporters, de Valera founded the American Association for the Recognition of the Irish Republic in November 1920. The new organization soon outstripped the rival Friends of Irish Freedom in membership and influence, and gave valuable support to the Irish cause.

The Irish president originally planned only a short visit to the United States, but the fight with the old guard and the urging of the Dail Cabinet caused him to prolong it. The Cabinet felt that de Valera was doing important work and would surely be arrested if he returned to Ireland. At the end of November 1920, however, de Valera learned that Griffith had been arrested, and news also reached him of British peace feelers and plans for intensified coercion. He therefore decided to return to Ireland without delay and arrived in Dublin secretly on December 23.[70]

Although he failed to win recognition of the Republic, de Valera's

American mission was more a success than a failure. He won widespread popular sympathy and obtained millions of dollars for the Irish cause, as well as helped to focus world attention on his country's struggle. His activities gave much-needed hope to his followers at home and a bad case of nerves to the British government. The fact that both the Irish and the British overestimated America's emotional involvement in Irish affairs was partly a tribute to de Valera's success.

Had the president remained in Ireland, he could hardly have rendered such signal service to his nation's cause. But if de Valera influenced America, it also influenced him. The fight with Cohalan and Devoy made him more cautious in expressing his views and more sensitive to criticism. His amazing reception as "President of the Irish Republic" deepened his sense of the responsibility of that office and made him more aloof from his colleagues. His determination to have things his own way when he returned home, even though he was out of touch with events, was partly the result of his transatlantic experience.

The American mission had served Ireland well; whether it served de Valera well is open to question.

Chapter 4
The Last Phase:
January-July 1921

President de Valera returned to Ireland with two major proposals. The first was that Collins should visit the United States to help restore Irish-American unity and obtain more financial aid. Second, his absence from Ireland would preclude a clean sweep of the revolutionary leadership by Britain. Although the Cabinet agreed to the idea, Collins protested strongly, convinced that Brugha and Stack were behind the proposal and that the war effort would suffer badly if he left his post. Eventually, he agreed to go to America, but by then peace negotiations appeared imminent and de Valera decided he could not be spared. However, the abortive plan probably caused the first serious misunderstanding between the two leaders.[1]

The president also wanted to reduce the level of terrorism. Concern about the burden guerrilla warfare imposed on the people and its adverse effects on public opinion led him to suggest that the IRA should fight fewer and more conventional engagements. Both the Dail and the leaders of the army appreciated the realities of the military situation, however, and when they strongly opposed this proposal, de Valera withdrew it.[2] This defeat made the president all the more determined to refute British charges that the IRA was nothing more than a "murder gang." On March 30, 1921, with the Dail's authorization, he declared that the IRA was a national defense force, and the Republican government took full responsibility for its actions. At the same time, de Valera unequivocally endorsed the Volunteers' tactics, contending that ambushes were fully justified to repel the invaders' unjust attacks on the Irish people and their government.[3] In later statements he repeated his assertion that the Dail controlled the IRA, both to spike rumors of division and to refute allegations that the IRA ran the government.[4]

While the president defended them, the Volunteers stepped up operations. The number of ambushes increased and road-cutting and destruction of loyalists' homes became common. In Dublin, 120 IRA members seized and burned the Customs House on May 25, destroying vital tax and local-government records. The action proved costly, for about seventy Volunteers were captured and six were killed, but the sacrifice was justified. By dramatically demonstrating the failure of British pacification efforts, the daring assault scored a resounding progaganda success.[5]

As the military conflict intensified, casualties rose steeply. From January to July 1921, 228 police and 96 soldiers were killed, half again as many fatalities as during the previous two years. Irish deaths from January 21 to March 31 were estimated at 317 Volunteers and civilians, a considerable increase over any comparable period since 1916. When the British began to execute prisoners under martial law regulations, the IRA shot hostages; presumably, it also shot most of the seventy-three "spies" killed in the first four months of 1921.[6] Inevitably, violence made life cheaper. Young men were growing accustomed to the use of guns and bombs, and children played games of ambush and assassination.

England got a taste of the war as it moved toward its climax. Late in 1920, the IRA prepared plans for the destruction of English docks, bridges, warehouses, power houses, reservoirs, and railways. In the months that followed, there were outbreaks of arson or attempted arson in Liverpool, Manchester, London, and other areas. In April, attacks were made on railway signal boxes near London and Manchester, and hundreds of telephone wires were cut in different parts of the country.[7]

In its attempts to mount a maximum effort, the IRA faced serious obstacles. The government's inability to provide adequate funds for the army was partially offset when local units resorted to systematic levies on the populace.[8] But the shortage of arms and ammunition remained a pressing problem, with lack of ammunition hindering operations and posing a grave threat to active units in the weeks before the truce.[9] Loss of experienced men was an added difficulty. By June, over 3,000 rebels were in internment camps, and hundreds more were in British jails. If more units had taken part in the fighting, the situation would have been less critical; but outside Dublin and the southwest, most areas were relatively inactive, sometimes because of a lack of guns but often because of the local commander's timidity or incompetence.

The Crown forces also had problems. The Cabinet's decision to impose martial law only in Munster and part of Leinster left two kinds of law operating within a few miles of each other. Lacking effective control of adjacent counties, the army was hardpressed to prevent rebel movements in and out of the martial law areas. And with most of the country remaining under civil administration, the military could not establish the strict controls needed to crush rebellion.

A more critical handicap was the shortage of trained infantry. By 1921 there were 40,000 troops and 15,000 police in Ireland. But Macready could neither control nor rely on the RIC, and the slowness of postwar recruiting, coupled with depletion from overseas drafts, had reduced the garrison's fifty-one infantry battalions to half strength. This left Macready with only about 25,000 infantry effectives, and a sizable number of them were required for guard duty and for peacekeeping in Belfast. Of the 250 to 300 men per battalion who could be employed against the IRA, a large majority were young recruits who lacked the expertise in marksmanship and skirmishing essential to counterinsurgency operations. With an unseasoned offensive force of perhaps 15,000 men, Macready had to fight 3,000 to 5,000 active guerrillas and to police an area of over 30,000 square miles. The odds in his favor were not enough to ensure victory.

Despite these difficulties, Macready was guardedly optimistic. Whatever its limitations in practice, martial law expanded military powers over a large area. Moreover, the army adopted new methods as it took a larger role in the Irish troubles. Training in counterinsurgency tactics was introduced. In Dublin, foot patrols were used more extensively, and sizable captures of rebel arms and ammunition were made, a clear indication that military intelligence was becoming more effective. Collins continued to lead a charmed life, but a very narrow escape convinced him there was a traitor in his organization. Viewing the general situation as much more hopeful than in 1920, Macready believed the IRA might be crushed before the new year ended.

Military prospects continued to improve as summer approached. Long nights and bad weather favored the IRA, but now the days were growing longer and sunnier. In April, the British staged the first of a series of sweeps in the midlands and west, surrounding and searching a sizable area. These exercises were not immediately productive, because the concentration of forces alerted the local IRA, but they provided experience in combined operations and kept the rebels on the move. Had the sweeps continued through the summer, it seems likely they would have brought more positive results.

Much more dangerous to the IRA were roving patrols, sometimes without uniforms, which moved by night through the countryside. Such a patrol might stay out as long as two weeks, converging with other patrols on an area frequented by rebels or lying in wait for an IRA column or dispatch rider. Such tactics threatened the IRA's control of rural areas and, if properly coordinated with sweeps, could run the rebels into the ground. By June 1921, large reinforcements were arriving in Ireland, and the weight of the army was being swung against the southwest. Short of guns and desperately short of bullets, the IRA faced a long hot summer against an enemy much more formidable than the RIC.[10]

Although Britain's military position improved in 1921, protest against the government's policy became impossible to ignore or silence. Irish Home Rulers, southern Unionists, and labor leaders denounced "Black and Tannery" and urged a settlement based on some form of Dominion status, a demand strongly supported by Liberals opposed to the coalition

government. The British Labor Party sent commissions of inquiry to
Ireland in 1919 and 1920, and their reports constituted a comprehensive
and cogent indictment of the government's pacification methods. Early
in 1921, the Labor Party staged a nationwide peace campaign, which
urged withdrawal from Ireland and a peace based on self-determination.
Twenty thousand copies of the Labor Commission's 1920 report were
sold, and seven million pamphlets on the Irish situation were distributed.[11]

Within the coalition, Liberals were restive about mounting violence
and police misconduct, while such prominent Conservatives as Lords
Hugh and Robert Cecil, Lord Henry Cavendish-Bentinck, and Oswald
Mosley went into opposition over Ireland. Cavendish-Bentinck and
Mosley played leading roles in the Peace with Ireland Council, an influential nonparty organization founded late in 1920. A small but growing
group of moderate Conservatives, including such promising politicians
as Edward Wood (the future Lord Irwin and Viscount Halifax) and Sir
Samuel Hoare, were thoroughly disillusioned with what they regarded
as a bankrupt policy, based on crime and lies. Hoare even began work on
his own peace plan, convinced he could win the support of most coalition
MPs for it. Conservative criticism reflected mounting unrest among
back-benchers and boded ill for the government.

Leading literary figures and intellectuals, as well as clergymen of all
denominations (especially the Church of England), joined the chorus of
protest. Like their counterparts in Parliament, these critics were repelled
by IRA terrorism, but they were even more outraged by the misdeeds
of those who acted in the name of the Crown. No one expressed this
moral indignation better than Randall Davidson, archbishop of Canter-
bury, when he warned the government it could not cast out devils by
calling in the devil, and any peace won in this way would not be worth
having.[12]

No attacks hurt more than those of the press, in part because they
were led by the highly respected editors of the country's two most presti-
gious newspapers—C. P. Scott of the *Manchester Guardian* and Wickham
Steed of the *Times*. Much of the ammunition used by the press was
supplied by journalists such as Hugh Martin of the London *Daily News,*
who reported British outrages despite threats by the Tans and Auxies.
Among the magazines that played an important part in the peace campaign were the *Nation*, the *Contemporary Review*, the *New Statesman*, and
the *Round Table*.[13]

From the Dominions came more loud protests. Canada and Australia,
which had large Irish populations, made plain their opposition to coercion, while Premier Jan Smuts of South Africa warned: "Unless the Irish
Question is settled on the great principles which form the basis of this
Empire, this Empire must cease to exist."[14]

The hostile attitude of the United States caused special concern because American policy on naval armaments and war debts was of crucial importance to Britain. Angry American reaction to police outrages in Ireland and de Valera's warm reception in the United States alarmed the Cabinet in 1919 and 1920. Although it became clear in 1921 that the United States was not going to intervene in Irish affairs, the troubles in Ireland remained an acute embarrassment to Britain. Over $5 million was raised in America for the relief of Irish distress, and the one-sided report of an American commission of inquiry on Ireland provided still more ammunition for Sinn Fein. Unless Britain could somehow resolve the Irish Question, there was slight prospect of harmonious Anglo-American relations.[15]

Even in the palace, the protest movement found support. King George V rarely intervened in politics, but he had received distressing reports about Ireland from many sources and felt obliged to voice his concern. In May 1921, Lord Stamfordham, the king's private secretary, wrote to Greenwood: "The King does ask himself, and he asks you, if this policy of reprisals is to be continued and, if so, to where will it lead Ireland and us all? It seems to His Majesty that in punishing the guilty we are inflicting punishment no less severe upon the innocent."[16]

A month earlier, the prime minister had attempted a comprehensive defense of government policy in an open letter to Protestant church leaders who denounced reprisals and urged a truce. Lloyd George admitted that the Crown forces had been guilty of "deplorable excesses" but denied that these had been authorized or condoned by the government. He claimed that action had been taken to rid the RIC of undesirables and punish misconduct, and he maintained that discipline was improving despite extreme provocation by the rebels.

Reviewing events since 1918, the prime minister held Sinn Fein mainly responsible for the sad state of Irish affairs. Liberals and Home Rulers had agreed with Unionists that Ulster must be safeguarded and, subject to this condition, the government had offered Home Rule. But Sinn Fein's Republican demand had prevented a settlement and divided Ireland more deeply. Charging that threats and terror partly explained Sinn Fein's hold on the Irish people, the prime minister rebuked the churchmen for refusing to condemn rebel violence unequivocally. He also argued that a truce and negotiations would serve no purpose so long as Sinn Fein insisted on complete independence. An Irish republic would be incompatible with Britain's security and the Commonwealth's existence, and it would precipitate civil war between Ulster and the rest of Ireland.

Repeating a favorite theme, Lloyd George contended that the present struggle was not about the Home Rule Act at all. Basically, the issue was the same as in the American Civil War: the British government was striving to preserve the union of two islands, strategically and economically interdependent, while Sinn Fein was fighting for secession. He maintained that the British ideal of combining unity with Home Rule was a finer and nobler ideal than "that excessive nationalism which will take nothing less than isolation, which is Sinn Fein's creed today, and which if it had full play would Balkanize the world." The clergymen could best promote peace by making clear to the Irish that they could not gain their ends by crime, that secession was impossible, and that Ulster could not be coerced. Once the Irish understood these essential points, a settlement would be possible.[17]

On behalf of the churchmen, the bishop of Chelmsford replied, denying that they had condoned Sinn Fein's outrages and pointing out that crimes committed by those charged with maintaining law and order stood in a class by themselves. The clergymen's main criticism of the government still stood. Its policy had made the Irish situation worse, and an agreed settlement seemed impossible without some initiative by Britain. Like the prime minister, the bishop and his associates opposed Ireland's secession from the Empire or coercion of Ulster, but an agreed solution seemed possible within the limits defined by the government. Unless a deliberate and patient effort to reach such a settlement were made and failed, many people in Britain would be unable to acquiesce in any alternative policy.[18]

Future British policy depended on the fate of the Government of Ireland Act, which would be decided by elections in May. On April 21 the Cabinet conceded that Sinn Fein would win the election in southern Ireland but decided that nothing was to be gained by postponing the election or seeking a truce.[19] The government's only conciliatory gesture was the appointment of a Catholic viceroy, Lord Fitzalan, a gesture the Irish failed to appreciate.

The Republican government decided to contest the Home Rule election to renew Sinn Fein's mandate, taking care to discourage opposition from other interests. The appeal for a united front had the desired effect in southern Ireland, but in the northeast the Home Rule Party refused to stand down and again divided with Sinn Fein the seats to be fought against the Unionists. In the south, 124 Sinn Feiners were nominated for an equal number of seats and were returned unopposed. The four remaining seats were filled by independent Unionists from Trinity College. These four members of the House of Commons and fifteen senators nominated by the viceroy were the only representatives to attend the formal opening of the Parliament of Southern Ireland on June 28. After a brief meeting, it adjourned *sine die*.[20]

In contrast to the south, northern Ireland provided a number of sharp electoral contests. Polling day in the north fell on May 24, which was also Empire Day. In Belfast, voters trooped to the polls through loyalist neighborhoods lavishly decorated with Union Jacks. Carson warned that

"Ulster must be saved from the assassin vote," while Craig declared: "The Union Jack must sweep the polls." Despite some rioting and disorder, 90 percent of the electorate voted, and the result was a solid Unionist victory. Loyalists won forty of fifty-two seats in the northern House of Commons, while Sinn Fein and the Home Rulers evenly divided the remainder. Tyrone and Fermanagh remained nationalist, with an antipartition majority of almost 8,000 votes.[21] On June 7 the Belfast Parliament opened with only Unionist members in attendance. They chose Sir James Craig as prime minister, and he formed an all-Unionist government. Ironically, by participating in the Home Rule elections, Sinn Fein recognized partition and assisted in the establishment of a separate government for the six counties.[22]

May and June 1921 marked the final and most critical phase of the Anglo-Irish war. Sinn Fein had again demonstrated its political dominance outside the six counties, and the IRA, though hard pressed, seemed resolved to fight on. After endorsing intensified coercion, however, the British Cabinet was forced to acknowledge that repression could not be continued in defiance of public opinion. Consequently, it initiated a decisive shift in policy by opening peace negotiations with Sinn Fein, thereby transforming a military into a diplomatic struggle.

On May 12, after exhaustive discussion on the question of a truce, the Cabinet resolved that "it would be a mistake for the Government to take the initiative in any suspension of military activities in Ireland, and that the present policy in that country should be pursued."[23]

All the Liberal ministers except Lloyd George and Edward Shortt, the home secretary, favored a truce, while every Conservative who was present voted against it. Balfour, the most irreconcilable Unionist minister since ill health had forced Bonar Law's retirement in March, spoke strongly against a cease-fire. Austen Chamberlain, Law's successor as head of the Conservative Party, together with his fellow Tories, Lord Curzon, the foreign secretary, and Sir Robert Horne, chancellor of the exchequer, had originally favored a truce; but the views of the Irish administration and some of their Cabinet colleagues caused them to change their mind. The prime minister helped ensure the moderates' defeat, arguing that a truce would only encourage Sinn Fein to demand Dominion status or a republic. He urged continuing coercion, claiming it would eventually restore order.[24]

On May 24 the Cabinet again considered the situation. The Government of Ireland Act provided that if less than half the members of either Irish House of Commons failed to swear allegiance to the king within two weeks of its first meeting, the assembly would be dissolved, and the viceroy would rule by Crown Colony government. Since it was known that Sinn Fein would boycott the southern Parliament's opening on June

28, Crown Colony government would go into operation by July 12 in the twenty-six counties. Important decisions were therefore imperative.

In making them, the Cabinet weighed disturbing reports from the secretary of state for war, Sir Laming Worthington-Evans, and from Wilson and Macready. All three men agreed that the army's position was unsatisfactory and urged that an intensive effort be made to stamp out rebellion during the summer. The troops' morale, health, and discipline were excellent, but they were weary from constant strain. If their well-being and discipline were to be preserved, drastic measures must be taken against the rebels. In Macready's opinion, which Wilson endorsed, the IRA must be defeated by October or virtually the entire garrison would have to be relieved.[25]

Impressed by these pessimistic conclusions, the Cabinet at once made preparations for an all-out military effort. All available reinforcements were to be dispatched as soon as possible. The service departments were to determine the number of reinforcements, and a reconstituted Irish Situation Committee would consider their proposals. At the same time, the Irish Executive should make every preparation for Crown Colony government and martial law in southern Ireland in the event that Sinn Fein refused to work Home Rule. The Irish Situation Committee would decide to what extent martial law should be imposed after July 12 and report to the Cabinet.[26]

On May 25 the Cabinet agreed on the essential elements of a peace settlement. Britain must retain control of the Irish coastline, and Ireland could not have separate armed forces. Ireland must also make a fair contribution toward Imperial expenditures (i.e., the 1914–1918 war debt and the cost of Britain's armed forces). Finally, the Irish should not be allowed to place customs duties on British goods, although Churchill and two other Liberal ministers dissented from the decision to withhold customs control in all circumstances.[27] The Irish Situation Committee met on May 26 and reported next day, recommending martial law if the southern Parliament did not function and the dispatch of maximum reinforcements without delay. The Cabinet approved the substance of these recommendations on June 2.[28]

General Macready was most disturbed by the Cabinet's decision that the military would remain subject to the civil authority after the extension of martial law. To Macready, martial law meant undivided military authority; to the Cabinet, it meant what the House of Commons would support. Convinced that martial law would not be rigorously enforced, Macready wrote Greenwood that he was becoming "thoroughly fed up with this business." By mid-June, the government's continued "political wobblings" had brought Macready and Wilson to the brink of despair.[29]

Frustration led Macready to express his views very forcefully. On June 15 he informed the Cabinet's Irish Committee that while he did not believe coercion would resolve the problem, it could not succeed even militarily if it were applied halfheartedly. Martial law must be vigorously enforced. Rebel leaders must be tried for treason. Those who were captured in the field would be court-martialed and shot, and the same applied to rebels caught in possession of arms, ammunition, or explosives. As many as 100 men might be shot in a week, and the government must not tell him after the first week that he had to stop. Ministers had to realize what coercion must entail, if it were not to be self-defeating. Speaking bluntly, Macready declared: "It was a case of 'all-out' or 'nothing.' Could the government go 'all out'?" Sir John Anderson and Worthington-Evans strongly supported Macready. Chamberlain, the committee's chairman, responded that while the Cabinet was grateful to Macready and anxious to give him the fullest support, it had to consider public opinion. It would not help Macready to take measures which the public would not support. The general ended the discussion by requesting a Cabinet decision not later than July 5.[30]

On June 20 Macready drove home his arguments in a letter to the prime minister. He said he felt coercion was a mistake; it might produce an "apparent calm" but not a lasting settlement. If the Cabinet decided on coercion, he would do his best to carry it out; but to be of any use, it must be drastic and have active public support. Without such support, trying harsh measures would only destroy the confidence and morale of the Crown forces. If the government opted for drastic action, Macready urged that it announce, at the same time, exactly how far it was willing to amend the Government of Ireland Act. A pledge to liberalize Home Rule might rally moderates and help restore order; it would also make good propaganda.[31]

A growing number of ministers shared Macready's reservations. Winston Churchill, the colonial secretary, and most of the other Liberal members of the Cabinet favored a brief truce, accompanied by the most generous offer of self-government and the threat of drastic coercion if it were refused. The prime minister was prepared "to fight the matter out at all costs," relying on Conservative support; but with Ulster safeguarded, such leading Conservatives as Chamberlain and Lord Birkenhead showed sympathy for Churchill's approach.[32] After a vigorous debate, the Cabinet had approved more drastic measures; but Lloyd George could not ignore his colleagues' misgivings. Churchill was a brilliant, if erratic, politician, with some knowledge of military affairs; Chamberlain was leader of the dominant party in the government and Parliament; and Birkenhead, the lord chancellor, was clever and was influential in Unionist circles.

In April, Lloyd George had remarked that shrewd observers said it would take a year to crush Sinn Fein, and he wondered if the British people were willing to continue coercion that long.[33] It now seemed doubtful whether his colleagues were prepared to do so.

Although the government made no serious overture until late June, peace feelers were put out to Sinn Fein almost continuously from the end of 1920. Lloyd George seemed to be probing for a weakness he could exploit to bring the rebels to terms. De Valera realized this and made plain that if the prime minister wanted to discuss a settlement, he should publicly propose a meeting for that purpose. If this were done, de Valera promised a public reply; but until then, the Irish people should be wary of attempts to divide them by vague offers of peace. On Cope's initiative, de Valera and Craig met in May, but nothing came of their interview. Craig felt the Sinn Fein leader was a visionary, obsessed with past grievances, while de Valera came away from the meeting convinced that only direct negotiations with Britain could secure peace.[34]

Real peace efforts originated with Premier Smuts of South Africa, who arrived in London in June for the first postwar Imperial Conference. Smuts was known to be sympathetic to Irish national aspirations, and like-minded acquaintances persuaded him to use his influence for peace. On June 13, Smuts saw the king, who expressed concern about his imminent visit to Belfast to open the northern Parliament. The king had not yet seen the speech he was to deliver and feared that nationalists would view his visit as a deliberate insult. Smuts told him he could perform a great service by making his speech an appeal for peace. Impressed by this suggestion, George V asked Smuts to draft a speech incorporating his ideas. Smuts did so and then sought Lloyd George's approval for his approach, since the advice of the king's British ministers must rule in Irish affairs.

On June 14 Smuts sent his draft to the prime minister, together with a harsh criticism of the government's Irish policy. Although that policy was "an unmeasured calamity" for the whole Empire, and a failure as well, Smuts saw two hopeful elements in the situation. First, Ulster's position had been safeguarded, and this left the way open to a settlement with the rest of Ireland. Second, the king's visit to Belfast would be fully justified if he made an appeal for peace, a move Smuts felt sure the Dominion premiers would support.[35]

Lloyd George was favorably impressed by the South African leader's suggestions, and Chamberlain held a meeting of the Irish Committee to discuss the king's speech. The committee agreed that the object of the royal visit to Belfast was to inaugurate a great enterprise, and the prime minister concurred when he joined the committee's deliberations the following day. He feared Sinn Fein would not listen to any appeal; "nevertheless, it was an occasion for a big gesture" (but not for an offer of Dominion status, as he made clear to Smuts).[36]

Lloyd George presented the committee-approved speech to the king, who warmly approved it. Four days later, on June 22, George V delivered the address in Belfast. He spoke of the importance of the occasion for Northern Ireland, for Ireland as a whole, and for the Empire. With moving sincerity, he appealed for peace:

> I speak from a full heart when I pray that my coming to Ireland today may prove to be the first step towards the end of strife amongst her people, whatever their race or creed.
> In that hope I appeal to all Irishmen to pause, to stretch out the hand of forbearance and conciliation, to forgive and forget, and to join in making for the land they love a new era of peace, contentment and goodwill.

He concluded by voicing the desire that a Southern Irish Parliament would soon be opened and that the Irish people—under one Parliament or two, as those Parliaments decided—would work together in a common love of their country, based on mutual justice and respect.[37]

Reaction to the speech was universally favorable, and the king returned to a triumphant reception in London, where his ministers offered warm congratulations. Lloyd George wrote to him: "None but the King could have made that personal appeal; none but the King could have evoked so instantaneous a response." He promised that the Cabinet would spare no effort to bring about an Irish settlement.[38]

On the morning of June 23, Chamberlain saw the prime minister and urged a final attempt at peacemaking before applying more coercion. Lloyd George seemed impressed and, shortly afterward, Birkenhead told Chamberlain that he too favored a peace overture. The next day, Lord Stamfordham conveyed to Lloyd George the king's urgent desire that the government not lose the favorable opportunity created by his speech.[39]

Late that afternoon, the prime minister met with Chamberlain, several other ministers, members of the Irish administration, and Smuts to discuss a peace offer. Macready observed that although this was a political matter which did not affect him directly, an invitation to parley would make his position easier if more blood had to be shed. Anderson shared his view, and there can be no doubt that Chamberlain, Smuts, and Cope pressed for a peace initiative.[40]

While this conference was still in session, the prime minister summoned the Cabinet to obtain approval for a formal offer of negotiations. He opened the meeting by reminding his colleagues of the enthusiastic response to the king's speech and informing them of His Majesty's anxiety for positive action. It appeared de Valera might now settle for less than a republic and might abandon his demand for separate armed forces and fiscal autonomy. Though none of this was certain, Lloyd George thought it only fair to the king to try for an accommodation with Sinn Fein; he therefore proposed inviting Craig and de Valera to a conference in London. To avoid giving Sinn Fein advance notice, the invitation would not be published, nor would it contain specific terms, in view of the general nature of the king's appeal. However, the government's terms would be based on the guidelines laid down by the Cabinet on May 25. The Cabinet resolved unanimously to try negotiations. Lloyd George read the letter he proposed to send Craig and de Valera, and various amendments were made. While agreeing to omit any reference to a truce, the Cabinet authorized the prime minister either to make an informal intimation to de Valera on the subject or leave it for conference discussion. The Cabinet also empowered the prime minister to publish the invitation whenever he saw fit.[41]

De Valera's arrest on June 22 caused the government momentary alarm but did not disrupt its plans. Cope arranged de Valera's release, and Lloyd George's letter was delivered on June 25. Once this was done, the prime minister published it.[42]

June 24th, 1921

Sir,

The British Government are deeply anxious that, so far as they can assure it, the King's appeal for reconciliation in Ireland shall not have been made in vain. Rather than allow yet another opportunity of settlement in Ireland to be cast aside, they felt it incumbent upon them to make a final appeal, in the spirit of the King's words, for a conference between themselves and the representatives of Southern and Northern Ireland.

I write, therefore, to convey the following invitation to you as the chosen leader of the great majority in Southern Ireland, and to Sir James Craig, the Premier of Northern Ireland:—

(1) That you should attend a conference here in London, in company with Sir James Craig, to explore to the utmost the possibility of a settlement.

(2) That you should bring with you for the purpose any colleagues whom you may select. The Government will, of course, give a safe conduct to all who may be chosen to participate in the conference.

We make this invitation with the fervent desire to end the ruinous conflict which has for centuries divided Ireland and embittered the relations of the peoples of these two islands, who ought to live in neighbourly harmony with each other, and whose co-operation would mean so much not only to the Empire but to humanity.

We wish that no endeavour should be lacking on our part to realise the King's prayer, and we ask you to meet us, as we will meet you, in the spirit of conciliation for which His Majesty appealed.

I am, Sir,

Your obedient servant
[signed] D. LLOYD GEORGE[43]

Even though powerful forces inside and outside the government had prepared the way for this dramatic policy shift, it was sudden and unexpected so far as the public was concerned.[44] Almost overnight, the king's speech created both the opportunity and the irresistible pressure for a formal peace overture.

Lloyd George was not at all sure that de Valera would accept his invitation, but he and his colleagues were sure that it would strengthen their position. As Birkenhead remarked: "If he comes it is a gain. If not, it is to the good. Before we brace ourselves for what is to follow it will be useful to have this."[45] Accepting the necessity of a new departure and trying to soften ultra-Unionist reaction, the prime minister confided to Carson: "The game is up. We shall have to give in."[46]

Of course, an invitation to parley did not mean complete surrender. The government remained as firmly opposed as ever to an Irish republic or coercion of northeast Ulster. Indeed, the Cabinet contemplated nothing more than a liberalized Home Rule settlement for Southern Ireland, and its Conservative members only agreed to negotiations after the Six Counties had been safeguarded by partition. Lloyd George was careful not to state the government's peace terms in his invitation precisely because this would invite immediate rejection and demands for greater concessions. By offering peace without stating his conditions, the prime minister raised hopes everywhere and forced the Sinn Feiners either to disappoint these hopes by rejecting his offer or risk compromising their demand for unity and independence by accepting it.

De Valera was eager to discuss peace. He knew that Sinn Fein could not force Britain to recognize a completely independent republic and that this demand also impeded Irish unification. Negotiations might win for Ireland what no state had so far been willing to grant: recognition of the essential attributes of national self-determination. Moreover, a truce would give both the IRA and the people a badly needed respite. Finally, rejection of Britain's peace overture would cost Sinn Fein badly needed public sympathy.[47]

However tempting the British invitation, de Valera felt that Sinn Fein must clarify its position before it accepted. After consulting his Cabinet, de Valera replied to Lloyd George on June 28, indicating that while Sinn Fein desired peace very much, its leaders saw no way to reach a settlement if the British government denied Ireland's essential unity. The president added that before replying more fully, he was seeking a conference with representatives of the loyalist minority. Craig refused de Valera's invitation, but at Lloyd George's urging the earl of Midleton and three other prominent Southern Unionists accepted. When they arrived at Dublin's Mansion House on July 4, the Unionists were cheered loudly by a war-weary crowd outside.[48]

At the outset of the meeting, de Valera declared he could not go to

London to discuss peace with Craig, or with anyone else who represented part of the country of which he was president. He then insisted
on guarantees that the British would not use the negotiations to improve
their military position. Midleton knew that Macready felt the same anxiety about the IRA, and after two days' discussion he crossed to London
to obtain the government's consent to a truce and negotiations without
Craig.[49]

Before Midleton left for London, Smuts arrived in Dublin at de Valera's invitation. On July 5 he told de Valera that the British desire for
peace was fervent and almost universal. When the president replied that
he suspected Lloyd George was trying to play him off against Craig and
that he intended to refuse the invitation, Smuts warned that this would
be a terrible mistake. Refusal to discuss peace would lose Sinn Fein the
sympathy of the whole world, including Ireland. Partition had removed
the main obstacle to settlement; Sinn Fein should accept the loss of the
northeast and talk to the British about Southern Ireland.

But de Valera refused to accept partition, blaming it and Ulster's
hostility on the British government. When Smuts asked for his solution
of the Irish problem, the president replied, "A Republic." When Smuts
inquired if de Valera really believed the British people would agree to
this, de Valera countered that an Irish republic would be willing to be
bound by a treaty with Britain. He based his argument for a republic on
the principle of natural right, while Smuts argued against it in terms of
political experience. The Boer Republics' treaty of association with Britain had not worked, and the war which resulted had devastated Smuts's
country. He implored de Valera not to accept a republic bound by treaty
to Britain, even if the British should offer it; such an association would be
more restrictive than the freedom conferred by Dominion status and
guaranteed by the other Dominions.

When Smuts asked whether Ireland would accept Dominion status, de
Valera replied that the offer would be submitted to the people, but he
emphasized that it must include no restrictions on Irish sovereignty. If
Britain refused to recognize Irish freedom, Sinn Fein would fight on for
a republic, which de Valera believed would be won eventually. Smuts left
Dublin feeling that de Valera would attend a peace conference and
support a Dominion settlement.[50]

Whatever the good effects of Smuts's mission, it was Midleton who
opened the way to direct negotiations. At their first meeting, Lloyd
George readily agreed to exclude Craig from negotiations with de Valera, but he claimed the Cabinet had decided no truce could be considered.[51] Midleton argued that nothing further could be done without a
truce. Rebel outrages would continue, the Crown forces would retaliate,
and this would destroy any peace talks that might be held. The prime
minister seemed adamant, but he presented Midleton's requests to a

meeting of fellow ministers, Irish officials, and Smuts. This group agreed to both a conference without Craig and a truce, although the latter was to be a "gentlemanly understanding" rather than the formal agreement Macready preferred. When Lloyd George met the anxious Midleton again on July 7, he agreed to his requests and gave him a letter acknowledging the necessity of a truce for fruitful negotiations. If de Valera agreed to enter into peace talks and order the IRA to end all acts of violence, the British government would order the Crown forces to suspend active operations.[52]

On July 8, Sinn Fein leaders and Southern Unionists discussed a truce. At Midleton's request, Macready submitted his terms and came to the Mansion House to expedite agreement. As he approached the lord mayor's residence, he was wildly cheered by the large crowd outside, who sensed his appearance meant an end to hostilities. After Macready's arrival, truce terms were quickly arranged. The British agreed to stop raids, searches, and similar activities, to confine military operations to support of the police in their normal functions, to maintain order in Dublin through the city police force, and to remove curfew restrictions. Only routine troop movements and training would be carried on and reinforcements from England (except those already en route) would be stopped. For its part, the IRA was to cease all attacks on Crown forces or civilians, prohibit the use of arms, halt all maneuvers and interference with government or private property, and prevent any disturbance that might require British military action. During the truce, the IRA would not occupy abandoned police stations or quarter troops in new areas, unless this were absolutely necessary. Liaison officers were to be appointed to investigate breaches of the truce and restore peace. Hostilities were to cease at noon Monday, July 11.[53]

Once this agreement on the truce had been reached, the conference released the news, announcing that publication of the terms was expected the following day. Macready telephoned Lloyd George to inform him of the agreement, while de Valera wired his willingness to discuss peace in London. The next day, Lloyd George replied that he would welcome de Valera and his colleagues on any day during the coming week. De Valera informed the prime minister that he would confer with him on Thursday, July 14.[54] On July 8 Macready ordered his troops to abstain from unnecessary activity in view of the truce agreement. The IRA, on the other hand, kept up its attacks until the last moment to demonstrate its capacity and willingness to carry on the fight.[55] But when the Volunteers finally ceased fire, a large part of the Irish problem was at last on its way to solution.

The Anglo-Irish war occasioned a number of savage incidents but there were almost no large-scale encounters, and the number of casualties was small. Probably not more than 2,000 people were killed between Easter Monday 1916 and the truce, and almost all of them died during Easter Week and in 1920–21. British casualties from January 21, 1919, to July 16, 1921, were 405 police killed and 682 wounded and 150 soldiers killed and 345 wounded. Exact Irish figures are not available, but the IRA estimated that about 650 Volunteers were killed between January 1919 and the peace treaty of December 1921. Another Irish source claims that 752 Volunteers and civilians were killed and another 866 wounded from January 1919 to July 1921, but it admits this estimate is probably too low because numerous casualties were not reported. The British government reported 196 civilians killed and 185 wounded during the same period. But to these figures must be added the 82 civilians killed and the hundreds injured during the Ulster riots of June–September 1920.[56]

Both sides gained and lost by the truce, and at first glance it would seem the Irish benefited much more than the British. Though the IRA had harassed the Crown forces, it could not expel them from Ireland, and the Volunteers were fast approaching the limits of their endurance in the summer of 1921. Six thousand Republicans were imprisoned or interned, many of them active guerrillas, and those who were still at liberty were desperately short of ammunition. By mid-July the British garrison had been reinforced by nineteen infantry battalions, three cavalry regiments, and a strong force of marines, bringing the total military establishment to seventy infantry battalions, nine cavalry regiments, and the necessary support units. There were now about 70,000 troops and police in Ireland, and about half this number were infantry effectives.[57]

The IRA was no longer confronted mainly by Tans and Auxies but by the "organized strength" of the military, which Collins rightly considered far more dangerous than the police. He and other IRA leaders welcomed the truce precisely because they feared they could not hold out against a determined summer offensive by the army.[58] British intelligence and counterinsurgency operations were becoming more effective. Had troop reinforcements been accompanied by a stringent nationwide application of martial law and intensified operations in the southwest, the army might well have broken the back of the IRA by October, the target date set by Macready. But the British government was no more sure of military success than of public support, and it therefore shelved repression in favor of negotiations. However reluctant this decision, it was certainly wise. Military victory could not solve the Irish problem, only a political settlement could do that.

But if the truce saved the rebels from a real threat of military defeat, it also made successful renewal of resistance virtually impossible. A brief cease-fire would not give the IRA the relief it needed, and an extended cease-fire would erode popular support for further fighting. The jubilation which greeted the truce clearly showed the people's deep desire for peace.[59] The longer the truce lasted, the stronger that desire became, and without popular support the IRA was helpless. This was the most important setback of the truce, but by no means the only one. Rebel leaders who had escaped the British dragnet because of their anonymity now became known to enemy intelligence as they were identified and repeatedly photographed. Collins told a close friend, "Once a truce is agreed and we come out into the open, it is extermination for us if the truce should fail." He confided to another intimate during the truce, "If this fails, we're done."[60] Another unfortunate result of the truce was the demoralization of the IRA, which not only reduced its military effectiveness but posed a dangerous threat to the Irish people, as shown in the next chapter.

To the British, agreement to a truce on equal terms with the rebels may have seemed the final humiliation, but this was a small price for the advantage it conferred. The government now had a chance to negotiate a settlement which would rid Britain of a very troublesome problem without sacrificing national security or prestige. If it failed to achieve this result, the government could renew the war with greater assurance of popular support because of its efforts for peace. War would be costly and unpleasant, and it would not resolve the Irish Question, but it seemed a lesser evil than recognition of an Irish republic. If the British made this quite clear to Sinn Fein and also drove home the fact that Ireland would suffer much more than Britain from resumption of hostilities, they were likely to get most of what they wanted in the way of a settlement. Thus the truce placed powerful weapons in Britain's hands at the cost of some loss of face. But while the British gained greater freedom of action as a result of the truce, the Irish simply exchanged one set of limitations for another. Despite appearances, therefore, the British won the advantage by agreeing to a cease-fire.

Chapter 5
Preliminary Negotiations:
July-October 1921

De Valera met with Lloyd George four times—July 14, 15, 18, and 21. All four discussions took place at No. 10 Downing Street, and the prime minister conducted the opening discussion with great showmanship, greeting de Valera warmly as a brother Celt and using all his charm and eloquence to win over the cautious and formal Sinn Feiner. Describing the evolution of the British Empire, Lloyd George said that its representatives were presently meeting on equal terms in an Imperial Conference, and a place in those deliberations was reserved for Ireland. When de Valera did not respond, the prime minister resorted to menace, warning that if the conference failed, the situation would become much more terrible than before the truce. De Valera accused him of threatening coercion, but Lloyd George replied that he was simply predicting what must happen if no settlement were reached. He also made clear that there could be no question of recognizing an Irish Republic. After the interview ended, Lloyd George believed that progress had been made toward an understanding.[1]

At their second meeting, the prime minister found de Valera a trifle more rigid and attributed this to consultation with his colleagues. The Irish president continued to press for an independent but associated Republic, but Lloyd George reiterated that Britain would never agree to this. In the interval between the second and third meetings, Lloyd George saw Craig but made no headway toward securing Irish unity. Smuts, meanwhile, tried to impress on de Valera the seriousness of the Ulster problem for the British government, but de Valera thought the British were using Ulster solely to frighten him.[2]

When the two leaders met again, the prime minister offered an outline of peace terms, which de Valera criticized as inadequate, emphasizing Sinn Fein's demand for a united Ireland. Lloyd George warned that attempts to force Ulster into an Irish state could lead to a civil war which would involve the whole Empire. De Valera maintained that the South would never allow itself to become involved in civil war; it would rather let Ulster alone. Lloyd George countered by asking why Sinn Fein would not leave Ulster alone now. Eventually, de Valera said he must consult his Cabinet about the British proposals, and Lloyd George agreed to send him a draft of the terms before their next meeting.[3]

On July 20 the prime minister summarized his interviews with de Valera and Craig for the British Cabinet. He thought both men wanted a settlement but were afraid of their followers. Ulster seemed the real obstacle to settlement, and it was hard to see how Irish unity could be achieved. A statement of terms, drafted by the prime minister, Chamberlain and Balfour, was distributed and minor amendments were made. After some discussion, the Cabinet approved the use of the word "treaty" in the terms, despite its connotation of an agreement between sovereign states. The prime minister was also empowered to publish the terms at his discretion.[4]

The British proposals of July 20 offered a highly qualified form of Dominion status, which represented only a small advance beyond the Government of Ireland Act. Southern Ireland was to have full control of its internal affairs, including taxation, finance and land defense, but its local defense force must be of "reasonable" size compared to those of Britain and Northern Ireland. More important, sea defense was to remain the exclusive province of the Royal Navy, using whatever Irish bases it required. Southern Ireland must also grant Britain all necessary facilities for development of air defense and communication, British recruiting in the South was to continue, and the hope was expressed that Southern Ireland would make a voluntary contribution to the maintenance of Britain's armed forces. Free trade between the two countries would continue, and Southern Ireland was to assume responsibility for a share of the United Kingdom's debt and liability for war pensions, the share to be determined (in default of mutual agreement) by an independent arbitrator from within the Empire. Finally, Sinn Fein must recognize "the existing powers and privileges of the Parliament of Northern Ireland, which cannot be abrogated except by their own consent." The British government expressed the earnest hope that Ireland would eventually achieve national unity, but that could be attained only by consent and not by force. Britain would help in any way possible and give effect to any agreement made between North and South. If the Irish people accepted the principle of the proposals, details could be worked out through negotiation and the results would be embodied in a treaty.[5]

De Valera received these terms late the same evening. He and his colleagues examined them closely, and next day he told Lloyd George that he could neither accept the proposals nor advise the Irish people to do so. According to the prime minister, de Valera demanded full Dominion status for all of Ireland, with British security requirements to be settled at a later conference. If northeast Ulster were excluded from the Irish state, Southern Ireland must have complete independence. The prime minister told de Valera that the government could not consider these alternatives; if this were Sinn Fein's last word, the only question remaining was the exact time for terminating the truce. Although doubtless upset by the threat of war, de Valera refused to knuckle under. Once this was clear, Lloyd George tried a different tack, declaring he would publish the British offer so the Irish people could see how liberal it was. Reproaching the prime minister for breaking his pledge to publish nothing except by mutual agreement, de Valera warned that if the terms were made public, he would publish his refusal. The Irish leader was ready to depart, but again Lloyd George shifted his approach, appealing for a considered reply to his offer. De Valera agreed to this, provided he was given time to consult his colleagues and nothing was published in the meantime. Lloyd George assented and de Valera left Downing Street and returned to Dublin the following day.[6]

Though Lloyd George had little hope that the Irish counterproposals would prove acceptable, he was confident of a favorable public reaction to the government's offer, as were the king and Chamberlain.[7] However, the sessions with de Valera had exhausted Lloyd George and, in the end, he felt he had made no impression. Like Craig, he had had to endure a long recital of English misdeeds in Ireland. To intimates, the prime minister confided that talking with de Valera was like trying to catch up with a horse on a carousel or trying to pick up mercury with a fork.[8]

The Cabinet thought the peace offer was very generous, and Sir Henry Wilson angrily concurred, describing it as "an abject surrender to murderers." When the aged nationalist politician Tim Healy learned of the terms, he reflected that "the Sinn Feiners won in three years what we did not win in forty."[9] Despite such judgments, Lloyd George's pessimism was justified. Sinn Fein had not fought for a liberalized form of Home Rule for a truncated Ireland, and there could be no settlement unless both sides were prepared to make greater concessions.

After discussing the British offer, the Irish Cabinet voted unanimously to reject it and authorized a reply based on a draft submitted by the president.[10] While he prepared this letter, Smuts wrote to him, urging acceptance of Britain's terms. De Valera answered that only recognition of an all-Ireland Republic would produce agreement. In a second letter, Smuts again argued that Southern Ireland should accept Dominion status as the best possible settlement; freedom within the Commonwealth would lead to Irish unity. Immediately after writing this letter, Smuts returned to South Africa. In a sharp move, Lloyd George published it on August 14, revealing that Southern Ireland had been offered Dominion status, but not mentioning the offer's restrictions or Irish criticisms of it. Sinn Fein protested, but the damage had been done.[11]

In his August 10 reply to Lloyd George, President de Valera had reiterated that neither the Dail nor the Irish people would accept Britain's peace proposals (although the Dail had not yet been consulted and the people would not be). Britain did not fully recognize the right to national self-determination, which Ireland could not and would not surrender. The solution must be amicable but absolute separation, with reasonable guarantees for British security; the idea of Dominion status for Ireland was illusory. Remoteness from Britain safeguarded the Dominions' freedom more than laws and treaties; the most explicit guarantees, including the Dominions' acknowledged right to secede from the Empire, would be necessary to secure equal freedom for Ireland. Instead, Britain insisted on restrictions which would reduce Ireland to helpless dependency. The Republican government was prepared to negotiate a treaty of association with the Commonwealth, if this would secure a united Ireland. Questions dealing with trade, armaments, and communications could be freely negotiated, and Irish liability for a share of the British debt could be determined by arbitration, but the Irish people must settle the question of partition themselves. Their representatives could not admit Britain's right to partition Ireland, either in its own interests or those of a political minority within Ireland. Sinn Fein agreed that force would not solve the problem, and was willing to submit it to foreign arbitration if North and South could not agree on unity. The president concluded by expressing readiness to agree to any terms which were reasonable and just.[12]

The British Cabinet found the meaning of de Valera's letter obscure. On one hand, it rejected the government's proposals and seemed to offer Irish independence as an alternative basis of negotiations. On the other hand, it showed some evidence of substantive agreement, that is, the suggestion of association, the pledge not to coerce Ulster, and the proposals on trade, debt liability, arms limitation, and communications. Information from Cope and other sources indicated that the letter was not intended as a final rejection of British terms. Ministers agreed that their response should be brief, clear, and precise. It should explicitly repudiate the suggestion that Ireland could be outside the Empire or that Irish questions could be submitted to foreign arbitration, and it should point out that essential naval defense requirements had not been mentioned by de Valera. Sinn Fein should also be informed that all Anglo-Irish correspondence would be published on August 15.[13]

On August 13 Lloyd George replied to de Valera, following the Cabinet's guidelines.[14] When the correspondence was published, the prime minister's anticipation of public support was fully gratified. Although the *Times* and some Liberal newspapers conceded that the terms of July 20 might be improved on in detail, the press was virtually unanimous in contending that their substance was unalterable. Sinn Fein was warned not to insist on a republic.[15] Although there was no parliamentary debate on the peace proposals, Lloyd George explained the government's position on August 19. Opposition leaders gave him strong support and Parliament recessed with the assurance it would be recalled if negotiations broke down.[16]

On August 16 the Second Dail, elected the previous May, assembled in Dublin. President de Valera declared that its predecessor had been elected in 1918 in a plebiscite on the nation's future. This vote had not been so much for a form of government—"because we are not Republican doctrinaires"—as for independence, which could best be realized through a republic. Britain's peace proposals had been rejected because they did not recognize Ireland's right to freedom.[17] The next day, de Valera explained that his ministry was prepared to make concessions to win freedom and unity, such as association with the British Empire and accommodation of any reasonable British claims.[18]

Five days later the Dail met in private session and unanimously rejected the British terms. In the course of this discussion, the president warned that if the Dail insisted on recognition of the Republic, Ireland would face a war of reconquest. When the time came for final decision, the Dail must realize the gravity of Ireland's position. De Valera also clarified his position on Ulster, rejecting absolutely the use of force and supporting the idea of exclusion by county option if the Republic were recognized. Several deputies disagreed with the president on this question, but the matter was not pursued.[19]

In private session the following day, de Valera read the reply he proposed to send Lloyd George. It informed him that the Irish people would not surrender their right to independence by accepting unjust terms. However, a just, honorable, and lasting peace could be negotiated on the basis of the principle of government by consent of the governed. If Britain accepted that principle, Dail Eireann would appoint plenipotentiaries to arrange its application in detail.[20] At the same session, de Valera explained that if he were reelected president, he would represent the whole nation rather than a party. His only pledge was to do his best for the Irish people, and if the Dail should reject his peace proposals, the government would resign. De Valera made plain that he must be free to consider each question in the negotiations as it arose, and the government must remain free to explore all avenues toward peace, including exclusion by county option.[21] This speech, together with the president's earlier remarks on Ulster and his contention that refusal to compromise meant all-out war, shocked many deputies, but it did not impair their confidence in his leadership.[22]

On August 26, after submitting his government's resignation, de Valera was unanimously reelected president of the Republic (a title belatedly formalized by the Dail the day before). Responding warmly to this vote of confidence, de Valera declared the government would continue to work as a team and so would the nation.[23] Griffith became minister of foreign affairs in the new Cabinet and Collins (finance), Brugha (defense), Stack (home affairs), and Cosgrave (local government) retained the offices they had previously held. Robert Barton was named to the new post of minister of economic affairs, and twenty-nine-year-old Kevin O'Higgins was reappointed assistant minister of local government.[24] The well-known Cosgrave had been "on the run" much of the time, and O'Higgins had played a large part in making that department a success. When he returned from America, de Valera recognized O'Higgins' ability and invited him to take part in Cabinet meetings (but not to vote).[25]

Opinion in the British Cabinet was divided on whether de Valera's letter of August 24 was a definite refusal to discuss any terms involving allegiance to the Crown or merely an attempt to save face. Most ministers, including Lloyd George, inclined to the latter view. It was generally agreed that the government should not be drawn into a series of interminable exchanges, that it should conclude negotiations by a definite date—to prevent Sinn Fein's using the truce to consolidate its authority —and that it should strive to retain public support. The Cabinet laid down guidelines for the reply to de Valera and approved the prime minister's draft on August 26.[26]

In his letter, Lloyd George claimed that Britain's terms were magnanimous and consistent with de Valera's demand for government by consent of the governed. In demanding that Ireland be treated as a separate power, Sinn Fein claimed what the most famous Irish leaders of the past had explicitly disavowed. The government offered more than they had asked, and it was "playing with phrases" to claim that the principle of government by consent compelled recognition of Ireland as a foreign power. There was no political principle, however clear, which could be applied without regard to limitations imposed by physical or historical facts. Ireland must accept allegiance to the Crown and membership in the Empire, or there would be no settlement. The time had come when definite and immediate progress must be made toward a basis for further negotiations, and if de Valera was prepared to examine how far British requirements could be reconciled with Irish aspirations, a conference could be held.[27]

De Valera's answer reached Lloyd George at Gairloch, on the west coast of Scotland, where he was on holiday. The president stated that the two essential conditions of the situation were Ireland's declaration of independence and Britain's refusal to accept it. Britain offered Ireland a status definitely inferior to the Dominions' free and equal partnership in the Commonwealth, leaving Ireland with neither the geographical distance nor the constitutional rights that secured the formers' freedom. The proposed terms, also, would divide Ireland into two artificial states, both subject to British control. The main historical and geographical facts of the situation were not in dispute, but each country interpreted them differently. Ireland was convinced that its interpretation was true and just, and was willing to let an impartial arbitrator judge the question.

Britain refused and threatened to impose its view by force. This would not solve the problem—any more than it had in the past—and threats must be abandoned. Only acceptance of the principle of government by consent of the governed, which the British claimed as their invention and as the foundation of the Commonwealth, offered a basis for fruitful negotiations. On that basis, the Irish government was ready to appoint plenipotentiaries for a peace conference.[28]

Lloyd George summoned the Cabinet to Inverness to discuss the latest communication from Sinn Fein. On the morning of September 7 he had an interview with the king, who was vacationing nearby. His Majesty urged a conciliatory reply and an invitation to an immediate conference, suggestions which Lloyd George promptly transmitted to his colleagues.[29] Two courses were open to the Cabinet. It could propose a conditional conference on the basis of Crown and Empire, or it could offer to resume unconditional negotiations, referring only briefly to the British terms rather than stating them specifically.

Opinion was almost equally divided on the advantages of each course. Churchill, Birkenhead, and several other ministers urged a conditional conference, claiming that an open invitation would seriously weaken Britain's position. On the other hand, a majority of ministers, including Chamberlain, supported an unconditional conference, contending that extremist pressure would prevent de Valera's agreeing to a conditional one. And in a conference, the Irish leader might well make concessions which he could not make publicly in advance. Edwin Montagu, the Liberal secretary of state for India, argued that insistence on a conditional conference might abort negotiations and lead to war, and waging war because Sinn Fein rejected an invitation that imposed preconditions would be difficult. Montagu suggested an invitation that stated the government had defined its position so clearly as to make further correspondence superfluous.

Having heard out his colleagues, the prime minister warned that an unconditional conference would lower British prestige everywhere and enable de Valera to postpone acceptance of Crown and Empire until he learned the British position on other matters, particularly Ulster. If the conference broke down on the issue of partition, the government would find it far more difficult to rally public support than if the break came on Crown and Empire. But despite his misgivings, Lloyd George was impressed by the strength of the "no conditions" party and reserved final judgment for the moment. After lunch there was further discussion, and the Cabinet eventually agreed on an unconditional conference.[30]

On September 7 the prime minister replied to de Valera, pointing out that further correspondence was futile and asking whether Sinn Fein would agree to a conference whose purpose was "to ascertain how the association of Ireland with the community of nations known as the

British Empire can best be reconciled with Irish national aspirations." If the answer were affirmative, Lloyd George suggested the conference should meet at Inverness on September 20.[31]

De Valera responded on September 12, accepting the invitation but reaffirming Ireland's independence: "Our nation has formally declared its independence and recognizes itself as a sovereign State. It is only as the representatives of that State and as its chosen guardians that we have any authority or powers to act on behalf of our people."[32]

This statement outraged Lloyd George. He could not confer on any such basis, the prime minister informed the two couriers who delivered the letter. Unless the offending passage were altered, all hope of peace would be lost. Despite arguments and entreaties, however, the two Sinn Feiners held firm. They could not change the letter—and alteration would do no good because the Dail was to meet next day to approve it. Lloyd George insisted that this must be prevented at all costs, pointing out that no part of the correspondence was to be published without mutual consent. The couriers agreed to report the prime minister's objections by telephone and then return to Dublin to explain the situation fully. Lloyd George was satisfied with this, and the couriers left at once for Inverness and the nearest telephone. When de Valera received their message he became angry, thinking his emissaries had somehow been taken in by Lloyd George.

Meeting the Dail in private session, he emphasized the necessity of restating the Irish position clearly before entering a conference, even though doing so could mean war. The Dail endorsed the letter without dissent and it was published without alteration. At the same time, to help keep negotiations alive, the president had the Dail approve the plenipotentiaries chosen by the Cabinet and he released their names to the press.[33]

Despite de Valera's conviction that he had acted rightly, publication of his letter almost wrecked the plans for a conference. On September 15 Lloyd George canceled the conference and repeated that Britain would never agree to a conference which entailed recognition of an Irish republic.[34]

Cancellation of the Inverness conference set off a rapid exchange of telegrams between de Valera and Lloyd George. Replying to the latter's wire of September 15, de Valera expressed surprise that offense had been taken at the Irish government's clarification of its position. The British had taken care to define their own, and if the two positions were not so opposed, there would be no problem to discuss. To reach a settlement, the negotiators must meet unrestrained by any conditions except the facts as they knew them. Lloyd George responded that acceptance of de Valera's claim to independence would constitute recognition of Ireland's secession from the Empire. To this, the president replied that his government had not asked the British to abandon any principle, "but surely you must understand that we can only recognize ourselves for what we are."[35]

The king informed Lloyd George that he thought de Valera's latest telegram was intended to be conciliatory and showed his eagerness for an immediate conference. Bonar Law, Anderson, Cope, and Tom Jones also urged patience and restraint on the prime minister.[36] Nevertheless, Lloyd George held to a hard line in his next message. From the outset of the negotiations, he declared, the British had made clear that Crown and Empire formed the unalterable basis of their proposals. The status claimed by de Valera was a repudiation of that basis, and unless he withdrew his claim there would be no conference. De Valera's response had an anxious tone. The Irish government had no thought of insisting on preconditions to a conference, but a conference was impossible if Britain demanded surrender of Ireland's position as a prerequisite. Was the prime minister's letter of September 7 intended as such a demand or was it an invitation to an unconditional conference? If a free conference were intended, the Irish government confirmed its acceptance of the invitation: its representatives would meet the British at any time designated by the prime minister.[37]

At this juncture, Lloyd George took counsel with several members of the Cabinet, including Churchill, Montagu, and Greenwood. He told them his last message to de Valera had produced quite a different tone of response; it seemed that de Valera was losing public support and dividing his followers. However, the prime minister warned, it would be a mistake to assume that a conference would solve the problem, and the government should not put itself in a false position merely to have one. He was willing to help save de Valera's face if it were merely a question of extricating him from difficulties caused by an unwise choice of words. But if the claim to Irish independence were a reality, it would be better to fight the matter out now.

The assembled ministers again weighed the merits of an unconditional versus a conditional conference. In support of the former, it was pointed out (very probably by Montagu) that if Britain could enter a conference without recognizing an Irish republic, all would be well; even if the meeting failed, the government would not have compromised its position. Moreover, the public had set its heart on a conference, and if failure to hold a conference caused a rupture, it would be said that a meeting might have saved the situation. The government might not have general support if it broke off negotiations because Sinn Fein refused to accept Crown and Empire as prior conditions for a conference. The prime minister maintained that the correspondence with de Valera since September 7 was not a suitable basis for negotiations. On the other hand, suggesting a new conference would free the Irish leader from the unacceptable position he had assumed in the last two weeks. The meeting provisionally agreed on a conciliatory reply.[38]

On September 28 the British informed Sinn Fein that they could not enter a conference based on the correspondence since September 7. However, the government still was anxious to explore every possibility of a settlement by personal discussion, and it therefore proposed a conference in London on October 11 to ascertain "how the association of Ireland with the community of nations known as the British Empire may best be reconciled with Irish national aspirations." De Valera replied the next day, declaring "our respective positions have been stated and are understood," and accepting the invitation.[39]

The preliminaries were over and the long-awaited conference was about to begin. However, fully to understand the circumstances that determined its outcome, we must further examine the background of the conference. From the start of the truce, the Republican government made every effort to consolidate its authority. Dail Eireann met openly, approving new loans and receiving reports on the peace negotiations, while the Irish ministry tightened its control over local government and administration of justice. Republican courts sat freely, their decisions enforced by the IRA in rural areas. Maintenance of the truce compelled British authorities to deal directly with IRA officers, thereby affording implicit recognition of their belligerent status. Up and down the country, the Crown forces stood by while the IRA drilled, trained, and levied taxes. The government in London was well aware that such a state of affairs could not be tolerated indefinitely. If Southern Ireland were not to become a republic by default, negotiations must be concluded with reasonable dispatch.[40]

The impact of the truce on the IRA posed a problem for the Irish as well as the British. For months, many active Volunteers had lived "on the run" from the Crown forces. With the cease-fire they returned home, to be lionized by the people and politicians as the men who "won the war." Bristling with guns, youthful IRA members swaggered about, attended dances and concerts, basked in the glow of worshipful gazes. Commandeering cars for "military business," they "tore up and down the little country roads with girls all the hot bright days of summer; stopped at wayside pubs and swanked."[41] Full of self-importance, they assumed control of local affairs, collecting taxes for the army, policing their districts, arbitrating all manner of disputes. In such an atmosphere it was easy for impressionable youths to forget their desperate plight on the eve of the truce, to come to believe that they had beaten the British Empire and could do so again if they had to. Although the IRA appeared to make serious preparations for the resumption of hostilities, these were largely a sham. The Volunteers were part-time soldiers, and their discipline deteriorated rapidly in the absence of wartime conditions. An influx of "sunshine soldiers" or "trucers," spoiling for a fight now that the fighting was over, further demoralized the army.

The IRA's sense of superiority manifested itself in a growing tendency to "domineer over civilians and despise 'politicians.' "[42] Too many Volunteers came to regard politicians as timid and self-seeking and the people as sheep. Convinced of their own virtue, these patriots saw themselves as the incorruptible guardians of the Republic against the fainthearted, who would sacrifice it for peace.

This attitude was both unjustified and dangerous. The IRA could not survive without popular support, and freedom did not demand a republic. Political leaders should have warned the soldiers of the enemy's power, the limits of British concession, and the people's war-weariness; but they did not. Some were blind to reality; others were too busy trying to make peace or maintain a united front. Collins saw the danger and viewed the IRA's demoralization with mounting concern.[43] The military situation made a peace settlement essential, and if the army were to be brought under civil control, it must be concluded quickly. Otherwise, Ireland faced worse troubles than those from which the truce delivered it.[44]

Despite this urgency, dissension among Sinn Fein's leaders seriously hindered peacemaking. When the Irish Cabinet discussed the appointment of conference delegates, President de Valera astonished his colleagues by announcing he would remain in Dublin. Griffith, Collins, and Cosgrave protested this decision, but Brugha, Stack, and Barton supported the president, and he prevailed. De Valera proposed that Griffith lead the delegation, and the Cabinet agreed. He also insisted that Collins accompany Griffith, and over Collins' strong objections he again won his point. Barton was named the delegation's economic expert (like his cousin, Erskine Childers, Barton came of a Protestant landowning family and was a convert to republicanism). Two lawyers, Eamonn Duggan and George Gavan Duffy, were chosen to round out the team, and Childers, over Griffith's protests, was appointed its principal secretary. The Dail approved the delegation on September 14, with Collins again voicing his objections against going to London and de Valera his determination to remain at home.[45]

Once de Valera made this decision, Griffith was the natural choice to head the delegation. He was foreign minister, was widely respected, and had functioned well as acting president. Brugha and Stack detested his political moderation, but both refused to go to London themselves and neither challenged Griffith's selection. The appointment of Barton, Duggan, and Duffy likewise occasioned no controversy; each was chosen for his particular expertise and in the belief that he would work well with Griffith and Collins. De Valera also believed that Barton and Duffy would strengthen the delegation's Republican commitment.[46]

Childers' appointment was a different matter. He came of a distinguished Anglo-Irish family, had been educated in England and a member of the British civil service, and had been decorated for bravery in the South African and European wars. A convert to the nationalist cause, Childers had smuggled guns to the Volunteers in 1914. After serving as secretary to the ill-fated Irish Convention, he had despaired of British good faith toward Ireland and offered his services to Sinn Fein in 1919. His talents as a propagandist won him the respect of both Collins and de Valera, especially the latter, who was much impressed by Childers's knowledge of things British. But Griffith believed Childers was only a disgruntled English radical, who was motivated more by hatred of British imperialism than love of Ireland. While conceding that he could be useful, Griffith contended that no Englishman should be given a position of influence or authority in Sinn Fein. But the Cabinet overruled Griffith, and Childers became the delegation's secretary.[47]

Besides Childers, there were three other secretaries: John Chartres, Diarmuid O'Hegarty, and Finian Lynch. An English Sinn Fein sympathizer, Chartres was selected because of his legal and civil service experience. O'Hegarty was secretary to the Cabinet, clerk of the Dail, member of the IRB's Supreme Council, and a close friend of Collins. Lynch also was a friend of Collins, as well as a member of the Dail and a veteran of the 1916 rising.[48]

Collins's reluctance to serve as a delegate surprised de Valera. Arguing that he was a soldier, not a diplomat, Collins claimed that if he stayed at home the delegates could represent him as a diehard, whom only maximum concessions would placate. But de Valera maintained that Collins' presence would cause the British to go the limit to conciliate their most dangerous enemy. In the end, the Big Fellow went to London but remained unhappy, with good reason. For one thing, he was worn out and needed a rest. For another, he knew that Brugha and Stack were out to discredit him, and he was unsure of de Valera's attitude. Friends had warned him not to place himself in a position which his enemies could exploit. Privately, Collins remarked that he was being sent by others "to do what they knew must be done but had not the moral courage to do themselves" (i.e., abandon the demand for complete independence). He also felt that the reputations of all those involved in the negotiations would suffer, whether an agreement was made or not. For him, the conference was a trap from which there was no escape.[49]

The president's decision not to go to London was just as important as his decision to send Collins and Griffith. By remaining in Ireland, de Valera believed, he could emphasize his position as head of state and avoid any danger of compromising the Republic. Abstention would also enable him to guard against hasty decisions by the delegates and maintain unity at home. If the negotiations broke down, the Irish people would accept the failure more readily if a moderate like Griffith had led the delegation, and the president would be in a better position to reopen negotiations or rally the people for war if he were not directly involved in the rupture. Remaining at home would also give de Valera time to work out the details of his peace plan of "external association" and secure the assent of Brugha and Stack to it. And if the British accepted this plan, he would have a better chance of winning extremist support for it if he had not been directly involved in the negotiations which produced the final compromise.[50]

Notwithstanding these considerations, de Valera should have led the delegation. External association was his idea, and only he fully understood its principles, whose meaning and merit he could have expounded better than anyone else. Moreover, de Valera's meetings with Lloyd George gave him more knowledge of the Welsh Wizard's devious methods than was possessed by Griffith or Collins. The president's refusal to attend the conference appears totally incomprehensible in light of what he wrote to an American supporter shortly after a settlement had been reached:

> Having decided that I should remain at home, it was necessary that Collins and Griffith should go. That Griffith would accept the Crown under pressure I had no doubt. From the preliminary work which M. C. [Collins] was doing with the I.R.B., of which I had heard something, and from my own weighing up of him, I felt certain that he too was contemplating accepting the Crown, but I had hoped that all this would simply make them both a better bait for Lloyd George—leading him on and on, further in our direction. I felt convinced on the other hand that as matters came to a close we would be able to hold them from this side from crossing the line.[51]

Doubting their Republican commitment as he did, de Valera acted irresponsibly in sending Griffith and Collins to negotiate a settlement under the most difficult conditions possible. The kind of settlement de Valera sought was foreshadowed in his "Cuban interview" of February 1920, although it was not until June 1921 that the president broached the idea with his colleagues. After his talks with Lloyd George, he had hit upon the phrase "external association" to describe his plan and had won the Cabinet's unanimous acceptance of its basic principle. The president refrained from discussing his scheme in correspondence with Lloyd George because he felt such discussion would be premature. The references in his letters to a treaty of association were therefore couched in general and guarded language.[52]

External association was a novel and imaginative idea. It envisioned Ireland as a sovereign state, completely independent in internal affairs but voluntarily associated with the British Commonwealth in external affairs for matters of common concern. Although inhabitants of Ireland and the Commonwealth countries were to enjoy reciprocal citizenship rights, Ireland was to be a neutral state, with its neutrality guaranteed by members of the Commonwealth and, if possible, by the League of Nations and the United States.[53] The proposal offered real advantages for both Ireland and Britain. It not only preserved the Republic but it safeguarded British security. Limited association with the Empire offered assurance to Britain and the loyalist minority of Sinn Fein's desire for Anglo-Irish friendship without infringing on Ireland's internal sovereignty.

Despite de Valera's authorship of external association, he was unable to arouse his colleagues' enthusiasm for the idea or even to make clear his binding commitment to it. Griffith and Collins went to London believing that external association did not represent de Valera's last word, that he would support any terms they felt justified in accepting, even if these terms fell short of the compromise he had devised.[54] The president did not deliberately mislead them but he did leave them confused about his real intention, and the result was just as bad.

The Irish people were even more confused than their leaders as to what constituted acceptable peace terms. Politicians' speeches and the IRA's belligerence implied a policy of "no surrender," but peace rumors abounded, and few persons thought hostilities would be renewed. This public optimism was partly the result of wishful thinking, but the course of the preliminary negotiations encouraged it. The British left no doubt that allegiance to the Crown and inclusion in the Empire were essential conditions of a settlement, but the Irish position was much less clear. De Valera had never pledged to preserve the Republic in his letters to Lloyd George; in fact, he mentioned the word only twice in their correspondence. Furthermore, although the president had flatly rejected a restricted form of Dominion status, he accepted an invitation to a conference whose purpose was to associate Ireland with the British Empire. The people knew nothing about external association; de Valera refused even to discuss it in a private session of the Dail.[55] Naturally, like almost everyone else, they assumed that Sinn Fein was prepared to trade the Republic for the most generous measure of Dominion Home Rule it could get.[56]

What caused de Valera to disregard the public mood, to discount Ulster's implacable opposition to unification, to exaggerate the limits of British concession? The answer can only be that he was so preoccupied with his peace plan that he ignored almost everything else, including the need to make clear to his colleagues and the British that external association constituted his minimum terms for peace.

Dail Eireann met in private session on September 14 and approved the appointment of the peace delegation, whose members were empowered

as Envoys Plenipotentiary from the Elected Government of the REPUB-
LIC OF IRELAND to negotiate and conclude on behalf of Ireland with the

representatives of his Britannic Majesty, GEORGE V., a Treaty or Treaties of Settlement, Association and Accommodation between Ireland and the community of nations known as the British Commonwealth.[57]

These credentials were intended not only to enable the delegates to conclude a settlement but to obtain, for tactical purposes, British recognition of the Republic. The latter aim was not achieved. The credentials were not presented; in fact, Lloyd George never saw them.[58]

Instructions given the delegates by the Cabinet shortly before they left for London aroused considerable controversy during and after the conference. The instructions stated:

1. The Plenipotentiaries have full powers as defined in their credentials.
2. It is understood however that before decisions are finally reached on the main questions that a despatch notifying the intention of making these decisions will be sent to the Members of the Cabinet in Dublin and that a reply will be awaited by the Plenipotentiaries before the final decision is made.
3. It is also understood that the complete text of the draft treaty about to be signed will be similarly submitted to Dublin and reply awaited.
4. In case of [a] break the text of final proposals from our side will be similarly submitted.
5. It is understood that the Cabinet in Dublin will be kept regularly informed of the progress of the negotiations.[59]

These directions were designed to ensure that the delegates did not sign any agreement without the Cabinet's approval. But since the Cabinet could not limit powers conferred by the Dail, the instructions were really nothing more than suggested guidelines. In this sense, Griffith accepted them.[60]

However hard de Valera sought to maintain unity among his colleagues, there could be no real unity where even agreement on acceptable peace terms was lacking. And disunity increased as the negotiations progressed. Finding they held similar views, Griffith and Collins drew closer to each other and Duggan followed their lead. Opposition to these views led Duffy, Barton, and Childers to band together. Conflicts of personality and principle weakened the delegation, widened the gap between it and the Cabinet, and deepened already existing divisions within the Cabinet. Lack of clearly defined proposals further hampered the delegates in the early stages of the conference. The Irish Cabinet approved Draft Treaty A on October 7, but this was only an outline of external association. The Cabinet members in Dublin were to complete the draft and forward the results as soon as possible, while the delegates were empowered to fill in details as the negotiations proceeded.[61]

The British delegation's position was much stronger, partly because of its composition. Although the prime minister had chosen its leading members some time before, the British Cabinet formally approved the delegation only on October 6.[62] Lloyd George himself was its chief, seconded by Chamberlain, Birkenhead, and Churchill, with Greenwood, Worthington-Evans, and Sir Gordon Hewart, the attorney general, rounding out the negotiating team. Lionel Curtis, an expert on imperial affairs, and Tom Jones, assistant secretary to the Cabinet, were appointed as secretaries.

Given the importance of the negotiations, Lloyd George's participation was to be expected. The same could be said of his selection of Chamberlain, whose position made his support essential for the success of the conference. Circumstances likewise compelled the prime minister to include Birkenhead and Churchill. Their abilities, as well as their differences with Lloyd George on a number of issues, including Ireland, made it too dangerous to exclude them from the negotiations. But merely to admit them was not enough; the prime minister had to persuade them to support his efforts to reach a settlement. Soon after the start of the conference, he therefore came to terms with his two restless lieutenants and won their cooperation in return for giving them an equal voice with himself and Chamberlain in government policymaking. Although he supported Lloyd George, Churchill played only a minor part in the conference because he was reluctant to make further concessions to Sinn Fein. Once Birkenhead had been won over, however, he contributed decisively to the success of the negotiations.[63]

While not a delegate, Tom Jones also played an indispensable role in the conference. A former economics professor, Jones had spent some time in Ireland, was a student of Celtic lore and customs, and was sympathetic to Irish national aspirations. This sympathy, combined with his tact, discretion, and close association with his fellow Welshman, Lloyd George, made Jones an ideal intermediary with the Irish delegates.[64]

Other factors increased the advantage enjoyed by the British team because of its political skill and experience. The British delegation was united; the Irish were not. The British could use the excuse of other urgent business to set the timetable of meetings and could consult on important questions immediately; the Sinn Feiners had to refer to Dublin, which handicapped more than helped them. More important, Britain had clearly stated its terms for peace whereas Sinn Fein had not, leaving most people to assume it would abandon the Republic rather than renew the war. Not knowing how much they could safely concede also hampered the Irish delegates. And finally, the British were the stronger power, with the threat of war their ultimate weapon. The Irish might minimize this threat by astute maneuver, but they could never escape it. Brave and resourceful as they were, the Sinn Feiners faced a terribly unequal contest in London.

Of course, the British delegates also had problems. They had to placate a public eager for peace without alienating the Conservative Party, which would reject any settlement that compromised Crown, Empire, or Ulster. Having recovered from his recent illness, Bonar Law could provide the leadership for a Tory revolt. And he was sure to fight on Ulster, the one issue on which the delegates might be tempted to compromise. Despite these limitations, the British team held most of the high cards during the conference.

Chapter 6
The First Stage
of the Conference:
October 11-November 3, 1921

A cheering crowd greeted the Irish delegates when they arrived in Downing Street at 11 a.m. on Tuesday, October 11. After meeting and shaking hands with them as they entered the Cabinet Room, the prime minister directed the Sinn Feiners to their places and introduced them to their British counterparts across the table.[1] This exchange formally initiated almost two months of negotiations, which would include seven plenary sessions, twenty-four subconferences, and nine meetings of special committees. A series of nine informal interviews between Tom Jones and Griffith, sometimes accompanied by Collins or Duggan, played a vital part in these negotiations.[2]

If they were to reach agreement, the delegates had first to learn mutual respect and trust. Almost at once, Griffith and Chamberlain, so much alike in their integrity and loyalty, established a rapport. Lloyd George and Churchill shared Chamberlain's high regard for Griffith. At first, Griffith distrusted the prime minister, but came to have confidence in him as a result of their interviews and Tom Jones's powers of persuasion.[3]

Unlike Griffith, Collins felt that Chamberlain was aloof, patronizing, and not to be trusted. He initially viewed Churchill as an opportunist and jingoist, but learned to value his support after he knew him better. Churchill, for his part, was fascinated by Collins but, like Chamberlain, was repelled by Collins' association with "terrible deeds." The two men could work together, but the gulf between them could never be completely bridged. Collins never really trusted Lloyd George, regarding him as a crafty antagonist, who would do anything for political gain. He found the prime minister's comradely and benevolent air "particularly obnoxious" because he felt Lloyd George would cheerfully have had him hanged, if he could have managed it. At first, Lloyd George thought Collins more capable than Griffith, but once he began to make headway with Griffith, Collins seemed to have only the "simple sort of mind" befitting "a great military commander." Of all the British delegates, only Birkenhead won Collins' confidence, largely because they were kindred spirits, like Griffith and Chamberlain. Collins admired Birkenhead's clarity of mind, capacity for hard work, and refusal to be dominated by others. The lord chancellor was "a good man," who "always saw the point" and was "always loyal to the facts." Birkenhead reciprocated Collins' liking and trust, and their mutual understanding was crucial to the success of the conference.[4]

Not surprisingly, Griffith and Collins were the only delegates who made any impression on the British. Early in the game, Lloyd George wrote off Duffy and Duggan as "pigeons for the plucking," and soon formed an equally unflattering opinion of Barton. However, the British had a strong antipathy toward Childers, whom they considered a renegade and a fanatic.[5]

Lloyd George opened the conference by asserting his belief that both sides wanted peace. If the interests of Britain and Ireland could not be reconciled, it would not be the fault of their representatives, whose duty was to explore every possible approach toward peace. When the prime minister asked for criticism of the July 20 proposals, Griffith refrained from attacking their substance. Sinn Fein's strategy was to show a genuine desire for agreement and dispose of as many troublesome details as possible before arguing basic principles. Griffith therefore criticized the reservations on Dominion status, claiming they meant continued British domination. Lloyd George denied this vigorously, and when the Irish protested that Britain had violated previous treaties with Ireland, he countered that Ireland had never made a treaty with the British people before, only with ruling oligarchies. Discussing the Dominions' role in wartime, the prime minister stated that their participation was voluntary. If Ireland did not give its support freely, it would not be worth asking for. However, when Barton contended that a Dominion need not join in a British war, Birkenhead shot back: "That is not conceded." In defending free trade, the prime minister dwelt on the danger of tariff wars. Barton asked why he feared a tariff war if Ireland were so dependent on Britain. Rather lamely, Lloyd George answered that there were temptations on both sides, and he wanted peace. At a little after 12:30 p.m., the conference adjourned until 4 p.m.[6]

When the delegates reassembled, the prime minister suggested that objections to the proposed limitations on Dominion status could be answered satisfactorily with some clarification, which he promised to provide. The conference then agreed to set up a committee on financial relations.[7] In a discussion of defense, Griffith attacked the British demand for naval bases on the grounds that this would make Irish neutrality impossible. Lloyd George argued that Britain wanted Irish bases only for national security, and the Irish agreed to appoint a committee on defense. He also pointed out that as a Dominion, Ireland could not be neutral when Britain was at war. While Britain could not compel Irish support, a proclamation of neutrality meant secession from the Empire.

Collins recalled Bonar Law's statement that Dominions could vote themselves out of the Empire,[8] but Lloyd George rejoined that this meant
only that Britain might not employ military sanctions to prevent secession. When Griffith asked about the Dominions' future role in foreign
policy, the prime minister explained that Britain favored a common
policy for the Empire. Every Dominion had the right to express its
opinion, but Britain must conduct whatever policy was decided upon.
Again, he voiced the desire that Ireland enter the Empire freely; but
Griffith countered: "We have no free choice if the alternative is war."
Before the session ended, the two sides agreed to set up a committee on
observation of the truce.[9]

Griffith described the results of the first two sessions in a letter to de
Valera. Despite the fact that no headway had been made against the
demand for naval bases, he believed that the British wanted peace.
Crown and Empire were yet to be discussed, but Griffith felt that "on the
whole we have scored today." De Valera was less optimistic and replied
that Lloyd George was covering the same ground he had covered in July.
He warned that Griffith would have "to pick him up soon on this 'further than this we can't go' stunt," adding, "Two can play at that."[10]

The third plenary session opened at noon, October 13, with an argument over alleged truce violations, which were eventually referred to the
truce committee. The rest of the meeting was taken up with trade. Barton made a spirited defense of fiscal autonomy, asserting it would not
threaten Britain, but without it, Ireland could neither rule itself nor
develop its economy. Collins and Duffy supported Barton, and the
British conceded that certain Irish industries might be safeguarded by
tariffs.[11]

The Irish delegates had held their own in the first three sessions and
won time for de Valera to complete Sinn Fein's peace proposals. But the
conference had now to take up the two major issues: the Crown and
Ulster. The Republican Cabinet had decided that the Crown should be
left until last. Griffith therefore warned the president:

> Our tactics have been successful up to the present, but unless we can get in
> our Treaty proposals by Monday [October 17] the initiative will pass to
> them. If we cannot have the Ulster and other omitted clauses by ten o'clock
> Monday at the latest, we must fight them on ground of their own choos-
> ing.[12]

Ulster was the main topic at the fourth plenary session on Friday,
October 14, but since Griffith had not yet received de Valera's proposal
he could only play for time. He charged that the British were responsible
for partition because of their support of Ulster Unionists; if Britain
stood aside, Irishmen could settle the problem themselves. Lloyd George

was most conciliatory. He believed persuasion was the best way to bring about unity, and Britain would be happy if it were achieved. In the course of his remarks, the prime minister mentioned that the alternative to exclusion of the entire Six County area would have been boundary revision by a special commission. But this would have resulted in an excluded area with an overwhelming Protestant majority, solidly opposed to unification. Collins said there was another alternative: local option. If the South did not coerce Ulster, Ulster must not be allowed to coerce its own nationalist minority. Griffith agreed with Collins, while Lloyd George remarked that boundary revision by some form of popular choice would be fair if applied all round, that is, on both sides of the border.[13]

The session ended with Chamberlain pointing out the political risks the conference entailed for the British delegates, a theme he returned to in the next session.[14] Griffith was sufficiently impressed to write de Valera:

> The difficulties this British Cabinet has are real. They greatly exaggerate them to us for negotiating purposes, but it would be a mistake for the people at home to think there are none. The "Morning Post" party [the ultra-Unionists] at home is not without power, and it is obvious that both Ll. G. and Chamberlain are a trifle afraid, not of its present power, but of its potentialities.[15]

Lloyd George was pessimistic after the first four sessions. His experience with de Valera seemed to have been repeated; he could get nothing definite. The Irish delegates refused to make decisions; whether this was because they did not want to or were afraid to, he did not know.[16] Griffith, on the other hand, was optimistic, chiefly because of the British attitude on Ulster. He believed they would do anything short of using force to end partition and only wanted to save face.[17]

On October 14 de Valera wrote Griffith, urging forceful advocacy of a neutrality agreement, which would settle the issue of Ireland's relation to the Empire. At the same time, the president forwarded the Cabinet's proposal on Ulster. Under its provisions, existing constituencies of Northern Ireland's Parliament were to vote individually on direct representation in an all-Ireland parliament. Those constituencies that voted affirmatively were to be guaranteed fair representation and protection of local interests through arrangements with the Dublin government. Constituencies that refused direct representation in a national parliament (all of them or those which formed a contiguous unit) were to retain the Parliament and powers conferred on Northern Ireland in 1920. But the overriding powers reserved to the British Parliament under the Government of Ireland Act were to be transferred from Westminster to Dublin, and the constituencies that were excluded from direct rule by Dublin were to be given the same number of seats in the all-Ireland parliament that they held in the British Parliament.[18]

At the fifth plenary session, on October 17, there was another long discussion on Ulster. Using carefully prepared maps and statistics, Griffith laid claim to five of the province's nine counties on the basis of Catholic-nationalist majorities. He also declared that two more would vote for inclusion in a united Ireland, if given a free choice, because both contained large numbers of Protestant as well as Catholic nationalists. Growing weary of this recital, Lloyd George asked for Griffith's proposal. For some reason, Griffith did not present the Cabinet's Ulster clause; instead, he simply asked Britain to stand aside so that Sinn Fein could make the northeast a fair offer. This offer would probably produce agreement, but if it were rejected the people of the Six Counties must be allowed to decide their future by local option. Collins and Duffy supported Griffith, but none of the Irish delegates demanded that hard-core Unionist areas in the northeast be brought into an Irish state against their will. Indeed, Griffith said that any area which voted for exclusion should "go to Northern Ireland to enjoy the powers [which] they have there." The British probably inferred from this that Sinn Fein would settle for something less than unity if Northern Ireland refused its offer of safeguards.

The prime minister suggested that all nine counties of Ulster be allowed to vote together on unity versus partition. This would give the North a chance to gain three counties and the South a chance to end partition. Craig, of course, did not want the three additional counties, and Griffith was unwilling to risk any further loss of nationalist territory. He therefore insisted that the option units be local—either the 1918 parliamentary constituencies or Poor Law areas. Claiming that the province of Ulster was a logical unit, the prime minister admitted that the inclusion of only six counties in Northern Ireland was a compromise. But the result of local option would be another compromise that would leave minorities in both North and South and be no more logically defensible than the existing arrangement. Lloyd George did not see how Sinn Fein could end partition except by dealing directly with northeast Ulster, and he again pledged that Britain would sanction any agreement between North and South. However, the Sinn Feiners argued that this would give Ulster an unfair advantage. The British had created partition, and now they must help undo it by supporting freedom of choice for local areas within the Six Counties. When the Sinn Feiners warned that the Northern Parliament would never function because the nationalist minority would not obey it, the prime minister disagreed and asked whether Sinn Fein would prefer the *status quo* on the boundary or a vote by the entire province for or against exclusion. Griffith repeated his demand for local option, but Birkenhead declared this impractical;

the choice was exclusion for the Six Counties or option for the whole province. The Irish dissented, and on this note the meeting adjourned.[19]

At this juncture, external incidents threatened to end the negotiations. On October 19 Pope Benedict XV wired King George V his best wishes for an Irish settlement. The prime minister drafted the king's reply, which joined in the pope's prayer that negotiations might end the troubles in Ireland and open an era of peace and happiness for the king's people. After reading this, de Valera thanked the pope for his solicitude but pointed out that the troubles were not in Ireland; they were between Britain and Ireland. These troubles had sprung from Britain's attempt to impose its will on a people who had proclaimed their independence and owed no allegiance to Britain's king. The *Times* and other London newspapers branded de Valera's action irresponsible and harmful to prospects for peace.[20]

The British delegates agreed that the prime minister should call the Sinn Feiners' attention to serious breaches of the truce which had recently been uncovered—the seizure in Hamburg of an arms shipment destined for Ireland and discovery of an IRA bomb factory in Cardiff. He should also inform them that the hostile reaction to de Valera's message to the pope would make continuance of negotiations very difficult, if not impossible. It was therefore "absolutely necessary" that Sinn Fein state without further delay its position on the fundamental questions of Crown, Empire, and defense.[21]

When the sixth session opened at noon on October 21, Lloyd George launched his assault. To complaints about truce violations and de Valera's message he added a protest against the memorandum on defense presented by Collins, claiming that it challenged the entire British position on national security. The political risks taken by the British representatives to win a settlement had placed the life of the government in jeopardy, and Sinn Fein's provocative acts would make agreement impossible. The Irish must make clear their position on Crown, Empire, and defense by that afternoon, if possible, but by Monday, October 24, at the latest.

Griffith found himself in a tight corner. He knew nothing of the alleged truce violations, and he regarded de Valera's message as inopportune because it gave the British a chance to force the issue of Crown and Empire to the forefront of the negotiations.[22] Doggedly and skillfully, Griffith sought escape from a dangerous position, denying that arms importation was a violation of the truce and asserting that de Valera's cable had merely stated public facts. Sinn Fein's proposals would be submitted October 24, and then the conference could see whether a settlement was possible. Griffith reminded the prime minister that Sinn Fein did not yet know Britain's position on Ulster, that is, whether the British intended to use their influence to maintain (or alter) the *status quo.* As far as trade and defense were concerned, the problems were not insoluble.

Collins then argued the case on defense, contending that Irish neutrality would safeguard both British security and Irish independence. Churchill disagreed and claimed that the Irish memorandum on defense was a deliberate refusal of every British demand. Britain could not rely on Irish good will. It could not be sure that Ireland could or would preserve neutrality in a future war. Even if neutrality were effectively maintained, it would pose grave difficulties for Britain in wartime. Collins continued to press his claim that a friendly and neutral Ireland would be of great benefit to Britain, but made no headway.

Responding to Collins' arguments, Chamberlain observed that neutrality would put Ireland outside the Empire. Duffy said that Ireland could still be associated with Britain for certain purposes. Collins asserted that the conference was really discussing a new association, that the British Empire was developing into a partnership of free and equal states without centralized control. Lloyd George conceded the Dominions' growing autonomy, but the British remained unconvinced of the feasibility of Irish neutrality. Contending that Ireland was not being offered full Dominion status, Griffith pointed out that Ireland was denied the right to have a navy and thus was placed in a position inferior to other Dominions. The prime minister answered that all the Dominions had begun under such restrictions but, in time, Britain had invited them to undertake naval responsibilities. Ireland would travel the same road in a few years, once the memory of the Anglo-Irish hostilities faded. In the meantime, a government that was responsible for protecting over forty million people, many of them Irish, could not take risks.

At this point the British withdrew for consultation and returned to announce that they would be happy to receive the Irish proposals on Monday. The meeting closed with a heated exchange over the IRA bomb factory in Cardiff. Griffith denied this was a truce violation and Collins demanded to know the facts of the case. Lloyd George confessed he could not understand why Sinn Fein did such things when the only result was loss of public sympathy.[23]

It is impossible to ascertain how far Sinn Fein was guilty of deliberate truce violations. The evidence is not conclusive and the truce terms were ambiguous. Collins did his best to prevent flagrant breaches but his absence from Dublin diminished his authority, and he was unable to prevent several embarrassing incidents. Fortunately, such incidents were infrequent, and this fact, together with the British desire for settlement, kept them from destroying the negotiations.[24]

Based on Draft Treaty A, Sinn Fein's October 24 proposals emphasized that Ireland was not a colony but "an ancient and spirited nation." Its claim, therefore, was not Dominion status, but if it were, Britain's proposals would not confer that status. On the other hand, the Irish proposals would reconcile British demands for security with Ireland's demand for freedom, thereby laying the basis for a just and lasting peace. According to these terms, Ireland would adhere for all purposes of agreed common concern to the British Commonwealth. It was to be recognized as a "free State," with its freedom and integrity guaranteed by the British Commonwealth and, if they agreed, by the League of Nations and the United States. In return, Ireland would take no action inconsistent with its obligation to preserve its freedom and integrity. Although the "free State" would have complete autonomy in taxation and finance, it was prepared to conclude special conventions with Britain, ensuring reciprocal trade obligations and civic rights. The memorandum did not include the Cabinet's Ulster clause. Instead, it declared partition a domestic matter, but one for which Britain was responsible. Sinn Fein proposed to conclude an agreement with Ulster that would safeguard its lawful interests in a united Ireland. If agreement could not be reached, voters in Northern Ireland must be given freedom of choice on their political future.[25]

The memorandum did not offer acceptable answers on Crown, Empire, and defense, but the British felt the document was so ambiguous that the government could not count on united public support if it broke off negotiations. Sinn Fein's attitude on the three vital questions must therefore be clarified.[26]

When the seventh plenary session assembled at 5:30 p.m. on the 24th, Lloyd George declared that negotiations had reached a critical stage and discussion on vital questions could not be prolonged much longer. He wanted to know what the Irish meant when they said they would "adhere" for all purposes of agreed concern to the Commonwealth. Was Ireland prepared to accept membership in the Empire if all other conditions were satisfied? Griffith replied that this was "not quite our idea of association," explaining: "We should be associated with you—outside that a free people." When he added that the Dominions were bound by the link of the Crown, the Prime Minister quickly inquired: "By 'adhere,' you don't accept the link of the Crown?" Griffith answered that Ireland would accept the Crown as head of the association. "As allies?" Lloyd George asked, and Griffith responded: "Something more; permanent allies, not temporary." But not as members of the Empire, Lloyd George pressed. Griffith agreed, but added that Ireland would be represented in the Imperial Conference and would accept its decision in matters of common concern. The prime minister wanted to know what was meant by "common concern." Large issues such as war and peace and trade, Griffith replied; an agreed list would be included in the treaty.

When Lloyd George asked whether Irishmen would be British subjects or foreigners, Griffith explained: "We should be Irish and you would be British, and each would have equal rights as citizens in the country of the other." Birkenhead turned the discussion to defense, pointing out that if Ireland gave Britain the bases it demanded, no country would recognize Irish neutrality. Griffith and Collins contested this assertion, but Birkenhead bore down relentlessly. Although an enemy of Britain might not find it worthwhile to declare war on Ireland, neutrality would be "a meaningless trophy" under such circumstances. Griffith abandoned the struggle for neutrality by agreeing in principle that British security must be safeguarded, even though adjustment of details might be very difficult.[27]

The British withdrew for consultation and the plenary session adjourned. When Chamberlain observed that the Irish contemplated a situation where they would not be automatically at war if Britain were, Birkenhead remarked laconically: "They will give way on that." There was general agreement that Griffith's answers marked an important advance in negotiations. Lloyd George pointed out that the Irish had agreed to common and interchangeable citizenship (which was not quite the Irish position). He added that they would come into the mechanism of the Empire, into its common council for discussion of common purposes (true enough). Finally, he declared that they accepted the principle that Britain should occupy their ports for Imperial defense, even if exercise of that right meant war (not quite the case, but a fair assumption from Griffith's remarks). All this represented "a great advance," although Lloyd George admitted that the Irish did not accept the Crown and wanted to choose their own head of state. Birkenhead, hitherto skeptical about the value of the negotiations, confessed that the Irish answers had shaken him. An interview following the plenary session had been scheduled, in which the prime minister and Chamberlain were to meet with Griffith and Collins. Birkenhead thought it would be worthwhile for Lloyd George and Chamberlain to make plain that no agreement was possible without Irish allegiance to the Crown.[28]

The subconference on October 24 was the result of a British request for a private interview with Griffith and Collins that day. Ostensibly, the prime minister wanted to discuss matters without the presence of troublesome supporters, such as Greenwood and Worthington-Evans, but his real reason for seeking a small meeting was undoubtedly his belief that he could make more progress this way. He was bothered much more by Duffy, Barton, and Childers than by secondary members of his own team. Lloyd George knew that Griffith and Collins would talk more freely in private session and that this would make agreement on fundamentals easier. Indeed, it may well have been his knowledge that the two Sinn Feiners preferred small meetings that prompted the request for a subconference. Barton and Duffy did not like the idea but had no real grounds for objections. After all, Griffith and Collins were the delegation's leaders and had a perfect right to explore matters with their British counterparts.[29]

At the subconference, Chamberlain and Lloyd George emphasized that peace was impossible unless Ireland accepted the Crown. However, the most Griffith would promise was recommendation of "some form of association with the Crown," if all else were settled satisfactorily. He made clear that Sinn Fein would consider such association only as a concession to Ulster, in return for agreement on "essential unity." The four leaders decided to proceed with settlement of all other points and leave the Crown until last.[30]

As soon as the meeting ended, Lloyd George reported to his fellow delegates that Griffith would recommend acceptance of the Crown, provided all else proved satisfactory. Collins had shown more reluctance, asking whether an oath to the Irish Constitution might be substituted for one to the Crown. However, the prime minister thought he would come round if other problems were worked out. Chamberlain felt the Crown was the biggest problem. The two Sinn Feiners had dwelt on the idea of an elected head of state as the Crown's representative, and they seemed to contemplate a republic within the Empire.[31] Chamberlain's analysis was more accurate than that of Lloyd George, who tended to exaggerate Irish concessions throughout the conference.

The apparent success of the subconference led the British to adopt this *modus operandi* for the rest of the negotiations.[32] De Valera raised no objections, convinced that no important decisions would be made without consulting the Cabinet. If the president harbored any reservations about allowing the delegates the widest possible latitude, he soon found out they insisted on it. When de Valera learned that Griffith had offered some form of association with the Crown, he at once responded:

> We are all here at one that there can be no question of our asking the Irish people to enter an arrangement which would make them subject to the Crown, or demand from them allegiance to the British King. If war is the alternative, we can only face it, and I think that the sooner the other side is made to realize that the better.[33]

This apparent reprimand infuriated Griffith and Collins. Griffith threatened to quit unless his hands were left free; Collins swore he would resign, raging that the Cabinet was trying to put him in the wrong and get him to do its dirty work. This violent reaction may well have been caused by the two men's belated realization that de Valera would not, after all, agree to a Dominion settlement.[34] Barton and Duffy were not particularly disturbed but saw the need to explore all possibilities for a settlement; with Duggan, they agreed to sign a letter of protest written by Griffith. Collins signed reluctantly; he would have preferred to quit the delegation. In the letter, the delegates declared that the president's remarks tied their hands and were inconsistent with their powers and instructions, neither of which imposed limits on freedom of discussion. Without this freedom, they could not continue the negotiations. "Obviously any form of association necessitates discussion of recognition in some form or other of the *head* of the association." If interference from Dublin destroyed the "very slight possibility" of settlement, the responsibility for failure would not rest with the delegates. They urged the president to come to London privately, if he could; however, he should not come publicly unless they advised his presence was essential.[35]

Taken aback by this reaction, de Valera immediately wrote that there had obviously been a misunderstanding. There could be no question of limiting the plenipotentiaries further than by their original instructions. Unless he stated otherwise, his letters were only an attempt to keep the delegation in touch with the Cabinet's views on various points as they arose. It was most important that this be done, since the Cabinet would have to decide on policy when the delegation returned to Dublin. De Valera ended by confiding that his going to London privately was impossible. Griffith replied by expressing deep appreciation for the president's letter.[36]

This exchange of views helped clear the air, but had de Valera been aware of Griffith's concept of recognition of the Crown, he probably would not have voiced alarm in the first place. Limited recognition was first suggested by John Chartres, the delegation's second secretary, in an October 14 memorandum to Griffith. Chartres proposed that Ireland recognize the British king as head of the association to which Ireland would belong. The king would exist—so to speak—only for external purposes and would have no power of any kind in Irish internal affairs. Recognition might be made through an annual contribution to the king's civil list, which would represent payment for the interests Ireland would have in common with Commonwealth nations. Once de Valera fully understood the idea of the "Chartres Crown," he saw its merit and made it an integral part of his peace plan, winning Brugha's reluctant assent to the change.[37]

By late October the pattern of negotiations was becoming clear. The Irish delegates had abandoned their claim to neutrality and accepted in principle the British demand for naval bases. Given Britain's power and the fears aroused by Germany's submarine warfare, Sinn Fein's retreat on this issue was predictable. Trade and financial relations remained unsettled but agreement on them seemed likely. Inevitably, the Crown and Ulster had become linked issues. Griffith was making tentative concessions on Crown and Empire to win Britain's help for unity. If the British failed to persuade Ulster to join the South, Sinn Fein could break off negotiations with the assurance of world sympathy and only minimal risk of war. But Griffith had to be very careful. If he did not offer enough, the British would not pressure Ulster and might even break off negotiations, knowing that defense of Crown and Empire would win public support. On the other hand, if Griffith gave away too much, he would have surrendered the Republic without securing unity. He must therefore make his pledges on Crown and Empire tempting enough to induce the British to go all out for unity, but he must also keep these pledges consistent with external association.

The British delegates' task was as difficult as that of the Irish. They must do their best to obtain peace without compromising the all-important symbols of Crown and Empire (or jeopardizing national security) and without precipitating a Conservative revolt over Ulster. This meant extracting the maximum concessions from Sinn Fein while cautiously exerting pressure on Craig to secure unity. If they failed to convert Craig, the British must still try to reach agreement with Sinn Fein on the basis of a divided Ireland. If they failed in this as well, as seemed likely in October, they must make sure that the conference did not break down over partition but over allegiance. Of course, the government could resign if it failed to secure Irish unity, on the grounds that it was bound not to coerce Ulster and could not coerce Sinn Fein, given Ulster's stubborn opposition to unity. Rather than resign and admit failure, however, Lloyd George would do everything he could to overcome the Ulster problem. If he could accomplish this, other outstanding differences with Sinn Fein could probably be resolved.

On October 25 Griffith and Collins discussed Ulster with Chamberlain and Sir Gordon Hewart, who expressed willingness to help with the problem but made plain they were bound to maintain the area and powers of Northern Ireland. The Sinn Feiners again pressed for local option, but while the British admitted the justice of this demand they denied its practicability, again proposing the entire province as an option unit. Griffith rejected this idea; the vote must be limited to the Six Counties and taken by the 1918 parliamentary constituencies. Districts that voted for inclusion in an all-Ireland parliament would be placed under its direct rule. Those that voted for exclusion would retain the powers conferred by the Government of Ireland Act but would be subject to the overriding authority of the national parliament. Here, at last, was the Cabinet's Ulster clause, but the British gave it short shrift. With both sides standing fast, the discussion appeared to have reached an impasse. In an attempt to break the stalemate, the British suggested that the Six Counties retain both their Parliament and territory under an all-Ireland parliament. Chamberlain and Hewart explained that they had no authority for their suggestion; they were only discussing possible solutions. Griffith turned down the new proposal, although privately he and Collins thought it might form a basis for agreement. In the end, Griffith reiterated that any association with the Crown was contingent on Ulster's agreement to essential unity. "This," he wrote de Valera, "should put them up against the Ulster Die-hards."[38]

De Valera responded that the main thing was to close on the Ulster question without delay and obtain definite agreement on an all-Ireland parliament. After that, the "make or break" question of Crown and Empire could be dealt with. The president added that Sinn Fein should avoid any agreement which would compel nationalist areas to remain under the Northern Parliament without their consent.[39]

Despite Griffith's initial rejection of the idea, Chamberlain reported to his colleagues that Sinn Fein might agree to local autonomy for the entire Six Counties if Craig accepted unity. Churchill saw no reason why they should not press the North to accept an all-Ireland parliament, coupled with retention of its own area and powers. Birkenhead concurred, while the prime minister said it was time to review the whole situation. They should ask Sinn Fein for definite answers to vital questions, adding that they understood Sinn Fein's position on Ulster was "so and so." They should also affirm willingness to discuss Ulster's area and consider any machinery which would recognize and strengthen Irish unity. If the Sinn Feiners accepted everything else, subject to unity, the British could make proposals to Craig; if Sinn Fein refused to accept everything else, it could not break on Ulster.[40]

The memorandum that resulted from this meeting was delivered to the Irish on October 27. It stated that further progress depended on satisfactory answers to certain questions. Would Ireland maintain allegiance to the Crown and acknowledge the common citizenship and full partnership in the Empire it entailed? Would Ireland grant Britain the facilities necessary for common defense and accept prohibition of an Irish navy and air force? Finally, would the Irish accept free trade? No questions were asked about finance, since the matter was still under discussion, but the British restated their original position.[41]

As Frank Pakenham (Lord Longford) points out in his brilliant study of the negotiations, this memorandum was not really a rejection of the Irish proposals on strictly constitutional grounds, although the British tried to make it appear so. Their assertions represented only one interpretation of an unwritten Constitution, and neither that Constitution nor the British Empire was as simple and logical as the memorandum claimed since both were the product of historical evolution and compromises among many different interests. But although the Irish might have disputed their opponents' claims on constitutional and legal grounds, they were probably just as wise to forgo this approach and adhere to practical arguments in favor of external association. If British ministers rejected these arguments, they certainly would have rejected those which conflicted with their prejudices. Even if worsted in a debate on constitutional history and law, Lloyd George and his colleagues would simply have fallen back on the argument that the symbolism they insisted on was vital to any settlement because it was what Britons understood and revered. A republic, on the other hand, was as alien to British subjects everywhere as the Crown was to Irish rebels. No matter how much the Irish might argue, and whatever arguments they might use, a republic associated with the Empire, or even inside it, was just not practical politics in the 1920s.[42]

Before drafting a reply to the memorandum, Griffith and Collins met with Lloyd George and Birkenhead, who said that if Sinn Fein would accept the Crown, they would send for Craig and, as Griffith understood it, "force Ulster in." The two Irishmen declared they could not pledge acceptance of the Crown, but they might recommend some form of association if everything else, especially unification, were settled satisfactorily.[43]

Sinn Fein's official response was more an evasion than an answer. Under agreed terms of association, Ireland would accept the obligations of free partnership with the Commonwealth. Furthermore, if agreement were reached on all other issues, the Irish delegates would recommend that the government of a free and undivided Ireland "recognize the Crown as symbol and accepted head of the combination of signatory states." Since defense of the Irish coast was a matter of common concern, Britain should have such facilities as were mutually agreed upon, but only until Ireland could undertake its own defense. On trade, the Irish agreed to a free-trade convention which would not derogate from Ireland's fiscal autonomy (although surely it must have).[44] De Valera did not object to the defense concessions, but in reference to recognition of the Crown he noted to Griffith: "You know the view here" (on allegiance).[45]

While marking some advance in Sinn Fein's position, the October 29 memorandum was most disappointing to the British. Ultra-Unionists had just proposed a resolution condemning the negotiations, and before confronting them in Parliament Lloyd George wanted more concrete assurances from Sinn Fein. With a view to obtaining them, Tom Jones arranged a meeting of Griffith and Collins with the prime minister, Birkenhead, and Churchill at Churchill's house on the night of Sunday, October 30. The three British leaders, who had by now sunk their political differences, dined together, and shortly afterward, Griffith and Collins arrived. Since the two Sinn Feiners did not yet trust Birkenhead and Churchill, Griffith talked with Lloyd George privately. Collins, meanwhile, chatted with the other two men in another part of the house, laying the foundations of a closer relationship, especially between himself and Birkenhead.[46]

The prime minister and Griffith talked for forty-five minutes. Lloyd George said he was preparing his speech for a crucial debate the next day, but complained that he could not tell where he stood from the wording of the latest Irish reply. Griffith explained that since the British terms had obviously been framed for publication in the event of a breakdown, the Irish had responded in the same way. Turning to a familiar theme, Lloyd George declared that if Griffith would give him a personal assurance on Crown, Empire, and naval bases, "he would go out to smite the Die-hards and would fight on the Ulster matter to secure essential unity." Griffith reiterated that the delegates would recommend recognition of the Crown if they were satisfied on other matters. He also pledged to send the prime minister a letter of personal assurance on this point so as to strengthen his position with the Conservative Party. On the question of unity, Lloyd George said that he could carry a Six-County Parliament subordinate to a national Irish parliament. Alternatively, he promised that he would try to carry a revision of Northern Ireland's boundary or a vote by the entire province for inclusion or exclusion, but he was not hopeful of doing either. When Collins and Birkenhead joined them, both British ministers indicated that if they were certain of Irish good will, they would take risks and fight. The meeting ended on the understanding that the British delegates would come out strongly for peace in the debate next day.[47]

Even before he met Griffith on the 30th, Lloyd George thought the Sinn Feiners wanted to settle and would meet his major demands. But it looked as if they would demand a national parliament and the transfer of Tyrone and Fermanagh to direct rule by Dublin. The prime minister did not believe that Ulster would ever agree to these terms. Opinion was hardening against the rebels, but he wondered whether the British people would fight for Northern Ireland.[48] The interview with Griffith reinforced Lloyd George's belief that Sinn Fein would come to terms in return for unity. If the matter could be settled on those lines, he claimed he would resign rather than continue civil war.[49]

In the House of Commons on October 31, Tory die-hards vied with each other in denouncing the government's Irish policy. But the prime minister argued convincingly that the only alternative to negotiations was imposition of terms on Ireland. This would be costly and difficult, and people must be convinced there was no other way to resolve the problem. If Sinn Fein refused reasonable terms, Britain would do whatever was necessary to defend its safety and honor, but it was not yet certain that a just and honorable peace could not be made. If the House desired further efforts toward peace, it must uphold the government. The Labor and Liberal opposition gave the government valuable moral

support, Chamberlain summed up impressively, and the House defeated the proposed vote of censure 439 to 43.[50] With Parliament due to
be prorogued November 10, the government was free to devote more
time to the conference, although it was certain to face another challenge
at the Conservative Party convention in Liverpool on November 17.

At this time, President de Valera also was trying to rally his followers.
He told a secret session of the Sinn Fein Ard Fheis in late October that
Irishmen would not swear allegiance to the Crown, even if war were the
alternative, but association with Britain was a possibility if it safeguarded
Ireland's rights and interests. Warning of possible difficulties, the president explained that legitimate differences could arise in the Irish
Cabinet and the Dail over an agreement made by the plenipotentiaries.
If these differences spread to the people, any chance of a just peace
would be destroyed. There was also the danger that negotiations might
break down very soon, he said, with Britain renewing the war.[51] In
November, de Valera pressed for army reorganization, to improve military effectiveness and to tighten government control over the IRA so as
to prevent its opposition to a compromise peace. But GHQ blocked his
proposals, and the army remained essentially autonomous.[52]

On November 1 Griffith showed his fellow delegates the personal
letter of assurance he intended to give Lloyd George. In it, he repeated
his October 30 pledges on Crown, Empire, and defense, again making
them conditional on attainment of national unity. Barton, Duffy, and
Childers angrily protested the letter, but a heated exchange settled nothing. Duffy drafted a strong statement asserting that Griffith's letter
would weaken the stand taken by Sinn Fein in its formal proposals. If the
delegation decided a letter should be sent to the prime minister, it
should closely follow the phrasing of the last Irish memorandum, and it
should come from all the delegates, since all of them would be held
responsible for it.[53]

Barton and Childers endorsed Duffy's memorandum and, at their
request, Duffy went to Dublin on November 4 to warn the president that
the subconferences were dividing the delegation. But de Valera was
not alarmed; he himself had seen Lloyd George alone, and might have
done so again if he were leading the delegation. Moreover, the delegates were to make no important decisions without consulting the
Cabinet. Dismayed by their inability to influence events, Duffy and Barton considered resigning. They did not do so because this would only
advertise the split in the delegation and because they shared the president's conviction that, whatever happened in London, the Cabinet in
Dublin would have the last word.[54]

Needless to say, Griffith resented his critics' well-meant advice. It was
all very well for Duffy, Barton, and Childers to find fault, but they did
not bear the responsibility for diplomatic bargaining or appreciate its

difficulties. Griffith knew he had given away nothing essential. All he had done was try to make Sinn Fein's terms as attractive as possible to help secure peace and unity. These goals were well worth a few verbal concessions, and if the conference should break down, these concessions would give Sinn Fein a decided tactical advantage. Despite his irritation, Griffith agreed to redraft the letter to Lloyd George. It was sent from the whole delegation, and its language closely followed that of the official memorandum of October 29.[55]

Griffith and Collins delivered the revised letter to Birkenhead at noon on November 2. The lord chancellor suggested several changes, the most important of which was that the phrase "free partnership with the British Commonwealth" be altered to "free partnership within the British Commonwealth." Griffith refused to make this change because it would have meant Ireland was prepared to enter the Commonwealth. Unwilling to give up so easily, Birkenhead persuaded the two Irishmen to meet with Lloyd George and himself later in the day.[56]

The subconference lasted from 6:45 to 8:15 p.m., and Chamberlain joined it in progress. The British pressed for more definite commitments on Crown, Empire, and defense, claiming that these commitments would aid their efforts to secure unity. Six or seven alterations in the letter were suggested. Griffith and Collins accepted two, rejected one, and the other disputed points were redrafted to mutual satisfaction. The Sinn Feiners refused to change "a recognition of the Crown" to "recognition of the Crown" because this would imply allegiance rather than limited recognition. However, the British won another important point. The Irish leaders agreed that their country's association with the Commonwealth should be defined as "a free partnership of Ireland with the other states associated within the British Commonwealth." The British also scored an important gain on defense. Naval facilities in Ireland ceased to be those which "must be agreed to be necessary" and became such "as may be necessary," leaving the decision on this matter to Britain. The Irish position on Ulster was weakened by deletion of the letter's final phrase, which ruled out any association if unity were denied in form or fact. What remained was simply the statement that Sinn Fein's attitude on other vital matters was "conditional on the recognition of the essential unity of Ireland." The demand for unity was thus rendered less specific and less absolute.[57]

With some effort, Griffith won the assent of the entire delegation to the revised letter and sent it to Lloyd George at 11 p.m. on November 2. The next day he sent a copy of it, with a covering letter, to de Valera. Explaining that he had adhered to the basis of the Irish memorandum of October 29, Griffith pointed out: "You will observe my wording, which they accept, is consistent with external association and external recognition."[58]

In fact, Griffith agreed to one change that was not consistent with external association when he accepted the phrase "a free partnership of Ireland with the other states associated within the British Commonwealth" to define the form of association. The obvious interpretation of this phrase put Ireland inside the Empire. It is strange that Griffith did not see this, and stranger still that no member of the Irish delegation or the Cabinet grasped the significance of the verbal concession.[59]

On the morning of November 3, Birkenhead told Griffith and Collins that the government greatly appreciated the letter of assurance. The British intended to see Carson and Bonar Law before talking to Craig, to dissuade them from opposing efforts to secure Irish unity. If Ulster proved unreasonable, Birkenhead pledged that the government would resign rather than use force against Sinn Fein. For the moment, Griffith was well satisfied. It was now up to the British government to deliver Irish unity or resign; whatever happened, Sinn Fein's position seemed secure.[60]

Chapter 7
Advance and Retreat:
November 1921

British efforts to bring about Irish unity decisively influenced the negotiations with Sinn Fein, but not at all in the way Griffith had anticipated. At his first meeting with Lloyd George on November 5, Craig seemed receptive to the idea of an all-Ireland parliament with suitable safeguards for the northeast, but two days later he flatly rejected it. His opposition to unity had obviously been reinforced by Carson and Bonar Law, both of whom Lloyd George failed to convert. Carson opposed any concessions to the Sinn Feiners. Law would concede Dominion status to Southern Ireland, but he would not sacrifice Ulster for peace with Sinn Fein.[1] In a letter written November 12, Law expressed his views fully. If the government tried to coerce Ulster he would fight. If he failed to get a majority of Tory MPs on his side, he would withdraw from politics; but he believed that once the issue was clearly stated, he would have an almost unanimous party behind him. Law contended that coercion of Ulster would violate Conservative pledges, split the party, betray an area that was as much a part of Britain as Scotland, and precipitate civil war. He felt as strongly about Ulster as he had before the war, and nothing would change his position.[2]

Anxious about a breakdown of negotiations over Ulster, Chamberlain consulted his party's chairman and its chief whip. He asked whether the country would support coercion of Southern Ireland if the peace conference failed because of Ulster's insistence on exclusion from an Irish parliament. Their replies confirmed his own assessment: the country wanted peace and would not support intransigence by Ulster if Sinn Fein accepted Britain's essential terms and offered suitable minority safeguards. However, support for Ulster among Conservatives would cause a party split if the government tried to impose Irish unity.[3] Craig's intractable attitude thus placed Conservative ministers in an apparently impossible position. They could not coerce Ulster because of past pledges and because this would split their party. On the other hand, public opinion would not support coercion of Sinn Fein simply because it refused to accept partition. Under these conditions, resignation seemed the only way out.[4]

The same thought had occurred to Lloyd George. Stymied and depressed by Craig's "no surrender" attitude, the prime minister sounded his colleagues on the idea of resignation. Balfour agreed, but Churchill warned that resignation would be criticized as an abdication of responsibility and argued that the government must carry out the policy it believed in until it was defeated in Parliament.[5]

It is doubtful that Lloyd George seriously intended to resign. The suggestion reflected his frustration, but it was also designed to hold the Cabinet in line and show Law the futility of opposition. He told Law that a government formed to coerce Sinn Fein could count upon only the support of right-wing Tories.[6] At the same time, Lloyd George used the threat of resignation, coupled with warnings of an ultra-Tory government, to win Griffith's assent to a proposal designed to prevent any attempt to coerce Sinn Fein, but one which also fell short of securing unity. Griffith's tentative agreement had far-reaching ramifications, but its immediate result was to free the prime minister from his pledge to resign if he failed to deliver essential unity.

On November 10 Lloyd George informed the Cabinet of Ulster's obduracy, expressing his belief that Britain could not use force against either the South or the North. Lord Curzon said that Craig feared oppression by a Dublin parliament, as well as the loss of Tyrone and Fermanagh. The prime minister declared that Sinn Fein's claim to the two counties was "overwhelming," and if Northern Ireland refused unity, it must submit to boundary revision. However, if Ulster accepted an all-Ireland parliament, with safeguards, Sinn Fein might not press its claim to nationalist areas in the Six Counties. Other ministers admitted the dilemma over coercion. Chamberlain did not believe that his non-coercion pledge precluded putting maximum moral pressure on Ulster to help secure a settlement with Sinn Fein.[7]

Immediately after the Cabinet meeting, the prime minister submitted the government's proposals to Craig. In return for Sinn Fein's acceptance of Crown, Empire, and naval bases, Britain would create a national Irish parliament with sufficient powers to form an autonomous state. The government of Northern Ireland would retain the powers conferred on it in 1920, but would exercise them under the overriding authority of Dublin rather than Westminster. The question of what area would remain under Northern Ireland's direct rule would be open to discussion, as would further safeguards for Ulster's special interests, but creation of an all-Ireland parliament would facilitate a friendly settlement of such questions. The prime minister pointed out that the customs barrier necessitated by partition would penalize the North and the jagged frontier line would leave discontented minorities in both parts of Ireland. Moreover, the tax burden Northern Ireland would have to bear as part of the United Kingdom would almost certainly be greater than what it would bear as part of an Irish Dominion. Lloyd George concluded with an invitation to a conference for a "full and frank exchange of views."[8]

After consulting with his colleagues, Craig replied on November 11, reaffirming Ulster's desire for the closest possible union with Britain. He expressed surprise that Lloyd George thought it necessary to confirm Northern Ireland's retention of the powers granted in 1920 and voiced concern about possible revision of its statutory area. As for unification, the Council of Ireland constituted a mechanism for creation of an all-Ireland parliament whenever both parts of the country wanted it. But Ulster remained as opposed as ever to unification. No paper safeguards could protect it against maladministration, and local Unionist feeling was so hostile to unity that no government could even enter a conference if this point were open to discussion. To resolve the problems which would arise from the existence of two governments of unequal status in Ireland, Craig proposed that the North as well as the South be granted Dominion status.[9]

On November 12 the British delegates discussed Craig's reply. Lloyd George and Chamberlain agreed that his request for Dominion status would cause a great revulsion of feeling against Ulster, which had always claimed to be loyal to Britain. Lloyd George maintained that the proposal was motivated by a desire for lower taxes and would be rejected by Bonar Law. While appealing for patience with Ulster, Chamberlain declared that the North could not have its existing boundaries if it refused unity. Churchill urged creation of an all-Ireland parliament with the option of exclusion for Ulster. The prime minister closed the meeting by asking his colleagues to think over what reply should be sent to Craig.[10]

After an unproductive talk with Bonar Law, Lloyd George concluded that Craig would discuss nothing until after the Conservative Party convention. If the convention supported peace with Sinn Fein, he would be easier to deal with. The British delegates therefore rejected Craig's proposal for Dominion Home Rule and repeated the invitation to a conference.[11] In his reply, Lloyd George pointed out that Craig's proposal

would stereotype a frontier based neither upon natural features nor broad geographical considerations by giving it the character of an international boundary. Partition on these lines, the majority of the Irish people will never accept, nor could we conscientiously attempt to enforce it.[12]

On November 17 Craig responded, firmly restating his opposition to unity and again requesting Dominion status. He agreed to talk with Lloyd George, but nothing came of their meeting. Returning to Belfast, Craig announced on November 29 that within a week negotiations with Sinn Fein would either have broken down or the prime minister would send him new proposals for consideration. In the meantime, Lloyd George had pledged that Ulster's rights would not be compromised.[13]

The British press urged Ulster to accept unity in the interests of peace, and this campaign helped set off another round of violence in Belfast. The transfer of local powers from Westminster to Belfast, which began in November, made matters worse in some ways. On November 28 the nationalist-controlled Tyrone County Council pledged allegiance to Dail Eireann, declaring the people of Tyrone and Fermanagh would never submit to separation from the rest of Ireland. The Belfast regime at once ejected the council from its offices and seized its records.[14] Whatever Northern Ireland's immediate future, strife was sure to play an important part in it.

Although he had failed to win unity, Lloyd George was not yet ready to resign. He hoped that aversion to high taxation and boundary revision might lead Ulster Unionists to reconsider their position. But this kind of pressure did not guarantee unity, and if Griffith withdrew his concessions and demanded Lloyd George's resignation on the grounds that he had failed to deliver unity, the negotiations would be wrecked. Determined to avoid this disaster, Lloyd George set out to obtain Griffith's commitment to a compromise on Ulster.

On November 7 the prime minister described the impasse to Tom Jones, contending there was only one alternative to a breakdown of negotiations and resignation. This was Dominion status for the Twenty-six Counties, the *status quo* for the Six Counties, and boundary revision. Observing that he might be able to secure British approval for this arrangement if Sinn Fein would accept it, Lloyd George charged Jones with finding out if Griffith and Collins would agree to the proposal.[15]

The next afternoon, Jones told Griffith and Collins that Craig was "standing pat," rejecting both unity and boundary revision. The prime minister was going to propose that Northern Ireland accept an all-Ireland parliament with safeguards; if it refused, he would at once resign office and retire from public life. Collins was upset by this news, but Griffith calmly remarked that Lloyd George should stand up to the Ulster Unionists; they were bluffing, and an honest plebiscite would show an anti-partition majority in Northern Ireland. Jones replied that Lloyd George would fight as hard as he could, but the real possibility of failure must be considered. If the prime minister resigned, Chamberlain and Birkenhead might retire with him. Bonar Law might then form a militarist government to coerce Southern Ireland and, if he did, a Conservative majority in the Commons would support him. Jones said he cared too much for Ireland to allow this to happen if there were any way to prevent it, which meant Lloyd George must be kept in office. To this end, presenting the prime minister's proposal as his own, Jones suggested that Southern Ireland be given Dominion status, while a boundary commission should delimit Northern Ireland, the delimited area to be restricted to its powers under the Government of Ireland Act. Griffith replied that Sinn Fein preferred a plebiscite, while Collins protested that Jones's proposal sacrificed unity entirely. Jones agreed with Collins but claimed that the alternative to his suggestion was chaos, Crown Colony government, and civil war. Griffith was noncommittal, remarking only that the proposal was the British government's concern for the moment, and Sinn Fein would leave it in Lloyd George's hands. Jones promised to get the prime minister's opinion on the proposal and give them a reply the next day.[16]

Reporting to de Valera on the interview, Griffith expressed the conviction that Jones's dire predictions were "partly bluff, but not wholly." More important, he believed that the proposed boundary commission "would give us most of Tyrone, Fermanagh, and part of Armagh, Down, etc."[17] Griffith felt the conference might end within a week. If this happened, he thought it should end on the note of Ulster's unreasonableness so as to turn Dominion opinion against the North.[18]

On November 9 de Valera replied to all of Griffith's letters since October 30. He wrote that from the start of negotiations he had favored breaking on Ulster, if a break were necessary, provided only that Ulster could not raise the cry of loyalty to Crown and Empire and that Ireland's claim to unity and independence was not prejudiced. The delegates had managed to put Ulster in the wrong, and if a break came now, public opinion everywhere would condemn Ulster's intransigence.

> The danger now is that we should be tempted, in order to put them more hopelessly in the wrong, to make further advances on our side. I think, as far as the "Crown and Empire" connection is concerned, we should not budge a single inch from the point where the negotiations have now led us.[19]

This advice obviously pertained to Griffith's reports of the assurances given Lloyd George to aid him in dealing with Craig, but the president issued no warning against further concessions on Ulster.

Heartened by Griffith's mild reaction to his Ulster proposal, the prime minister lost no time in exploiting his advantage.[20] On November 9 Jones told Griffith and Duggan that Craig was standing firm and that Lloyd George was to secure the Cabinet's support against Ulster the next day. But the prime minister wanted to reinforce his position by playing a second and "absolutely last card," if Craig refused an all-Ireland parliament. Predictably, this "last card" was a Twenty-six County parliament, with powers mutually agreed upon, and "a Boundary Commission to delimit the six-county area . . . so as to give us the districts in which we are a majority." That part of Northern Ireland which remained after boundary revision would receive no powers beyond those conferred in 1920 and would have to pay British taxes. Jones asked Griffith and Duggan if they thought Ulster would accept this proposal. They were sure it would not, and he agreed. The plan, Jones explained, was a tactical maneuver to deprive Ulster Unionists of British support by showing how utterly unreasonable they were in attempting to coerce Northern nationalists.

> He asked us would we stand behind such a proposal. We said that it would be their proposal—not ours—and we would not, therefore, be bound by it but we realised its value as a tactical manoeuvre and if Lloyd George made it we would not queer his position. He was satisfied with this.

Although Sinn Fein would prefer a plebiscite, Griffith said that a boundary commission was very much the same thing in substance. He stipulated that it would have to cover all six counties and not just Tyrone and Fermanagh. Jones said that Griffith's limited assurance on the boundary commission was enough for him and vowed that the prime minister would fight as hard as he could on the main proposals. Before he left, Jones again emphasized how beneficial the new plan would be for Sinn Fein. It would show Ulster's demands to be intolerable, keep Lloyd George in office, and prevent any attempt to renew coercion in Southern Ireland.[21]

The prime minister was "perfectly satisfied" with Jones's report of his second interview with Griffith, although he insisted that boundary revision must apply to all of Ulster's nine counties rather than just the six northeastern ones (which meant that Sinn Fein could lose as well as gain from it). Jones informed Duggan of this the next day, and Lloyd George's optimism increased when there was no objection. On several occasions during the next few days, he expressed confidence that his alternative proposal would compel Ulster to accept unity.[22]

In talking with his associates, it is not surprising that Lloyd George dwelt on the threat of high taxation rather than boundary revision as the most effective means of exerting pressure on Northern Ireland. For one thing, he took this view himself. More important, the tax threat was unlikely to cause trouble with Bonar Law and his followers, especially since Law himself had originally suggested the idea to Lloyd George.[23] To minimize the risk of confrontation with Conservatives over boundary revision, Lloyd George soft-pedaled it in discussions with British leaders who were not directly involved in the negotiations. Indeed, he even withheld knowledge of the proposed boundary commission from Craig, explaining to Griffith that mention of it would only increase support for Ulster at the upcoming Conservative convention.[24]

But while the idea of boundary revision involved some risk for the British government, it also offered a chance to break the deadlock over Ulster. For the same reasons it alarmed Craig, boundary revision strongly appealed to Sinn Fein. Furthermore, Conservative ministers did

not regard it as coercion and were prepared to support it. Writing to the
prime minister on November 11, Chamberlain claimed that in the subconference of October 25

> Griffith and Collins had clearly in mind the possibility that Ulster would
> refuse any form of United Parlt. and that they said that in that case they
> expected us to allow a vote by constituencies or poor-law areas. They were
> sure that the vote would give them more than 2 counties and would leave
> "Ulster" economically paralysed.
>
> We should have to discuss how far we can put pressure on Craig in this
> matter of boundaries; but obviously Bonar and Carson feel the weakness
> of his case there, and all Carson's talk points to agreement on a Boundary
> Comn.
>
> I beg you therefore in talking with Griffith to remember that the pre-
> sumption is that Sinn Fein would accept
> (a) Dominion Home Rule (as defined by us) for the South
> (b) a Boundary Comn. or new delimitation by some other machinery[,]
>   upon condition that
> (c) We do not give *new* powers to Ulster.[25]

On November 11 Craig and his Cabinet formally refused to consider
an all-Ireland parliament. Jones at once relayed the bad news to Griffith,
informing him of the prime minister's belief that Craig was being encouraged by British supporters, who hoped to win a vote against Sinn
Fein at the Conservative convention. But Chamberlain had told the
Cabinet, the day before, that he thought the Sinn Fein delegates sincere
and honorable men, and he planned to speak strongly for an Irish
settlement at the convention. Griffith was jubilant when he heard this
and wrote de Valera that there could be no more pressure on Sinn Fein
until Ulster had agreed to unity: "The 'Ulster' crowd are in the pit that
they digged for us, and if we keep them there we'll have England and
the Dominions out against them in the next week or two."[26] But Griffith
was wrong. Jones's visit was designed to set the stage for a binding
commitment to Lloyd George's "tactical manoeuvre" on Ulster.

Jones saw Griffith again on the morning of November 12. After showing him Craig's last reply, Jones said that if Sinn Fein cooperated with
the prime minister, Irish unity might be achieved "before many months
had passed."[27] He then invited Griffith to meet Lloyd George that afternoon. Griffith agreed, and when he arrived at the appointed rendezvous, the prime minister brought him up to date. Craig's request for
Dominion status had astounded the Cabinet and surprised even Bonar
Law. Lloyd George's reply would reject the Dominion proposal and
offer instead the creation of an all-Ireland parliament from which
Northern Ireland might withdraw. However, if Northern Ireland chose
exclusion, a boundary commission would delimit its area to make the

boundary conform as closely as possible to the wishes of the population, and the delimited area would be subject to the same financial burdens as Britain. If Ulster refused this offer, as he believed it would, Lloyd George declared that he "would fight, summon Parliament, appeal to it against Ulster, dissolve, or pass an Act establishing the all-Ireland Parliament."[28] When the prime minister asked his opinion of this strategy, Griffith replied:

> I told him it was his proposal, not ours. He agreed, but he said that when they were fighting next Thursday [at the Conservative convention] with the Die-hards and "Ulster" in front, they were lost if we cut the ground away behind them by repudiating the proposal.
>
> I said we would not do that, if he meant that he thought we would come out in public decrying it. It was his own proposal. If the Ulstermen accepted it, we would have to discuss it with him in the privacy of the Conference. I could not guarantee its acceptance, as, of course, my colleagues knew nothing of it yet. But I would guarantee that while he was fighting the "Ulster" crowd we would not help them by repudiating him.

This satisfied Lloyd George, but he pledged Griffith to secrecy about their meeting to protect himself from charges of conspiring against Ulster.[29]

According to Griffith's account of this interview, he had promised Lloyd George no more than he had promised Jones three days before; that is, Sinn Fein would not publicly repudiate Lloyd George's Ulster proposal when it was offered to Craig. However, the prime minister gave Chamberlain a different version shortly after the interview. Lloyd George said he had told Griffith he planned to offer Craig the choice of an all-Ireland parliament or a boundary commission; if both were refused, he would proceed with the latter. The prime minister then explained to Griffith that he would be much criticized for taking this course and could succeed only if his plan for boundary revision was the one compromise acceptable to Sinn Fein. Before sending Chamberlain and Birkenhead to the Conservative convention to risk their political careers over Ireland, he must be sure of Griffith's support. He did not expect or as yet need the support of the other Irish delegates, or even active support from Griffith. What he needed was a personal pledge that if he offered Ulster the alternatives described, Griffith would not repudiate him or break off negotiations then or later on this issue. Griffith, Lloyd George claimed, had agreed not to let him down on the Ulster proposal. This meant he would not break off negotiations despite Lloyd George's failure to secure unity, as long as the prime minister carried through his plan for boundary revision. Even before Chamberlain arrived, Lloyd George jubilantly informed his confidante, Frances Stevenson, that Griffith would agree to his new scheme and the Ulster Unionists would be "done in."[30]

How could the usually astute Griffith have failed to make clear to Lloyd George the crucial distinction between acquiescence in the boundary commission as a tactical maneuver and agreement to it as a solution to the Ulster problem? He may have felt that Jones had already explained his attitude to the prime minister and that it was therefore unnecessary to define it in detail. Or he may have thought Craig's rejection of boundary revision would kill the idea. He may even have been so attracted by the apparently favorable prospects of boundary revision that he neglected to stress the qualified nature of his assent to it. Whatever the reason for Griffith's failure to clarify his position on November 12, Lloyd George believed he had obtained Griffith's pledge to accept as part of a general settlement a proposal which did not guarantee unity. Henceforth the prime minister, as well as Chamberlain and Birkenhead, acted on the assumption that Griffith would not break off negotiations on the issue of partition.

The British advantage was quickly consolidated. On Lloyd George's instructions, Jones drafted a summary of the proposal agreed to by Griffith, which Chamberlain put into final form. On the evening of November 13, Jones showed Griffith this statement, and he assented verbally to its terms. These provided that if northeast Ulster did not accept at once the principle of an all-Ireland parliament—with retention of the local legislature and powers conferred in 1920 and whatever other safeguards were agreed on—the British would still create a national parliament but would allow northeast Ulster the option of exclusion from its jurisdiction. If Ulster chose exclusion, it would retain the local autonomy within the United Kingdom conferred in 1920 but would continue to be subject to British taxation. Moreover,

> it would be necessary to revise the boundary of Northern Ireland. This might be done by a Boundary Commission which would be directed to adjust the line both by inclusion and exclusion so as to make the boundary conform as closely as possible to the wishes of the population.[31]

Griffith did not mention this document to his colleagues or to de Valera. There was no reason why he should have, since he felt that it only confirmed the limited pledge he had already described to them.[32]

As the date of the Conservative Party convention in Liverpool approached, Chamberlain and Birkenhead became increasingly anxious. Lord Derby, Lancashire's most eminent Conservative, nervously reminded party leaders that they could trigger a revolt if they pushed Ulster too far in their efforts to placate Sinn Fein. Sir Archibald Salvidge, the powerful party boss of Liverpool, shared Derby's fears of a split, and his attitude was crucial because of the influence he would wield over the convention. Although strongly pro-Ulster, Salvidge made up his mind not to attack the government while the Irish negotiations were in progress, and he made his position clear in a letter to the prime minister and a statement to the press on November 14.[33]

Unaware of this statement, Birkenhead journeyed to Liverpool and met secretly with Salvidge on the morning of November 15. The lord chancellor admitted that he had originally regarded the negotiations as a waste of time, but had become more hopeful and more interested as they progressed. He had come to realize how important the conference was and to believe that the Irish delegates were honorable men who would keep any treaty they made. The government asked that Northern Ireland join the new Irish Dominion, with safeguards for its local interests. But the government would not try to coerce Ulster, nor would it consent to any settlement which did not include Irish allegiance to the Crown, membership in the Empire, and British control of Ireland's naval defense.

A settlement on these lines was almost reached; it required only the blessing of the Liverpool convention to bring it to fruition. Birkenhead asked Salvidge to help win that endorsement, reminding him that the alternative settlement was terrible war. Convinced of Birkenhead's absolute sincerity, Salvidge showed him the morning newspapers, with their announcement that he would not oppose the government. Neutrality was not enough, the lord chancellor contended; the party leaders must have a clear mandate for continuing the negotiations. Salvidge agreed to give the government strong support, and a grateful Birkenhead returned to London.[34]

Eighteen hundred delegates converged on Liverpool for the all-important convention, which opened November 17 with the diehards' shrill denunciations of the government's Irish policy. Colonel Gretton moved a vote of censure on the negotiations, but Salvidge proposed an amendment, endorsing a settlement that safeguarded the Crown, the Empire, the Southern Unionists, and Ulster. Derby and Worthington-Evans gave Salvidge impressive support and the amendment was carried almost unanimously. The diehards were momentarily silenced and Chamberlain triumphantly closed the convention with an eloquent and forceful address.[35]

Lloyd George was immensely gratified at this result, but it was not devotion to him or the coalition that produced it. The convention endorsed the negotiations because of the country's strong desire for peace and probably an even stronger desire not to split the Tory party. But the price of unity was a settlement that clearly safeguarded Crown, Empire, defense, and Ulster.[36]

Another possible obstacle to peacemaking was removed a few days

after the convention when Chamberlain explained the government's position to Bonar Law. Once he made clear that the government had never
contemplated forcing Ulster into an all-Ireland parliament, Law was
satisfied. He would not object to anything the government proposed to
give Southern Ireland and would not support Ulster's claim to remain
part of the United Kingdom without bearing the full burdens of citizenship. Finally, if Ulster stood firm on exclusion from an all-Ireland parliament, Law would advise Carson and Craig that they could not expect
the British government to fight, nor could they themselves fight, to
maintain Northern Ireland's existing boundary.[37]

On November 15 Lloyd George told Griffith that he would receive
the latest British peace proposals the next day. The draft arrived on
schedule but it lacked any heading, signature, or address. Griffith sent a
copy to de Valera, saying he thought the terms should be rejected and
the British informed that Sinn Fein would shortly submit counterproposals. The British memorandum offered Ireland Dominion status,
with its constitutional position to be as nearly as possible that of Canada,
subject to certain special conditions. In default of mutual agreement,
Commonwealth arbitration was to determine Anglo-Irish financial relations. Britain would defend the Irish coast until it was mutually agreed
that Ireland should assume this function. Ireland was to furnish whatever defense facilities Britain might require, and its army was to be
limited to 40,000 men. Although the two countries would maintain free
trade with each other, they might impose duties to prevent dumping and
unfair competition. Northern Ireland could exclude itself from the Irish
Dominion, but if it did, a boundary commission was to revise the Irish
boundary in accordance with the wishes of the inhabitants.[38]

De Valera wrote Griffith that it was time to send the British the final
word, which could best be done by presenting Draft Treaty A, "modified
somewhat to meet the exact position."[39] Griffith responded that the
British proposals were not a treaty draft after all, only a set of suggestions.[40] He believed that the Irish reply should follow the British example and be an informal rather than a final offer. He also told de Valera
that Sinn Fein, instead of Ulster, was now in confrontation with the
British. "The crucial question—'Crown and Empire'—must be met next
week. If 'Ulster' gets us to break on them, she will have re-won the
game."[41] Divergent views within the delegation hampered the drafting
of a reply. Aided by Barton and Duffy, Childers prepared a draft, which
was offered as the work of Barton to avoid arousing Griffith's wrath.
After some revisions, it was delivered on November 22.[42]

The memorandum was based on the assumption that Ireland's essential unity would be maintained. It stipulated that political authority in
Ireland was to be derived exclusively from the Irish people's elected
representatives. Ireland was to be associated with the Commonwealth

for purposes of common concern, and for these purposes the Crown would be recognized as symbol and accepted head of the association. Ireland's rights and status in respect to matters of common concern were to be the same as those of other Commonwealth members, and it would undertake such concerted action as the associated states might decide. Ireland would also provide its own defense as far as its resources permitted and would not allow itself to be used in any way inimical to Britain. Defense facilities required by Britain should be precisely defined, and Ireland would take full responsibility for its own defense in five years. As Britain requested, the ratio between the Irish and British armies would be the same as that between the populations of the two countries. An arbitration tribunal would settle outstanding financial questions. An agreed list of free-trade commodities was to be drawn up, but in all other matters Ireland was to enjoy fiscal autonomy. If Northern Ireland accepted unity, it would retain its local Parliament and powers and be given whatever safeguards it required.[43]

Even though the memorandum was very similar to his own draft, Childers complained that only the clauses on the source of political authority and the settlement of financial questions were fully consistent with Ireland's claim to complete independence. Barton and Duffy supported Childers, but Griffith was outraged and accused him of working against a settlement. When Childers angrily demanded that this accusation be put in writing, Griffith apologized, but his dislike of Childers was doubtless intensified.[44]

Despite his impatience with dissent in the delegation, Griffith knew that the Cabinet's attitude was the real problem. Collins felt the same way, and when Griffith asked him what terms they could accept, he wondered, fearing that acceptance of any terms would bring allegations of treason. A dozen times a day, Collins asked himself what they had come to London for, and he blamed the Cabinet for confusing rather than instructing the delegation. Miserable in the artificial atmosphere of the conference, he raged: "If we had the guns there'd be no negotiations." But Sinn Fein did not have the guns. Tired and worried, Collins asked himself again and again: "What do we accept?"[45]

The British delegates were even more unhappy than Childers with the memorandum of November 22. With the full support of Chamberlain and Birkenhead, an irate Lloyd George instructed Jones to tell the Irish that their proposals were wholly inadmissible and that if this offer were their last word, he would have no choice but to break off negotiations.[46]

Jones quickly conveyed the message. He appealed to Griffith to withdraw the memorandum or at least substitute more moderate terms. Griffith refused, arguing that the memorandum constituted "a great advance" toward peace. It offered a form of association honorable to both sides. If the defense clauses were unclear, it was because the Admiralty had failed to define its requirements precisely. The trade proposal was reasonable and rectified Britain's attempt to subordinate Ireland economically. As for Ulster, Sinn Fein had made "a great offer."

Privately, Jones shared Griffith's view that the proposals marked a considerable advance on previous offers, but since his superiors disagreed, he could only play desperately for an opening that would avert a collapse of negotiations. He pointed out that the memorandum contained no list of specific safeguards for Ulster such as the prime minister had requested. Griffith replied that Sinn Fein had promised all the safeguards Ulster required, asking only that these be named. Jones confessed the prime minister had misunderstood that point, and there might be others.[47] But Griffith was not yet ready to discuss possible misunderstandings. Instead, he accused the British of trying to get Sinn Fein's full agreement to their terms before Craig made any concessions. If Sinn Fein agreed, and the prime minister told Craig, Craig would concede nothing and would announce that Sinn Fein had betrayed its followers. The Irish delegates would not dare face their people after having given so much away without being sure of getting anything in return. While admitting the force of this argument, Jones vigorously denied that the British were playing Craig's game. They only wanted to be sure how far Sinn Fein was willing to go before they negotiated with Craig. Agreement on major issues would enable them to defy Craig and his supporters.

At about this point, Collins joined Griffith and Jones, and Jones repeated the substance of Lloyd George's message. Neither Irish leader had any suggestions on how to prevent a rupture, but Jones did. He felt there were explanations of the offending memorandum that would modify British objections and suggested a meeting of the principals the following day. Griffith agreed and wrote de Valera: "We shall urge the acceptability of the arrangement *re* association we have proposed, but I have little hope of any good result." If he failed, he believed Lloyd George would end the negotiations.[48]

Jones gave as favorable an interpretation of the interview as he could to the prime minister, but Lloyd George remained worried and irritable, almost worn out by the difficulties encountered in the protracted negotiations.[49] Every time he thought he had pinned Griffith down, the stolid Irishman somehow managed to escape and resume an impossible position.

The British wasted no time on November 23. They told Griffith, Collins, and Barton that they must fight on the issue of the Crown, and they summarily rejected the Irish counterproposal on this issue. However, the meeting cleared up some misunderstandings on trade and defense, and seemed to clarify Sinn Fein's position on Ulster.

On Ulster Lloyd George declared that I had assured him I would not let him down, if he put up the proposals subsequently embodied in their memorandum to Craig, and complained that we had not embodied them in our memorandum. I said I had given him that assurance and I now repeated it, but I told him at the time it was his proposal—not ours. Therefore, it did not appear in our document. Our proposal was, in our opinion, better but it was different.

He was satisfied. He had misunderstood us in this instance and said as much. He would put his proposal to Craig from himself only.[50]

Actually, this exchange only confirmed the confusion over Ulster. Griffith implied that Sinn Fein would accept the British proposal if Craig did. But since he did not expect Craig to agree either to unity or boundary revision, he felt he could still break off negotiations on Ulster if the need arose. However, Lloyd George was prepared to implement his alternative proposal (i.e., boundary revision) even if Craig rejected it. He assumed that Griffith realized this and was willing in the final analysis, to settle for less than "essential unity." The prime minister therefore saw no need, at this stage, to remind Griffith more explicitly of his pledge of November 12–13.

After consulting briefly with Chamberlain and Birkenhead, the prime minister returned to announce that he must know where he stood before seeing Craig again. If he had to fight on fundamentals, there was no help for it, but it would be a tragedy if negotiations broke down on misunderstandings. Lloyd George suggested that Griffith and Collins meet with Birkenhead to review Griffith's November 2 letter of assurance. This would ensure that the British understood the exact Irish position on Crown and Empire. Once a meeting was arranged for the following day, Lloyd George agreed to postpone his interview with Craig to await its result. According to Jones, the prime minister was now in a "much milder mood."[51]

Griffith and Collins brought Duffy and Chartres to the November 24 meeting, and Hewart accompanied Birkenhead. The Crown was the sole topic of discussion. A memorandum submitted by Chartres pointed out that Ireland lacked the protection against British interference which distance gave the Dominions. If the Crown were to exist in Ireland, Irish freedom could only be assured by written guaranties that it would never function. Since this would expose the monarchical principle to ridicule and contempt, the British would be better advised to accept an associated republic. The Irish government would formally recognize the Crown as head of the association by something like a small annual contribution to the king's civil list.[52]

When Hewart asked whether this meant that the Crown should not function in Ireland, Chartres replied that it would not even exist. Birkenhead was most conciliatory. The treaty could include a provision that the Crown should not act except on the advice of its Irish ministers. He emphasized that Ireland's status would be the same as that of Canada, and when Chartres reminded him of the qualification, "as nearly as may be," the lord chancellor said that these words could be dropped if there were a strong objection to them. Chartres was not so easily pacified and turned to the problem of royal symbolism. Even if the Crown were not made the instrument for interference in Irish affairs, the symbol itself was offensive because of its past associations. Birkenhead contended that the Crown's value as a symbol of Commonwealth unity was tremendous. But why must Ireland accept the Crown, asked Chartres, if it were no more than a symbol? Because, answered Birkenhead, the British people were deeply attached to that symbol. The Sinn Feiners failed to inquire how this fact justified imposing the Crown on Ireland. By now, Griffith and Collins were convinced that if the British refused to accept limited recognition, there was no point in challenging their belief in the Crown as a mystical symbol of unity and tradition, a concept which found expression in the oath of allegiance.

Griffith tried another approach, offering an annual contribution to the king's civil list. Birkenhead admitted that this would be a fine gesture, but it would not answer the main problem. Duffy declared it would do no good to make peace based on a lie. Even if a settlement that included allegiance were approved in Ireland, it would drive Republican opposition underground and would not bring lasting agreement. Collins added that Ireland was offering a great concession to British sentiment for the sake of a real peace.

Earnestly and forcefully, Griffith again unfolded the advantages of external association. What was needed now, he contended, was a "big gesture" by Britain, like that which had extended autonomy to South Africa shortly after the Boer War. Were hostilities to be resumed on a technicality? Ireland would recognize the Crown for external affairs while retaining the Republic for internal affairs. If the British preferred to translate the Republic's official title, *Saorstat na hEireann,* as "Free State" (of Ireland), Griffith would not quarrel with their translation. Birkenhead commented suavely: "The title, Free State, can go into the Treaty." Griffith finished by asserting that the Irish proposals were a *via media* between two apparently irreconcilable positions. They preserved the honor and interests of both peoples and satisfied the pride of both; they could end the struggle of centuries.

Hewart intervened to assure the Irish that the British government was not contemplating war, but Birkenhead at once corrected him. On all other issues, he said, there was substantial agreement, but the question of allegiance was vital. The Sinn Feiners were left to draw the inescapable conclusion that failure to agree on this point meant war. Griffith and Duffy made final appeals, but to no avail. Birkenhead asked that the proposal for recognition of the Crown be formulated in writing, and the

Irish agreed. When Lloyd George heard the lord chancellor's report of the subconference, he believed a break was imminent.[53]

The Sinn Feiners returned to Dublin to consult the Cabinet in formulating proposals on the Crown. On November 25 the Cabinet unanimously resolved

(a) That Ireland shall recognize the British Crown for the purposes of the Association as symbol and accepted head of the combination of Associated States.

(b) That an annual sum be voluntarily voted to the civil list.[54]

It was a tribute to de Valera's persuasive powers that Brugha and Stack agreed to this compromise.

On November 28 the Irish delegates submitted their proposal on the Crown, set forth in three clauses.

1. The legislative, executive and judicial authority of Ireland shall be derived exclusively from the Elected Representatives of the Irish people.

2. Ireland will agree to be associated with the British Commonwealth for all purposes of common concern, including defence, peace and war, and political treaties, and to recognize the British Crown as Head of the Association.

3. As token of that recognition, the Irish legislature will vote an annual contribution to the King's personal revenue.[55]

This was accompanied by a note which put the case for external association forcefully and skillfully. It bore Griffith's signature but it clearly reflected Childers' views. After summarizing the arguments against the Crown as a historical symbol of repression in Ireland, the note again pointed out that Ireland was denied the protection against British interference which distance gave the Dominions. Voluntary acceptance of the Crown in any capacity was a "momentous step" for the Irish people in view of history and geography, and showed their sincere desire for a friendly and lasting settlement.[56]

When Lloyd George saw the Irish reply, he remarked to Jones, "This means war."[57] Chamberlain's initial reaction was more prudent. Though no more satisfied than Lloyd George with external association, he thought the document still showed "a *real* desire for peace." "We *cannot make peace on these terms*," he wrote, "but we *must not break on this document*" (emphasis in original). Chamberlain appreciated the Irish fear that the Crown's power would continue to be used by British ministers, but he believed that this problem could be resolved by finding words which would guarantee Ireland against this "fancied danger."[58] This appeal for a moderate response was well advised, and Chamberlain's suggested solution proved to be the way to break the deadlock on the Crown.

On the night of November 28, at the prime minister's request, Griffith and Duggan (Collins was still in Ireland) met with him, Birkenhead, and Sir Robert Horne, the chancellor of the exchequer. Lloyd George opened the meeting by declaring that the latest Irish note was "impossible," and any British government which tried to propose the abrogation of the Crown would be "smashed to atoms." Griffith replied that he could negotiate only on the basis of exclusion of the Crown from purely Irish affairs. In the discussion that ensued, the British "knocked out" the Irish argument on the Crown by offering "to put in any phrase in the Treaty we liked to ensure that the function of the Crown in Ireland should be no more in practice than it is in Canada or any Dominion." The British followed this concession with one of almost equal importance. Although it would be "an immense difficulty" for them, they would try to modify the traditional oath of allegiance if this would help the Irish delegates. They also promised that the Crown's representative would be appointed only in consultation with the Irish government. Moreover, they guaranteed that he would be only a symbol and that no one the Irish objected to would ever be appointed to the post. After two hours of conversation the Sinn Feiners departed, and the prime minister went to bed, remarking to Jones that the situation was better.[59]

The British concessions were confirmed next day. Lloyd George, Birkenhead, and Chamberlain specifically offered Griffith, Collins, and Duggan a phrase in the treaty which stipulated that the Crown would have no more authority in Ireland than in Canada. They also offered an oath of allegiance different from the one in use in Britain and the Dominions. The Irish did not accept it, but asked for more time to consider the question. Although rejecting an appeal for an elected representative of the Crown, the British again promised that the king's representative would be appointed only after consultation with the Irish government and that its will would prevail in any dispute with him. The delegates went over trade and defense again, and the prime minister informed the Sinn Feiners that final proposals would be sent to them and to Craig not later than Tuesday, December 6. Griffith voiced the fear that the terms would become known throughout Ulster before Sinn Fein made its decision on them and asked that his delegation be given the proposals before Craig. The British agreed to try to deliver the terms to Sinn Fein on the evening of December 1, deferring formal presentation until December 6. Griffith wrote de Valera that it was essential to discuss the British proposals, and he asked the president to call a Cabinet meeting for the morning of Saturday, December 3.[60]

Chapter 8
The Final Rounds:
December 1-6, 1921

The British proposals arrived ahead of schedule, on Wednesday evening, November 30. According to these terms, the Irish Free State was to have the same national status as the other Dominions, and its relationship with the Crown and the Imperial Parliament was to be governed by both the law and the practice of Canada. The oath of allegiance was much like that suggested on November 29, while the financial and trade provisions were largely the same as those of the previous offer. Naval facilities that were required in peacetime were listed in an annex, but Britain was to have whatever defense facilities it needed in time of war or strained relations. Also listed were the safeguards guaranteed Northern Ireland if it joined the Free State: control of local patronage, tax collection, and local militia, as well as a veto on duties affecting local products. If the North rejected unity, a boundary commission would determine its boundaries in accordance with the wishes of the inhabitants, "so far as may be compatible with economic and geographic conditions." The draft concluded with a description of the procedure for establishing an Irish Provisional Government to implement the treaty.[1]

At 6:15 p.m. on December 1 Griffith and Collins presented Lloyd George with an altered oath of allegiance:

> I . . . do solemnly swear to bear true faith and allegiance to the Constitution of the Irish Free State as by Law established and that I will be faithful to H. M. King George in acknowledgement of the Association of Ireland in a common citizenship with Great Britain and the group of nations known as the British Commonwealth.

They also pointed out that although the proposals mentioned Ireland's undertaking its own defense in the future, there was no indication of when this was to happen. The prime minister reported their suggestions to his fellow delegates at 7:45 p.m. They rejected the Irish oath but agreed to a review of the defense question in ten years, and accepted other minor amendments. At a 9:30 meeting with Griffith and Collins, the British agreed to a few further changes.[2]

On the morning of December 2 Griffith left for Dublin with a copy of the revised terms. Late the same evening he presented them to de Valera, explaining that he viewed them favorably and would not break on the Crown. The president declared that he could never accept such terms. The two men argued until well past midnight, but neither was able to convert the other.[3]

Members of the Irish Cabinet and delegation assembled at 11 a.m. on Saturday, December 3. Their first session lasted until 1:30 p.m.; at 3 p.m. they resumed discussion for three and one-half hours.[4] Ministers and delegates alike were in poor condition for a long meeting in which vital decisions had to be taken. De Valera and Brugha had returned hurriedly from a military inspection tour the day before. After driving a car from Clare to Dublin in bad weather, the weary president met with an almost equally exhausted Griffith. Collins, Duffy, and Childers had almost no sleep the night before the meeting because of a collision at sea which delayed their arrival in Dublin.[5]

When the president opened the meeting by inviting opinions from the delegation on the British offer, Griffith strongly supported acceptance. No better terms could be obtained; this was Britain's final offer. Barton disagreed. The terms guaranteed neither Dominion status nor unity, and the British would not make war over allegiance. Duffy took the same line. The British were bluffing, and Sinn Fein could win acceptance of its terms with a few small concessions. Duggan backed Griffith, and so did Collins. In Collins' opinion, refusal of the terms would be a gamble because Britain could make war in a week. The sacrifices to Ulster were made for the sake of essential unity and were justified. With pressure, further concessions could be obtained on trade and defense. The oath should be rejected, but the Dail should ask the people's opinion on the treaty as a whole. Childers came out firmly for rejection, concentrating his objections on the defense provisions, which robbed Ireland of sovereignty and would involve it in every British war.

Trade caused a long argument. Barton pressed for full fiscal autonomy, but the other delegates did not think the British would agree to it. So involved did the discussion become that the delegates could not agree on exactly what had been decided once they were back in London. At one point in the meeting, with Griffith repeating he would not break on the Crown, Brugha asked who had been responsible for dividing the delegation, so that Griffith and Collins did most of the negotiating and the other delegates lacked full information. He was told that the British were responsible but that the entire delegation had approved the arrangement. Brugha commented acidly that the British government had selected its men. On Griffith's demand, Brugha retracted this statement, but hard feelings remained.

After the withdrawal of delegates who were not Cabinet members, the meeting continued, with de Valera contending that the terms should be rejected. He could neither subscribe to the oath nor sign an agreement that allowed the Six Counties to vote themselves out of the Irish state. Having done their best, the delegates must now show the British that if the terms were not altered, Ireland was ready to face the consequences: war or no war. De Valera would treat the present offer just as he had that on July 20; he would state that it could not be accepted and submit counterproposals. Griffith admitted he did not like the British terms, but he did not think them dishonorable. They practically recognized the Republic, and primary allegiance would be to Ireland. If the terms were rejected, the people had a right to know the alternative. They would not fight on the question of allegiance, and there would be a split. He suggested the delegates sign the treaty and leave its rejection to the president and the Dail. Brugha was in full agreement with de Valera, except on the point of recognizing the king as head of the Associated States.

Debate resumed after lunch, when the delegates rejoined the Cabinet. Griffith maintained he would sign the terms rather than risk war. Barton appealed to de Valera to go to London, saying it was not fair to place responsibility on Griffith when the latter was so unwilling to risk war. Griffith declared that he would get as many concessions as he could, and when Craig accepted the final terms, he would sign them and submit them to the Dail, which was the body to decide for or against war. Brugha exploded, saying Griffith would split the country "from top to bottom" by signing. Struck by this prediction, Griffith promised that he would not sign the document but would submit it to the Dail and, if necessary, to the people. This pledge mollified Brugha and satisfied other opponents of the proposals. Convinced that nothing would be signed which committed Ireland to allegiance or inclusion in the Empire, de Valera abandoned any idea of going to London.[6]

When Griffith *did* sign an agreement accepting Dominion status, his foes charged he had broken his pledge, and this allegation provoked a bitter controversy. Griffith maintained that the British concessions of December 5 substantially altered their previous proposals and nullified his promise not to sign. In fact, the situation was changed much more by unforeseen events which rendered Griffith's pledge irrelevant.

In the discussion of counterproposals, the question of an oath was the main topic. Cosgrave declared that he would not take the one proposed by the British, while de Valera and Brugha objected to any form of oath. Collins argued that an oath was to be the "sugar coating" which would help the British people swallow the treaty. The president conceded that an oath to the treaty would be unobjectionable and, after brief reflection, he suggested one that would be consistent with the principle of external association. Both O'Murchadha and Barton took down his words. O'Murchadha's version (with Barton's divergences in parenthesis) stated:

I . . . do solemnly swear true faith and allegiance to the constitution of the Irish Free State (Ireland), to the Treaty of Association and to recognize the King of Great Britain as Head of the Associated States (Association).

Brugha refused to subscribe to such an oath, but there were no other dissenters. Stack even tried to persuade Brugha to agree to it.

As the delegates made ready to return to London, the Cabinet confirmed its main decisions:

1. The delegates were to carry out their original instructions with the same powers.
2. They were to tell the British that the Cabinet would not accept the oath of allegiance unless it were amended, and they were to face the consequences, assuming that Britain would declare war.
3. The present oath of allegiance could not be subscribed to [unanimously agreed].
4. Griffith was to inform Lloyd George that the document could not be signed, to state that it was now a matter for the Dail to decide, and to try to place the blame for a break on Ulster.
5. The delegates were empowered to meet Craig if they thought it necessary [Brugha and Stack dissented from this decision].
6. The President would not join the delegation in London at this stage of the negotiations.

Childers sought clarification. Did the demand for alteration of the oath mean rejection of Dominion status? De Valera said it did, which meant that external association must be presented again. The meeting ended with the delegates scrambling for their coats to catch the night boats to Britain.[7]

In retrospect, it is clear that the oath of allegiance dominated the December 3 meeting. De Valera recalled: "The oath crystallized in itself the main things we objected to—inclusion in the Empire, the British King as King in Ireland, Chief Executive of the Irish state, and the source from which all authority in Ireland was to be derived."[8] On his return to London, Collins noted privately that the oath was the "greatest difficulty" and the "worrying point," adding "Adjustment of wording—text reviewed. Otherwise . . ."[9]

This preoccupation was at least partly responsible for the Cabinet's failure to clarify its position on Ulster. Although de Valera and Brugha were plainly dissatisfied with the British proposal on Ulster, they offered no alternative, even though Sinn Fein's proposal had been flatly rejected by Craig. Griffith himself failed to suggest an alteration in the Boundary Commission clause to correct a flaw pointed out to him by a friend on his journey to Dublin.[10] In the end, the Cabinet gave the delegates neither an alternative proposal on Ulster nor even explicit instructions to turn down the British proposal; this would make it very hard to stage a break on the issue of partition, however desirable that might be.

Early in November, Collins remarked to a friend that the Cabinet was confusing rather than instructing the delegates.[11] After a long day's wrangling, climaxed by last-minute decisions, he was more confused than ever. As he rode to the night boat, he complained bitterly to a close friend: "I've been there all day and I can't get them to say yes or no, whether we should sign or not."[12] When he had left London the day before, Collins' spirits had been high; now they were very low indeed.

On the morning of December 4 Childers, Barton, and Duffy revised the British proposals to bring them into line with external association. The opening clauses of the British offer were replaced by the November 22 statement on association. In like manner, de Valera's oath supplanted the proposed oath of allegiance. The memorandum conceded defense facilities for five years, pending the creation of Ireland's own coastal defense forces; it also accepted the limitation on the size of the Irish army. Coupled with these concessions was a reassertion of Ireland's obligation to provide for its own defense by land, sea, and air. The Irish terms were identical with those of Britain on financial relations and approximated them on trade relations. The counter-proposals did not mention Ulster since the delegates had no specific instructions to do so. Logically, the British assumed that the absence of a counterproposal on Ulster meant the Irish were satisfied on this question.[13]

Although Griffith, Collins, and Duggan had prepared no proposals of their own, they objected strongly to certain parts of their colleagues' memorandum. In fact, it took some time to persuade them that the Cabinet had authorized another presentation of the full demand for external association. An argument over trade ended with Barton finally accepting the others' contention that the Cabinet had not insisted on complete fiscal autonomy.[14] The terms of the oath caused further debate. Barton, Duffy, and Childers claimed that the king was to be acknowledged as head of the association, while Griffith, Collins, and Duggan argued that "Associated States" was the phrase used by the president. Since Barton and his allies were unable to prove their assertion by reference to his abbreviated note of the oath, they gave way, even though their interpretation of de Valera's intention was undoubtedly correct. Recognizing the king as head of the Associated States meant that he would be head of the Irish state, and this violated the essential principle of external association. But Griffith and Collins doubtless hoped this wording would help placate the British.[15]

By the time the delegates agreed on the proposals, it was almost 5 p.m., but Griffith, Collins, and Duggan refused to take part in a scheduled meeting with the British, maintaining that those who wanted a rupture should present the terms previously rejected. Griffith reversed himself as Barton and Duffy prepared to leave for Downing Street and accompanied them in his usual role as chief spokesman. But Collins remained behind.[16] He later claimed that he had fully discussed all points with the British and therefore had urged Barton, who had not, to see what he could achieve. Collins also maintained that his abstention won more concessions than his attendance could have, because the British thought it meant he was ready to resume hostilities.[17] (But this explanation will not do. Collins knew that Barton could not win better terms than he and Griffith had. Moreover, the British rightly assumed that Collins' absence meant he opposed a break, and Collins must have realized they would draw this conclusion.)

At 5 p.m. the Irish party met Lloyd George, Chamberlain, Birkenhead, and Horne, and for the next two hours Griffith employed all his skill as an advocate. Carefully avoiding any statement that might give the British a chance to break on the Crown, he concentrated his objections on Ulster. However, when Griffith argued that Sinn Fein was not responsible for the British proposal on Ulster, the British declared that they intended to carry it out even if Craig rejected it, and they reminded Griffith of his pledge not to let them down on this. Griffith confirmed his pledge, but asserted that, without any guarantee of Craig's acceptance, Sinn Fein could not be held responsible for endorsing a proposal that might well involve partition. He had offered association and recognition of the Crown in return for unity; so Craig should now accept unity. Patiently, the British replied that Craig would not do this, but reiterated that they would implement the Ulster proposal and the rest of the treaty once Sinn Fein agreed.

After a discussion of proposed Irish amendments, the British held a brief consultation. When they returned, the prime minister denounced the Irish proposals as wholly inadmissible and a complete departure from the previous week's discussions. (They were, in fact, the same proposals that had already been considered and rejected.) The Sinn Feiners pressed the case for external association but made no headway, nor was Griffith successful when he tried to work back to Ulster. Eventually, the prime minister asked what the difficulty was about coming into the Empire with Canadian status. Duffy answered that Ireland would be as closely associated with Britain in important matters as were the Dominions, but "our difficulty is to come inside the Empire, looking to all that has happened in the past." As if on signal, the British jumped up with cries of "That ends it" and "In that case it is war." The meeting ended abruptly, with the Irish agreeing to send their final proposals the next day and the British promising to send back a formal rejection.[18]

As they drove away from Downing Street, the three Sinn Feiners were a thoroughly unhappy lot. They had failed to make peace or to stage a break on Ulster. An angry Griffith vented his rage on Duffy, whose verbal misstep had given the British their chance to break on the Crown. But although prospects for peace had never seemed more dismal, Lloyd George had not abandoned hope. Before the afternoon meeting, the British had learned (probably from Cope) that while the Irish Cabinet had rejected their offer, Griffith, Collins, and Duggan favored acceptance. They had also been informed that Collins was "fed up" with the differences in the delegation and had sent Barton and Duffy to the meeting to see if the prime minister could convert them. The time had come for Jones to retie the broken threads of the negotiations, and Lloyd George lost no time in setting him on this.[19]

Jones saw Griffith at midnight and talked with him for an hour. Speaking with "the greatest earnestness and unusual emotion," Griffith told Jones that while he and Collins believed Lloyd George wanted peace and was doing his best to secure it, their colleagues in Dublin did not agree. However, both he and Collins were convinced that this fear and distrust could be overcome by Ulster's consent to unity. Griffith pleaded with Jones to persuade Lloyd George to get Craig's conditional acceptance, however shadowy, of unity in return for Sinn Fein's acceptance of the Empire. If Craig would agree, Sinn Fein would give the North all the safeguards it wanted and would not ask for a boundary commission— a very difficult concession because it would leave Tyrone and Fermanagh under Belfast's direct rule. Agreement to unity would give Griffith *"something"* to take back to the Dail, and he and Collins could then push the treaty through the Dail in a week. But if unity were not secured, Griffith did not think that he and Collins could carry more than about half the Dail. He confided that the British need not worry about Barton, Duffy, and the doctrinaires, "with their protective duties"; 90 percent of the "gunmen" would follow Collins.

The upshot of the talk, Jones wrote Lloyd George, was that Griffith was appealing to the prime minister for help. Griffith warned that if the war were renewed, the people would obey the Dail, but emphasized that he and Collins trusted Lloyd George. He asked Jones if the prime minister would see Collins and have a "heart to heart talk" with him. Jones said that Lloyd George would see Collins the next morning. He concluded his report of the interview by urging the prime minister to send for Craig and make one more effort for peace.[20]

Jones stated Griffith's position accurately enough, but whatever Griffith thought, it is unlikely that Collins trusted either Lloyd George or Jones; and once out of the negotiations, Collins was most reluctant to become involved again. However, Griffith and Jones appealed to him to talk with the prime minister, and Jones apparently held out the promise of tangible gains. An entry in Collins' diary for December 5 reads: "Jones to see me. Subject: Enlarging of ours by inclusion of most of Fermanagh and Tyrone—Boundary Commission?"[21] In the end, Collins agreed to see Lloyd George, and their meeting took place at 9:30 a.m.[22]

The prime minister opened the interview by saying he was meeting the Cabinet at noon and would explain that the conference had broken down on the question of Ireland's membership in the Empire. Collins was equally blunt, voicing his dissatisfaction over Ulster and his desire for a definite answer from Craig on the question of unity. Lloyd George countered by recalling that Collins himself had pointed out (on a previous occasion) that the North would be forced economically to unite with the South. Collins confirmed this, but said that recent troubles in the North made him anxious to secure an answer from Craig, adding that rejection was as agreeable as acceptance. "In view of the former we would save Tyrone and Fermanagh, parts of Derry, Armagh and Down by the boundary Commission, and thus avoid such things as the raid on the Tyrone County Council and the ejection of the staff." Another such incident would trigger conflict throughout the country. Lloyd George said that these views might be put to Craig, and if he agreed to unity, North and South could work out safeguards.

Collins gave Lloyd George a copy of a new form of oath, suggested to him by a legal friend. But the prime minister insisted that Sinn Fein must definitely accept Dominion status before the oath could be discussed. Turning to defense, Collins objected to Britain's exclusive role because it implied Ireland could build no naval craft. He also wanted responsibility for coastal defense transferred to Ireland in ten years. On trade, Collins pressed for abolition of restrictions on Ireland. Lloyd George made notes of Collins' objections and suggested a meeting of delegates at 2 p.m.; Collins tentatively accepted. The prime minister concluded by pledging that if the Irish delegates accepted the treaty's clauses on Dominion status, he could delay action until they had submitted the treaty to Dail Eireann and the country.[23]

Both parties were encouraged by this talk. To Lloyd George, a settlement now seemed possible because Collins appeared willing to accept Dominion status.[24] For his part, Collins got the impression that Sinn Fein might win major concessions on the oath, trade, and defense. Most important, he was apparently convinced that Lloyd George shared his view that Ireland's unification was inevitable. In fact, the prime minister had only quoted Collins' opinion and refrained from challenging his prediction on boundary revision, but this was enough for Collins. He was back in the negotiations, and he brought the Irish delegation with him.

Collins' influence and popularity made his attitude toward a settlement as crucial as de Valera's. Although he believed peace was vital, he had little time to think about its actual terms before he went to London. Once there, however, he concentrated on this question, working out his gen-

eral ideas in a memorandum that was presented to the British on
November 24. In it, he sketched the history of Anglo-Irish relations and
pointed the way to reconciliation in a Commonwealth of completely
autonomous nations. Collins contended that while Britain had accepted
the growth of practical independence in its colonies, it had refused to do
so in Ireland. Now, Ireland had at last won independence, and the
problem of Anglo-Irish relations, like that of Anglo-Dominion relations,
urgently needed a solution. Ireland and the Dominions were restive
under any form of British control, but they were willing to cooperate
freely with Britain in matters of common concern. This meant that if
Britain's association with these states were to continue, it must be based
on full and formal recognition of their sovereignty.[25]

This view of an evolving Commonwealth was based on wide reading,
which included the incisive memorandum on Dominion status drafted
by Lionel Curtis early in the negotiations. According to Curtis, the
Dominions and Britain were now on a footing of full equality in external
as well as internal affairs. While there were still some legal restrictions on
Dominion powers, Curtis demonstrated that they were purely formal
and were never exercised.[26] Collins understood the trend of Commonwealth development, and he felt sure a Dominion settlement would give
Ireland virtual sovereignty and open the way to full independence. He
was equally certain that the Irish people would approve it and that it was
the most they could hope for in the immediate future. On the other
hand, he realized many extremists would oppose the British terms, and
this made him reluctant to endorse them. While he saw the wisdom of
accepting Dominion status, Collins would assume responsibility for this
decision only if he had no other choice.[27]

Following his interview with Collins, Lloyd George saw the king, then
hurried to a session with his fellow delegates, and finally presided over a
noon Cabinet meeting.[28] He described to the Cabinet the latest British
offer, emphasizing that it gave Ireland full control of internal affairs and
that Collins and Griffith seemed willing to accept it. The Cabinet approved the oath submitted by Collins, agreeing that as long as the clauses
on Dominion status remained unaltered, the precise terms of the oath
were immaterial. The meeting ended with three decisions. The delegates
should try to conclude a Dominion settlement at their afternoon session
with Sinn Fein; Churchill should secure Irish agreement to the substance
of the defense clauses; and the Cabinet would meet again later that day,
if necessary.[29]

The decisive session of the long negotiations began at 3 p.m. on
Monday, December 5. Present in the Cabinet Room were the prime
minister, Chamberlain, Birkenhead, Churchill, Griffith, Collins, and
Barton. Ulster dominated the first part of the meeting. Griffith and
Collins did their best to withhold response to the British terms until

Craig had given his reply, but they were outmaneuvered by Lloyd George, who pinned Griffith down on his pledge of November 12–13 and thereby destroyed any chance of a break on Ulster by a united delegation.

The prime minister first asked if Sinn Fein accepted Dominion status, to which Griffith replied that he would accept it if Ulster and other points were cleared up. Lloyd George said he must know once and for all exactly where the Irish stood on the Ulster proposal Griffith had agreed to. Griffith declared that before he gave a decision on other vital issues, he must know Craig's position on unity. Collins took the same line, but Lloyd George and Chamberlain denounced this attitude as inadmissible and contrary to Griffith's pledge. Had they known the Irish held this view, they would not have risked their political futures in pursuit of peace. Griffith repeated he would accept inclusion in the Empire if Craig agreed to unity. Lloyd George retorted that this meant Griffith was going back on his promise to accept Britain's Ulster proposal whatever Craig did. Griffith said that if the British stood by the boundary commission, he stood by them, but he contended it was not fair to ask his colleagues for their answer before Craig replied. The situation was serious, Lloyd George declared. He had promised to send Craig news of the negotiations that night; was his message to announce peace or war? Were the Irish delegates prepared to face their diehards, as were the British? Griffith said he was, but Collins contended that agreement to Britain's terms before Ulster accepted unity would surrender Sinn Fein's "whole fighting position." The British had Sinn Fein's conditional agreement to Crown and Empire; it was just as easy to get Craig's conditional agreement to unity.

At this point Lloyd George grew excited, declaring that the Irish were trying to stage a break on Ulster because their Cabinet had refused membership in the Empire. Collins' proposal, he asserted, was not the one Griffith had agreed to. As he spoke, Lloyd George produced the written summary of that proposal and waved it at the Irish. He said he had told Chamberlain and Birkenhead about Griffith's pledge, and Jones had shown Griffith a statement of the agreed terms, which he accepted as correct. In a last, desperate bid to save Sinn Fein's position, Griffith appealed to the prime minister to ask Craig if Ulster would accept unity on condition Sinn Fein accepted Crown and Empire. Lloyd George brusquely refused. The agreement between Griffith and himself was that he should submit to Craig the alternative proposal embodied in the written statement of November 13.

> You agreed to our proposal, and you now put a totally different one to us. If you say now that you are not going to accept the preliminary conditions which to us are fundamental, we are not going to put the rest to Ulster.

Collins and Barton watched this exchange in amazement. Noticing their mystification, Lloyd George asked Collins if Griffith had not told him about the document under discussion. When Collins said nothing, Chamberlain passed a copy of the proposal to the Irishmen. It provided that Northern Ireland could exclude itself from an all-Ireland parliament, but if it did, a commission would adjust the Irish boundary to make it conform as closely as possible to the wishes of the population.

Confronted with written evidence of his pledge, Griffith was beaten. He may well have felt that Lloyd George had tricked him, but he could not be sure that he himself was not to blame for what had happened. To the charge that he had broken his word, there was only one response for a man of Griffith's integrity, and he made it: "I said I would not let you down on that and I won't." Lloyd George counted on this reaction. Exploiting both Griffith's sense of honor and overriding desire for peace with his well-timed thrust, the prime minister destroyed Griffith's chance to break on Ulster and ensured his acceptance of the treaty. However, though Griffith confirmed his commitment, he also suggested that it was not unreasonable for Sinn Fein to require at least a reply from Craig before accepting or rejecting the treaty. This made sense, for if Craig opposed boundary revision as stubbornly as he had unity, he might frustrate the former proposal as effectively as he had the latter. But Lloyd George rejected the suggestion. The only alternative to unity was the boundary commission, and the British government would carry out that proposal whatever Craig said about it.

With Ulster out of the way, the prime minister announced that he and his colleagues would like to hear any further objections to their proposals. He insisted, however, that the clauses on Dominion status were essential and not open to discussion. The oath was settled quickly. Birkenhead produced the version submitted by Collins that morning, which he had altered slightly and the Cabinet had approved. Two minor changes were made, and the resulting oath became part of the treaty.

> I . . . do solemnly swear true faith and allegiance to the Constitution of the Irish Free State as by law established, and that I will be faithful to H. M. King George V, his heirs and successors by law, in virtue of the common citizenship of Ireland with Great Britain and her adherence to and membership of the group of nations forming the British Commonwealth of Nations.

After a brief and unproductive discussion of financial relations, the delegates spent considerable time on defense. Eventually, the British agreed to remove the word "exclusively" in reference to their naval defense of Ireland and to add a provision allowing the Irish to build ships for revenue and fisheries protection. Soon afterward, the British withdrew for consultation. While they conferred, the Irish decided that their final word would be to demand an appeal to the Dominion premiers, if the British broke on Sinn Fein's refusal to reply to their terms before Craig had done so.

When the British returned, Churchill moderated his earlier opposition to any naval concessions by agreeing that the review conference on coastal defense should be held in five instead of ten years, with the intention of giving Ireland a share in its own defense. On trade, Lloyd George finally conceded what Barton had so long demanded: fiscal autonomy—playing this high card for all it was worth. Frankly admitting that he had been its strongest opponent, the prime minister offered this concession as a last sacrifice to secure peace, but only on condition that the treaty be accepted without further delay. One minor matter remained: the time period of Ulster's exclusion option. At Sinn Fein's request, the British agreed to shorten it to one month, to minimize uncertainty in the South and antinationalist violence in the North.

Both sides now withdrew to consider the amended treaty. When the delegations returned to the conference room at about 7 p.m., the prime minister asked if the Sinn Feiners were prepared to stand by the agreement whatever choice Ulster made. Griffith answered that he would, but said it was unfair to demand an answer from his colleagues before Craig replied, because they were not a party to his pledge. Considerable discussion ensued on this point, but Griffith stood firm. Weary of fencing, the prime minister issued an ultimatum. He had thought Griffith spoke for the entire delegation; however, the Irish delegates were plenipotentiaries, and each of them must make up his own mind on the issue of peace or war. In dramatic fashion, Lloyd George produced two letters; holding one in each hand, he delivered his ultimatum:

> Is it a bargain between Sinn Fein and the British Government? I have to communicate with Sir James Craig tonight. Here are the alternative letters which I have prepared, one enclosing the Articles of Agreement reached by H. M. Government and yourselves, the other telling Sir James Craig that the Sinn Fein representatives refuse allegiance and refuse to come within the Empire, and that I have no proposals to make to him. If I send this letter it is war—and war within three days. Which of the two letters am I to send? That is the question you have to decide.

He demanded their answer by 10 p.m. A special train and a destroyer were waiting to carry the news to Belfast. If the letter were to reach Craig before the Ulster Parliament met the next day, it must go soon.

There can be no doubt of the impact of Lloyd George's performance. In Barton's words, the prime minister

> with all the solemnity and the power of conviction that he alone, of all men I met, can impart by word and gesture—the vehicles by which the mind of

one man oppresses and impresses the mind of another—declared that the signature and recommendation of every member of our delegation was necessary or war would follow immediately.[30]

Outwardly calm, Griffith outlined his understanding of the procedure to be followed if the treaty were signed. The agreement would be submitted to both the British and the Irish parliaments as soon as possible, and once they ratified it, steps would be taken to establish a Provisional Government and withdraw British troops from Southern Ireland. On that understanding, Griffith would do his best to secure ratification, but this was only his personal pledge. Lloyd George inquired: "Do I understand, Mr. Griffith, that though everyone else refuses you will nevertheless agree to sign?"[31] "Yes, that is so, Mr. Prime Minister," was Griffith's answer. It was surely this statement that led Chamberlain to remark: "A braver man than Arthur Griffith I have never met."[32] But while Lloyd George fully appreciated Griffith's moral courage, one signature was not enough. The British delegates were united in their obligation, he declared; they demanded the same of the Irish. If all the Irish representatives signed, their British counterparts would do their best to carry the agreement through, even to the point of the government's defeat and dissolution of Parliament. But if they did not all sign, there would be no agreement. On their answer, he reiterated, hung the issue of peace or war. Saying his delegation would reply by 10 p.m., Griffith and his two colleagues prepared to leave. According to Churchill, "Michael Collins rose looking as if he was going to shoot someone, preferably himself. In all my life I have never seen so much passion and suffering in restraint."[33]

At about 7:15 p.m. the Irishmen left Downing Street, but they did not return until well past the appointed hour of 10 p.m. The British idled away this interval, none of them in a hopeful mood. Churchill recalled that they expected only Griffith to sign the treaty, and one Irish signature would not make a valid agreement. Birkenhead had prepared a speech for delivery the following day, calling for national support to suppress the rebels. Lloyd George told one of his secretaries that he had given the Sinn Feiners an ultimatum and it was up to them to choose between peace and war. If only Collins had as much moral as physical courage, there would be a settlement. But moral courage was a much higher quality than physical courage, he observed, and one that brave men often lacked.[34] Lloyd George had accurately diagnosed Collins' dilemma, but by that time the Big Fellow had made his decision.

As the Sinn Feiners' taxi rolled through London's dark streets on its way to their residence, Collins announced he intended to sign the treaty.[35] Barton's astonishment showed how carefully Collins had concealed his thoughts from everyone but Griffith. The decision was agonizing, but the only one Collins felt he could make. He was convinced that Ireland could not get substantially better terms and that the alternative to settlement was war and defeat. Collins knew what the people had endured and was unwilling to commit them to a further ordeal. The people themselves or their representatives, not the delegates or the Cabinet, must decide whether to accept or reject the treaty, and only by signing could he give them the chance to make that decision.[36]

At their residence, the wrangle that began in the taxi continued. Duggan supported Griffith and Collins while Duffy and Childers agreed with Barton that the delegates should refuse to sign. No one questioned Lloyd George's demand for an immediate decision by arguing that Craig could wait a few more days to learn the outcome of the negotiations. (After all, he had been waiting since July, and was in no position to set deadlines. The British could hardly have resorted to war because Sinn Fein refused to decide Ireland's future before it knew the position of northeast Ulster.) But the prime minister had set the stage with a master's touch—special letters, special messenger, special transport—and the Irish delegates never thought of delay. They did not even think of using the telephone to escape their predicament: of asking the British to call Craig to explain the situation, or trying to reach de Valera themselves.[37]

For over three hours there was heated debate, with Griffith and Collins concentrating their arguments on Barton. He was a member of the Cabinet; if they could persuade him to sign, Duffy could not hold out alone. The two leaders warned that refusal to sign would cause killing and destruction on a scale much greater than before the truce. Their arguments echoed Lloyd George's warning and left Barton badly shaken. His position was vulnerable and he knew it. He was only a subordinate delegate, and a year's imprisonment had put him out of touch with the situation at home. If Collins were for peace, what right had he to risk war? If he refused to sign, what chance would a divided and disheartened people have against a massive British onslaught? Nevertheless, despite tremendous pressure, Barton clung tenaciously to the Republic. Three times Griffith, Collins, and Duggan started to leave for Downing Street; three times Barton pulled them back to continue the terrible debate. On Childers' suggestion, he argued that the Irish should sign the treaty with a formal declaration that they acted under duress. But it was clear the British would not allow this. In the end, it was Duggan who broke Barton's will. Before Barton's eyes, the humble solicitor relived the nightmare of final conversations with condemned rebels. He pleaded with Barton not to throw away the freedom those men died for and renew the vicious cycle of killing. Duggan's anguished appeal moved Barton as nothing else could, and he agreed to sign. Left isolated, Duffy caved in shortly afterward and a united, if miserable, delegation was prepared to accept the treaty.[38]

At 10:15 p.m. word reached the British that the Sinn Feiners' return would be delayed. An hour later, Griffith, Collins, and Barton marched into the Cabinet Room and quietly lined up opposite Lloyd George, Chamberlain, Birkenhead, and Churchill. After a brief pause, Griffith announced that the delegation was ready to sign the treaty, but there were a few points of drafting which they wished resolved. With the main issue out of the way, the two delegations concentrated on details for the next two hours, carefully avoiding any mention of vital questions.[39]

Although the Irish failed to obtain deletion of the clause providing for the appointment of the Crown's representative in the Free State, the British agreed to remove the words "Governor-General" and allow the Irish to determine the title of the office, excluding that of "President." Collins got the British to drop the word "local" from the description of the Irish military defense force, thus giving it the status of a regular national army. A few more minor changes were made, and at Collins' request, Birkenhead drafted a memorandum explaining the procedure for the transfer of power to the Provisional Government. When this had been done, the prime minister asked if the Irish delegation were prepared to accept the Articles of Agreement. Griffith replied: "We do." "Then," said Lloyd George, "we accept."[40]

It was 1 a.m. While stenographers typed final copies of the Treaty for signature, the two delegations separated. Shortly after 2 a.m., two final copies of the agreement were brought into the Cabinet Room, where the seven delegates read them over and signed them.[41] Afterward, the British lined up to shake hands and say goodbye to the Irishmen, expressing the hope that together they had laid the foundation of permanent understanding and friendship between their peoples.[42] "As lighthearted and as happy as a boy coming out of school," the prime minister gave his secretary the message for Craig. Then he retired, while his messenger sped northwest through the winter night on the mission that could not be postponed.[43]

In an excited mood, Griffith returned to the delegation's London residence, where he forecast to his wife the great prospects ahead. The North would join the Free State, and Irish businessmen would support it. There was much to do, but it could all be cleared up in a few months. His wife would have her wish: he would retire from politics the following August. For hours he walked the floor of her room, talking of dreams whose realization now seemed possible.[44]

Meanwhile Collins, who had fallen into a mood of deep depression, poured out his troubled thoughts in a letter to a close friend.

When you have sweated, toiled, had mad dreams, hopeless nightmares, you find yourself in London's streets, cold and dank in the night air.

Think—what have I got for Ireland? Something which she has wanted these past seven hundred years. Will anyone be satisfied at the bargain? Will anyone? I tell you this—early this morning I signed my death warrant. I thought at the time how odd, how ridiculous—a bullet may just as well have done the job five years ago.

I believe Birkenhead may have said an end to his political life. With him it has been my honour to work.

These signatures are the first real step for Ireland. If people will only remember that—the first real step.[45]

Chapter 9
The Treaty:
Reflections and Reactions

Like any other compromise, the Treaty had defects and virtues. On the one hand, it failed to unify Ireland, left it liable to involvement in British wars, and imposed an odious symbolism on Republicans. More important, it gave most of Ireland complete independence in domestic affairs and considerable freedom in external affairs. After decades of struggle, nationalist Ireland had won the right to decide its own destiny.

The Treaty offered symbolic as well as substantial gains. Its official title, Articles of Agreement for a Treaty between Great Britain and Ireland, constituted recognition of Irish sovereignty (see appendix II). While it is true that the British did not regard the Treaty as a pact between sovereign states, they never revealed their reservations to the Irish, who insisted that the Treaty was a full-fledged international agreement. In the end, the British government had no choice but to accept the Irish interpretation, although it refused to admit that Britain had in any way recognized the Republic in 1921.[1]

In attempting to appease Irish sentiment, the British had so modified the traditional oath of allegiance that it was almost devoid of meaning. Republicans attacked that oath on the grounds that it imposed a primary and binding obligation of loyalty to Crown and Empire, while ultra-Unionists angrily alleged that it entailed no obligation at all.[2] The only point to emerge clearly from the acrimonious debate over the oath is that symbols wield much more influence over many minds than reality. Further evidence of the new Dominion's uniqueness can be found in the provision that Anglo-Irish relations were to be governed in accordance with the law, practice, and constitutional usage governing British relations with Canada. This provision constituted the first official British recognition of the supremacy of popular authority in the Dominions.

Both the oath and the explicit statement of constitutional status show that the Treaty was much more radical in implication than either its Irish critics or British supporters were willing to admit. Supporters in Ireland and enemies in Britain came much closer to assessing the Treaty's true significance when they proclaimed that it gave Ireland the power to gain complete independence. Instead of disarming Irish national aspirations, the achievement of Dominion status strengthened them and opened the way to the Republic.

Despite the impressive powers conferred by the Treaty and the pressure exerted to secure their assent, Griffith and Collins would have refused to sign it if they had not felt certain it would end partition.[3] Admittedly, this conviction was partly self-induced. The large nationalist population of the Six Counties made them sure that boundary revision would cripple Northern Ireland and compel Craig to seek unity. But their belief was confirmed only after the British assured them that the Boundary Commission would do what they expected it to do. Lloyd George, Churchill, and Birkenhead led Griffith and Collins to believe that Craig's government would be left with only three or four counties after boundary revision and that British pressure would force this rump to join the South. Because public pledges of this kind would have precipitated a Tory revolt and wrecked the negotiations, these assurances were conveyed informally and indirectly, through Tom Jones and Tim Healy, a Sinn Fein sympathizer and former nationalist MP, as intermediaries.[4] Lloyd George himself seemed to underwrite these pledges in his interview with Collins on December 5.

It is easy to dismiss such assurances as a calculated deception, but the truth seems more complex. Both Sinn Fein and the British government desperately wanted a lasting peace, and both believed a united Ireland would be the strongest foundation for one. The British delegates were fed up with Craig's "no surrender" attitude. They could not openly coerce Ulster, but they may well have felt that a successful settlement with Sinn Fein would enable them to apply legitimate forms of pressure, such as high taxation and the threat of boundary revision, to promote unification. On November 10 Lloyd George told the Cabinet that if Ulster insisted on exclusion, Sinn Fein was entitled to Tyrone and Fermanagh. And when he, Birkenhead, and Churchill publicly expressed the post-Treaty view that all or most of these two counties preferred union with the South, they seemed to be setting the stage for large-scale land transfers unfavorable to Northern Ireland.[5] The general reaction to these statements showed that both friends and enemies of Ulster anticipated this result.

Fulfillment of British pledges, however, depended largely on Sinn Fein's reception of the Treaty. If all went well, the Free State could be established quickly and boundary revision carried out in an atmosphere of Anglo-Irish harmony and good will. Under these conditions, there was every reason to expect that the Boundary Commission award would reflect the popular mood and transfer predominantly nationalist areas in the Six Counties to the Free State. And if this happened, Craig and his supporters would find it hard to block the award. Of course, a substantial reduction of Northern Ireland's area might not produce unity but, even so, it would make partition much more equitable and strengthen the Treaty settlement. As it happened, however, events took quite a different turn in the post-Treaty period, and the Boundary Commission changed nothing.[6]

This result might have been avoided had Griffith and Collins insisted on a precise definition of the Boundary Commission's functions, instead of accepting a loosely worded formula in the belief that it would be interpreted in Sinn Fein's favor. If they (and their colleagues in the delegation and the Cabinet) had been more astute and aggressive, they would have demanded that the boundary be redrawn in accordance with plebiscites in specified local units—without introduction of limiting factors, such as economic and geographic considerations, which could be used to nullify the popular will. Detailed arrangements for proper supervision of plebiscites (on the model of the European peace treaties) could have been included in the Treaty, as could provision for Dominion arbitration in default of agreement on the Boundary Commission's award. The British delegates would have found it hard to resist such a demand. After all, Sinn Fein was prepared to accept terms which did not guarantee unity and, having pledged not to coerce Ulster, it had every right to ensure that Ulster did not coerce nationalists. Once such a demand was embodied in the Treaty, it would have been difficult to prevent sizable gains by the Free State, whatever the political situation in Britain.

Ironically, the kind of boundary revision anticipated by Griffith and Collins would have strengthened rather than weakened Northern Ireland. Loss of its nationalist areas would not have destroyed Northern Ireland's economic viability, because this was something it never had. Nor would extensive boundary revision have eased the plight of Belfast's Catholic minority. But it would have left Northern Ireland a more compact and homogeneous unit with fewer economic and political problems. Unfortunately for all parties concerned, Ulster Unionists refused to concede this and remained unalterably opposed to major territorial changes.

Despite the shortcomings of the Treaty's Ulster provisions, there was very little nationalist criticism of them.[7] While the reluctance of the Treaty's supporters to voice such criticism was natural enough, the reticence of its opponents is harder to understand. Why should they have accepted reports of private British assurances about boundary revision, when they rejected public British pledges on every other matter relating to the Treaty? In private session, de Valera told the Dail that the Ulster problem should be separated from Anglo-Irish differences. To that end, he prepared to accept the *fait accompli* of partition, while making clear that this acceptance did not recognize the right of any part of Ireland to secede from the nation.[8] But de Valera's argument that Ulster was a domestic matter is singularly unconvincing. For one thing, he held that the British were responsible for partition and must help undo it. For another, the British government, not Craig, had negotiated the Ulster provisions of the Treaty and would play the decisive role in boundary revision. If de Valera and other foes of the Treaty believed that the Boundary Commission was a fraud, they should have attacked it as remorselessly as they did the Treaty's other alleged shortcomings. Such an assault surely would have helped defeat an agreement they held to be both disastrous and dishonorable for Ireland.

In all probability, the real reason why the Treaty's opponents failed to criticize its Ulster clauses was that they had no practical alternative to offer. De Valera strongly opposed coercion and had even stated his willingness to allow exclusion by county option.[9] Such a policy was very similar to the one advocated by Griffith and Collins. Of course, lack of a better proposal need not have ruled out an effective attack on the Boundary Commission, but the anti-Treaty forces apparently felt it did. So they talked about winning external association by another round of negotiations or the isolated Republic by another round of war, while studiously ignoring partition.

Although most members of the Dail wanted and hoped for unity, there were deputies on both sides of the Treaty debate who had already written off Northern Ireland. However, knowing that this view was unpopular, they remained silent. In the last analysis, then, lack of criticism of the Treaty's Ulster provisions can be ascribed to support of them, inability to devise a better alternative, or simply the belief that there was no solution to partition.

In any discussion of alternatives to the Treaty, external association must be considered. Compared with the Treaty, it had several distinct advantages and disadvantages. External association would make possible Irish neutrality in British wars. Furthermore, by excluding British symbolism from Ireland's internal affairs, it preserved the Republic. And whatever the advantages of Dominion status, it did not confer full recognition of Ireland's nationhood. Dominion Home Rule offered a convenient solution to a British government groping for some answer to the Irish Question, but it was not what Sinn Fein sought, nor did it seem an appropriate status for a nation as old as Britain. Exclusion from the Dominion of the one part of Ireland that might be regarded as a British colony simply underscored this fact for many separatists. Ireland might become a Dominion constitutionally but, in their view, it could never be one psychologically. The dividing line between supporters of the Treaty and supporters of external association was narrow but sharply defined, and it could not be bridged.[10]

External association had serious defects, however. The Treaty conferred fiscal autonomy, external association did not. De Valera's plan made Irish neutrality possible, but Ireland would still be tied to Britain in matters of common interest, and an externally associated Republic could

not count on the self-interested support of the Dominions in its inevitable disputes with Britain over questions of defense and foreign affairs.
Moreover, external association would be more morally binding than the
Treaty as a final settlement of Ireland's claims; an imposed settlement
could never limit Irish political development as much as one proposed
by Ireland itself. The worst defect of external association, however, was
that the British turned it down. It was an ingenious compromise, but too
novel, subtle, and abstract to win either British acceptance or Irish enthusiasm. From the start of negotiations, the British government made
plain that its fundamental conditions for peace were Irish acceptance of
Crown and Empire. Repeated rejections of external association, whatever modifications were made in it, only confirmed the fact that the
British would have no part of it.

War was a much more likely alternative to the Treaty than external
association. Lloyd George's ultimatum has often been denounced, and it
was certainly short sighted because of the resentment it was bound to
cause in Ireland. On the other hand, it is possible that an ultimatum was
the only way to secure a settlement, presenting both Republican and
Tory diehards with a *fait accompli* that would be difficult to undo. Whatever evils followed in its wake, it should be remembered that Lloyd
George's threat of war *did* break a deadlock and produce an agreement
which gave most of Ireland independence. Viewed from this perspective, the British ultimatum can be better understood and even partially
justified.

From a practical point of view, the important question was not
whether the ultimatum was justified but whether it really represented
the British government's intention. A definitive answer to this query is
impossible, but the evidence suggests that war would have followed rejection of the British terms. On December 2 Lloyd George told C. P. Scott,
editor of the *Manchester Guardian,* that coercion was the alternative to
settlement. Three days later, he informed Scott that the Irish had gone
back on all their pledges and that agreement on their terms was impossible. The threat of war that evening may have been bluff, but Lloyd
George repeated its substance to one of his secretaries shortly after he
delivered it, with no suggestion it was a trick. The ultimatum had been
foreshadowed in speeches made by Worthington-Evans and Birkenhead
the previous week, and Birkenhead was ready to issue a call for war if the
Irish refused to sign the Treaty.[11]

The draft reply that was prepared after the abortive subconference on
December 4 provides further evidence that war was imminent. It announced the termination of negotiations on the grounds that Sinn Fein
had definitely and finally repudiated allegiance to the Crown and membership in the Empire. Reviewing their own terms, the British emphasized their attempts to meet Irish demands for autonomy. During

five months of negotiations and nearly two months of conference, the government had searched for any clue that could lead to a settlement but had been given only proposals that would break the Empire in pieces, dislocate society in the Dominions, and destroy forever the hope of Irish unity. In these circumstances, further negotiations were useless. If Sinn Fein did not accept the British terms, the government would have no choice but to institute Crown Colony government in Southern Ireland.[12]

While the Cabinet did not discuss war plans during the truce, its Irish Committee made policy recommendations that were largely accepted by the War Office and incorporated with General Macready's military plans.[13] Shortly after the opening of the London conference, Worthington-Evans submitted a detailed outline of the War Office's suggested plan of action if war were resumed. This plan called for Macready to take the offensive as soon as hostilities were renewed, supported by large reinforcements, an extension of martial law, intensive propaganda and recruiting campaigns, and other measures designed to facilitate successful counterinsurgency operations. Macready's plan of action called for hard-hitting and incessant attacks on the IRA, coupled with tight military controls over almost every aspect of Irish life.[14]

Intent on making peace and unwilling to prejudice the negotiations, the government took no action on these recommendations, which meant it could not wage "immediate and terrible war" if the Irish failed to sign the Treaty. To this extent, at least, Lloyd George's threat was a bluff. Moreover, it must be conceded that the British press generally opposed war and urged continued efforts to reach a settlement, taking a position that probably reflected the views of most of its readers.[15]

Nonetheless, it is hard to see how war could have been avoided if Sinn Fein rejected the Treaty. Violations of the truce mounted steadily during the negotiations. If the peace conference broke down, clashes between the IRA and the Crown forces would probably have escalated into war. Macready warned the government at the beginning of December that if the truce were not more strictly observed, British forces would either take action on their own against the rebels or become completely demoralized.[16] Britain could not stand by and allow Sinn Fein to establish a *de facto* Republic. If its terms were not accepted, the government would have to assert its authority or withdraw, and withdrawal was unthinkable.

A final argument for war is the government's willingness to use force to prevent repudiation of the Treaty. It is clear that the British were prepared to fight in 1922 to keep Southern Ireland in the Empire and to protect Northern Ireland, and they almost certainly would have done the same in 1921, if Sinn Fein had rejected their terms. In substance, then, Lloyd George's ultimatum was no bluff. However contrived the performance, his threat reflected political realities.

On December 6 Lloyd George summarized the Treaty's major points for the Cabinet and thanked its members for their trust and loyalty during the negotiations. Lord Curzon expressed the Cabinet's gratitude to the delegates and spoke of the beneficial effects the Treaty would have on Britain's foreign relations, especially with the United States. The Cabinet approved the Treaty unanimously and next day approved the release of 4,000 internees to help secure its acceptance in Ireland.[17]

In the days following the signing, the prime minister was deluged with good wishes from almost every quarter. The king offered heartfelt congratulations, and leaders of other states were quick to follow suit. At home, the press applauded the settlement, and its praise was echoed abroad, especially in the Dominions and the United States.[18] Inevitably, there was some dissatisfaction. The Admiralty wished for an absolute and permanent prohibition of any Irish naval force.[19] Field Marshal Wilson recorded his disgust in his diary: "The agreement is a complete surrender. 1. A farcical oath of allegiance; 2. Withdrawal of our troops; 3. A rebel army, etc., etc. The British Empire is doomed."[20] Similar views were expressed by other diehards and their mouthpiece, the London *Morning Post,* but these protests were drowned in a chorus of praise.

The Treaty's reception in Ulster was much less favorable. Local loyalists feared the British meant to desert them, and Craig warned that the North would oppose any boundary revision that threatened it with substantial loss of territory. Indeed, he claimed hostility to the Treaty was so intense among loyalists that they might sweep his government aside and declare Northern Ireland independent.[21]

Anxious about minority safeguards, Southern Unionist spokesmen were reassured by Griffith during the negotiations. Meeting them again on December 6, he promised that the minority's interests would be adequately protected by its representation in the Free State Parliament, and he repeated his pledge in a letter to Lloyd George.[22] However, the Southern Unionist representatives complained to the British signatories that the Treaty contained no minority safeguards, and they urged its amendment. The British refused, suggesting that the former loyalists should seek the guarantees they desired in the Free State Constitution. It was agreed that Griffith's letter of assurance would be published, together with a reply from the prime minister expressing the minority spokesmen's satisfaction with Griffith's pledge but noting that they had raised other points which he trusted Griffith would consider. While by no means wholly satisfied, moderate loyalists remained hopeful and generally welcomed the Treaty.[23]

On December 14 Parliament met in special session to approve the Treaty. Opening the debate, the prime minister expressed the view that the settlement had been made at just the right moment, when both parties had become convinced that compromise was inevitable and when the position of Northern Ireland had been safeguarded by the Government of Ireland Act. Northern Ireland had not been coerced, but if it chose exclusion from the new Dominion, its boundary should be revised to produce a more homogeneous population. (Although refusing to predict the outcome of such revision, Lloyd George strongly implied that Tyrone and Fermanagh should be transferred to the Free State.) He assured the House that the Free State Constitution would include the terms of the Treaty and be subject to parliamentary approval. In the course of his remarks, the prime minister expressed the guarded hope that the answer to the Irish Question had at last been found.[24]

The diehards vied with each other in condemning the Treaty as a betrayal of British interests and predicted that Sinn Fein would use it to secede from the Empire. The government and the press were denounced for trying to coerce Ulster, and the prime minister for agreeing to a Boundary Commission that might destroy it.[25]

While Labor and the opposition Liberals warmly endorsed the Treaty, it was Bonar Law's support that assured overwhelming approval. Law admitted he did not like the agreement, but he saw no reasonable alternative. He hoped posterity would see the Treaty as a permanent triumph for Lloyd George but warned that its legislative approval would not settle the Irish Question. Ireland was demoralized and chaotic, and great difficulties lay ahead; still, he believed the Irish signatories meant to carry out the Treaty and should be given the chance to do so.[26] After three days' debate, the House of Commons approved the Treaty by a vote of 401 to 58.

Opposition was more formidable in the Unionist-dominated House of Lords, where Carson delivered a philippic against the government and its cowardly surrender. He singled out Birkenhead, a prewar champion of Ulster, for special abuse as an unprincipled opportunist who had abandoned Ulster once it ceased to serve his ambition.[27] In response to Carson's fulminations, Birkenhead offered a restrained and carefully reasoned defense of the government's policy.[28] Bowing to the Conservative leadership's endorsement of the Treaty, the Lords approved it, 166 to 47, on December 16. But dissolving the Union at the behest of men who were pledged to maintain it must have angered many of the Tory peers who voted for the Treaty or abstained.

In Ireland, the nationalist press was jubilant over the settlement. Leading newspapers in Southern Ireland hailed it as a great advance that would bring freedom and, it was hoped, unity. The *Irish News,* principal organ of Ulster's nationalists, likewise applauded the agreement and pointed out to Northern loyalists the wisdom of joining the Free State.[29] Catholic bishops supported the Treaty, not only because it held out the prospect of national freedom and unity but also because it promised an end to the violence which seriously threatened morality and clerical authority. An impressive number of public and private bodies also expressed approval of the settlement. The Labor movement was more cautious because it feared a split in its own ranks over the Treaty, and the *Voice of Labour* advised workers not to take sides on the issue but to leave the decision to the Dail and the voters.[30]

The Irish people took the news of the agreement very calmly. Their apparent apathy was largely due to the fact that the truce had already convinced them the war was over. This conviction gained strength with each passing week and made the peace settlement seem almost anticlimactic. However, there was never any doubt about the people's attitude toward the Treaty. When they heard the news, they filled the churches to offer thanksgiving.[31] Even the Treaty's enemies were compelled to admit the people wanted it and wanted it badly.

De Valera was well aware of the popular desire for peace and it deeply disturbed him. In late December he wrote an American supporter that his talks with Lloyd George had convinced him that the British would offer Ireland ("on paper at least") Dominion status, except as pertained to Ulster and naval defense. With war the only alternative, he felt sure the people would be willing to accept this offer. To those who thought a Republic unattainable or impracticable, to those who believed it would confirm partition, and to Unionists (groups which de Valera feared were a majority of the nation) "the only way out seemed Colonial Home Rule."[32] A week before the Treaty was signed he wrote Harry Boland in America:

> As things stand today it means war. The British ultimatum is allegiance to their King. We will never recommend that such allegiance be rendered. . . .
> Without explanation you will understand that if I appear with those who choose war it is only because the alternative is impossible without dishonour. As far as I am concerned it is now, External Association, YES; Internal Association involving Allegiance, NO.[33]

After the Cabinet meeting on December 3, de Valera resumed his western inspection tour, proclaiming that Ireland would fight on, whatever the cost, until it won complete freedom. He spent the night of December 5 in Limerick and was preparing to return to Dublin when news reached him that an agreement had been signed. Assuming that the delegates had signed without consulting the Cabinet only because they were sure of its approval, he concluded they had won external association. Surprised but happy, the president remarked he had not thought the British would give in so soon.[34]

Arriving in Dublin in midafternoon, de Valera spent a few hours with his family and then went to the Mansion House, where he was to preside over a symposium honoring Dante. Brugha and Stack met him as he entered the building at 7:15 p.m. Eagerly, the president asked if there were any news, and Stack answered affirmatively. "Good or bad?" de Valera inquired. "Bad," Stack replied, handing him an evening paper which contained a summary of the Treaty. As de Valera examined this, Duggan arrived from London, bearing a copy of the Treaty, which he asked the president to read. Disappointed and angry, de Valera inquired why he should read it. Duggan said that the delegations had arranged for publication of the full Treaty in London and Dublin at 8 p.m. Astonished at this, the president asked if the Treaty were to be published whether he had seen it or not, whether he approved it or not. Duggan answered uneasily that that was the agreement. In response to Stack's angry query why the delegates had signed the Treaty, Duggan asserted: "It was war in five minutes unless we signed." As de Valera read the terms of the Treaty he seemed to Stack "an almost broken man." Crushed and silent, he made his way to the stage and throughout the proceedings which followed betrayed no sign of his inner torment. Afterward, he met again with Brugha and Stack, but all three men were numbed with grief.[35]

Three weeks later, de Valera confided to Joe McGarrity the full extent of his disappointment at the delegates' decision. When Griffith and Collins had argued on December 3 that holding out for external association was a gamble, de Valera had begged them to take the risk.

> A win meant triumph, definite and final. If we lost, the loss would not be as big as it seemed, for we would be no worse than we had been six months ago. To me the win seemed almost a certainty, but they could not see it, and a great occasion was missed—great not merely for Ireland but for England too, and for the world.

The desire of both peoples for peace, inclusion of the Tories in the government (which precluded their opposition to a settlement), Lloyd George's political needs and imagination, and the readiness of extreme Republicans to accept external association constituted a unique combination of factors in favor of a just and lasting peace. This priceless opportunity was lost because of Lloyd George's trickery and because the Irish delegates "were not bold enough to dare 'to make one heap of all their winnings' and stake it."[36]

On December 7 de Valera met with the Cabinet and announced he intended to call for the resignations of the three ministers who had signed the Treaty. Cosgrave maintained that it would be wrong to condemn the delegates without a hearing. Realizing that if Cosgrave supported the Treaty there would be a Cabinet majority in its favor, the president decided caution was essential. The minister-delegates were summoned for a meeting the next day so that a Cabinet decision might be taken on the Treaty.[37]

The meeting lasted five hours. All the Cabinet members were there, as well as Duggan, Duffy, Childers, and Kevin O'Higgins. The delegates insisted that war was the alternative to the Treaty, although they held different opinions about the agreement itself. According to Stack, Griffith emphasized the Treaty's merits and refused to admit British duress. Collins conceded only "duress of the facts" while Barton and Duffy said they had been forced to sign. Griffith would recommend the Treaty on its merits to the Dail and the people. Collins and Barton, supported by Cosgrave, would recommend its acceptance as the best way out of an impossible situation. De Valera, Brugha, and Stack tried hard to persuade the delegates not to recommend the Treaty to the Dail, or at least not to use their full influence on its behalf. But the delegates felt they had done all they could in London and refused to dishonor their signatures. In the eventual vote, Griffith, Collins, Barton, and Cosgrave voted for the Treaty, de Valera, Brugha, and Stack against. The Cabinet summoned the Dail to meet December 14. It also empowered the president to issue a statement explaining his position and agreed that the government should remain in office to carry on essential services.[38]

In his public statement, de Valera condemned the terms of the Treaty as "in violent conflict with the wishes of the majority of this nation as expressed freely in successive elections during the past three years." Neither he nor the ministers of defense and home affairs could recommend its acceptance. The Cabinet would carry on until the Dail decided the issue, and the army would continue under the same orders and control, unaffected by the political situation. The message ended with an appeal for popular discipline:

> The greatest test of our people has come. Let us face it worthily, without bitterness and, above all, without recriminations. There is a definite constitutional way of resolving our political differences—let us not depart from it, and let the conduct of the Cabinet in this matter be an example to the whole nation.[39]

The hostile or uncomprehending reaction of the strongly pro-Treaty press to this proclamation was predictable.[40] The president himself was partly to blame because he had hitherto failed to make his position clear on the issue of Republic versus Dominion. On the other hand, if the Cabinet was divided over the Treaty, the people had a right to know. Moreover, the president's remarks about the IRA, constitutional settlement of differences, and the need for national discipline were sensible and necessary reminders to a people whose political disagreements had too often been the occasion of vilification and even violence. It is doubtful that the Treaty was really "in violent conflict" with the people's wishes, since the great majority of voters were not committed Republicans in 1918 or 1921. Yet, in fairness to de Valera, the people had endorsed the Republican demand on more than one occasion.

When de Valera denounced the agreement, his immense prestige and the authority of his office caused some people who had initially accepted it to have second thoughts.[41] He created or confirmed misgivings about the settlement in the minds of many and encouraged them to voice their opposition. Very quickly, a sizable party rallied behind the president of the Republic.

De Valera's order to Harry Boland to denounce the Treaty ended initial Irish-American rejoicing and opened a split like the one in Ireland.[42] Devoy and Cohalan endorsed the agreement, but McGarrity and other leaders supported de Valera. In England, the Irish Self-Determination League split.[43] And so it went in every Irish community in the world, once news of the division among Sinn Fein's leaders was made public.

In Ireland, both sides busied themselves in winning support. Griffith replied to de Valera's manifesto by praising the Treaty and obtaining further assurances from Lloyd George. In a letter on December 13, the prime minister offered guarantees of Irish rights and powers in such matters as appointment of the Crown's representative, arbitration of Ireland's financial liability, membership in the League of Nations, and the drafting of the Free State Constitution. He also promised that British evacuation would begin as soon as the Irish ratified the Treaty.[44]

Although Griffith appeared imperturbable, he was deeply hurt by friends' opposition to the Treaty and the estrangements which inevitably resulted.[45] Collins was even more tormented, and found it harder to conceal his feelings. Calling on his good friend Batt O'Connor after the divisive Cabinet meeting, he was miserable, and in response to O'Connor's warm welcome he unburdened himself. He doubted that he could win the Dail's approval of the Treaty over de Valera's opposition. If the Treaty were defeated, the war would be resumed and Ireland would be beaten in two weeks. O'Connor impressed on Collins that the people wanted the Treaty, that they looked to him for leadership, and that he must not desert them now. Collins calmed down, and before he departed promised he would see the Treaty through the Dail, making sure its terms were fully discussed and put before the people clearly. Whatever the popular verdict, he was ready to abide by it.[46]

With the tide running strongly in favor of the Treaty, de Valera decided that the best way to defeat it was to offer an alternative. With the aid of Childers, he drafted what became known as Document No. 2 (to distinguish it from the Treaty). In essence, it was external association modified to meet the situation created by the Treaty. It offered Britain the same defense facilities as the Treaty, but only for five years. On northeast Ulster, it duplicated the Treaty's provisions, basing acceptance of partition on sincere regard for internal peace and unwillingness to employ coercion. But this concession was qualified by refusal to recognize the right of any part of Ireland to be excluded from the Irish state. Thus de Valera accepted *de facto* partition but rejected *de jure* division of the country. Although he had drafted his proposal hastily and was unhappy with its Ulster clauses, he hoped it would serve as a basis for restoring nationalist unity and achieving a just peace. If the Dail approved his proposal, he believed the British would accept it rather than make war against a united people.[47]

Of all Irish reactions to the Treaty, the IRA's was most crucial. Collins believed that de Valera would strongly influence the IRA and feared that extremists might use the army to wreck the settlement. He knew he could count on his close associates in the Squad and at GHQ, but the army as a whole was strongly Republican and its local units were largely a law unto themselves.[48] What influence Collins possessed had suffered from his preoccupation with the negotiations, and he could not be sure how much weight his views would carry in the struggle for the IRA's support.

Knowing most GHQ officers shared Collins' general estimate of the military situation, Griffith persuaded de Valera to meet with them, hoping their views would moderate his opposition.[49] When the president asked the staff officers what they would do if the Dail rejected the Treaty, Collins said he would fight as an ordinary soldier but would accept no military responsibility. Richard Mulcahy was equally blunt. The IRA could maintain resistance for six months or so, but it could not defeat the British. He felt he must tell this to the Dail and could therefore not continue as chief of staff if the Treaty were rejected, although he would serve in any other useful capacity. Other staff members were generally pessimistic about resuming hostilities but agreed to carry on their work, whatever the Dail decided. De Valera assured them that if the Treaty were approved, he would not tolerate mutiny in the army.[50] Convinced that GHQ was under the sway of Collins and the IRB, the president wrote angrily to a supporter: "Tho' the rank and file of the army is right, the Headquarter[s] Staff [has] clean gone wrong—a part of the machine. Curse secret societies!"[51] Feeling as he did, de Valera ignored GHQ's assessment and continued his efforts to defeat the Treaty.

Pro-Treaty staff officers tried to prevent a mutiny by maintaining that the Volunteers would obey the Dail and their military superiors, regardless of personal opinions.[52] Dan Breen, the man who had staged the Soloheadbeg ambush in January 1919, was one of the first soldiers to contest this view. On December 7 he urged Liam Lynch, commander of the 1st Southern Division, to end the truce at once by attacking the

British. Breen hoped such action might maintain army unity and prevent the politicians from betraying the Republic. When Lynch rejected his advice, Breen left for the United States, predicting civil war within a year.[53]

Although most officers were slower to take an extreme position, anti-Treaty sentiment in the IRA began to crystallize rapidly once de Valera condemned the agreement. On December 10 senior officers of the 1st Southern Division unanimously adopted a resolution urging the Dail to reject the Treaty. Shortly afterward, divisional headquarters informed Dail deputies from Cork that failure to vote against the settlement would be considered treason to the Republic.[54]

Through the influence of the IRB, Collins hoped to overcome opposition from the army, whose upper ranks had been systematically infiltrated by the secret society. During the London negotiations, he had kept in close touch with members of the Supreme Council, which met in Dublin on December 10 to decide its policy on the Treaty. As president, Collins pressed for endorsement of the agreement, contending that Ireland could not win the Republic by war but that the Treaty made possible its peaceful attainment. He may even have suggested that the "dark hand" of the IRB within the Free State government would guarantee progress toward that goal.[55] Only Liam Lynch declared his opposition to the Treaty at this meeting. Two days later, the Supreme Council issued the following statement to division and county leaders of the Brotherhood:

> The Supreme Council, having due regard to the Constitution of the Organisation, has decided that the present Peace Treaty between Ireland and Great Britain should be ratified.
> Members of the Organisation, however, who have to take public action as representatives are given freedom of action in the matter.[56]

This directive left Dail members who belonged to the IRB free to vote as they wished, but it also made clear that those who opposed the Treaty rejected the Supreme Council's judgment.

De Valera deplored Collins' attempts to use IRB influence on behalf of the Treaty, and he and others claimed that it would have been defeated in the Dail but for these tactics.[57] The evidence does not sustain this charge, however. During the final phase of the struggle with Britain, the IRB's influence had sharply declined. Its diminishing importance was partly due to the conditions of guerrilla warfare, which necessitated a high degree of local military autonomy. The Supreme Council might dominate GHQ, but neither body could control IRA units. The IRB's decline also owed something to the oath its members took to the Dail and, more important, to the Republic in 1920, which weakened their loyalty to the Brotherhood. By the time of the truce, many of the IRB's units had been inactive for months, and the secret society's functions had been largely assumed by the Volunteers and the Dail. In plain fact, the IRB was obsolete and constituted no real threat to either the British or the Republican government.

Of course, Collins held a very powerful position in the revolutionary movement, but his influence owed much more to his work in the IRA and the government than to his role as IRB head center. And even within the Brotherhood his power had limits, as the Treaty controversy demonstrated. Four members of the Supreme Council opposed the Treaty;[58] in all probability, so did most of the organization's rank and file; and in the Dail, such IRB men as Harry Boland, Austin Stack, and Con Collins spoke and voted against it. It is true that more IRB Dail deputies supported than opposed the Treaty. But of the Supreme Council members who sided with Collins on this issue, only Richard Mulcahy and Gearoid O'Sullivan were deputies, and their votes in both bodies were clearly decided as much by their assessment of the military situation as by ioyalty to Collins. The same was true of other IRB soldier-deputies, such as Sean MacEoin and Eoin O'Duffy. Furthermore, the speeches made in the Dail by such Brotherhood stalwarts as Patrick MacCartan, Sean McGarry, and Alec McCabe strongly suggest that they supported the peace settlement for reasons much more compelling than IRB pressure. Finally, it must be remembered that many deputies, including de Valera, Griffith, Brugha, Cosgrave, Barton, Childers, and Eoin MacNeill, as well as all six women in the Dail, did not belong to the secret society.

By all odds, the IRB made only a marginal contribution to the Dail's decision on the Treaty. Its influence was exaggerated by the anti-Treaty forces to convince themselves and their supporters that only the machinations of a powerful clandestine organization could subvert the Dail's allegiance to the Republic.[59]

Chapter 10
Dail Eireann and the Treaty:
December 1921-January 1922

The Dail was ill prepared for the responsibility thrust on it by the Cabinet's split over the Treaty. Most deputies had not been selected for office because of their political experience or mature judgment but because of their separatist credentials and willingness to follow orders. The Cabinet had concluded a truce without consulting the Dail and rejected Britain's original peace proposals before consulting it. Most deputies were not even aware of the Cabinet's peace proposals during the London negotiations. What had been a rubber-stamp assembly was suddenly charged with making a decision of paramount importance.[1]

The Treaty debate took place in the Senate Chamber of University College, Dublin. After a short public session on December 14, the Dail went into private session to discuss confidential matters. Public meetings resumed on December 19 and lasted four days, with a brief private session on military affairs on the 20th. The Dail recessed on December 22; debate resumed on January 3 and lasted five days. After the vote on the Treaty on January 7, two more public sessions were held on January 9 and 10 to discuss matters arising from the vote.

President de Valera opened the first day's debate by claiming the delegates had failed to carry out their instructions by not consulting the Cabinet before signing the Treaty.[2] At the same time, he declared that the Treaty should be discussed on its merits and he offered to answer any questions about the negotiations. Griffith and Collins challenged de Valera's contention that the delegates had somehow exceeded their powers, and Collins urged that the Cabinet's final proposals be made public so they could be compared with the Treaty. The Dail then decided to go into private session to discuss the negotiations.[3]

In its private meetings, the Dail heard a long and involved account of the final stages of negotiations from Cabinet members and delegates, with copies of relevant documents circulated for the deputies' consideration. The president spoke often and at length to explain his position and to dispel any suspicion that he had "let down" either the Republic or the delegation. While admitting that he had "battered down the wall of the isolated Republic," he maintained that peace could only be negotiated through some sort of association with Britain. He conceded the people would accept the Treaty under British duress, but it would split the nation and would not bring peace. Offering his alternative proposal, Document No. 2, de Valera urged the Dail to adopt it instead of the Treaty.

Griffith and Collins rejoined that the British had already turned down external association and that the only alternative to the Treaty was war—real war. In their reactions to the two proposals, deputies generally assumed the same attitudes they adopted in the public debate, although a few foes of the Treaty (Liam Mellows, Seamus Robinson, and Sean Etchingham) made plain that they stood for absolute independence, that is, the isolated Republic, and they threatened civil war if the Dail approved the Treaty.[4]

Dismayed by the opposition to his plan, de Valera withdrew it, asking that it be treated as confidential until he reintroduced it publicly. Griffith and Collins strongly objected, arguing that confidentiality would prevent their showing the people that the alternative to the Treaty was another compromise. While agreeing to respect the president's request as far as he could, Griffith declared he would not conceal the proposed alternative from the people.[5]

When public sessions resumed on the 19th, Griffith moved the Treaty's approval. The agreement was not ideal, he admitted, but it was honorable and it safeguarded Ireland's vital interests. If the Dail rejected the Treaty, it would misrepresent the people's will and lose all authority. The difference in the Cabinet and the Dail was between "half-recognizing the British King and the British Empire" and going into the Empire "with our heads up." It was essentially a "quibble of words," which did not justify rejecting the Treaty and going to war.

President de Valera told the Dail that acceptance of the Treaty would bring neither freedom nor peace. It did not do "the fundamental thing," and by approving it, the Dail would presume to set bounds to the march of the nation. Stack supported the president's appeal, denouncing the oath and demanding full national independence.[6]

After a luncheon recess, Collins made an impassioned speech, declaring he had signed the Treaty not because of bluff or threats but because he thought it the best thing to do. He admitted that the agreement was a compromise, but the same would be true of any settlement. There would have been no conference had the Cabinet demanded recognition of the Republic as a precondition; instead, it compromised by accepting a conference based on the idea of association with the Empire. Of the Treaty itself, Collins declared: "In my opinion it gives us freedom, not the ultimate freedom that all nations desire and develop to, but the freedom to achieve it." The agreement would end British military occupation and enable Ireland to end British economic exploitation. With the other Dominions serving as guarantors of Irish freedom, Ireland would share in the development of Dominion status, expanding the powers it had won. The Treaty made an effort to deal with the problem of partition, which he believed would lead quickly to good will and unity. While this policy might not be ideal, it was up to others to devise a better one, if northeast Ulster were not to be coerced. In making its decision, Collins urged the Dail to consider the will of the people, for it was their right to decide the question of peace or war.[7]

Childers denied the Treaty gave Ireland Dominion status. Its defense provisions gave Britain control of the country; but even without these restrictions, Ireland lacked the guarantees of distance and sentiment that protected other Dominions from British interference. He profoundly regretted the Treaty had been signed, but an honorable peace could still be made on the basis of external association. Whatever the alternative, the Dail would not and could not abandon national independence. Such an act would be unprecedented in the history of democratic nations.

While acknowledging that the Treaty was not the Magna Carta of Irish liberty, Kevin O'Higgins contended that it gave Ireland a great deal, and he hoped what remained to be achieved might be won by peaceful political evolution. The Dail was not entitled to reject the agreement unless there were a reasonable prospect of obtaining more. Since the alternative to acceptance was war, neither honor nor principle could justify rejection. After all, the welfare and happiness of the Irish people must take precedence over political creeds and theories.

Robert Barton declared that while he and Duffy had argued for refusal of the British terms, he could not accept responsibility for war. He had therefore signed the Treaty and now fulfilled his obligation to recommend it to the Dail.[8]

When its members assembled the next day, the Dail learned that President de Valera intended to move the adoption of his alternative peace proposal after the vote on the Treaty.[9] The speeches in the morning session offered no surprises. In the early afternoon, the Dail met privately to discuss military affairs. Most of the high-ranking officers who were deputies agreed that a return to the conditions existing before the truce was out of the question.[10]

When the public session resumed, Sean Milroy, a close friend of Griffith, attacked de Valera's tactics. He protested the president's refusal to make public his peace proposal, charging he was trying to persuade deputies to vote against the Treaty in the hope that something better would follow. When Milroy read the oath agreed to by the Irish Cabinet on December 3, in order to show how little difference there was between the Treaty and the president's proposal, de Valera objected. But Milroy brushed aside the protest, warning that the alternative to the Treaty was war and chaos.[11]

Gavan Duffy opened the debate on December 21, recommending the

Treaty because he saw no alternative. The agreement gave Ireland real power; rejection would be a gamble; and it must be ratified in the interest of the people. Eamonn Duggan denied Duffy's contention that the delegation signed the Treaty because of personal intimidation or demoralization. He had signed because Britain was more powerful than Ireland, and war was the alternative. Listing the advantages of the Treaty, Duggan asserted that if the Irish people could not achieve freedom under its terms, it would be their fault and not the Treaty's.[12]

Challenging Childers' interpretation of the Treaty, Cosgrave argued that it would give Ireland almost complete freedom and that its defense provisions were a reasonable arrangement for a new state which lacked a navy. On a more basic question, Cosgrave declared the people had the right to decide whether they would accept or reject the Treaty. He also put the case that pressing economic and social problems made its acceptance imperative. The day's proceedings ended with a three-hour tirade by Mary MacSwiney, sister of the martyred lord mayor of Cork. She predicted that if Ireland stood by the Republic, world opinion would not allow England to exterminate the Irish. Again and again, MacSwiney appealed to the deputies not to abandon the Republic because of British tyranny and trickery.[13]

On December 22, sadly but calmly, Richard Mulcahy told the Dail that he would vote for the Treaty because he saw no alternative. The president's peace proposal had not been treated fairly by either side, in his opinion, but neither the president nor his supporters had shown how the objective he sought might be attained. There was "no solid spot of ground upon which the Irish people can put its political feet but upon that Treaty." Admittedly there were defects in it, but the IRA could not drive the British from the Treaty ports; in fact, it had been unable to drive the enemy from anything but a good-size police barracks. Mulcahy did not believe that the agreement prejudiced the Ulster problem, because he saw no solution to that problem for the moment. To him, the issue was clear: the Treaty, with complete control of the country's resources, or the risk of war, with all its waste and misery, against a much stronger power.[14]

At the close of the day's debate, the Dail voted to adjourn over the Christmas holidays. The adjournment was moved by Collins, who doubtless felt that the Treaty had a better chance for approval if voters brought pressure to bear on their representatives.[15]

Popular opinion made itself felt during the Christmas recess. By January 7, 1922, 369 elected and other bodies had endorsed the Treaty and only fourteen had declared opposition. Most of the county councils and borough corporations, as well as a large number of urban and rural district councils, Sinn Fein clubs, farmers' associations, and some labor organizations, came out in support of the settlement. In de Valera's constituency, the Clare County Council endorsed the Treaty by a vote of 17 to 5 (later reaffirmed 18 to 1) and urged the president to do his best to maintain national unity. Liam Mellows, an extreme Republican, found public opinion in his Galway constituency overwhelmingly pro-Treaty.[16]

As public support for the settlement manifested itself, the opposition forces became more disheartened and bitter. In their opinion, turncoat Republicans, aided by Unionists, Home Rulers, the press, and the Catholic bishops, were exploiting the people's fear of war to win approval of the Treaty. The British were abetting this campaign by releasing internees and announcing preparations to evacuate Southern Ireland and begin the transfer of power as soon as the Irish ratified the agreement.[17]

Angry and dismayed at the course of events, de Valera wrote Joe McGarrity: "I have been tempted several times to take drastic action, as I would be entitled to legally, but then the army is divided and the people wouldn't stand for it, and nobody but the enemy would win if I took it."[18]

Some high-ranking officers experienced similar temptations; they talked of repudiating GHQ's authority and threatened armed resistance to the Treaty. However, Brugha and Mellows persuaded them to refrain from overt defiance for the time being.[19] Republicans found some release for their anger in the *Republic of Ireland,* which published its first issue on January 3, 1922. Edited first by Mellows and then by Childers, this weekly newspaper condemned the Treaty, heaped scorn on its supporters, and endorsed external association.[20]

While the South debated the Treaty, events in the North underscored the urgent problems facing the nationalist minority. On December 15 the Fermanagh County Council, by a vote of 13 to 10, pledged allegiance to Dail Eireann and announced it would hold no further communication with the local-government departments of Great Britain or Northern Ireland. The police at once seized control of the council's offices, and on December 23 the Belfast government dissolved the council and appointed a commissioner to discharge its functions.[21] Thus the Fermanagh County Council followed its sister body in Tyrone into oblivion.

On January 3, 1922, the Dail reconvened and Piaras Beaslai made what was probably the most moving speech of the entire debate. He asked how war could be avoided if the Dail rejected the Treaty—how two governments could restrain their armed forces from breaking a truce that had no objective. The Treaty was a solid fact and would enable Ireland to restore its nationhood and control its own destiny. Its opponents would throw all this away for a formula. Like so many other Irishmen, they had become so involved in the struggle against foreign oppression that they never visualized what freedom could mean. They lacked faith in the nation and all that it could be under the Treaty—free and Gaelic, progressive and prosperous. Recalling a line from a play of the Gaelic revival, he asked the opposition: "The nation, the nation—do you ever think of the poor Irish nation which is trying to be born?" To Beaslai, the nation was not an abstraction or a formula; it was the Irish people—all ages, all classes, all parties and religions. If the Dail rejected the Treaty, it would doom itself and the nation to division and chaos.[22]

Shortly after Beaslai's speech, Collins offered a plan to maintain unity. Ireland, he asserted, could not be weaker if it accepted the Treaty, and the opposition should allow it to be approved without a vote. If necessary, the anti-Treaty forces could fight the Provisional Government after it had taken power from the British. De Valera rejected the proposal on the grounds that the anti-Treaty party could take this course if it lost the vote in the Dail. Moreover, Collins' party had turned down a chance to make a real peace, based on external association, simply because "certain credits were involved."[23]

On January 4 Liam Mellows made a fiery appeal for the Republic. The people were being stampeded because of their fear of war. Approval of the Treaty would bring Ireland material advantages but would not bring peace, because the people would have to overthrow the Free State government to gain real freedom. Mellows begged the Dail not to surrender the noble position Ireland had won by its struggle but to defy Britain and stand by the Republic.[24]

In reply to another demand by Griffith that he publish his peace proposal, de Valera circulated copies of it and announced he would submit it formally to the Dail the following day. Collins urged a vote on the Treaty before any other document was considered, while Griffith claimed the proposal that was being circulated was not the president's original proposal; six clauses had been omitted. Accusing Griffith of quibbling, de Valera declared he had made only a slight change of form.[25] The difference between the two versions was that the second offered Northern Ireland privileges and safeguards as substantial as those in the Treaty, while the original had incorporated the Treaty's actual provisions on Ulster. The president had already announced this change in private session, explaining he felt it would be better to deal with Ulster directly on the matter of safeguards. But this move angered Griffith, who thought de Valera was trying to obscure his *de facto* acceptance of partition.[26]

Soon after assembling on January 5, the Dail adjourned so a few deputies could continue informal efforts to restore unity. The self-appointed committee reported in the afternoon that it was unable to reach agreement, but the Dail ordered the committee to meet again and report the next day.[27]

The main topic of discussion on January 5 was the *Freeman's Journal*, which had just published a savage editorial declaring that de Valera did not have the "instinct of an Irishman in his blood" and was being advised by a renegade Englishman. The president's initial peace proposal was printed next to the Treaty and dismissed as the product of his vanity and Childers' brain. The Dail denounced this vilification but refrained from any action which might infringe freedom of the press.[28]

Protesting the release of his original peace proposal to the press, the president said he had asked that it be kept confidential so it would not confuse discussion of the Treaty, and the Dail had agreed to his request. Griffith admitted he had released the document, but denied it was confidential. The president had asked only that it be treated as such, and Griffith had honored that request, even though it hampered arguments for the Treaty; but then de Valera had introduced a new document and accused him of quibbling when Griffith charged it differed from the original proposal. Griffith had therefore given the initial draft to the press so the people could judge whether he was quibbling or not. The argument ended when de Valera accepted Griffith's refusal to allow consideration of his proposal until after the vote on the Treaty.[29]

On January 6 the Dail discussed the work of its *ad hoc* peace committee privately. The committee had tentatively agreed on a compromise two days before by which de Valera's followers would abstain from voting against the Treaty, he would remain president of the Dail, and the Provisional Government would be responsible to the Dail. On January 5 Griffith and Collins accepted the proposal but de Valera rejected it, contending that it meant foes of the Treaty should allow the Free State to take root and then try to extirpate it.[30]

When the Dail met publicly on the afternoon of the 6th, President de Valera submitted his resignation, declaring he could no longer serve as head of a divided government. When his peace proposal was made public, he realized he could no longer have confidence in his fellow ministers, and he (and they) must resign. If the Dail reelected him president, de Valera pledged to throw out the Treaty and offer Britain a peace based on external association. If the British rejected it, he would use every available resource to defend the Republic. Asserting that his policy was rooted in his experience as Ireland's leader since 1917 and in his understanding of its people, de Valera declared: "Therefore, I know what I am talking about; and whenever I wanted to know what the Irish people wanted I had only to examine my own heart and it told me straight off what the Irish people wanted."[31]

Collins and Griffith at once protested de Valera's attempt to resign, claiming it was designed to confuse the Dail, and called for a straight vote on the Treaty before any other issue was discussed. Speaking frankly, Griffith said he did not understand why the debate should be interrupted to take a vote on President de Valera's personality, and he did not think the Irish people would understand it either.[32] In a mixture of annoyance and self-pity, the president told the Dail he was so sick and tired of the politics he had seen since the Treaty was signed that he intended to retire to private life no matter what happened. If the Dail wanted to vote on the Treaty, he did not want to interfere. "It is because I am straight that I meet crookedness with straight dealing always, and I have beaten crookedness with straight dealing."[33] Griffith agreed with the president's request for a vote on the Treaty within forty-eight hours, and the Dail decided it should be taken the next day.[34]

The debate resumed, and Seamus Robinson, an IRA officer from Tipperary, made an angry and menacing speech. He claimed that the army had been let down by its leaders, and he accused Collins of conspiring with Lloyd George to force the Treaty on their respective cabinets and countries. The Volunteers, he contended, were not a regular professional army, and they had a right to a general convention to state their political views. If such a convention were held, the IRA "would refrain from certain terrible action that will be necessary if the Treaty is forced on us without our consent as an Army of Volunteers."[35] In effect, Robinson threatened civil war if the Dail approved the Treaty, and there was no doubt he spoke for many in the IRA.

Just back from the United States, Harry Boland opened the final day's debate with a strong anti-Treaty speech. He conceded that American public opinion generally favored the settlement, but dedicated supporters of Ireland viewed it as a betrayal. Britain was too deeply involved in troubles overseas to make war if the Dail rejected the Treaty. Moreover, world opinion would turn against Ireland if it accepted the Treaty without meaning to abide by it.[36]

In the early evening, the long talk moved toward its close with speeches by Brugha and Griffith. Brugha began with a savage attack on Collins, alleging the press had greatly exaggerated his wartime role. Collins had done no fighting and was "merely a subordinate in the Department of Defence," who held a very high opinion of himself. Many deputies were shocked by the vehemence of Brugha's remarks, and several called upon him to stop. But Brugha refused, and one observer claimed that his attack on Collins swung at least two votes for the Treaty. Collins sat calmly through the onslaught and harbored no ill will toward Brugha because of it. After he had finished with Collins, Brugha denounced several other deputies and then turned his fire on the Treaty, condemning the oath, common citizenship, and British control of Irish coastal defense. He emphasized his fundamental disagreement with Griffith's political views but appealed to him and the other delegates not to vote for the Treaty. Only if it were turned down could unity be restored and a just peace made.[37]

Griffith wound up the debate with a long and effective address. He began by rejecting Brugha's suggestion that he refuse to vote for the

Treaty and by praising Collins as "the man who won the war." Reviewing
the history of the negotiations, Griffith maintained that the delegates
had been sent to make a compromise which would give Ireland substantial freedom. They believed they had done this, although many people
disagreed. These people, however, had attacked the delegates instead of
discussing the Treaty. It was not ideal, but it was a signed agreement
which served Ireland's interests. It was not dishonorable and "it has no
more finality than that we are the final generation on the face of the
earth." Ireland could use the Treaty to attain whatever status its people
desired, but if it were rejected, the country would be thrown back into
the political futility that existed before 1916. On one occasion, Griffith
recalled, he had asked the Irish Cabinet what the alternative to the British
terms was, since no Cabinet member held that Ireland could expel the
British by force. He had been told that this generation might go down
but the next generation might do something or other. "Is there to be no
living Irish nation? Is the Irish nation to be the dead past or the prophetic
future?" The Dail had a duty to the Irish people to do the best it could
for Ireland while keeping the nation's honor safe. Ireland's leaders had a
duty not to demand of the people something they knew the people could
not do, in order to save their own faces at the expense of the people's
blood.

Turning to the president's alternative proposal, Griffith said it was a
compromise that secured neither the Republic nor more freedom than
the Treaty and one that the British had already rejected. The people
wanted the Treaty, and every member of the opposition knew it. If the
Dail threw it out, the people would throw out the Dail. His guiding
principle was Ireland for the Irish people. If he could get that with a
republic, he would take a republic; if he could get it with a monarchy, he
would take a monarchy. He would not sacrifice his country for a *form* of
government. The Treaty gave the Irish people the freedom to shape
their destiny for the first time in centuries, and it was their right to have
it.[38]

When Griffith finished, de Valera rose to protest the assertion that
there was only a shadow of difference between his proposal and the
Treaty; his document would rise in judgment against the men who said
that. Collins answered: "Let the Irish nation judge us now and for future
years."[39]

The Speaker ruled that each deputy could vote only once, even if he
represented two constituencies. The roll was called and the vote was 64
to 57 in favor of the Treaty.[40]

When the result was announced, de Valera said he would resign the
presidency; but until the people voted to disestablish the Republic, it still
existed, with Dail Eireann as supreme national authority. Declaring he
did not regard the vote as a triumph for his side, Collins suggested

formation of a joint committee to supervise the transfer of power from Britain. However, before de Valera could respond to this appeal, Mary MacSwiney jumped up, denouncing the Dail's betrayal of the Republic and asserting there could be no cooperation between Republicans and the Free State.[41]

Collins again asked for cooperation to preserve public order, but there was no response. De Valera called for discipline. They had a glorious record of four years of magnificent national discipline, and the world was looking at them now. At this point, overcome by emotion, the president sat down, buried his face in his arms, and wept aloud. His action released the pent-up emotions of his fellow deputies, and almost every one of them soon was sobbing openly.[42] After four years of unity, they knew they had come to the parting of the ways. On this note, the Dail ended its most important session since its first meeting three years before.

Although Griffith and Collins had seized the initiative in rallying support for the Treaty, they were put on the defensive during the debate. To some extent this was inevitable, because they were proposing disestablishment of the Republic, but the two leaders added to their problem by initially agreeing to keep de Valera's peace proposal private. Had Griffith and Collins insisted on a public discussion of external association early in the debate, they would have shown clearly how far the entire Cabinet was committed to a compromise peace and how similar in substance external association was to the Treaty. Such a revelation would have forced de Valera and his supporters onto the defensive and done much to discredit them in the popular mind. It would also, probably, have driven a wedge between external-associationists and diehard Republicans. But Griffith and Collins held their hand; they had great respect for the president and, like him, still hoped that unity might somehow be restored. This meant that the Treaty's supporters spent much of their time in the debate either apologizing for its defects or trying to answer personal attacks, while the Treaty's real merits were not fully explored.[43] By the time de Valera's plan was made public, the long debate was almost over and it was too late to exploit the opposition's vulnerability.

Reviewing the debate, one finds de Valera's arguments negative, repetitious, and sometimes hard to follow; yet his passionate sincerity moved all who heard him. Griffith showed little emotion, but his solid and forceful presentation made an impact on the Dail and the crowded press gallery. Cosgrave showed flashes of wit and humor, while Brugha shocked the audience with his ferocious attack on Collins. Childers spoke like a "quiet ghost," "reflective in that pale, rather white, and keenly cold way of his." And always there was Collins—earnest, restless, incisive, at once aggressive and conciliatory. He spoke for the Treaty "passionately, eagerly, pervadingly," impatiently brushing back his unruly forelock. But outside the Senate Chamber, he paced up and down with a weary, defiant look as he witnessed the unity of the revolutionary movement being torn to shreds.[44]

Of the many factors that influenced the Dail's vote on the Treaty, only the most important need be mentioned here. The powers it conferred weighed heavily in the agreement's favor, as did the hope that it would lead to complete freedom and national unity. Equally important was the knowledge that the people wanted it and the belief that rejection meant war and defeat. Collins' advocacy also helped persuade many deputies that ratification was in Ireland's best interest. On the anti-Treaty side, the Republic and de Valera's prestige were the dominant considerations. The oath of allegiance was a major issue in the debate; partition was not.

When the Dail met on Monday, January 9, de Valera offered his government's resignation, turning down another invitation for political cooperation from Collins on the grounds that this would divide executive responsibility. The anti-Treaty party proposed de Valera's reelection as president of the Republic. He pledged that, if reelected, he would do his best to maintain the Republic, without actively opposing those who sought to implement the Treaty, until the people voted on the agreement in its final form in the Free State Constitution. Collins and Griffith strongly opposed the motion, contending it was an attempt to reverse the vote on the Treaty by setting up a Republican government. If successful, it would make the Dail a laughing stock and produce chaos in the country. In the vote that followed, de Valera was narrowly defeated, 60 to 58.[45]

De Valera announced his belief that the right thing had been done and expressed hope that no one would talk of "fratricidal strife." "We have got a nation that knows how to conduct itself. As far as I can on this side it will be our policy always." His party would try to help the Free Staters get the most out of the Treaty and would oppose them only if they threatened to injure the nation.[46]

The Dail then discussed Collins' proposal that Griffith form a provisional government. Griffith assured the opposition that the Republic would be maintained until the people disestablished it by their votes. However, anti-Treaty deputies protested that Griffith could not use the Dail to form a government that would subvert the Republic. De Valera warned that the majority party must elect a Republican president; otherwise, the Dail would cease to exist and Republican members would withdraw. Assailing the opposition for obstructionist tactics, Collins gave notice he would move his proposal formally the next day, and the Dail adjourned.[47]

On January 10 Collins moved that Griffith be elected president of Dail Eireann. The anti-Treaty party again protested possible use of the Dail to subvert the Republic, and de Valera pressed Griffith to promise he would function as president of the Republic if elected. Griffith replied that, if elected, he would "occupy whatever position President de Valera occupied." When de Valera asked if he would uphold his oath as president not to subvert the Republic, Griffith repeated he would maintain the Republic until the people decided its fate, but he added that he intended to carry out the Treaty. Again, de Valera objected, claiming Griffith's election would place him in an impossible position—pledged to subvert the Republic with one hand and maintain it with the other. In protest, de Valera led his followers out of the Dail.[48]

As the anti-Treaty deputies left the chamber, an angry exchange took place:

> *Collins:* Deserters all! We will now call on the Irish people to rally to us. Deserters all!
>
> *David Ceannt:* Up the Republic!
>
> *Collins:* Deserters all to the Irish nation in her hour of trial. We will stand by her.
>
> *Countess Markievicz:* Oath breakers and cowards.
>
> *Collins:* Foreigners—Americans—English.
>
> *Countess Markievicz:* Lloyd Georgeites.[49]

The members who remained unanimously elected Griffith president of Dail Eireann and approved his Cabinet nominations. Collins remained minister for finance and Cosgrave minister for local government. The other Cabinet appointments were Gavan Duffy, foreign affairs; Duggan, home affairs; O'Higgins, economic affairs; and Mulcahy, defense.[50]

That afternoon, the anti-Treaty deputies resumed their seats, and the Dail received a Labor delegation headed by Thomas Johnson, secretary of the Irish Labor Party and Trades Union Congress. Johnson warned the Dail that if grave social problems, such as unemployment and inadequate housing, were not dealt with quickly, the people would overthrow the government. They had played their full part in the struggle for freedom, and they meant to have it. President Griffith acknowledged the workers' patriotism and the urgency of the problems mentioned by Johnson, and he promised to appoint a committee to try to deal with unemployment.[51]

De Valera regretted he could not congratulate Griffith on his election. While promising that his party would do its best to help secure full national liberty, he warned that it would not recognize the Provisional Government and would do all in its power to prevent disestablishment of the Republic. Griffith asked for a fair trial for the new government in the terribly difficult work it must do. But he refused to answer Childers' request for more information about his policy, declaring angrily: "I will not reply to any damned Englishman in this Assembly." Childers tried to clarify the matter of his nationality, but the Speaker ruled the discussion out of order. Mulcahy assured the opposition that the army would remain the Army of the Republic, and the Dail adjourned until February.[52]

It has been suggested that Griffith and Collins should have adjourned the Dail *sine die* after it approved the Treaty.[53] Its continuance meant that there would be two governments in Southern Ireland, Dail and Provisional, and that the anti-Treaty party would have an official forum for criticism and obstruction. While it is true that an immediate election on the Treaty was the ideal course of action for Griffith and Collins, this was impossible. They needed British authority to hold an election and some way to persuade the IRA to allow one. Under the circumstances, prolonging the life of the Republican assembly was simply making the best of a difficult situation. This decision appeased foes of the Treaty and ensured that no rival government would be set up to contest the authority of the Free State regime. It also gave the Provisional Government time to consolidate its position in the country. In practice, the existence of two governments did not hinder implementation of the Treaty because their personnel were almost identical, and they met together to decide policy. Maintenance of a Republican facade did not deceive Republicans, and it was not a masterstroke of Free State policy, as one writer has claimed.[54] But even though the action was unavoidable, it had its advantages.

Chapter 11
The Way Ahead:
January-February 1922

In late December 1921, Lloyd George appointed a Cabinet Committee to supervise the transfer of power in Southern Ireland. The Provisional Government of Ireland Committee was headed by Churchill, who, as colonial secretary, was in charge of Anglo-Dominion relations. Procedural arrangements for the transfer were worked out following the Dail's approval of the Treaty.[1]

On January 12, 1922, Griffith, acting in his capacity as chairman of the Treaty delegation, summoned members of the House of Commons of Southern Ireland to a meeting on January 14. At 11 a.m. on the appointed day, sixty pro-Treaty deputies and the four representatives of Trinity College met at the Mansion House. Within an hour they had unanimously approved the Treaty and elected a Provisional Government. Having completed its assigned task, the assembly adjourned and never met again. Collins was chosen as chairman of the Provisional Government, with Cosgrave, O'Higgins, and Duggan occupying the same ministries they held in the Dail government. Neither Griffith nor Mulcahy joined the Provisional Government, but although they had no official connection with the authority charged with implementing the Treaty, both worked closely with it.[2]

On January 16 the new government formally took possession of Dublin Castle. However, Collins wisely chose to set up headquarters in City Hall, which allowed easy access to the Castle but was in no way identified with the old regime.

The Free State leaders faced a host of problems. They had to take over the Executive from the British, maintain public order during the transition period, and draft a constitution. They also had to prepare for an election on the Treaty and coordinate the work of Dail departments with those taken over from the British. O'Higgins later described the Provisional Government as "simply eight young men in the City Hall standing amidst the ruins of one administration, with the foundations of another not yet laid, and with wild men screaming through the keyhole."[3]

Collins, O'Higgins, and Duggan went to London late in January to work out the sequence of steps that would bring the Free State officially into existence. It was agreed that the viceroy was to act on the advice of the Provisional Government on general questions and on matters concerning individual departments as soon as these were transferred to Irish control. Amnesty, indemnity, and demobilization of the RIC were also covered under the working arrangements.[4]

British military evacuation began as soon as the Provisional Government took power. The British were anxious to expedite it, both to show good faith and to avert clashes with the IRA. Withdrawal was to take place in two stages. The first would remove all troops outside the cities of Dublin and Cork and the large base at the Curragh, in County Kildare. The second would complete evacuation of the Twenty-six Counties (except the Treaty ports) and would be carried out as soon as the political situation permitted. At first, it was hoped that the entire garrison might be withdrawn by Easter 1922, but events prevented this.[5]

By mid-February, all but a handful of troops had been moved east of the Shannon. As fast as they could be concentrated, they were moved to points of embarkation. Half of the RIC's Auxiliary Division left Ireland even before the Provisional Government took office, and the rest were gone by the end of January. The Black and Tans were also withdrawn as quickly as possible, while the regular RIC was concentrated in the larger towns, preparatory to demobilization. By the end of February the RIC had practically ceased to function as a police force in Southern Ireland.[6] Although Collins called publicly for rapid evacuation of the troops, he was not anxious for their departure. He expressed concern about the increased unemployment which evacuation would cause, but almost certainly he was more worried about his power to control the anti-Treaty IRA once the British were gone. However, Macready and Wilson were unwilling to use British soldiers to support Collins in an Irish quarrel.[7]

Although evacuation proceeded in good order, some posts were turned over to anti-Treaty Volunteers. British officers who took part in these transactions were satisfied that they were dealing with representatives of the Provisional Government, even though many of the involved IRA officers clearly regarded themselves as agents of the Republic. This confusion was inevitable. Collins had to assure the British that he controlled the IRA to ensure implementation of the Treaty, but he was unwilling to precipitate an open break with anti-Treaty units by demanding a pledge of loyalty to the Provisional Government as a condition of their occupying vacated posts. Collins therefore temporized by allowing them to take over posts in areas that were short of loyal troops.[8]

The British government chose not to question Irish assurances in this matter. Lloyd George and his colleagues knew that Collins and Griffith faced tremendous difficulties, and they were willing to wink at irregularities in the interests of harmony. Furthermore, it made much more sense for the British to concentrate and evacuate their forces, no matter who took over their former positions, than to leave them scattered about Southern Ireland. When they evacuated, the British took their arms and ammunition with them. On a few occasions the anti-Treaty IRA was able to capture war materiel from departing units, but such losses were minor.[9]

As the British moved out, it became increasingly clear that the fate of the Treaty depended as much on the IRA as on them. By the time the Dail debate ended, the split over the Treaty had infected almost every Volunteer unit, quickening the erosion of discipline begun by the truce. In other countries that have emerged from political upheaval, the army has often served as an essential stabilizing force, but in Ireland it was the main obstacle to restoring order.

On January 10 de Valera asked senior IRA officers to give Mulcahy, the new minister of defense, the same cooperation they had given Brugha, and he appealed to Mulcahy to take no action that would undermine discipline and widen the split in the army. Outspoken anti-Treaty officers, such as Liam Mellows, Rory O'Connor, and Ernie O'Malley, did not even attend the meeting with de Valera; Liam Lynch, who did attend, denounced the Treaty and spoke of refusing to obey GHQ's orders. However, Mulcahy again pledged that the army would remain Republican, and the anti-Treaty officers who were present agreed to cooperate with him on that basis.[10]

After further consultation, high-ranking anti-Treaty officers decided that the best way to prevent subversion of the Republic would be formally to reestablish the IRA's autonomy, and they agreed that a convention for this purpose should be held as soon as possible. On January 11 four GHQ staff members, six divisional commanders, and the two Dublin Brigade commanders requested an army convention no later than February 5. Its stated purpose would be to reaffirm allegiance to the Republic, elect an executive, and draft a constitution for the army.[11]

On January 13 Mulcahy replied that Dail Eireann was the government of the Republic and that the Cabinet had no constitutional power to approve any proposal which would transfer the Dail's control of the army to another body. On the same day, Rory O'Connor wrote the new chief of staff, Eoin O'Duffy, that the officers who demanded a convention intended to call one themselves, adding that they would act on O'Duffy's orders only when they were countersigned by himself. At an acrimonious meeting with Mulcahy on January 18, anti-Treaty officers argued that the IRA had a constitutional right to hold a convention and restore its autonomy. Mulcahy repeated that the Dail was the government, and the army was subject to its authority. The meeting finally agreed that a convention would be held within two months. Mulcahy realized that a convention would probably repudiate the Dail's authority, and he agreed to one only to prevent an open break with the dissidents.[12]

Whatever else might come of it, postponing a showdown strengthened the Free State. At the same time that they were taking over the machinery of government, the Free Staters were creating their own army. On January 31 an IRA detachment that was loyal to GHQ took over Beggar's Bush Barracks in Dublin from the British. As these troops swung past City Hall on their way to the barracks, the chairman of the Provisional Government stood on the steps to take their salute. The new Beggar's Bush garrison, composed of Collins' Squad and trusted members of the Dublin Brigade, formed the nucleus of the Dublin Guards, the first regiment of the Free State army.

The fiction that the new force that was taking shape was part of the IRA was studiously fostered by the Defense Ministry. Its members were pre-truce veterans who wore the dark green Volunteer uniform, complete with Republican insignia. But anti-Treaty members of the IRA were not enrolled in the new army, and recruits who expressed anti-Treaty views were dismissed. Members of this force were soon referred to as "Dail" or "Government" troops, while anti-Treaty Volunteers were called "Republicans" or "Irregulars." From its inception, the Free State army followed regular military procedure. Its soldiers wore uniforms, lived in barracks, learned drill and standard tactics, and were armed with British-supplied weapons. Organizational progress was slow at first. Trained staff officers and instructors were scarce; so were arms, uniforms, and equipment; and strict discipline could not be instilled in guerrilla warriors in a week or two. There were small-scale mutinies in the new force and a number of soldiers resigned, deserted, or were dismissed. Slowly but steadily, however, the army grew as loyal troops underwent training at Beggar's Bush and returned to their home districts. Pro-Treaty members of the IRA who could not be absorbed in the small force constituted a ready reserve.[13]

In another move designed to bolster its authority, the Provisional Government began formation of a regular police force. In late January GHQ ordered disbandment of the IRA's police units and the Provisional Government opened recruiting for the Civic Guards. Although there was no shortage of recruits, Republican opposition, poor leadership, and other problems made the force's early history an unhappy one.[14] Reorganization did much to solve the problems, but before the police could perform their duties effectively, the government had to suppress armed opposition to its rule.

The IRB was divided over the Treaty in much the same way as the IRA. A meeting of the Supreme Council with local leaders on January 10 produced no agreement, and two days later the council issued a statement intended to clarify its position and restore unity. This declared that the IRB had always made use of any instrument likely to aid in attaining a Republic. In December the council had decided that no organizational action should be taken on the Treaty. It informed members in the Dail that it supported ratification, but left them free to vote as they chose. The truce made a compromise settlement inevitable, and it would be inexpedient for the Brotherhood to interfere with a Treaty that might move Ireland closer to a republic. Once the Supreme Council had considered the Free State Constitution, future policy would be discussed. Until then, the Dail should be recognized as the government of the Republic, and IRB members in the IRA should obey the orders of their authorized military superiors.

This statement split the Brotherhood wide open. Many members rejected Collins' wait-and-see policy, arguing that the Republic was now a living entity, established and ratified by the people's votes. Whatever practical advantages the Treaty might offer, it was a betrayal of the Republic, the nation, and the IRB itself. On January 21 Cork IRB officers passed a resolution condemning the Supreme Council's statements of December 12 and January 12 as violations of the IRB Constitution. It branded members of the Supreme Council who authorized these statements as unfit for office and called on them to resign. A number of like-minded circles subsequently broke away from the Supreme Council and ceased to function.[15]

On the political front, a January meeting of the Sinn Fein Executive revealed a deep split, and it was decided to hold a special convention in February to consider the party's future.[16] Political turmoil aggravated serious economic problems. In the first two months of the new year, dockers, canal workers, and farm laborers struck against wage reductions, while another series of strikes tied up the railways. Intervention by the Northern and Southern governments was necessary to arrange a settlement between railway workers and management. With both parts of Ireland hard hit by economic depression, unemployment remained high.[17]

Spurred by workers' mounting discontent and Sinn Fein's inability to resolve economic problems, the Labor Party entered the political arena. At a special conference on February 21, party delegates called for a plebiscite on the Treaty and declared that Labor would take part in the next national election. Tom Johnson, the party's secretary, praised the Treaty but asserted that neither faction of Sinn Fein could achieve the ideal of a workers' republic. The time had come for Labor to enter national politics to attain this goal.[18]

Although the Provisional Government had more than enough trouble in Southern Ireland, renewed violence in Belfast forced Collins to turn his attention to Ulster. In an attempt to resolve the Northern problem, or at least relieve the sufferings of Catholics there, he held several meetings with Craig. On January 21 Churchill brought the two leaders together at the Colonial Office, and after some discussion they reached an agreement. By its terms, the Boundary Commission was to be set aside and the boundary determined by mutual agreement. Collins was to lift the Belfast boycott (which he did on January 24), and Craig promised to facilitate the return of Catholic workers to the Belfast shipyards as soon as economic recovery permitted. In the meantime, his government would increase relief for the jobless. The two men decided to meet again and to cooperate fully with each other and Churchill to solve mutual problems.[19]

The Craig-Collins pact was generally applauded in Britain and Ireland, but Northern nationalists were uneasy, fearing Collins' concessions would strengthen partition. When they voiced their alarm, Griffith gave them no encouragement; he would not jeopardize the Treaty for Ulster. Collins was more sympathetic, asserting he had made the pact to promote peace, but if it failed he was prepared to try stronger measures. Privately, however, Collins expressed some dissatisfaction with Ulster nationalists. If they expected help from the rest of Ireland, they should form a united front against the Belfast government.[20]

When Collins and Craig resumed discussions in Dublin early in February, their meeting quickly broke down over the question of boundary revision. Craig told reporters he had the British government's assurance that the Boundary Commission would make only slight changes. He had informed Collins in January he would agree to nothing more than this, and if North and South failed to agree, there would be no change at all. Now, however, Collins had produced maps which led Craig to the assumption that he "had already been promised almost half of Northern Ireland, including the counties of Fermanagh and Tyrone, large parts of Armagh and Down, Derry City, and Enniskillen, and Newry." Craig wanted peace, but not at that price.[21]

After consulting his colleagues, Collins also issued a statement. Refusing to admit any ambiguity in the Boundary Commission's functions, he said the question was one of local option, and majorities must rule. Anti-partitionists were in a clear majority in two of the six counties and in large parts of Down, Derry, and Armagh. Because the boundary question was an Irish matter that could be settled without British interference and because an agreed boundary was preferable to an imposed one, Collins had been willing to set aside the Boundary Commission; but Ulster had not responded generously. The South would not coerce the northeast, but it would not allow the Belfast government to coerce or discriminate against its nationalist minority. The real solution to the problem was unification, and Collins called for an all-Ireland parliament to draft a constitution for the whole country.[22]

Obviously, Collins was trying to mix threats and conciliation to secure a united Ireland. However, the stubborn resistance of Ulster Unionists and their British allies, coupled with the lack of clarity in the Treaty's

Boundary Commission clause, were formidable obstacles to the success of his policy. Yet despite its handicaps, the only alternatives to Collins' approach were inaction or coercion.

When British and Irish representatives met in London for further procedural talks on February 5–6, Lloyd George expressed the view that, for the moment, nothing could improve the Ulster situation. He had always doubted that direct negotiations could settle the boundary question and felt only the Boundary Commission could resolve it. Collins now took the same position, contending that Ulster should exercise its exclusion option as soon as the British ratified the Treaty. Boundary revision could then be carried out quickly, bringing Northern nationalists under Dublin's protection and reducing the risk of conflict. The British held, however, that Ulster's option should not be exercised until after Parliament ratified the Irish Constitution and officially recognized the Free State. With the help of their chief legal advisers, Sir Gordon Hewart and Hugh Kennedy, the two governments eventually reached agreement on procedure. The Irish Free State Agreement Bill would legalize the Treaty and the transfer of powers to the Provisional Government, and authorize the election of a Provisional Parliament to enact the Free State Constitution. Final ratification of the Treaty would be deferred until the British confirmed the Free State Constitution; only then would Ulster be allowed formally to exclude itself from the Free State.[23]

Lloyd George's pessimism about Ulster was fully justified; in fact, the situation immediately grew worse. On February 8 the IRA carried out a series of raids across the border, kidnaping forty-three Unionists. Their object was to force the Belfast government to reprieve three IRA members who were under sentence of death and to release some recently arrested Monaghan Volunteers.[24] The sequel to the raids was an outbreak of violence along the frontier, which reached its height on February 11 in the Free State town of Clones, where an armed clash left one IRA officer and four Ulster police dead.[25] Border outrages caused the Northern government to tighten security and appeal for British troops to guard danger points. The British government agreed to reinforce the police along the frontier, and it halted troop evacuation of Southern Ireland on February 13. Churchill warned Collins that unless he could preserve order on his side of the line, Parliament might demand that British troops do so, or the Ulster Unionists might take such action themselves. He coupled this warning with an assurance that Britain still stood by the Treaty.[26] The Provisional Government quickly disavowed the border raids, and Collins soon secured the release of the Unionist hostages, while Craig, in turn, released the Monaghan IRA men. But from February on, the border was strongly defended by the Special Constabulary, supported by large numbers of British troops.[27]

In Southern Ireland, February was a month of frenetic political activity as both factions of Sinn Fein vied for popular support. The Republicans opened their campaign for the anticipated election on the Treaty with a mass meeting in Dublin on February 12. The Free Staters quickly responded in kind, and on succeeding Sundays rallies were held up and down the country, with both sides making exaggerated claims and charges designed to win votes.

On February 21 the Sinn Fein Ard Fheis opened in Dublin, after a sharp campaign for delegates by the anti-Treaty faction.[28] De Valera, still president of the party, told some 2,500 delegates that an open organizational split was preferable to spurious unity and he urged support for a Republican resolution. Griffith, on the other hand, asked for approval of the Treaty and recognition of the people's right to accept or reject it. Collins appealed for unity to promote national reconstruction and unification. He wanted the people's verdict on the Treaty, but an election could be postponed if his party were not obstructed in its work. Although there were impressive demonstrations of Republican support during the convention, the delegates' overriding desire was unity. This was preserved when the party's leaders hammered out an agreement which the convention enthusiastically approved. Under its terms, the Ard Fheis would stand adjourned for three months. During this interval, Sinn Fein's officer board would act as a standing committee for the party; no adverse vote in the Dail would require the government's resignation; no general election would be held; and when one was held, the Constitution, in its final form, would be submitted to the electorate with the Treaty.[29]

Both de Valera and Collins felt that they had good reason to be satisfied with this pact. De Valera knew that an early election would mean an overwhelming victory for the Treaty. The IRA could prevent an election, but this would mean civil war, which he dreaded. De Valera did not believe Collins could deliver the Republican Constitution he promised, and he felt that once the people understood the limitations the Constitution placed on Irish sovereignty, they would reject the Treaty. Like de Valera, Collins thought an attempt to force an election would precipitate civil war, and he too was repelled by this prospect. Delay would allow the Provisional Government to demonstrate the reality of the powers conferred by the Treaty. It would also give Collins time to draft a Republican Constitution, and if he could win British approval for it, there was a good chance of averting civil war.[30] Some astute British observers realized that Collins had given away very little in the pact, and extreme Republicans took a pessimistic view of it. Like Griffith, they opposed delaying a showdown on the Treaty, but also like Griffith, they had no choice but to accept a compromise made by Collins and de Valera and approved by the public.[31]

Alarmed by the agreement, Cope wired Churchill it could threaten the Treaty. The Irish Committee discussed the matter and Churchill invited Griffith and Collins to London to review the situation. Accompanied by Duggan and Hugh Kennedy, but not by Collins, Griffith met with the British on February 26. They expressed the belief that postponement of the election strengthened the anti-Treaty forces, and voiced the fear that de Valera and not the Treaty party would get the legal authority Parliament was in process of conferring on the Provisional Government. Griffith proved equal to the occasion. He maintained that submitting the Constitution to the voters would nullify any protest by de Valera that the British could throw out the Constitution if the Irish people had not seen it in final form when they approved the Treaty. He also pointed out that since an election could not be held at once, the actual delay resulting from the pact was only six weeks. The agreement gave the Irish Cabinet security in office for three months, and during this period the Sinn Fein organization would remain neutral, while each party set up its own electoral machinery. Griffith claimed his party had won the best of the bargain, adding that some of de Valera's followers agreed.

Chamberlain wanted to know what de Valera would do if the voters endorsed the Treaty. Griffith replied that de Valera had said he would not oppose the expressed will of the people. If he opposed the government constitutionally, all would be well. In any case, the government intended to run the country. Chamberlain then inquired about the IRA's attitude, and Griffith claimed that the bulk of the army was remaining aloof from politics and following the orders of the minister of defense. The Irish representatives maintained that they could run the country and deal with disorder. Eventually, the British agreed to accept the pact. In return, Griffith was to issue a statement declaring that the Provisional Government had no secret agreement with de Valera, that the pact strengthened its authority, and that the draft constitution would need the British government's informal approval before it was submitted to the Dail.

Chamberlain reminded Griffith that it was important to placate the Southern Unionists because of their strong support in the House of Lords. Griffith and Duggan pledged to do their best in this regard. Churchill announced that troop evacuation would be resumed (after its two-week suspension) and that the units that would remain until June would be quickly withdrawn once the Free State was formally established. In the ensuing discussion about Ulster, the British pressed for a meeting of the two Irish governments as soon as possible. After some conversation about the Free State Agreement Bill (then before Parliament), the conference ended.[32] Churchill expressed the government's satisfaction with the meeting the next day in the House of Commons.[33]

Ten days before, he had introduced the Irish Free State Agreement

Bill in Parliament. In explaining its purpose, Churchill emphasized the importance of arming the Provisional Government with legal power. The bill also provided for an Irish election for three reasons. First, the people must render their verdict on the Treaty. Second, an adequate constituent assembly must be chosen; the present assembly simply would not serve. Third, the Provisional Government needed a popular mandate for the powers it exercised. In the unlikely event that de Valera's party won the election, Ireland's position would be weakened by its internal divisions and repudiation of the Treaty, while Britain's would be strengthened by its demonstrated good faith.[34]

Unappeased by Churchill, Unionist diehards mounted another assault on the government. Churchill did his best to defend Griffith and Collins, but he declared that British tolerance had definite limits and that the government would not permit an Irish republic under any circumstances.[35] After amending the bill to provide for a deferred election, the Commons passed it, and the measure became law on March 31.[36]

Chapter 12
Confrontation and Crisis: March 1922

As the Free State began to take root, the IRA translated vocal opposition into action. In February, Ernie O'Malley's 2d Southern Division repudiated the authority of both GHQ and Dail Eireann and carried out a series of arms raids. A sensational attack on an RIC barracks at Clonmel in South Tipperary on February 26 resulted in the seizure of a sizable quantity of guns, ammunition, and stores.[1] Some police were killed and wounded in these raids; but when Churchill complained about the Clonmel affair, Collins told him the British government had been careless.[2] And so it had. The British army could take care of itself but the demoralized and disgruntled RIC could not. In April, Churchill admitted that 600 rifles had been taken from the RIC since the Treaty.[3]

Hard on the heels of O'Malley's open defiance came a dangerous confrontation in Limerick. The British were scheduled to evacuate the city on February 23, and this posed a serious problem. Limerick was in a highly strategic position, commanding the Shannon estuary and vital to control of southwest Ireland. However, the local IRA unit was anti-Treaty and its commander had publicly repudiated GHQ's authority.[4] GHQ ordered General Michael Brennan, the pro-Treaty commander of the 1st Western Division, to move from Clare into Limerick and occupy the British posts until loyal elements of the local brigade could be organized to garrison them. O'Malley would have none of this, and anti-Treaty troops converged on the city with those of Brennan as the British began to pull out.

Churchill anxiously wired Cope, asking whether the Provisional Government intended to fight or parley,[5] but Cope was unable to give a definite answer. De Valera refrained from public comment but privately urged Mulcahy to do his best to settle the affair peacefully.[6] Mulcahy was doing just that. However, he had to contend not only with the firebrands like O'Malley but also with prominent Free Staters who were equally opposed to compromise. Griffith felt a clash with the Republicans was inevitable and that postponement would only make it worse. During the Limerick crisis, he told his fellow ministers that if they did not act firmly, they would be known as "the greatest poltroons in Irish history." Collins at first supported Griffith, and so did the rest of the Cabinet (except Mulcahy). Mulcahy urged conciliation, contending that the government's troops were neither psychologically nor militarily prepared for war. Mulcahy knew that Liam Lynch was eager to avoid conflict, and he quickly won Collins over to a policy of compromise, leaving the other ministers no choice but to acquiesce.[7]

Mediating at GHQ's request, Lynch and Oscar Traynor (O/C Dublin Brigade) worked out an agreement that was accepted by both sides in Limerick and confirmed by GHQ. The police barracks were handed over to the city government, the two military barracks were occupied by local troops loyal to GHQ, and all other units evacuated the city. On March 11 the evacuation was completed and peace returned to Limerick.[8] Despite Griffith's aversion to compromise, peaceful resolution of the crisis kept Limerick out of Republican control and avoided an armed clash which could easily have wrecked the Treaty settlement.

Although disappointed at the Provisional Government's reluctance to assert its authority, Churchill tactfully wrote Collins on March 14:

> You seem to have liquidated the Limerick situation in one way or another. No doubt you know your own business best, and thank God *you* have got to manage it and not we. An adverse decision by the convention of the Irish Republican Army (so called) would, however, be a very grave event at the present juncture. I presume you are quite sure there is no danger of this.[9]

Churchill's concern was shared by the Irish government, which prohibited the IRA convention and thereby precipitated another crisis. On Mulcahy's recommendation, the Cabinet had given permission for the convention on February 27, but new information from the minister of defense caused the Cabinet to reverse its decision on March 15. Mulcahy explained that extremists were working to get the IRA to repudiate GHQ and prevent an election on the Treaty. He had no hope of controlling the convention and could not guarantee that it would not set up an autonomous military authority. On the evening of the 15th, the Cabinet's decision and the reasons for it were communicated to a meeting of senior officers who were preparing the convention's agenda. President Griffith's order, prohibiting the convention on the grounds that it sought to remove the army from the Dail's control, was published the next day.[10]

At this point, pro-Treaty officers withdrew their support from the convention, but anti-Treaty army leaders decided to proceed with their plans. Fifty-two officers, including Lynch, O'Connor, Mellows, and O'Malley, issued a summons to all IRA units to meet in Dublin on March 26. Efforts at compromise failed, and on March 23 Mulcahy declared that the proposed convention was a "sectional" assembly, called against GHQ's orders, and that any man who attended it would sever his connection with the IRA.[11]

Responding to the government on behalf of the conventioneers, whom he claimed represented 80 percent of the army, Rory O'Connor denounced the Treaty. In voting for it, he told a Dublin press conference, a majority of Dail members had violated their oaths to the Republic, just as the defense minister had broken his pledge to maintain the IRA as a Republican force by enlisting its members in the Free State army. O'Connor declared that the IRA repudiated the Dail's authority and would henceforth decide its own policy. When a reporter inquired if this meant a military dictatorship, O'Connor answered: "You can take it that way if you like." An American journalist pointed out that the IRA would be taking on a grave responsibility if it tried to impose its ideas on an unwilling people, but O'Connor contended that the responsibility would be no greater than that taken by the leaders of the 1916 rising. The people, he said, did not understand the Treaty, but the IRA did. Even if the Volunteers had not read and analyzed it, they were right to oppose it, because they were not going into the British Empire.[12]

A total of 223 delegates attended the convention, which met in private session at Dublin's Mansion House. Reaffirming allegiance to the Republic, the delegates vested control of the army in an elected executive and empowered it to draft a constitution, which would be submitted when the convention met again on April 9. The question of establishing a military dictatorship was also referred to the executive.[13] On March 28 the executive proclaimed that the minister of defense and the chief of staff no longer exercised any authority over the IRA and that recruiting for the Provisional Government's military and police forces was to stop. At the same time, the executive ordered all IRA units to reaffirm allegiance to the Republic on April 2.[14]

The most important fact to emerge from the army split was that a large majority of its members opposed the Treaty. The seven commanders who signed the convention summons headed units representing 55–65 percent of the pre-truce Volunteers. Together, Lynch's and O'Malley's divisions made 35–40 percent of the IRA's strength in July 1921, and officers in these divisions were almost solidly anti-Treaty. British military intelligence estimated that at least 75 percent of the IRA in Munster opposed the Treaty, and in Dublin the proportion was much the same.[15] The fact that opposition was strongest among the units that had been most active in the struggle against the British only made the situation worse for the government. For obvious reasons, Collins and Mulcahy could not admit that the IRA was largely anti-Treaty, but the British government had only to heed its own agents to know the truth.

The IRA lost no time in asserting its independence after the convention. On the night of March 29, executive forces smashed the presses of the *Freeman's Journal* on the grounds that it had published a misleading account of the convention's proceedings, which had been distributed by the Free State GHQ.[16] While the newspaper's account is open to question, the IRA's reprisal underscored its contempt for civil liberty. On March 29 the rebels also seized a ship bound from Cork to Britain with a cargo of arms and ammunition. Collins was extremely upset by this incident, suspecting the British of trying to encourage an Irish civil war for their own advantage. However, Churchill was as disturbed as Collins by the event, and he issued orders for strict precautions to prevent such losses in the future.[17] But this tardy action could neither dispel Collins' mistrust nor diminish the IRA's jubilation.

When the IRA repudiated the Dail's authority, it put de Valera in a dilemma. He had often proclaimed his support of the supremacy of civil authority and in January had appealed to senior army officers to remain obedient to the new government. In the weeks that followed, the ex-president remained free of any involvement with the IRA so that he might find a way to resolve the problems that were dividing the army and Sinn Fein. But while he took no part in the convention, and privately disagreed with its declaration of independence, de Valera was aware of the danger of splitting the anti-Treaty forces and probably felt the army's bold action would strengthen his hand. In the end, Republicanism triumphed over constitutionalism, and de Valera defended the convention. He later regretted he had not condemned it, but by that time he was a prisoner of the events which his support of the IRA had helped set in motion.[18]

Early in March the ex-president organized a new Republican party to contest the forthcoming general election.[19] Following this, he embarked on a speaking tour of Munster, where he painted a frightening picture of the future if the people accepted the Treaty.

At Dungarvan, County Waterford, on March 16, de Valera declared that the Treaty "barred the way to independence with the blood of fellow-Irishmen," for its acceptance would mean that freedom could only be won by civil war. Warning the people that if they did not fight today they must fight tomorrow, he proclaimed: "When you are in a good fighting position, then fight on."[20]

On St. Patrick's Day at Carrick-on-Suir, County Tipperary, the ex-president told a large audience, which included 700 young men of the IRA:

> If the Treaty was accepted the fight for freedom would still go on; and the Irish people, instead of fighting foreign soldiers, would have to fight the Irish soldiers of an Irish Government set up by Irishmen. If the Treaty was not rejected, perhaps it was over the bodies of the young men he saw around him that day that the fight for Irish freedom may be fought.[21]

The same day, at Thurles, County Tipperary, de Valera spoke to a crowd composed mainly of Volunteers, about 200 of whom carried rifles.

If they accepted the Treaty, and if the Volunteers of the future tried to complete the work the Volunteers of the last four years had been attempting, they would have to complete it, not over the bodies of foreign soldiers, but over the dead bodies of their own countrymen.

They would have to wade through Irish blood, through the blood of the soldiers of the Irish Government, and through, perhaps, the blood of some of the members of the Government in order to get Irish freedom.[22]

On March 19 at Killarney, County Kerry, again in the presence of armed men, de Valera asserted:

Therefore, in future, in order to achieve freedom, if our Volunteers continue, and I hope they will continue until the goal is reached—if we continue on that movement which was begun when the Volunteers were started, and we suppose this Treaty is ratified by your votes, then these men, in order to achieve freedom, will have, [as] I said yesterday, to march over the dead bodies of their own brothers. They will have to wade through Irish blood.[23]

It was in this speech that de Valera declared "the people had never a right to do wrong."

These speeches were widely stigmatized as incitements to civil war and assassination.[24] Griffith vowed that he would not sit in the same room with de Valera until he withdrew this incitement.[25] Collins pointed out that a leader must not be unmindful of his words, especially in time of crisis. He also observed that

while it was perfectly justifiable for any body of Irishmen, no matter how small, to rise up and make a stand against their country's enemy, it is not justifiable for a minority to oppose the wishes of the majority of their own countrymen, except by constitutional means.[26]

The ex-president and his supporters protested that his speeches were neither threats nor incitements but responsible and fair warnings. If the people accepted the Treaty, the nation's pledged word, backed by the full force of an Irish government, would bar the way to freedom.[27] One of de Valera's biographers has written that he was "merely syllogizing" in these speeches,[28] while others have echoed de Valera's own defense that he was only warning and prophesying, not inciting. They find no evidence that his speeches stirred up violence, as his critics alleged. Instead, they indict British politicians, along with Griffith and Collins, for intimidating Ireland with threats of war if the Treaty were not accepted.[29]

The historian's verdict can only be that de Valera's remarks, whatever their intent, were irresponsible and dangerous. The Irish people were only too well aware of the threat of civil war and needed no warnings about it. Certainly, excitable young men with guns in their hands did not need the kind of warning de Valera gave. For a leader of his stature to utter prophecies of bloody domestic conflict only increased its likelihood. Only two months before, de Valera had declared: "I hope that nobody will talk of fratricidal strife. That is all nonsense. We have got a nation that knows how to conduct itself. As far as I can on this side it will be our policy always."[30] By ignoring his own counsel, de Valera encouraged others to do the same—with guns as well as words.

On occasion, de Valera could still reassert his commitment to constitutional and democratic government:

> Everybody regards the will of the Irish people as supreme. I do for one. Not merely do I say I for one hold that this nation, taking away all force, should have the right to do with itself what it wants, but I would say further, that even in the circumstances of the moment—even with the threat of war—the Irish people would have the right, even [sic] if they wanted to, to avoid war by taking another course.[31]

But the ex-president's inner struggle to uphold constitutional principles was a losing one. Two weeks before he made the statement just quoted, he asserted that the people had no right to do wrong. Two weeks after it, he declared that if the army could save Ireland from the calamities which would arise from acceptance of the Treaty, he would consider the army justified in doing so.[32]

Despite his militant rhetoric, de Valera made no attempt to assume leadership of the IRA. He disagreed too much with its methods and its contempt for civil authority to ally himself with its extremists openly. But he hoped that their defiance would cause Griffith and Collins to scrap the Treaty, rather than precipitate civil war. If the government backed down, de Valera would be ready, with his plan of external association, to reunite the nationalist movement. But he misjudged the situation badly. Griffith and Collins would fight rather than abandon the Treaty, and IRA militants were not interested in any compromise peace plan. Since the ex-president refused to lead them, the extremists soon ignored him, having no further use for him except as a symbol. Having done his best to rally the people to the Republican cause and to encourage resistance to the Treaty, de Valera could hardly protest when bolder spirits pushed him aside. But in the end, both he and Ireland paid a high price for his support of the IRA.

As de Valera abandoned his role as national leader, Collins moved to fill it. On March 5 he implored foes of the Treaty to forswear armed resistance before it was too late for them and for Ireland:

> War, though necessary and noble, for necessary and noble ends, has terrible effects incidental to it, not only material ruin, but moral effects when prolonged unrighteously; a tendency to lose balance and judgment, to

forget or misinterpret the real object of the national struggle, to grow to believe that strife, even fratricidal strife, is noble in itself. Such things must cease as soon as freedom is secured or the nation will perish.[33]

In Cork, a week later, he made a moving appeal for a common effort:

We have a chance now of giving our people a better life, we have a chance of doing the things that the people require. We have a chance of securing that the people shall no longer live the life of beasts. We have a chance of ending our slums. We have a chance of ending the hovels of some of our country places. We have a chance now, not by travelling any soft road, God knows, but by a hard, united effort to make Ireland something for the next generation, which it was not for ourselves.[34]

In the same vein, he wrote:

Believe me, the Treaty gives us the one opportunity we may ever get in our history for going forward to our ideal of a free independent Ireland. This cannot be gained without very much work yet—very hard work and perhaps more than hard work. And it is not by dissipation of the national energy that we can gain this. It is not by acts of suppression and it is not by denial of liberty that we can reach liberty.[35]

Struggling to reconcile opposing forces and exploit the opportunities offered by the Treaty, Collins showed the same capacity for growth that had marked his career as a guerrilla leader and negotiator.

Frustrated by problems in Southern Ireland, Collins was tormented by the sufferings of Northern nationalists. The IRA was partly to blame for the violence there, but the Ulster Special Constabulary bore the main responsibility. Many "Specials" were fanatic Orangemen who equated Catholicism with disloyalty and maintenance of law and order with terrorism. Griffith likened the part-time, undisciplined "B Specials" to an army of London slum dwellers, while Lloyd George thought the Italian *fascisti* a more exact analogy.[36] Instead of trying to curb violence, the Specials often incited it, with the aim of cowing or expelling "subversive elements."[37] Catholics fought back, and sometimes took the offensive, but their position was hopeless. Unionists outnumbered them two to one (three to one in Belfast), controlled the machinery of government, and were supported by Britain.

Although deeply disturbed by the Ulster violence, the British government seemed unable to control it. The Cabinet's Irish Committee considered introducing martial law in the worst districts of Belfast, but both Craig and Macready opposed this step. Craig claimed it would make loyalists look as bad as their enemies, and Macready did not think it practical or necessary. The Special Powers Bill, just passed by the Belfast

Parliament, would give the police ample authority, in Macready's opinion, and martial law would have little more value, unless drastically enforced.[38]

Under the terms of the draconian Special Powers Bill, *habeas corpus* was suspended, and a special court of summary jurisdiction was set up to try specified offenses. Penalties were stringent, that is, death for bomb throwing and flogging for unauthorized possession of arms or explosives. Moreover, the minister of home affairs was empowered to do whatever might be necessary to preserve the peace, issuing additional regulations under the new law for this purpose and delegating his powers to any police officer. The bill overruled individual rights in the name of state security, leaving the ordinary citizen no legal protection against search, seizure, or imprisonment.[39]

Protesting bitterly to Churchill, Collins called this bill a new means to persecute Northern nationalists. If it became law, the consequences would be awful; the Provisional Government would be forced to take countermeasures to protect fellow nationalists and divisions between North and South would be deepened.[40] Notwithstanding Collins' objections, the king assented to the bill on April 7 and Craig's government soon employed its extraordinary powers.

Collins' fears for Ulster Catholics were heightened by knowledge that Sir Henry Wilson was advising the Belfast government on police matters. Upon retiring from the army early in 1922, Wilson had accepted an Ulster seat in the House of Commons, where he could freely attack the government. He also agreed to serve as an adviser to Craig's government. Wilson opposed using undisciplined Protestants as special police, recommending instead that the new police force should be organized on military lines and impartially administered. This plan had considerable merit (in fact, Macready had already urged such an approach) but unfortunately, it was never carried out. The regular police force acquired greater effectiveness but not impartiality, and rigorous discipline was never applied to the B Specials. Ironically, many nationalists blamed Wilson for the excesses of the police.[41]

In late March the government decided to invite Craig and Collins to London for another try at peacemaking. Both men accepted and a conference headed by Churchill, Craig, Collins, and Griffith met on March 29–30. The result was a new Craig-Collins pact, providing that both Irish governments would cooperate to restore peace in unsettled areas of the North. To this end, special police in mixed religious districts of Belfast were to include equal numbers of Catholics and Protestants, with special arrangements for other city districts. Strict regulations were to be imposed to ensure that the police did not abuse their powers, and arrangements were to be made to guarantee fair trials and reduce sectarian animosity. IRA activities in the Six Counties were to cease; once this happened, the special police throughout Northern Ireland were to be organized like those in Belfast. Refugees were to be restored to their homes, and release of political prisoners was to be negotiated by the two Irish governments. The British government was to ask Parliament for £500,000 for relief works in Belfast; one-third of this sum was to be used for the benefit of Catholics, and the Belfast government was to do its utmost to secure reemployment of expelled workers. On the all-important question of the boundary, it was agreed that during Ulster's option month, representatives of both Irish governments would determine whether any means could be devised to secure unity and, if not, whether agreement could be reached on the border without recourse to the Boundary Commission.[42]

The new pact was widely acclaimed. The Unionist *Belfast Telegraph* endorsed it wholeheartedly and urged moderates to implement it. Other British and Irish newspapers took the same line. Craig wrote Collins, expressing optimism about the agreement's prospects and asserting he was carrying out both its spirit and letter. Griffith declared that the pact would lead to a united Ireland. Collins was more circumspect, observing that everyone must wait and see how the agreement worked out and that it was nothing to be enthusiastic over.[43]

This cautious attitude proved justified. The pact changed nothing, and within a month Craig and Collins were blaming each other for its failure. But the real blame lay with extremists on both sides of the border. Given Unionist prejudices and economic depression, Craig had little chance of getting jobs for Catholics, and their implacable hostility compounded his difficulties. Collins' freedom of action was likewise circumscribed by the opposition of hard-line nationalists to any accommodation with the Northern government. Moreover, he himself was impatient for results from the pact, and when they were not forthcoming, Collins tried fighting fire with fire. Instead of trying to restrain the IRA, he encouraged both its factions to step up their campaign against the North, in the hope that this would check persecution of Catholics. Like Craig, Collins wanted peace. But both men were too much the prisoners of their heritage to implement a policy that might have secured it.

IRA planning for offensive action against Northern Ireland began before the army convention and continued until June, with Mulcahy, O'Duffy, Lynch, and Frank Aiken (commander of the IRA's 4th Northern Division) as protagonists. Apparently, Collins was not directly involved, although it is certain his associates would not have embarked on such a dangerous enterprise without his blessing. According to the agreed strategy, the IRA in the North was to be reinforced with men and guns for attacks on Crown forces. Mulcahy could not supply these weapons directly because Free State arms were provided by the British and could be identified if captured. So Lynch and O'Malley agreed to furnish the guns for the campaign, on the understanding that the Provisional Government would replace them with British-supplied weapons. Thus Collins was technically correct when he assured Churchill that no Provisional Government arms would be used against Ulster.[44]

Macready voiced the suspicion that Collins and his followers were involved in the IRA's activities in Ulster, and some Cabinet members shared this view.[45] However, the British government did nothing. It would not be easy to prove Collins' complicity, and British ministers were not eager to try. They had staked their political reputations on the Treaty and were determined to make it work. While it was more than willing to help settle differences between North and South, the British government would not intervene directly in Ulster unless the situation got completely out of hand or the IRA launched an invasion.

Their awareness of this attitude doubtless encouraged Collins and Mulcahy to try coercion against the North. They also hoped that joint action in this area would help reunite the IRA. At the same time, both of them realized that if they went too far, Britain would be compelled to intervene; this probably explains why so much talk produced so little action. A big offensive was scheduled for early May, but it was postponed. When the offensive did take place, it turned out to be only a series of small-scale actions, which received no support from GHQ, despite O'Duffy's prior approval and promises of aid. And the so-called invasion of the Pettigo-Belleek triangle in late May was nothing more than a minor incident. In the end, only a few men were sent North to work with local IRA units, and probably only a few of the guns destined for Ulster ever got there.[46]

Despite their unwillingness to press operations against the Six Counties, the involvement of Free State military leaders in such schemes was a reckless venture. Attacks by the IRA only laid Catholics open to vicious reprisals which the IRA could not prevent. Moreover, such attacks could have escalated into a war which would have wrecked the Treaty, and this was the last thing Collins and Mulcahy wanted. Whatever subterfuge they used to mask their cooperation with Republicans, they were in constant danger of exposure by their allies—and were, in fact, dangerously compromised by statements Lynch and Mellows made in April.[47] The Republicans had nothing to lose by attacking the North, the Free Staters everything. Collins' anguish over the sufferings of fellow nationalists and Mulcahy's desire for army unity led them up a blind alley. Only a timely retreat saved them from the consequences of their irresponsibility.

Although March was an ordeal, the Provisional Government made real progress. By the end of the month the British had completed evacuation of Connaught and Munster, except Cork. Disbandment of the RIC began on March 29, and the Dublin police were ready for incorporation in the Civic Guards. Under Sir John Anderson's skillful supervision, Irish ministers gradually assumed control of Dublin Castle's administrative machinery. The Irish Free State Agreement Act legalized the Provisional Government's position, and on April 1 an order in council formally transferred control of the Revenue departments and set guidelines for the transfer of other powers. Regular military and police forces were being organized, and the Dail's court system functioned effectively. The government ended a railway strike, averted one by postal workers, and persuaded the British to postpone closing the Haulbowline dockyard. Great difficulties lay ahead, but the outlines of solid achievement were visible as March turned to April.

Chapter 13
What Price Peace?
April-May 1922

On April 9 the IRA adopted a constitution that committed it to maintain the Republic and the rights and liberties of the Irish people, and to serve an established Republican government that upheld these aims. Lynch, O'Connor, Mellows, O'Malley, and twelve other officers were elected to a new executive, which in turn appointed an Army Council of seven men and named Lynch chief of staff. After discussing the proposal to set up a military dictatorship, dissolve the governments in both parts of Ireland, and prevent an election on the Treaty, the convention rejected it by a narrow margin and again referred the question to the executive. The executive decided not to declare a dictatorship or try to overthrow the existing governments, but it opposed any election on the Treaty in the near future.[1]

Mellows stated the executive's terms for army reunification on April 14 in a letter to the Dail. The Republic must be maintained, with the Dail as its government and the IRA under the control of its own executive. The Civic Guards must be disbanded, leaving the IRA to police Southern Ireland, and the Dail must pay all the army's expenses. Finally, there must be no election on the Treaty while the British threat of war remained. The letter evoked no response, despite its warning that this was probably the Dail's last chance to avert civil war.[2]

On the night of April 13 the executive occupied Dublin's Four Courts, the seat of the country's highest judicial tribunals, as a military headquarters and its forces soon seized other buildings in the capital. The government's only response was to occupy several important buildings with its own forces.[3] Outside the capital, the IRA seized a number of barracks held by Dail troops, and in some instances fighting took place. Early in May there was a sizable skirmish in Kilkenny when Free State troops defeated a Republican attempt to take over the town. By May 5 military clashes between the two army factions had left eight killed and forty-nine wounded, over 60 percent of them Free State troops.[4]

The IRA attacked barracks because it lacked accommodations and supplies; its members turned to robbery because they needed money. The executive justified raids on banks and post offices by claiming that the government had not kept its promise to pay all army debts incurred before the convention split. The IRA also commandeered supplies and transport, mainly through enforcement of the Belfast boycott.[5] Robbery and commandeering inevitably intensified public resentment against the Republicans.

While the IRA was the government's major problem, there were others almost as pressing. Unsettled political conditions gave rise to all kinds of disorder. There was a sharp increase in crime, especially armed robbery. In some areas, farmers withheld land-purchase annuities from the government, and there were many cases of cattle stealing and land seizure. As in 1920, Ireland seemed threatened with a land war, but now there was no united national leadership to prevent it. Closely allied with agrarian disturbance was the opportunistic Marxism practiced by some workers, who formed soviets to run local businesses. Most of these communistic experiments quickly collapsed, but agrarian discontent was not so easily disposed of and caused considerable trouble before a combination of force and concessions smothered it in 1923.[6] Fortunately for the government, neither the Republicans nor the Labor Party exploited economic discontent. The Republicans concentrated on political issues while most labor leaders refused to support violent assaults on the capitalist system. Even so, things were bad enough for the new regime.

The government's difficulties in trying to maintain order were matched by those it encountered in trying to lay its case before the voters. The IRA had no intention of allowing free speech for "traitors." At Castlebar, County Mayo, and Killarney, County Kerry, railway lines and roads were blocked and telegraph lines cut to prevent Collins from addressing meetings during April. When these tactics failed, Republicans in the audience caused a commotion, fired shots, and shouted Collins down. Physical assault on the speaker was narrowly averted on both occasions. Following the stormy meeting at Castlebar, the local anti-Treaty IRA commander prohibited all meetings in the area, "solely in the interests of peace." Undeterred, Griffith announced he would speak as scheduled at Sligo on April 6. General Sean MacEoin, a hero of the Anglo-Irish war and a strong supporter of the Treaty, accompanied Griffith and ensured an orderly meeting by making a determined show of force.[7]

On April 5 Churchill reviewed the Irish situation for the Cabinet. He explained there was no reason to doubt the Provisional Government's good faith and every reason to believe the Irish people approved of the Treaty. But the Provisional Government seemed unable to control the IRA, which might try to overthrow it before an election could be held. If the Republicans staged a coup in Dublin, Macready would proclaim martial law and attack them, whatever the Provisional Government's attitude. On the other hand, if the anti-Treaty forces set up a government outside the capital and the Free State regime offered no resistance to the rebels, the British should hold Dublin and perhaps occupy other ports, while British flying columns should attack the centers of Republican authority. For Ulster's protection, the British army should hold the best military defense line in the North, presumably the water line from Dundalk (County Louth) to Ballyshannon (County Donegal). Intercourse with disaffected counties would be stopped by British orders, and foreign powers would be notified of the blockade. The juridical conditions of such a conflict would be much like those in the American Civil War, that is, military recognition for rebels in uniform but no recognition of Irish sovereignty or belligerent rights.[8]

In the discussion that followed Churchill's report, the ministers agreed that a major difficulty arose from the fact that Griffith and Collins considered it essential to avoid striking the first blow against the Republicans or taking any provocative action. British armed support would therefore prove disastrous to the Provisional Government. However, the Cabinet expressed approval of the prime minister's declaration

> that the British government could not allow the republican flag to fly in Ireland. A point might come when it would be necessary to tell Mr. Collins that if he was unable to deal with the situation the British Government would have to do so.

At length, the Cabinet approved the issue of arms requested by the Provisional Government and recommended by Macready and General Lord Cavan, the new chief of the Imperial General Staff. But Churchill was to formally call the Provisional Government's attention to the very serious state of affairs in Southern Ireland and ask how it proposed to deal with the situation. The Cabinet also ordered the appointment of a subcommittee of the Committee of Imperial Defense to consider what measures would be required to meet the contingencies specified by Churchill. To counter any coup that might be imminent, the Cabinet approved the army council's instructions to Macready. If a republic were declared outside Dublin, he was to forward to the War Office all the information he could obtain from the Provisional Government. But if a republic were declared in Dublin, he was to declare martial law and concentrate his forces in the city.[9]

On April 12 Churchill wrote Collins, informing him of the Cabinet's anxiety. He conceded that economic deterioration could aid the Provisional Government up to a point, by rousing all classes to defend their interests. But in the long run the government must assert its authority or perish. The Irish people had a right to expect such leadership, and history would never forgive a failure to provide it. While reiterating that the British government would fulfill the Treaty, whatever the risk, Churchill warned that it would exert all its influence against any violation of the agreement. Opposing any further delay of the election, he said he expected it not later than the first week of June.[10] At the end of the month Churchill wrote again, congratulating Collins and Griffith for defending the right of free speech and expressing his belief that Irish opinion continued to swing toward the Treaty. He was disturbed, however, about Collins' public hostility toward Craig, who was honestly trying to fulfill his agreement with Collins. Progress took time, and quarrels between the two Irish governments only aided extremists on both sides. The business of statesmen was to put aside personal feelings and work for the general good.[11]

While the British were discussing how to deal with civil war in Southern Ireland, the Irish were trying desperately to avert it. A final initiative by the IRB was one of several peacemaking efforts in April. When IRB leaders met in Dublin, Collins explained that the Supreme Council still felt the Free State Constitution might provide a basis for unity and he suggested appointment of a committee to study the document. Lynch rejected the proposal and threatened action unless he were guaranteed a Republican constitution. However, Florence O'Donoghue, a more moderate anti-Treaty officer, called for a committee to try to restore army unity, because the IRA split posed the gravest threat of civil war. After some discussion, a committee was appointed, but failed to reach agreement. Its pro-Treaty members maintained that nothing positive could be achieved until the Constitution became available, except to arrange a truce between the IRA's two factions, a move they deemed essential for the success of any peace negotiations. Lynch responded by repeating his demand for a Republican constitution, and the committee adjourned. Although it failed in its purpose, this discussion spurred creation of an open committee of IRA officers to carry on peace negotiations.[12]

Efforts to prevent civil war came from outside as well as inside the revolutionary movement. In their Easter statement, the Catholic bishops reaffirmed their support of the Treaty, but admitted the issue could only be settled by an election. Condemning those who had forsaken reason for force in the dispute, they asserted that there could be no question about the nation's supreme authority as long as the Dail and the Provisional Government acted in unison. Political leaders from both sides should meet again and at least agree "that the use of the revolver must cease, and the elections, the national expression of self-determination, be allowed to be held, free from all violence."[13] De Valera paid no attention to this pronouncement, except to rebuke the bishops for their failure to recognize the Dail's authority during the struggle with Britain. The *Republic of Ireland,* however, launched an assault on the hierarchy for its allegedly anti-nationalist record and condemned the bishops for again proving false to every tradition of national sovereignty.[14]

While conventions of taxpayers and farmers joined the bishops in denouncing violence and calling for free elections, the Labor Party matched words with action. Its executive demanded that the IRA recognize the people's sovereignty and that the Dail both assert its authority and enact the social reforms promised in 1919. To support its protest, the executive called a one-day general strike in the Twenty-six Counties. The strike came off as scheduled on April 24 and 75,000 workers took part.[15]

In another peace initiative, Dublin's lord mayor and its archbishop sponsored a conference in which Sinn Fein's leaders tried to resolve their differences with the aid of Labor representatives. However, the conference ended in failure on April 29. During its sessions, Griffith and Collins offered several proposals, one of which was a June election on both the Treaty and the Constitution. If his party won, Griffith promised to enact the Constitution, introduce full adult suffrage, and hold another election on the Constitution in final form. Alternatively, he offered a June election on the Treaty alone, followed by enactment of the Constitution and adult suffrage, with a second election to accept, reject, or amend the Constitution. De Valera rejected both plans, on the grounds that they involved acceptance of partition, an election on an invalid register, and a breach of the Ard Fheis agreement (which called for an election on the Treaty and the Constitution in its final form). Griffith and Collins then proposed a plebiscite on the Treaty within one month, with all persons over twenty-one eligible to vote, supervised by the Catholic clergy, the Labor Party, and other public bodies. But de Valera turned this down as well, alleging the plebiscite would be conducted with "Stone Age machinery."[16]

The ex-president argued that only British dictation required a June election, and he urged a six-month postponement. This delay would allow time for tempers to cool and fundamental differences to be appreciated, while national reconstruction was begun and normal conditions were restored. If the election were postponed, de Valera was willing to accept proposals such as those offered by the Labor Party. At the same time, he warned that there could be no free election while the threat of war with England remained, and he contended that a minority had the right forcibly to oppose any attempt to surrender national sovereignty. Not surprisingly, Griffith and Collins rejected de Valera's plan.[17]

The Labor Party's proposals were designed to avoid controversy by shelving the Treaty. Dail Eireann, as the supreme governing authority, was to coopt representatives of various interests to help frame a constitution and was to appoint a council of state that would govern the country and control the IRA. The Provisional Government would accept the transfer of powers from Britain, while a reunited IRA confined itself to preparations for national defense and a civil police force kept order under the supervision of local authorities.[18] However, none of these suggestions resolved the central issue of the Treaty; so Griffith and Collins vetoed them and ended the peace conference.

In the midst of the peacemaking efforts, the Dail reassembled on April 26, having met briefly and unproductively in February and March.[19] President Griffith made an opening statement in which he assailed the opposition for political obstruction and interference with civil liberties, as well as attempts to seduce the army and terrorize the people. He also denounced those who were trying to reimpose the Belfast boycott, for causing resumption of the Orange pogrom.[20]

On April 27 de Valera replied with an attack on the ministry for its refusal to acknowledge the Provisional Government's responsibility to the Dail. He also accused the government of dividing the army and trying to create a rival armed force. Discussion of the Dail's sovereignty reopened argument about the 1921 negotiations, and this produced an angry exchange between Griffith and de Valera over who was responsible for surrendering the Republic. Griffith also crossed swords with Childers, claiming he had spent his life in the British secret service and accusing him of inciting the assassination of the Treaty's Irish signatories. By the time the Speaker intervened to end the futile bickering, the two sides were further apart than ever.[21]

While the Dail wrangled, a handful of IRA officers tried to halt the drift to civil war. In late April, Collins conferred with Humphrey Murphy, a ranking anti-Treaty officer in Kerry, about working out a peace pact. Murphy in turn spoke with some of the more moderate anti-Treaty officers in Munster, including Sean O'Hegarty, Dan Breen, and Florence O'Donoghue, a leader in the IRB's abortive peacemaking efforts. O'Hegarty, Collins, and Mulcahy then decided to get a few officers from each side together, who appreciated the need for a workable agreement. The group came to terms on May 1 and gave its proposals to the press. The army committee's statement stressed the need for unity to avoid civil war, and proposed

1. Acceptance of the fact—admitted by all sides—that the majority of the people of Ireland are willing to accept the Treaty.
2. An agreed election, with a view to
3. Forming a Government which will have the confidence of the whole country.
4. Army unification on [the] above basis.[22]

The IRA executive denounced these proposals, even though three of its members had signed them. The army council declared that any agreement for army unification must be based upon maintenance of the Republic and be authorized by the executive; attempts to make "deals" with individual soldiers could only intensify disunity.[23]

Despite this criticism, the *ad hoc* committee decided to make the most of its initiative. On May 3 Sean O'Hegarty addressed the Dail as the committee's spokesman and appealed for adoption of its proposals. Pro-Treaty deputies moved their approval and the formation of a committee to consider them in detail. Although several anti-Treaty deputies attacked the proposals, their party agreed to creation of a joint committee to explore possible avenues of agreement. O'Hegarty urged the necessity of a truce, and the Dail agreed that its committee should try to make one. Next day, a four-day truce was arranged, and on May 8 it was extended indefinitely so that peacemaking efforts might continue.[24]

On May 10 the peace committee reported failure to the Dail. Its pro-Treaty members had insisted that any agreement contain some admission that the country accepted the Treaty, but the Republicans refused to allow this. The Dail adjourned for a week so that the committee might continue to seek a solution. On May 17 the committee again reported failure. Setting aside the Treaty, it had discussed the details of an election. Both sides agreed that each should nominate its candidates for a national panel and that every other interest should be free to contest the election. They also agreed to the formation of a coalition government after the election and to a second election if the coalition proved unworkable. But the Republicans rejected a proposal that the ratio of candidates be set at 5 to 3 or 6 to 4 against their party, because this would constitute an admission that the country approved the Treaty. They maintained that provision for a coalition government ensured executive stability and provision for another election covered future contingencies. At this point the conference broke down.[25]

The Dail engaged in a long discussion of the committee's reports, in the course of which de Valera offered to join a coalition government as long as this action did not commit his party or the people to the Treaty. Griffith replied that he wanted de Valera's cooperation if he would not obstruct an election on the Treaty, but not otherwise. Gavan Duffy contended that any election must be on the Treaty, whatever the two parties decided. A Republican deputy agreed and argued that the Treaty party needed no advance guarantee to be assured a majority of seats. Outside interests would contest the election and draw their strength from the anti-Treaty side of the national panel, so that supporters and opponents of the Treaty would be returned in proportion to their popular strength. The government would therefore lose nothing by making this symbolic concession to the Republicans. Collins made a strong defense of the government's position and the people's right to vote on the Treaty. At the same time, he made a final appeal for cooperation and pledged to carry out any agreement made with the opposition. De Valera reiterated that his party would enter the government if it was not compelled to accept the Treaty. The Dail adjourned, and Collins and de Valera met to seek an agreement.[26]

Their efforts were initially unsuccessful. Collins apparently insisted that his party have a working majority of at least fifteen in the new Dail, but de Valera refused to agree.[27] On May 19 Griffith moved that the Dail approve an election for June 16, asserting the question was whether Ireland would be governed by the ballot or the bullet. The opposition had rejected every offer of reasonable compromise, and the government would be guilty of the worst kind of cowardice if it submitted to a tyranny that was "just as mean and less supportable" than English rule. Other deputies supported or opposed Griffith's motion in a wide-ranging discussion, and it was eventually decided that Collins and de Valera should report on their conversations the next day.[28]

When the Dail assembled the following afternoon, an agreement made by Collins and de Valera was submitted for approval. Griffith amended his election motion to include it, the amended motion passed unanimously, and the Dail adjourned.[29] The terms of the Collins-de Valera pact were:

(1) That a National Coalition Panel for this Third Dail, representing both Parties in the Dail, and in the Sinn Fein Organisation, be sent forward on the ground that the national position requires the entrusting of the Government of the country into the joint hands of those who have been the strength of the national situation during the last few years, without prejudice to their present respective positions.

(2) That this Coalition Panel be sent forward as from the Sinn Fein Organisation, the number for each Party being their present strength in the Dail.

(3) That the Candidates be nominated through each of the existing Party Executives.

(4) That every and any interest is free to go up and contest the election equally with the National Sinn Fein Panel.

(5) That constituencies where an election is not held shall continue to be represented by their present Deputies.

(6) That after the election the Executive shall consist of the President, elected as formerly, the Minister of Defence, representing the Army, and nine other Ministers, five from the majority Party and four from the minority, each Party to choose its own nominees. The allocation will be in the hands of the President.

(7) That in the event of the Coalition Government finding it necessary to dissolve, a General Election will be held as soon as possible on Adult Suffrage.[30]

Griffith accepted the pact with the greatest reluctance. Since the April peace conference, he felt that nothing good could come from negotiating with de Valera, whom he regarded as dishonest as well as wrong. When Collins told the Cabinet that the pact represented the best terms he could get and that he wanted it approved, Griffith was obviously upset. Asked for his opinion, he at first remained silent. Then, hands shaking with emotion, he removed his glasses and slowly polished them. Having put them on and adjusted his tie, he again removed them and said simply: "I agree."[31]

Exactly what Collins had in mind when he made the pact is impossible to say. He certainly viewed it as a last effort to avert civil war.[32] At the same time, he must have realized that some such agreement was the surest way to save the Treaty. The election that had been agreed upon would not be entirely free, but other interests could contest it, and it seemed certain that they would. Their participation was almost sure to produce a solid pro-Treaty majority in the new Parliament. If this happened, Republican leaders might refrain from pressing opposition to the Treaty to the point of civil war. The evident unwillingness of some IRA officers to defy the people's will offered some basis for this hope. Collins gambled that the British, like Griffith, would accept the pact rather than break with him. And if he could win their approval of an essentially Republican constitution, as well as win the election, his hope of peacefully implementing the Treaty might well be realized. Even if the pact did not avert civil war, an electoral victory would give the government the moral authority Collins felt it must have to fight fellow Irishmen.

Of course, there was always the chance that the Sinn Fein panel might sweep the election, thereby necessitating an attempt to form a coalition government. But if such a government proved workable, Collins would be better able to deal with Craig and nonpolitical disorder in Southern Ireland. Whatever the results of the pact, Collins could hardly be worse off, and there was a good chance it would improve his position. The pact made the British take a more demanding attitude toward the Free State Constitution; but since, in any case, they would not have agreed to the kind of constitution Collins wanted, the pact made only a marginal difference.

De Valera later wrote that he was more afraid of the pact than of anything he had ever done. It meant acceptance of the people's vote as the final decision on the Treaty, that is, defeat for the Republicans, unless Collins stood up to Lloyd George and secured a Republican constitution.[33] Not only did the pact cast the anti-Treaty party in a minority role, it created the possibility that independent candidates would overwhelm the Republicans at the polls. Moreover, after all his protests, de Valera had agreed to an election for only the Twenty-six Counties on what he claimed was an invalid register. His action was motivated by a desire to avert civil war, as intense as that of Collins. But unlike Collins, de Valera could strengthen his position only if the pact worked, and he did not believe Griffith and Collins would try to make it work. Thus he regarded the pact "tho' apparently a victory, as really a defeat for the Republic."[34]

The *Republic of Ireland* felt the same way, declaring the agreement might weaken the Republican ideal. Sooner or later, principle must fight expediency, and postponement of conflict only played into the hands of the Free Staters. Not surprisingly, Craig disagreed, denouncing the pact as a surrender to the Republicans. He declared his government would not deal with a coalition that contained Republicans and would refuse to cooperate with a boundary commission.[35]

On May 25 the Sinn Fein Ard Fheis approved the pact, with de Valera appealing to all Sinn Feiners to live up to its spirit and support only panel candidates. Collins claimed the pact was perhaps a better way to determine the people's will than a violently contested election, but pointed out it was not intended to deny voters the right to support whomever they wished.[36]

In the period just before the pact, the British became increasingly anxious about the possibility of a compromise that would wreck the Treaty. Early in May, when Collins asked for arms to attack rebel strongholds outside Dublin, Churchill refused, declaring further arms issues were contingent on the Provisional Government's attacking O'Connor's forces in the capital. A few days later, Churchill warned Collins that the British could not regard any sort of agreed election "as a basis on which we could build." Such a farcical arrangement would outrage democratic principles and justify the protests of those who claimed the Irish could not govern themselves.[37]

On May 16 the colonial secretary again reviewed the situation for the Cabinet. Ireland, he said, was in process of rapid social disintegration. There were not yet any clear-cut issues on which Britain could act, but it had good reason to complain of the Provisional Government's policy. Collins had been given authority, arms, and property, but the Irish people had not yet been given a chance to vote on the Treaty. Churchill warned there was serious danger of O'Connor's forces trying to provoke British military intervention in order to reunite the IRA. In his opinion, Irish government leaders should be invited to London and told they would get no more large issues of arms until they had shown they intended to reply forcefully to the Republicans' challenge. The Cabinet agreed that the Irish ministers should be asked to discuss matters as soon as they settled the question of a truce with the Republicans.[38]

Just prior to the Collins-de Valera pact, the British evacuated Cork and the Curragh, leaving the 5,000 troops in Dublin as their only remaining garrison in Southern Ireland.[39] Announcement of the pact indicated that these troops might soon face real trouble. Speaking in Parliament, Churchill said of the agreement: "It would appear to raise very serious issues affecting not only the character and validity of the election contemplated in the Irish Free State Agreement Act, but also affecting the Treaty itself."[40] The government had therefore invited the Irish Treaty signatories to London to discuss these issues.

On May 23 the first formal meeting of the British Treaty signatories since December 7 took place, with Balfour, Macready, and Fitzalan (the viceroy) present by request. Summarizing the situation, Churchill emphasized Collins' failure to take stern measures to implement the Treaty, while noting his urgent desire to avoid making martyrs of the Republicans. In Churchill's view, Britain would not be confronted with any sudden breakdown of the Treaty settlement on a very definite issue; instead, the Free Staters would "slide into accommodation" with the Republicans. Discussing the pact, he pointed out that the British government had no right to demand an election; the Treaty did not prescribe one, only the Irish Free State Agreement Act. Were the proposed election *bona fide,* the Free State leaders could pressure the government to stretch the Constitution to suit the Irish view. But since no election of value was contemplated, the British could be much more exacting in their examination of the Constitution. The pact might promote stability and make possible a free election later, and that might be the Irish defense. All the same, the British position must be stated unequivocally. First, if a republic were declared before or after the election, it meant war. Second, the British government would not allow itself to be gradually committed to a republic; at a certain stage, it would lose confidence in the Provisional Government. Finally, Parliament could not ratify the Constitution until after an election in which large numbers voted and real issues were decided.

Chamberlain said he trusted Griffith but was losing confidence in Collins. In Macready's opinion, Collins was not deliberately treacherous, but he was in the hands of de Valera and let matters slide. The prime minister thought Britain was drifting into a position where it must either abandon or reconquer Ireland. He opposed abandonment, but before they faced reconquest they should make plain to the world that the present situation was not Britain's fault. The British must not appear to take advantage of Ireland's inexperience with self-government the moment the Irish acted foolishly. If Britain acted precipitately, the world would say it had never meant to give the Irish self-government but had only used the Treaty to trap them. He feared stern action might have to be taken and asked Churchill to survey the various contingencies. But he opposed using threats unless the government meant to carry them out. The Irish ministers should be told the government's views and given a chance to put matters right.

Churchill explained that he had had the military and blockade questions explored by two committees, adding he would draw up a summary of the main complaints against the Provisional Government. Lloyd

George remarked that he could not see a very clear issue of Treaty violation, and any violation must be so obvious it could not be argued about. The Irish leaders would claim that Britain had left Ireland in a state of complete lawlessness and expected them to correct two or three years' disorganization in six months. He repeated that Britain must have a complete case, and Churchill agreed that one did not exist as yet. However, Macready and Chamberlain pointed out that the Irish situation had gone from bad to worse since the Treaty, and Chamberlain added that the pact could not be squared with the Treaty. Balfour expressed general pessimism about the Treaty's prospects, Collins' capacity for leadership, and military reconquest. Churchill countered by arguing for a blockade if the necessity arose. Britain should hold Northern Ireland and Dublin, cut off the rest of the country from the outside world, declare adherence to the Treaty, and express willingness to deal with any body of responsible Irishmen who would try to carry it out. Lloyd George again reminded his colleagues that they must have a clear issue if they broke with the Irish.[41]

When the Irish ministers received the invitation to confer, they decided Griffith must lead their delegation. The British trusted him, and he was the man most likely to make a good impression on them. At first, the president was outraged by the suggestion that he should defend the pact. However, he quickly calmed down and listened carefully to the case his colleagues made. In the end, he agreed to go, asking that Collins, Duggan, Cosgrave, and O'Higgins go with him. Hugh Kennedy and Diarmuid O'Hegarty accompanied the delegation as legal adviser and secretary. The Irish Cabinet agreed that the delegates should maintain the pact was necessary to carry out the Treaty and restore order, making clear that the Provisional Government was determined to stand by the Treaty. But they should also take the offensive on Ulster, pointing out that British policy there endangered the Treaty, that Craig had broken his agreement with Collins, and that he had publicly stated his intention to violate the Treaty by repudiating the Boundary Commission.[42]

Griffith, O'Higgins, Duggan, and Kennedy arrived in London a day before Collins and Cosgrave and met with Churchill on May 26. He quickly briefed them on British objections to the pact, warning that if the upcoming election were not *bona fide* it could not be the basis for parliamentary action on the Constitution and the Boundary Commission. Defending the pact, Griffith contended that the Treaty issue was implicit in the election, that it dwarfed all other issues, and that the government was sure to gain at least a few additional seats. Duggan said the Republicans were coming back as a minority and more or less accepting the Treaty position. O'Higgins claimed that many people had supported de Valera because they believed he was going to follow a constitutional course. They had taken a wrong position, but if the government had forced the issue, it would have faced disastrous consequences. By compromising, the government had undercut Republican opposition; two-thirds of de Valera's followers felt the pact had extricated them from a "damned bad mess." Griffith pointed out that the government lacked sufficient forces to protect all the polling stations in Southern Ireland; the Republicans could easily have attacked enough of them to invalidate half the elections. Churchill clung to his main objection: the election would be the result of a "deal." It might help the Free State leaders solve their internal problems, but it did not put the Treaty before the voters, and it did not enable the government to base its authority on the will of the people. O'Higgins repeated that people wanted the government to avert civil war and were satisfied the pact had done so. Theoretically, the Provisional Government ought to have gone straight ahead, but politics was not an exact science.

Turning to the question of the projected coalition government, Churchill asked whether its Republican members would sign the required declaration of acceptance of the Treaty. Griffith replied that Cabinet members would do so, but the four Republicans would be "External Ministers." Churchill said this would contravene the Treaty, which stipulated that every member of the Provisional Government must signify acceptance of the Treaty in writing. He reminded the Irish that British opinion was becoming increasingly disenchanted. The government had made a large concession to Southern Ireland, evacuating its garrison and transferring its authority to the Provisional Government, on condition there would be no republic. But the Free Staters had made repeated surrenders to the Republicans and had not obtained the people's verdict on the Treaty. Consequently, there was a "fierce scrutiny" of the British government's actions by its own people. He appreciated the Irish ministers' difficulties, but he did not believe that all of them were inevitable. On essentials, the British government was just as stubborn as de Valera or O'Connor, and it intended to fight if necessary. If Republican members of a coalition government did not signify acceptance of the Treaty, that would violate its terms; and if the Treaty lapsed, he would not like to contemplate the situation. Griffith said the subject had not been discussed with Republican leaders, but he conceded they might refuse to sign so as to save face.[43]

When Churchill reported on the meeting to his fellow signatories, Lloyd George contended that the pact did not constitute the clear issue that was necessary for a break. If a break occurred, it would mean a long and difficult struggle in which Britain's only weapon (blockade) would hurt its own people as much as the Republicans. The one issue on which the government could fight with the support of the whole Empire was allegiance to the king, and further discussion should be postponed until they had seen the Constitution. If it were republican, that would be a clear violation of the Treaty. The British decided the Law Officers should examine the draft when it was delivered next morning and report at 4 p.m., after which a full meeting with the Irish would be held.[44]

Outraged protest was the initial British reaction to the Constitution, which was essentially Republican in form and substance. An interview with Griffith and Collins on the afternoon of May 27 did nothing to improve the situation. After their departure, Churchill urged postponement of the election. Chamberlain was miserable and very angry about the Constitution and the pact. Lloyd George wanted to keep the two issues separate so as to minimize the danger of alienating Dominion opinion. British interference with a Dominion's election arrangements would be regarded as very high-handed procedure. Birkenhead supported the prime minister, but Chamberlain and Churchill remained unconvinced.[45]

At 6 p.m. that evening the two delegations met, and the prime minister opened the assault on the Constitution by calling it "a complete evasion and a complete negation of the Treaty." While reaffirming adherence to the Treaty, he warned that the issue would be joined if the Constitution represented Ireland's last word, and he announced that a formal statement of objections to the draft would be presented on May 29. Griffith repeated his earlier assertion that Ireland also stood by the Treaty, and he expressed willingness to make the Constitution conform to that agreement if it did not yet do so. But he added that he did not see how it diverged from the Treaty. This remark doubtless astonished the British, but Lloyd George ended the discussion by declaring that their statement would show in detail how it diverged.

With the Constitution temporarily out of the way, discussion turned to the pact. In response to Churchill's questions, Griffith insisted that the British would not be committing themselves to the pact by allowing the election to proceed, that the Treaty was the election issue, and that the pact had been made to permit holding an election without the turmoil which would invalidate it. The presence of Republicans in a coalition government would not violate the Treaty, because they would not be members of the Cabinet and hence not required to give written assent to the Treaty. Lloyd George challenged the last statement, but Collins interjected that the British ministers were members of a coalition who had not been asked to surrender their party principles when they joined the government. A coalition might cause parliamentary problems in Ireland, but it could also restore public order. Chamberlain would have none of this. There was a good deal in the Treaty he did not like, but it was a signed agreement and must be kept by both sides. Collins and Griffith affirmed that it would be kept.

Churchill expressed inability to understand why the election could not be postponed a bit. If the government allowed it to proceed now, Parliament would accuse it of endorsing the Collins-de Valera agreement. But if the matter were put off for a few days, they could reach an accord on the Constitution which would overshadow the pact. Griffith explained that postponement would enable Republicans to charge he was a British puppet. Eventually, the Irish convinced the British that an agreed election was not in itself a violation of the Treaty, and the British would not be compromised by allowing it to proceed. But the British made clear that if any Irish ministers did not give written assent to the Treaty, they would feel perfectly justified in taking steps to resume some of the powers handed over to the Provisional Government.

The way was now open to an understanding. Churchill suggested he would tell Parliament that the Irish election was perfectly constitutional and in accordance with the Treaty but that other things, not in accordance with it, might arise, and the government would not countenance them. Birkenhead commented that Churchill's statement should include the phrase "without prejudice to such points as we may desire to raise as to the nonconformity of the Constitution with the Treaty." The prime minister said that the government agreed to allow the election to proceed so that it could not be said Britain was interfering in a Dominion election, but only on the definite assurance that Griffith and Collins intended to make the Constitution conform to the Treaty. Griffith assented to this condition. The conference also agreed that the government's decision did not commit it in any way to the pact. Further discussion was adjourned until the Irish had considered the statement of objections to the Constitution, at which time legal advisers from both governments would consult together.[46]

Heightened violence in Northern Ireland aggravated Anglo-Irish tensions during May and June. The truce in the South facilitated IRA action in Ulster, and this intensified the Orange pogrom. As the death toll rose in Belfast, hundreds of Catholics fled to Dublin or across the Irish Sea to escape mob violence.[47] On May 30, while Lord Chief Justice Hewart and Hugh Kennedy discussed the draft Constitution, Collins and Griffith denounced the pogrom to Lloyd George and Chamberlain. Chamberlain thought the Irish leaders realized the Constitution created an unbridgeable gap between them and the government, and decided they must therefore quarrel with either the British or de Valera. The fact that Griffith and Collins had requested an interview and used it to denounce anti-Catholic violence in the North seemed to support this theory, as far as Chamberlain was concerned. Lloyd George and Birkenhead took a similar view of the matter.[48]

Admittedly, Griffith and Collins exploited the Ulster disturbances for political advantage, but this made their anger no less genuine. According to the prime minister, they talked about the "extermination" of North-

ern Catholics, and Collins talked of nothing else.[49] Charging that the
murders in Belfast were part of a deliberate war on Catholics, they
demanded that the British make an impartial inquiry into the Ulster
troubles and impose martial law. Chamberlain asked Collins whether he
would disavow the IRA in the North and order it to obey Craig's government, pending the results of boundary revision, if the British instituted an inquiry. Collins answered that he was willing to carry out his
March agreement with Craig but would not support the Ulster government while Catholics were being murdered.

In the Cabinet's discussion of this interview, Lloyd George expressed
anxiety about the case that could be made against Britain in the North.
Catholics had been the first victims there, and Catholic deaths consider-
ably outnumbered those of Protestants, but no one had been punished
or even arrested for the murders. Moreover, the British government
had agreed to arm Protestants to help maintain order. Britain must
maintain a stern impartiality between all races and creeds in the Empire
and should avoid a rupture on an issue like Ulster. If a break came on
"Republic versus Monarchy," the government could count on solid support at home and abroad. But if it came on Ulster, those who demanded
strong action would soon turn against the government, and religious
communities would oppose it as well. Democratic societies were senti-
mental and would not allow a policy of repression to be carried through
on a doubtful issue, such as Ulster. Supporting Griffith's and Collins'
demand, the prime minister proposed a judicial inquiry into the Ulster
troubles. Craig should not object to this, especially since his government
wanted £5 million for its Special Constabulary. During the inquiry,
neither side would want to look bad; so outrages might be stopped for a
time and other issues might develop.

Churchill argued that an inquiry in the North would generate public
pressure for one in the South. Balfour added that Ulster should not be
placed on trial with the South as a witness. The prime minister reminded
them that the South was a Dominion and Ulster was not. Moreover,
the IRA was clearly to blame for the trouble in the South; so there was
nothing to investigate. Chamberlain supported the prime minister, but
Churchill favored martial law for parts of Belfast or a return to the
Craig-Collins pact, rather than an inquiry. Eventually, the Cabinet decided that Churchill should invite Craig to come to London at once to
present his views and that the prime minister should propose a judicial
inquiry.[50]

Next day, Churchill defended the government's policy in the House of
Commons as Griffith and Collins listened in the gallery. He concluded
by expressing unreserved good faith in their sincerity. While their policy
and methods were admittedly open to question, the government believed that the two leaders were doing their best to carry out the Treaty.

If they failed to honor the agreement, it would be they, not the British, who would suffer disgrace. Britain's good faith and forbearance placed it in the strongest position, with the greatest worldwide support, to deal with whatever events might arise. In answer to diehard attacks, and in an obvious effort to allay the doubts of moderate Conservatives, Churchill repeated that the government would not tolerate an Irish republic. If one were set up, the British garrison would hold Dublin, since its control would be an essential preliminary step in military operations.[51]

After the debate, Collins told Churchill he had no quarrel with the speech: "we have got to make good or go under." The two men argued briefly about Ulster; then Collins became somber, saying: "I shall not last long; my life is forfeit, but I shall do my best. After I am gone it will be easier for others. You will find they will be able to do more than I can do."[52] Churchill assured him that all would be well in time, but Collins' prophecy proved correct. In three months he would be dead.

A series of incidents along the Irish border in late May and early June threatened to precipitate the conflict Lloyd George was so anxious to avoid. These events took place in a triangular section of County Fermanagh, cut off from the rest of the Six Counties by Lower Lough Erne and the River Erne. One of the two main villages in the triangle, Pettigo, lay mostly in Donegal. Belleek, the other village, was wholly inside Fermanagh, but an old stone fort in Free State territory over-looked it.

In late May, IRA parties moved into the triangle and fired on Ulster Specials in Pettigo. Police reinforcements skirmished with the IRA and called for military aid. Some troops were sent, but on May 30 a reconnaissance party, advancing on Pettigo, was fired on from the Free State and retreated. Churchill demanded and received Collins' assurances that no Free State troops were involved in this foray. On the same day, Craig denounced the incursion into Fermanagh, reaffirming his pledge that Ulster would never be coerced.

The British quickly retaliated against the IRA. On June 1 orders were issued to clear the Pettigo-Belleek area of all intruders, and on June 3 British troops moved down the lake and landed in the triangle. Both that day and the next, the troops were fired on from Donegal. On June 4 another British column came under heavy fire as it advanced on Pettigo from the east, but suffered only one casualty. Occupying the village, the British captured a few IRA prisoners, some guns, and a police car that had been taken at Belleek a few days before. The troops continued to occupy Pettigo and the high ground in Donegal west of it, allowing local inhabitants to return to their homes.

Collins wired Churchill on June 5, demanding an immediate joint inquiry into the Pettigo action, protesting British occupation of Free State territory, and calling for a suspension of action against Belleek

until Churchill had consulted with the Provisional Government. When
the Cabinet's Irish Committee met on June 6, the war secretary revealed
he had suspended further operations at Belleek in compliance with Collins' request. On Churchill's urging, however, the committee approved
the occupation of Belleek and endorsed a telegram, drafted by him,
setting forth the British position. The wire informed Collins that operations in the triangle had been carried out at the express orders of the
British government. There would therefore be no inquiry, but operations would cease with the occupation of Belleek unless there were
further provocation from the Free State side of the border. Collins replied by again protesting further British operations and repeating his
demand for an inquiry.

A meeting of the Irish Subcommittee of the Committee of Imperial
Defense on June 7 confirmed the decision to proceed against Belleek,
but agreed that the action should be carried out with extreme caution,
which was desirable on both military and political grounds. On June 8
British forces encountered hostile fire in their advance on Belleek. With
the aid of artillery, they dislodged their opponents and occupied both
the village and the old fort overlooking it with little difficulty. Local
people reported that about 200 IRA men had been collected in the
neighborhood, but claimed there were no Free State troops among
them. Macready reported that British operations appeared to have had a
good effect. Free State and Irregular troops had withdrawn from the
Fermanagh-Donegal border, and the military situation was easier
throughout the Six Counties.[53]

The Pettigo-Belleek affair was only a "tempest in a teacup," which
caused far more alarm to Churchill and Ulster Unionists than among
British military authorities.[54] A motley force of anti-Treaty IRA had
moved into the Fermanagh triangle and exchanged fire with some Ulster Specials. Craig's government had at once raised the cry of invasion,
which was taken up by his British allies, and Churchill had overreacted.
British troops were sent into the disputed area before Collins could
withdraw local IRA units to positions well back from the border, and the
result was some wild shooting, with little loss of life or property. Collins
was rightly concerned because he feared the skirmishing might trigger
general fighting along the border, which would destroy the Treaty.[55]

Lloyd George shared Collins' fears, and on June 7 he instructed the
Cabinet Office to send Tom Jones to his country residence at Chequers
with all the papers relating to the Pettigo-Belleek affair. Churchill sent a
letter defending British action with Jones, who had argued heatedly with
him on the question. As soon as Jones reached Chequers, he alerted the
prime minister to the explosive nature of the situation in the triangle,
and Lloyd George became very angry with Churchill's impulsive behavior. On June 8 he wrote the colonial secretary, warning him of the

danger of upsetting negotiations on the Constitution and causing a break on Ulster. "Let us keep on the high ground of the Treaty—the Crown, the Empire. There we are unassailable. But if you come down from that height and fight in the swamps of Lough Erne you will be overwhelmed." The prime minister begged Churchill not to squander by precipitous action what he had gained by his skill and patience in negotiations, however alluring the immediate prospect might be.[56]

Churchill's defense of his action was that the government could not have faced the House of Commons with the admission it did not know what was going on in a "British village" and did not dare to find out. After the event, he argued that the results had been good. Ulster was reassured that the British would protect it from invasion, and both the IRA and the Free State government had learned that the border could not be violated with impunity.[57]

This was true, but the same results could have been gained without hasty, large-scale military action. If they had deferred action for a few days, the British could have occupied the Pettigo-Belleek area with a handful of troops and without resistance. There was no military danger in delay, and it was highly desirable from a political point of view. The whole affair not only endangered Anglo-Irish peace, it made the British government ridiculous in the eyes of many observers. The ultra-Unionist *Morning Post* put the campaign in true perspective in its mocking description of the "battle of Belleek":

> Altogether, it was one of the most charming, bloodless battles in history. The weather was perfect, the scenery ideal, the artillery shooting masterly, the troops good-humoured, the roll of the gunfire among the splendid hills of Donegal and Fermanagh poetic to a degree, and best of all, nobody was hurt.[58]

Lloyd George did almost as well at Churchill's expense. Once it was clear that no real damage had been done, the prime minister amused his guests at Chequers by singing Burns's "Scots wha hae" to celebrate the victory of Belleek, putting in Churchill's name wherever he could.[59]

Chapter 14
The Constitution:
January-June 1922

The draft Constitution was largely the creation of a committee appointed by the Provisional Government. Griffith had urged Collins to appoint the well-known literary figure and Sinn Feiner, Darrell Figgis, as its chairman. However, Collins distrusted the erratic Figgis and took the chairmanship himself, naming Figgis as his deputy. Thus, although he did not have time to attend the committee's sessions, Collins retained ultimate control of the drafting process. The man Collins really wanted to head the committee was James Douglas, a Dublin businessman and organizer of the Irish White Cross relief work in 1920–21. Douglas served on the committee and was Collins' principal liaison with it; he also persuaded Collins to name C. P. France, an American lawyer (who also was active in White Cross work), as legal adviser, and France soon became a full member of the committee. Other members included James MacNeill, brother of Eoin MacNeill and former Indian civil servant; Hugh Kennedy, K. C., legal adviser to the Provisional Government; Kevin O'Shiel and John O'Byrne, barristers; and James Murnaghan, a Dublin law professor. Appointment of Alfred O'Rahilly, a Cork physics professor who was deeply interested in Catholic social-justice teachings, completed the roster.[1] In general, the appointments were well advised. All the committee's members supported the Treaty but only Collins and Figgis were partisan figures. The others were legal and administrative experts or men who had won the nation's gratitude for their successful efforts to relieve distress.

The Constitution Committee began work in late January and finished in early March. Griffith and Collins attended the opening session, and although they gave no detailed instructions, they left the committee in no doubt as to the kind of constitution they wanted. Their intention was that the document ignore the formal law governing Anglo-Dominion relations in favor of constitutional practice and usage. Griffith told the committee he wanted as little as possible of the Canadian Constitution in that of the Free State.[2] Collins went further, telling the group to bear in mind not past legalities but future practicalities, and to produce a "true democratic constitution."[3] He made clear to Douglas that he wanted a constitution which would be short, simple, and easy to change as Ireland moved to complete freedom. It should not treat Anglo-Irish relations, which were already covered by the Treaty, but should deal only with the establishment of domestic authority, derived exclusively from the people. Executive power was not to be vested in the king, nor were the oath of allegiance or the Crown's representative to be mentioned. Hugh Kennedy had told Collins that, in his opinion, the oath was not mandatory and need not be part of the Constitution. Collins instructed the committee accordingly, and he informed de Valera of this point.[4]

In the course of its deliberations, the committee studied a number of constitutions, including those of the United States, Canada, republican Germany, and Switzerland. Its members were unable to agree on a single plan, but a majority found substantial agreement on all but three major points: the structure of the Executive, the Senate, and the Supreme Court. Professors O'Rahilly and Murnaghan differed fundamentally with their colleagues and produced a draft constitution that strongly reflected O'Rahilly's religious conservatism and advanced ideas on social justice. The Provisional Government ignored this document, Draft C, when it was presented with the other two drafts in March.

Draft A, the work of Figgis, MacNeill, and O'Byrne, was the more conservative of the two major proposals. It gave greater power to the Senate than did Draft B, the plan of Douglas, France, and Kennedy.[5] Drafts A and B gave the highest courts the power of constitutional review but differed on their structure. The main difference between the two drafts related to the composition of the Executive. Draft A provided for Cabinet government on the British model, though without the king. Draft B stated that some ministers were to be chosen from outside the Dail. These "External Ministers" were to be elected by the Dail, and could sit and speak there, but not vote. Resignation of the Cabinet or dissolution of the Dail would not affect their tenure, but they could be removed from office by the Dail for specified offenses. The proposal for a dual Executive was designed to bring nonpartisan experts and minority party members into the government; it might also open the way to office for Republican leaders.[6]

The Constitution Committee presented its three drafts to Collins on March 8.[7] None was made public, and the Irish people were left in ignorance except for promises that the Constitution would be that of a free and democratic nation. De Valera remained patient, but neither he nor Childers believed the Constitution would go beyond the terms of the Treaty.[8] When Collins went to London on May 26, he took with him what was essentially Draft B, amended in certain respects by the Provisional Government. Although the Cabinet approved a preamble that forcefully asserted Irish sovereignty, the delegates deleted it from the final draft, doubtless to avoid needlessly offending the British.[9]

Section I of the draft Constitution, titled "Fundamental Rights," set forth in general terms the rights of the state and its citizens. Echoing the language of the 1916 Proclamation and the Democratic Program of 1919, article 1 declared that the nation's sovereignty extended to all material resources and that the right of private property was subordinate to the national welfare. Article 2 proclaimed that all citizens must give allegiance and service to the state, and the nation must ensure to all citizens opportunities for such service. Article 3 reiterated the fundamental proposition advanced by Sinn Fein during the Treaty negotiations: "All powers of government are derived from the people of Ireland. All persons who exercise the authority of Saorstat Eireann, whether legislative, executive or judicial, do so by virtue of the power conferred on them by the people."

Conditions for citizenship were spelled out in article 4, with no mention of common citizenship. Article 5 declared both Irish and English to be official languages, and article 6 stated that no titles of honor were to be conferred by the state. Articles 7 through 10 set forth individual rights: due process of law, freedom of conscience, speech, association, and assembly. Article 11 affirmed the right of all citizens to free elementary education, and article 12 asserted that the state could not alienate natural resources whose use was of national importance.

The Constitution's second section dealt with Legislative provisions. The Oireachtas/Parliament was to be composed of a Dail Eireann/ Chamber of Deputies and a Seanad Eireann/Senate. All citizens aged twenty-one years and over were eligible to vote, by secret ballot. Parliamentary rules were closely modeled on those of Britain (articles 13–25). Dail members were to be elected on the basis of proportional representation, with each deputy representing 20,000–30,000 people. The Dail could not be dissolved during its four-year term except by its own motion. The Senate was to be composed of forty members, aged thirty-five and over, with a normal term of twelve years. Senators were to be citizens who had done honor to the nation or who represented important aspects of national life. The Dail was to nominate candidates and elect one-fourth of the senators every three years by proportional representation from an electoral area comprising the entire Free State (articles 26–33).

The Constitution gave the Dail exclusive authority over taxation and appropriation, but stipulated it could appropriate monies only upon the Executive Council's recommendation. The Senate could delay a money bill for only fourteen days and other bills for six months. Parliament was given power to create subordinate legislatures with local powers and to establish vocational councils, but it alone was to raise, maintain, and control all armed forces (articles 34–43). Articles 44 and 45 provided the options of popular referendum and initiative in lawmaking. Article 46 guaranteed that the Free State should not be committed to take part in any war without the consent of its Parliament, except in case of actual invasion. Article 47 provided that Parliament could amend the Constitution, but required that every amendment be submitted to a referendum in which a majority of registered voters took part and be approved by a majority of those registered or by two-thirds of those voting.

Section III dealt with the Executive. The source of its authority was the Aireacht/Executive Council, which was to be responsible to the Dail and consist of not more than twelve ministers. Four of these, including the president and vice-president, had to be members of the Dail, and three more might be, while the rest were to be external ministers. After his election by the Dail, the president would appoint the vice-president and the other internal ministers (articles 48–49). Ministers who were not members of the Dail were to be nominated by a committee of that body. Each external minister should be the responsible head of some Executive department(s). He would hold office for a specified period and could be removed by the Dail only for certain serious offenses. Only ministers who were members of the Dail were responsible for external affairs. Subject to this provision, the Executive Council should meet and act as a collective authority, with each minister individually responsible to the Dail for his department(s). Ministers who were not members of the Dail should possess all the rights of members except the right to vote. Parliament was to be summoned by the president for each session (articles 50–58). Articles 59–62 covered administration of national finance.

Section IV was devoted to the Judiciary, which was to be composed of Courts of First Instance and a Court of Final Appeal. The former were to include a High Court, invested with full original jurisdiction over matters of law and fact, civil or criminal, as well as courts of local and limited jurisdiction with a right of appeal as determined by law. The High Court was to exercise original jurisdiction in all questions involving the constitutionality of laws and the interpretation of treaties, while the Court of Final Appeal, or Supreme Court, was to exercise appellate jurisdiction over the High Court. Its decisions were final and could not be reviewed by any other authority (articles 63–65). Articles 66–72 dealt with judicial organization and procedure, the appointment and independence of judges, and guaranties of legal due process.

The fifth section covered External Relations.[10] Article 73 declared that they were to be governed by treaties or agreements made between the Free State and other contracting parties, but none of them was to be valid unless approved by the Free State Parliament. Article 74 stipulated that Parliament and the Executive Council should respectively pass the necessary legislation and do all other things required for implementing the Treaty of 1921. Article 75 stated that while relations with the British Commonwealth were regulated by the Treaty, the Crown's representative should be styled "Commissioner of the British Commonwealth" and appointed with the previous assent of the Free State's Executive Council.

The commissioner should automatically signify the king's assent to laws submitted by the Executive Council.

Section VI dealt with transitory provisions designed to bridge the gap between the official establishment of the Free State and its normal functioning. Laws that were not inconsistent with the Constitution should continue in force after its adoption, until amended or repealed by the Free State Parliament. The Constituent Assembly could exercise the power conferred on Dail Eireann by the Constitution for up to one year from the date of the Constitution's enactment. After the expiration of this period, an election should be held as soon as possible. The first Senate should be set up immediately after the adoption of the Constitution, with the Dail electing thirty members and the president of the Executive Council choosing the other ten, the latter group to be selected with special regard to providing representation for minority groups (articles 76–78).[11]

A hostile British reaction to the draft Constitution killed any hope of inducing the Republicans to accept the Treaty peacefully. According to Darrell Figgis, Collins blamed the Republicans themselves for the British refusal to approve the Constitution in its original form. He felt that, had the first draft been submitted two or three months earlier, it would have been substantially confirmed. But growing Republican opposition to the Treaty weakened the Provisional Government's negotiating position. Figgis and Gavan Duffy felt there was some truth in this,[12] but Ernest Blythe and Kevin O'Higgins disagreed. In Blythe's opinion, the draft Constitution went outside the Treaty, and he agreed to its presentation only because it left room for bargaining.[13] O'Higgins likewise maintained that substantial revision was inevitable. Without Republican opposition, the government could have secured "a more pleasantly worded Constitution," but not one basically different from that which it brought back from London.[14]

This analysis was more realistic than that of Collins. Both the personal convictions and the political survival of the British signatories made it imperative that they insist on the inclusion of the Treaty's essential provisions in the Constitution. The only explanation for Collins' optimism is that his legal advisers were breathing the rarefied air of constitutional theory, untainted by political realities, while he himself ignored those realities because of his desperate desire for a Republican constitution.

Griffith and Collins got an angry reception when they met the British signatories on May 27. Lloyd George claimed that the Irish Constitution was not that of Canada but of a republic in disguise. It stripped the monarchy of any influence or prestige and made it ridiculous. It did not even mention the Treaty's oath of allegiance, nor did it make provision for judicial appeal to the king's Privy Council. In external affairs, the Constitution repudiated the idea that there must be a common foreign policy for the Empire, with Britain as the instrument of that policy; instead, it gave the Free State complete autonomy in foreign affairs. Replying calmly to this formidable indictment, Griffith confessed that the Constitution had been drafted in a hurry, but he and his colleagues intended to make it conform to the Treaty. Indeed, they had consulted eminent Irishmen who believed that it did conform, and he would like specific citations of alleged violations. Further discussion was deferred until the British consulted their legal advisers.[15]

When the British reviewed the situation among themselves, Lloyd George angrily declared that they were back where they had been at the start of the Treaty negotiations. The Constitution was "a complete evasion of the Treaty and a setting up of a republic with a thin veneer." Under its terms, the Crown's representative would be appointed with the previous assent of the Irish Executive. By a process of exclusion, the Irish could insist on appointing de Valera or nobody. Although the British government consulted the Canadian government about appointment of a governor general, and the British Constitution was based on popular authority, the mystic power of the Crown was held in reserve for possible use. However, the prime minister cautioned that this question must be handled carefully with the Irish, so as not to challenge the democratic sentiment of Australia and Canada.

Lloyd George asked his colleagues to consider the Constitution carefully. He believed that Griffith was "straight" and that he meant it when he said he stood by the Treaty and was willing to discuss the Constitution. But Collins had remained silent, and Lloyd George thought his silence ominous. When Churchill referred to the pact, the prime minister said he never thought there was much to worry about in that, but the Constitution was an evasion of the Treaty in writing, and they would be traitors to the king if they agreed to it. Were the Irish prepared to accept the constitutional position of the other Dominions or not? That was the issue. Churchill pointed out that if there were no agreement on the Constitution, Collins might resign and join de Valera. In that case, responded Lloyd George, there would be no doubt as to what action to take, but he wanted to think more carefully before discussing it. When they met the Irish again at 6 p.m., they should say: "This is a Republic under the thinnest of disguises. We will give you a considered statement in writing on Monday of our views on the Draft Constitution." The other signatories concurred, and the meeting adjourned.[16]

Although the main purpose of the evening conference on the 27th was to discuss the election, Lloyd George opened it with a stern lecture on the Constitution. After summarizing the British position, he said that a formal statement of objections would be given to the Irish in two days, and it was agreed they would need a few days to prepare their answer. After a lengthy discussion, the British allowed the election to proceed, on the understanding that this did not commit them to the pact and that the Constitution would be made to conform to the Treaty.[17]

After studying the draft Constitution on May 27–28, the Law Officers produced their critique. This statement, together with some observations on it by Sir Edward Grigg and Lionel Curtis, was discussed by the British signatories on the morning of May 29. They decided that it needed amendment. It was essentially a legal document, and Dominion citizens had more regard for constitutional practice than for the letter of the law. Publication of such a memorandum, without any real account of existing constitutional practice, would mislead Dominion opinion into taking the Irish side in the dispute over the Constitution. Grigg and Curtis were instructed to redraft the statement, giving greater emphasis to Canadian constitutional practice. After extensive revision, the document was sent to the Irish later that day, together with a Southern Unionist statement of objections to the Constitution's proposed minority safeguards.[18]

The British memorandum began by declaring that the Constitution must be in accordance with the Treaty and could not, therefore, contain anything inconsistent with it or omit any of its relevant provisions. The Treaty stipulated that the Irish Free State should have the same status as the other Dominions, and its position relative to the Imperial Parliament and government should be that of Canada in law, practice, and constitutional usage.

Summarizing the fundamental principles of the Canadian Constitution, the memorandum pointed out that executive authority was vested in the Crown, which acted on the advice of its Canadian ministers. The Crown appointed the governor general, the chief executive officer, in whose name all acts of state were performed. The Crown was also a constituent part of the legislature. Royal assent to bills was required, and Parliament was summoned and dissolved in the name of the king. Finally, the Crown was the fountain of justice, and all Canadians enjoyed the right to petition it for leave to appeal to the Imperial Privy Council against a decision of the Dominion's Supreme Court. The relationship thus established secured the king's constitutional position as head of the British Empire. The throne was the bond which knit together the Empire, and no constitution which was in form or substance republican could find a place within that community. Rising above political, national, and all other distinctions, the throne symbolized the common citizenship of all His Majesty's subjects and the Commonwealth membership of all His Majesty's governments.

Examined in the light of these principles, the Irish Constitution was a direct negation of the Treaty. Up to article 74, in fact, the Constitution was that of an independent republic, and it must be asked whether the inclusion of articles 74 and 75 was sufficient to make it conform to the

Treaty. Article 74 required the Free State to do whatever was necessary to implement the Treaty, while article 75 alone contained any reference to the king or his representative. It conferred the title "Commissioner of the British Commonwealth" on the Crown's representative, made his appointment subject to the previous assent of the Irish government, and compelled him automatically to assent to all bills. In practice, Dominion governments were always consulted in the choice of a governor general, but that was quite different from making the appointment legally subject to the government's prior approval. By constitutional practice, British veto of Dominion bills that dealt with domestic affairs was obsolete, but reservation of the veto was essential for measures affecting external relations, although it would be exercised only on the advice of the Imperial Conference. As for article 74, the Irish legislature could hardly correct any discrepancies between the Constitution and the Treaty because such changes would be amendments to the Constitution, and article 47 required that they be submitted to a popular referendum.

External relations were covered by article 73 of the Constitution, and it appeared impossible to reconcile the complete control conferred on the Free State in this area with article 2 of the Treaty. Moreover, independent treaty-making was opposed to the interdependence of member states of the Commonwealth and to the recorded views of Dominion governments at the most recent Imperial Conference. The king was and must remain the treaty-making power for states of the Empire, although he exercised this power on broad lines approved by the Imperial Conference and on the advice of all the governments concerned. Finally, the words of article 73 were open to the interpretation that the Treaty itself fell within the terms of the article and that the Irish Parliament could determine how far the Treaty was valid and binding on the Free State. In the same context, articles 64 and 65 entrusted interpretation of treaties to the final jurisdiction of the Irish Supreme Court. And under article 75, the duties of the Commonwealth commissioner continued only so long as Free State-Commonwealth relations were regulated by the Treaty of 1921.

Having demonstrated the inconsistencies between the Constitution and the Treaty, the memorandum pointed out that the Constitution omitted any mention of the specific restrictions and obligations imposed by the Treaty. The restrictions included limitations on the Free State's armed forces and the exercise of its powers in Northern Ireland, and prohibition of religious discrimination. In addition to the obligation to grant Britain naval and air bases, the Treaty required that all members of the Free State Parliament take an oath of allegiance to the Crown and that the Free State assume liability for a share of the United Kingdom's debt and pay compensation to retiring public officials in Southern Ireland. The only one of the required restrictions and obligations mentioned in the Constitution was that which prohibited religious discrimination, and even this provision fell far short of the Treaty requirement. As for the others, there was only the provision in article 74 enjoining the Free State to take the necessary steps to implement the Treaty. This general obligation was impossible of enforcement and was, in any case, no substitute for specific provisions in the Constitution which gave effect to Ireland's Treaty obligations. Certainly, the British could not approve the omission of so vital a provision as the oath. Even if it were argued that article 74 was sufficiently consistent with the Treaty so far as it imposed positive obligations, the British government could not accept a Constitution that was not expressly subject to the Treaty's restrictive provisions.[19]

On May 30 Hugh Kennedy and Lord Chief Justice Hewart tried to resolve the differences over the Constitution, but they were unable to reach agreement and adjourned the next day. Before they parted, Kennedy gave Hewart a memorandum of the Irish ministers' views on both the Constitution and the British criticism.

This statement was based on certain special considerations, the first of which was that Ireland was not a British colony like the other Dominions. It followed logically that the great body of laws, institutions, and forms called the "English Common Law" was not common law in Ireland but an alien system, imposed by statute. When the Treaty was signed, English statesmen expressed the hope that the Irish people would establish a constitution which would be wholly their own creation, fully in accord with their wishes and needs. Examination of the Treaty showed that its authors realized the true position. Unlike the other Dominions, Ireland was granted the substance of freedom without traditional British forms, which were meaningless to the Irish and liable to be misunderstood. This distinction was appreciated in Ireland, and much of the support for the Treaty was based on it. Apart from these considerations, the Irish ministers contended that the Dominions' status enabled them to alter their constitutions as they chose, even though they might produce constitutions different in principle from Britain's. The Irish Constitution had been framed to meet Irish conditions, and the Provisional Government could not concede that it was bound to adhere to the forms of English common law. There was no reason why it should and every reason why it should not, because Ireland differed from other Dominions in both history and tradition. The Irish memorandum was accompanied by a statement that the Free State Parliament was not to be summoned or dissolved in the name of the Crown, nor were ministers, judges, or other public officials to be appointed in its name.[20]

Hewart reported the deadlock with Kennedy to Tom Jones at 6 p.m. on May 31, and together they saw the prime minister. At a 7 p.m. meeting with these two men and Chamberlain, Churchill, and Curtis,

Lloyd George outlined the communication to be sent to the Irish, which asked plainly whether they meant to honor the Treaty. He also instructed Jones to inform Griffith and Collins that refusal to yield on the formula which excluded the king from the Irish Executive meant a break with Britain.[21]

When Jones conveyed the warning later the same evening, Griffith said very little. His main point was that the British insisted on putting the British North America Act of 1867 (Canada's written Constitution) into the Irish Constitution, whereas the Treaty gave Ireland Canadian practice and constitutional usage. Jones replied that the Treaty also stipulated that Ireland must accept Canadian law. Collins was in an irreconcilable mood, declaring the gulf was unbridgeable. He reverted constantly to the troubles in Ulster, blaming them on the British government and claiming its leaders seemed to want war with Ireland. Jones argued that British distrust was caused by developments in Ireland since the Treaty. When Griffith asked for suggestions, Jones proposed a meeting the next day with the prime minister and Birkenhead. Griffith readily assented but Collins agreed only reluctantly. Leaving the Irish a little after 10 p.m., Jones reported at once to Lloyd George, who remarked that it looked like a break.[22]

At noon on June 1 the prime minister reviewed the negotiations for the Cabinet, describing the situation as serious and requiring immediate decision. The Cabinet should ascertain whether the Irish intended to carry out the Treaty. It must also determine what action to take if the Irish refused to give way. After some discussion, the Cabinet decided that the Treaty signatories and Balfour should meet that afternoon and draft a statement of the government's position. The interview with Griffith and Collins was canceled, and the appropriate committees were directed to consider possible sanctions against Southern Ireland.[23]

At their afternoon meeting, the British approved a letter which was at once sent to Griffith. It declared that the draft Constitution was wholly inconsistent with the Treaty, demanded an explicit pledge that it would be made to conform to the British view, and insisted on definite answers to six questions:

(1) Was the Irish Free State to be within the Empire on the basis of common citizenship or merely associated with it?

(2) Was the position of the Crown in Ireland to be the same as in the other Dominions?

(3) Was the treaty-making power of the Free State to be the same as that of Canada?

(4) Were the Free State Courts to stand in the same relation to the King in Council [the Judicial Committee of the Privy Council] as did the Courts of the Dominion of Canada?

(5) Was the Treaty oath of allegiance to be incorporated in the Free
    State Constitution as the oath required of members of Parliament?
(6) Would all members of the Irish Provisional Government be required
    to sign the declaration of acceptance of the Treaty as stipulated in
    Article 17 of the Treaty?[24]

The letter was accompanied by a request for a full conference at 6:30
p.m. However, Collins complained that this arrangement left the Irish
less than half an hour to consider the letter, and he asked that they be
allowed to present a formal reply the next day. Lloyd George agreed to
this and to Collins' suggestion of an immediate interview with Griffith
and himself.[25]

In this meeting, Collins alleged that the British were acting like
Shylocks, demanding fulfillment of the letter of the bond. Lloyd George
countered that Britain had shown good faith by withdrawing its troops
and handing over Irish revenues to the Provisional Government. Were
they prepared to accept in return full membership in the Empire? Both
Irishmen answered affirmatively, but Collins added they were not prepared to have English common law forced upon them. The prime minister denied it was being forced upon them; they could abolish it whenever
they liked. The question at issue was a difference between republican
and monarchical institutions. Acts of state in Ireland must run in the
name of the Crown, a mystic term which stood for the power of the
people. Griffith replied that the Irish people regarded the Crown as a
symbol of tyranny, and some time must elapse before it would be regarded as an image of popular sovereignty.

Referring to the demand for Irish appeals to the Privy Council, Collins
contended that no one in Ireland would accept a system under which
men like Carson could sit in judgment on Irish cases. Lloyd George
assured him that no judge who had been involved in a controversy would
hear any cases connected with it. When the prime minister explained the
Free State's international position under the Treaty, Collins indicated he
was not much interested. Ireland had to get its own house in order
before becoming involved in external affairs.

Employing a personal touch, Lloyd George remarked that, as a Celt
himself, he was eager to see a Celtic nation like Ireland enter international affairs. But if this were to be, the Treaty must be carried out in
spirit and letter. Were the Irish ready to honor their agreement? Collins
responded by demanding constitutional safeguards which would give
Ireland the protection that distance gave Canada. Griffith added that
Hewart had tried to force the Canadian position of 1868 on Ireland.
Weary of this fencing, the prime minister pressed for definite answers.
Did the Irish accept the monarchy? He was not trying to exact a pound
of flesh, as Collins had alleged, but the Treaty represented the extreme

limits to which Parliament would go. Collins declared hotly that they would not have signed the Treaty unless they had believed the British had had a change of heart. After a brief wrangle, the prime minister returned to his argument, supporting it by reading extracts from a comparison of the Canadian and Irish constitutions. Griffith argued that Ireland was entitled to the practice as well as the law of Canada. Lloyd George explained that safeguards as to practice could not be included in the Constitution; such objections should have been made before the Treaty was signed.

Collins repeatedly raised the question of Ulster, blaming the British government for the murder of Catholics because it paid the Special Police, who committed those murders. This was not like Canada, and he wanted an impartial inquiry. The prime minister countered that Ulster was part of the United Kingdom, not a Dominion, and the British government had agreed to the use of Specials as a substitute for troops which were not available. He also reminded the Irish that British troops had remained in Canada for a generation after creation of the Dominion. Ireland was getting not only the British North America Act of 1867 but all the usage that had since accumulated. When discussion turned to the royal veto, Lloyd George explained it was no longer used in Dominions' domestic legislation but only for measures affecting imperial or foreign relations. Britain had never quarreled with any Dominion over it; indeed, Dominions were sometimes glad to have rash measures wiped out by the veto.

Winding up the interview, the prime minister tried to impress on the two Irish leaders that they had the best chance ever given of securing real liberty for their country, in an association of free nations which filled a great place in the world. If the Treaty survived, the names of its signers would be inscribed in gold letters; but if it perished, not only Irishmen, but all friends of Ireland, would be stricken with sorrow. If, through impatience or folly, Griffith or Collins dishonored their signatures, Ireland would never forgive them. The two men received these observations in silence, but did not appear to resent them. Griffith promised an answer to the prime minister's letter the next day, and the Irishmen took their leave.[26]

After the meeting, Lloyd George was in a good mood, despite the gravity of the situation, but he regretted that Griffith was the only real Irish leader; Collins "was just a wild animal—a mustang." Curtis compared negotiating with Collins to writing on water, and the prime minister added "shallow and agitated water."[27] One can understand the irritation which prompted these remarks, but they revealed a very limited understanding of Collins and of Ireland.

The following morning, Lloyd George described his interview to the Cabinet, predicting trouble over the oath, the Privy Council, and the position of Republicans in the coalition government. If the answers to his six questions were unsatisfactory, there would be a break. On the other hand, if they were satisfactory, there would be a break between Free Staters and Republicans. In the course of discussion, the prime minister remarked that the Irish were fed up with the Crown, and no wonder. Too often, in Ireland, the Crown had represented repression—Crown forces, Crown solicitor, Crown prosecutor, etc. Chamberlain wryly observed that the Irish were fortunate in having a Celt in the Cabinet to put their case against England.

Turning to Ulster, Balfour reported on the meeting with Craig that the Cabinet had asked him to arrange. He had warned the Ulster premier of the very difficult situation that would result from failure of the Treaty settlement, emphasizing the danger if Southern Ireland had any grounds for charging deliberate persecution of Catholics in Ulster. Craig blamed Sinn Fein propaganda for distortion of events in the North but agreed to a British inquiry to clear the record, if his government initiated the proposal. The Cabinet concluded that no decision could be taken on an inquiry until it received the Irish reply on the Constitution.

At this juncture, General Lord Cavan, C.I.G.S., entered the meeting and Churchill summarized the reports of the previous day's committee meetings on military and economic sanctions against Southern Ireland. The Cabinet agreed to defer decision on such measures but authorized Churchill to direct further inquiries (see appendix IV). The prime minister asked his colleagues to remain available in case another meeting proved necessary after receipt of the Irish reply.[28]

Jones saw Griffith while the Cabinet was in session and urged him to offer definite assurances to the prime minister's six questions. Late that afternoon he talked with Lloyd George, who asked if the Irish realized how near to a break they were. Jones said he had made clear to them that war was the alternative to agreement.[29] As in December, Griffith's and Collins' unwillingness to risk this alternative produced agreement.

Soon after Jones reported, the Irish reply arrived. Following a brief introduction on the history of the draft Constitution, Griffith took the prime minister's six questions in order. First, the Irish Free State was indeed to be a member of the Empire on the basis of common citizenship. As for the Crown, in all matters in which it was constitutionally effective (those arising from Commonwealth relations), its position would be the same in Ireland as in the other Dominions, but it would have no power in Ireland's internal affairs. To the third question, Griffith replied tersely that the Free State's treaty-making power would be the same as that of Canada. The Irish did not seek to exceed the position and would be glad to be shown how they had done so. On the matter of Irish appeals to the Privy Council, Griffith contended a matter of great delicacy was involved. The appeals question was being actively discussed throughout the Dominions, and many people believed they would be abolished in the near future; in Ireland, there were particular reasons for objections to the right of appeal. The Provisional Government wanted to know what guarantee of impartiality could be given in Irish cases. The possibility that the expense of appeals might be used to ruin poor suitors was also of special interest. It was not clear to the Irish that the right of appeal was a requirement of the Treaty, and, if it was, in what form it must be put. As to the oath of allegiance, Griffith declared that the Irish government was willing to include it in the Constitution and require that it be taken by all members of Parliament. On the sixth query, Griffith confirmed that all members of the Provisional Government would sign a declaration of adherence to the Treaty. He closed his letter with a pledge that he and his colleagues would amend the Constitution to make it conform with the Treaty, insofar as it could be shown there was conflict between the two.[30]

Upon receipt of the reply, Lloyd George called the Cabinet together and its members expressed general satisfaction with Griffith's letter. Further elucidation would be necessary on certain important issues, especially the Crown's position and the right of appeal, but there was nothing in the letter to warrant breaking off negotiations. Griffith was leaving for Dublin that night, but the prime minister said he would return to London in three days to discuss the Constitution further, if this were desired. The Cabinet instructed Lloyd George to inform Griffith of the government's willingness to resume conversations on June 6, using the Irishman's letter as their basis. It was also agreed that Griffith should be told informally his reply had created a favorable impression.[31]

In Dublin, the delegates reviewed the negotiations for their colleagues and the Cabinet decided that if the British insisted on including Canadian law in the Constitution, the Free State should demand the inclusion of Canadian practice.[32]

Griffith returned to London on June 6, seeing Jones first and then Churchill. He urged that Kennedy and Hewart redraft the Constitution, using his letter as the basis for revision. Hewart agreed, and by June 9 he and Kennedy had produced the first redraft.[33] A major change was the inclusion of a preliminary statement declaring that the Constitution was to be construed with reference to the Treaty, which was given the force of law in the Free State. Any provision of the Constitution or any law made under it that was repugnant to the Treaty was absolutely void and inoperative. At the same time, the first two articles of the original draft were deleted because of their strong expression of national sovereignty and were replaced by an unequivocal statement of Irish membership in the Commonwealth. However, the Irish refused to strike the third article, which asserted the sovereignty of the people, and the British yielded on this point.

This setback was one of the few suffered by the British in the revising process. As a result of the initial redrafting, the king was made part of the Legislature (article 13). The Treaty oath was made mandatory for all members of Parliament (17A), which was to be summoned and dissolved in the king's name (24). Bills were to be presented to the Crown's representative for approval, but he might withhold the Royal Assent or reserve a bill, if he acted in accordance with Canadian law, practice, and constitutional usage. A reserved bill would not become law unless it received the assent of the king in council within one year of its presentation (39A). Save in a case of invasion, the Free State was not to be committed to "active" participation in war without consent of its Parliament (46). Executive authority was to be vested in the king and exercised in accordance with Canadian law and practice (48). Hewart also obtained reluctant agreement to appeals to the Judicial Committee of the Privy Council (65).[34] Finally, the Irish agreed that all judges should be appointed by the Crown's representative on the advice of the Executive Council (67). After hearing Hewart's report, the British signatories approved the amendments and informed him what further changes were desirable.[35]

Either before or during the first stage of redrafting, the Irish abandoned their claim to independence in foreign affairs, and further changes led to deletion from the Constitution of the entire section on External Affairs. British arguments, Collins' relative lack of interest in the matter, and the apparent inconsistency of the Irish claim with the Treaty and other amendments explain this retreat.

One of the areas of disagreement remaining after the initial revision was the question of British honors for Irish citizens. The British decided to try for a compromise which would allow the king to honor Irishmen for services outside the Free State. They were also unhappy with the provision that Dail Eireann could be dissolved only by vote of its members, even though the Irish had agreed that the Crown would be the instrument of dissolution. Fearing that a hostile majority might refuse to dissolve, the British wanted dissolution only on the advice of the Executive Council. In addition, they wanted the Treaty's limitation on the Free State's armed forces included in the Constitution, and they decided to make clear that the Constitution could be amended only within the terms of the Treaty. While the Irish wanted the Crown's representative to be called the "High Commissioner," the British opposed the use of this title, because it differed from the standard title of Governor General and because it was the designation of Dominion representatives in London. They agreed to press for the title "Governor-General."

Another thorny point was the omission from the Constitution of any acceptable provision for administration of the law during the transition period preceding establishment of Free State courts. Hewart had suggested that the existing British courts bridge this gap, but the Irish protested this would make impossible the already difficult task of abolishing the Republican courts. Hewart therefore asked Kennedy to propose a suitable alternative. Last, but by no means least, was the question of safeguards for Southern Unionists. The British signatories judged it most important to placate parliamentary opposition on this issue, and they instructed Churchill to arrange a meeting with Griffith and Southern Unionist leaders.[36]

Hewart and Kennedy carried out the second redraft on the afternoon of June 9, and Hewart reported the next day that most of the desired changes had been made. Amendments to the Constitution must be within the terms of the Treaty (Preliminary, article 47). Irish armed forces should be such as were authorized by the Treaty (43). External ministers must take the oath of allegiance to the Crown (53). A suitable compromise had been arranged on the judiciary's transition period (76) and some minor changes had been made in reference to the Senate and appeal to the Privy Council. However, the Irish had stood firm on the issues of honors and dissolution of the Dail. The British decided that the prime minister should try to convert Griffith on the honors question. They still opposed dissolution of the Dail by its own vote but were willing to accept it if the Irish insisted.[37]

On the afternoon of June 10 Lloyd George, Churchill, and Hewart met with Griffith, O'Higgins, and Kennedy. The Irish decided to allow the Crown to confer honors on Free State citizens for services to the Empire, and they accepted the title Governor-General. They also agreed to pay the Crown's representative the same salary as his Australian counterpart. After some discussion, the British won their point that the Executive Council should have the exclusive right to decide the dissolution of the Dail.[38]

The Irish Cabinet met on June 12 to consider the changes that had been made in the Constitution. It approved the revised draft, with some suggestions for minor alterations designed to emphasize Dominion constitutional practice and deemphasize formal law. These suggestions were partially adopted when Kennedy met with British officials to carry out final redrafting on June 14.[39]

Until the last stage of the negotiations on the Constitution, the Southern Unionists were virtually ignored. The earl of Midleton had complained first to the Constitution Committee and then to the British about the lack of effective minority safeguards. But the loyalists got no real hearing until the British had secured the changes they wanted in the Constitution. On June 10 Churchill and Chamberlain argued the loyalists' case with Griffith, O'Higgins, and Kennedy. Two days later, Churchill and the three Free Staters met with four minority spokesmen, who objected to the Senate's limited powers and its election procedure.[40]

On June 13 Collins joined the meeting and an agreement was reached which enlarged the Senate, strengthened its legislative powers somewhat, and altered the electoral process to increase minority representation. Despite these concessions, the four Unionists remained dissatisfied. Under British pressure, they acknowledged the conciliatory disposition of the Provisional Government, but still voiced the belief that no popularly elected Senate with strictly limited powers could afford genuine protection to minorities. A letter expressing these views was published on June 16, the same day as the Constitution.[41]

In the final analysis, the Southern Unionists took an impossible position by demanding safeguards neither the Dail nor the Irish people could agree to.[42] While their past hostility to Irish nationalism made the loyalists anxious for protection, that very hostility argued against granting their demands, especially when these demands were incompatible with democratic government. As it turned out, Unionist fears were largely illusory. Some loyalists saw their homes destroyed in the troubles of 1916–1923, political jobs changed hands in the new state, and some laws were passed that reflected the majority's religious and social conventions; but on the whole, members of the former ascendancy were treated with much more consideration than Catholics in Northern Ireland or minorities in other newly liberated nations. This enlightened policy was the product of several factors. Not only was fair treatment of the minority morally right, it would promote good relations with Britain and might help end partition. Also, it would aid in keeping badly needed Unionist capital at home and would pay the nationalist debt to Protestants—from Swift to Parnell—who had led the struggle for Irish liberty. Finally, of course, reasonable concessions to a minority of less than 10 percent posed no threat to majority rule. If the Anglo-Irish had some reason for complaint in the new Ireland and failed to play the prominent role some of them had hoped for, this was due as much to their own shortcomings as to those of their fellow countrymen.

On June 15 the British signatories and Law Officers agreed that the revised Constitution conformed with the Treaty, and the Cabinet formally approved it on June 16, the same day it was published in Dublin and London.[43] As it appeared only on the morning of polling day, the Constitution probably had very little influence on the outcome of the election. Republicans attacked Griffith and Collins for making the document public only at the last minute, but the time factor made earlier publication difficult if not impossible. Moreover, it seems unlikely that earlier publication would have altered the election results significantly. Most voters supported the Treaty and, unlike Collins, they probably felt that acceptance of the Crown was the price for peace and self-government. As for the Republican minority, they would have voted for anti-Treaty candidates in preference to any others, whatever form the Constitution took.

Publication of the Constitution evoked a wide variety of responses. The *Sunday Times* (London) declared triumphantly: "Instead of weakening the Treaty, as was generally expected in Ireland, it underwrites the Treaty and underscores the Treaty in a most emphatic manner. The English victory is plain." De Valera agreed, saying he did not believe the Dail would pass the document as it stood because it would exclude from public service and practically disfranchise every honest Republican. The *Republic of Ireland* called the Constitution a "shameful document" and an abject surrender to England, while Rory O'Connor angrily declared: "The thing is too rotten to talk about." Griffith, on the other hand, hailed the Constitution as that of a free and democratic state which gave Ireland the power to control its own destiny. O'Higgins was more reserved when he introduced the document to the Dail three months later, admitting that the government had not gotten all it sought in its original draft. But if the Constitution was a strict interpretation of the Treaty, he claimed it was also a fair one, and it gave the Irish people real freedom.[44]

While the negotiations on the Constitution may seem an English victory, that victory was more apparent than real. As with the Treaty, both Britain and Ireland paid a price for peace, and—once again—the British paid more. In his searching examination of the Constitution, Dr. Leo Kohn summarized its essence as follows:

> The constitution was a most comprehensive and, in spirit, essentially republican constitution on continental lines. It had the characteristic dogmatic ring of all constitutions which embody not the legislative crystallization of an organic development, but the theoretical postulates of a revolutionary upheaval. It mocked the time-honored empiricism of the British constitution by the enunciation of basic principles and the formation of dogmatic definitions. It postulated fundamental rights. It defined in detail the scope and the functions of the several constitutional powers. It reduced to precise terms the conventional rules of the British constitution. Its archaic symbols had to be introduced, but their meaninglessness for Ireland was writ large on every page. The monarchical forms paled into insignificance in the light of the formal enunciation of the principle of the sovereignty of the people as the fundamental and the exclusive source of all political authority.[45]

According to the Constitution, the Irish Free State was a member of the British Commonwealth and the king was head of state. But it also declared that the Irish nation and people were sovereign. Doctrinaire assertions of democratic authority and fundamental rights made strange companions for the formal law of the British North America Act of

1867. But these assertions had strong support from the Irish government and people and, reinforced by Canadian practice, they made monarchical forms more a mockery than a splendid show. Unquestionably, "popular sovereignty dominated the life of the Free State from the very beginning."[46]

Even in 1922, some astute British observers perceived that the Irish were the real victors in the struggle over the Constitution. A. Berridale Keith, an expert on constitutional history and law, declared that the Constitution undoubtedly recognized the sovereignty of the Irish people and left Anglo-Irish relations entirely vague. Arguably, the Treaty gave Ireland the right to secede from the Empire; if so, that right was accentuated by the Constitution's wide claim of popular sovereignty. Canadian constitutional usage nullified royal veto power and, in effect, Irish legislation would be "utterly unfettered" by the British government or Parliament. Attempts to safeguard appeals to the Privy Council were inadequate, and it was likely that the Irish Parliament could abolish the limited appeal that existed, if it wished. Anticipating future events, Keith asked if the Constitution of the Commonwealth were not elastic enough to include a republic.[47]

These assessments were vindicated during the next fifteen years. The imposition of British constitutional law on the Irish was a futile gesture when they were given Dominion constitutional practice as well. Persistently and skillfully, the Free State exploited its own powers and the awakened nationalism of its fellow Dominions to secure abolition of the symbols of British rule. In the process, the Irish weakened British dominance in the Commonwealth and loosened its ties, repaying in kind those who forced Crown and Empire on Ireland.

Chapter 15
The Coming of
Civil War

While the London negotiations proceeded, the election campaign ran its course. On May 29 the viceroy dissolved the Parliament of Southern Ireland and summoned a Provisional Parliament. Republicans called this assembly the Third Dail while Free Staters referred to it as the Parliament to which the Provisional Government would be responsible.

From the moment the Collins-de Valera pact was signed, the press urged independent interests to contest the election. Little encouragement was necessary, and by June 3 forty-four non-panel candidates were nominated.[1] The anti-Treaty party was understandably upset, since all these candidates were pro-Treaty. On June 5 de Valera and Collins again appealed for support of the pact.[2]

Tom Johnson replied by asserting that Labor should be directly represented in the new Dail; a freely elected assembly could protect the people's rights better than a single political party. Predictably, Labor's platform was oriented to social and economic issues, such as land settlement, housing, and unemployment. It pledged that the party's representatives would work to prevent strife between the two wings of Sinn Fein and achieve national unity through an all-Ireland labor movement. Although Labor was not officially committed to the Treaty, its leaders' pro-Treaty stance was well known.[3]

Although the Republicans were unhappy with Labor's attitude, they used only verbal arguments to change it. They were well aware of Sinn Fein's debt to Labor and had no desire to alienate a party that contained a large number of Republican sympathizers. However, less tolerance was shown to other non-panel candidates. Darrell Figgis had his impressive red beard cut off by political foes, both for encouraging opposition to the panel and for running as an Independent. This indignity upset the former Sinn Feiner much more than verbal abuse, but it probably gained him popular sympathy and helped him win election. Some opponents of Sinn Fein fared worse. When appeals to patriotism did not persuade them to withdraw, threats and sometimes physical intimidation were used. Several candidates of the conservative Farmers' Party were threatened or attacked by armed men, and one was reported to have been shot and seriously wounded. Some Farmer nominees withdrew, and in other constituencies the party decided not to contest the election.[4]

Despite arguments and intimidation, a large number of non-panel candidates remained in the race. Thirty-four Sinn Fein candidates, seventeen from each faction (including de Valera), ran unopposed. But there were contests for ninety seats in twenty of twenty-seven constituencies, in which ninety panel candidates were pitted against forty-seven who represented other interests. The non-panel slate included eighteen Laborites, twelve Farmers, and seventeen Independents. Four more Independents were returned unopposed from Trinity College, Dublin.[5] Thus as many as 51 of 128 members in the new Dail might not belong to Sinn Fein.

As the election campaign neared its climax, Collins threw over the pact. On June 14, the day of his return from the London negotiations, he told a large crowd in Cork City:

> You are facing an election here on Friday, and I am not hampered now by being on a platform where there are Coalitionists, and I can make a straight appeal to you, to the citizens of Cork, to vote for the candidates you think best of, whom the electors of Cork think will carry on best in the future the work that they want carried on. When I spoke in Dublin I put it as gravely as I could that the country was facing a very serious situation, and if that situation is to be met as it should be met, the country must have the representatives it wants. You understand fully what you have to do, and I will depend on you to do it.[6]

Concern about Republican reaction to this speech probably led Collins to give the pact a moderate endorsement the following day, but it is doubtful that this lessened the impact of his Cork appeal.[7]

Both the *Irish Independent* and the *Freeman's Journal* reprinted Collins' repudiation of the pact on election day. The *Daily Mail* (London) commented that after Collins' Cork address, the pact could only be described as breaking up. General Macready felt this speech confirmed that the pact had been a "slim move" on Collins' part, rather than a sign of weakness. The *Republic of Ireland* denounced Collins' defection, and de Valera later observed: "England dictated the breaking of the Pact."[8]

Although it was an oversimplification, de Valera's explanation was essentially correct. The British accepted the pact's election provisions, but they insisted that Republicans be barred from the Provisional Government. More important, they took a firm stand on the Constitution. The British foresaw that if Collins complied with their demands, he must break with de Valera; in this sense, they dictated the breaking of the pact.

But even though the British government's attitude forced Collins' hand, virtually everything that had happened since he made the pact convinced him it could not succeed. Griffith put no faith in it. The partners in the proposed coalition could not even agree on the name or nature of the new assembly, let alone the composition and policy of the government. In any case, there was little chance the IRA would obey the new assembly. Negotiations for army unity had all but broken down in early June, and a sizable faction of the anti-Treaty IRA wanted an immediate attack on the British. Failure to secure a Republican constitution was the final blow to Collins' hope for the pact. By the time he left London, he realized that only a resounding popular endorsement of the Treaty might avert civil war. His appeal at Cork was thus both a desperate emotional plea and an astute political move. Made only when he despaired of cooperation with the Republicans, it caught them off guard and won an additional advantage for pro-Treaty candidates.

On polling day there were a few outrages, some intimidation, and a good deal of impersonation, with the anti-Treaty faction outdoing its panel partner. In most places, however, voting proceeded without disturbances. The low turnout—less than 60 percent of registered voters—can probably be attributed more to the limited number of contests than to intimidation.[9]

Because of the complex system of voter preferences under proportional representation, the final results of the election were not announced until June 24. The total popular vote was 620,283, of which panel candidates secured about 60 percent. The government party won 239,000 first-preference votes and the anti-Treaty party 130,000.[10] Labor won 132,000 first-preference votes, the Independents 63,000, and the Farmers 51,000. The government party would hold fifty-eight seats in the new Dail; seventeen of its nominees had been returned unopposed and eight were defeated. The anti-Treaty party elected thirty-six candidates, including seventeen unopposed, while twenty-two of its nominees were beaten. Labor elected seventeen of eighteen candidates; the Independents, six of seventeen; and the Farmers, seven of twelve. Counting the four Independents from Trinity College, nonpanelists would control thirty-four seats in the Dail, while the panel would have ninety-four.[11]

The government party outpolled the Republicans heavily in Leinster, the three Free State counties of Ulster, and the cities of Dublin and Cork. It beat the Republicans by a small margin in Munster and was narrowly outvoted by them in Connaught. The total vote for the Treaty, however, put the Republicans in a small minority everywhere, with just over 20 percent of the popular vote. Their defeat would have been even worse in an open election.[12]

One Republican apologist interpreted the results as a victory for the Sinn Fein panel, on the grounds that it won 60 percent of the vote and 73 percent of the Dail seats in an election in which the Treaty was supposedly not an issue.[13] But this explanation flouts the facts. Without question, the Treaty was the overriding issue in the election and its opponents were decisively repudiated. The total vote for the Treaty was 486,000, more than 78 percent of the poll, and 92 of 128 members of the new Dail, 72 percent of the House, supported the Treaty. Moreover, 71 of these deputies were elected over political opponents—almost one-third of whom were anti-Treaty while only 60 of the winning panel candidates faced opposition, and only 19 of these were foes of the Treaty.

Whatever they might say later, Republicans in 1922 had no doubt about their defeat at the polls. De Valera conceded defeat before the final returns were counted, blaming it on Britain's threat of war. The *Republic of Ireland* frankly admitted: "We have lost the election and must look beyond it." The editors claimed they were not surprised by the result and saw no reason for despair. Votes could not kill the Republican tradition, and its ultimate triumph was certain. But there would be no more pacts. Collins' treachery and the Constitution ended all chance of a coalition government.[14]

The press was understandably elated by the election results. Summing up the general attitude, a leading Dublin newspaper declared:

> The moral of the returns is threefold: first, that the Irish people approve the Peace Treaty; secondly, that they have made their protest against violence and intimidation; thirdly, that they will insist upon their right to have representatives ready to advance the business of the nation rather than men who would seek to flout the will of the electorate.[15]

While the election was held under far from ideal conditions, there was more freedom of choice than foes of the Treaty have ever conceded. The British threat of war if the Treaty were rejected, which the Republicans so roundly condemned, was offset by their own threat of civil war if the Treaty were accepted. And the Republicans employed much more direct methods than the British to impose their will. The voters' choice was not a pleasant one, but it was not dictated by any government or faction.

Collins was very much encouraged by the voting results. In West Cork, he topped the poll with over 17,000 first-preference votes, the largest total received by any candidate.[16] The people had given him the vote of confidence he wanted. Whether their mandate would secure peace was a question only the Republicans could answer.

By the time of the election, efforts to reunify the IRA had ended in failure. On May 4 army leaders agreed to a truce and both sides released their prisoners. Anti-Treaty units evacuated occupied buildings in Dublin (except the Four Courts) while the Free Staters agreed to stop occupying additional posts. Preparations for joint action against the Six Counties were also discussed. But the two sides proved unable to reach agreement on reunification. Free Staters rejected Liam Lynch's scheme for an independent Republican army and submitted counterproposals, but disagreement over who was to be chief of staff produced a deadlock.

Negotiations resumed following the Collins-de Valera pact. Lynch accepted Mulcahy's proposals on GHQ reorganization, and he was prepared to place the army under the authority of the Third Dail and the proposed coalition government. However, the IRA Executive was now more hostile than ever to compromise because three moderate members had resigned and been replaced by three extremists. After rejecting his offer, the Executive informed Mulcahy that army negotiations must cease; the Executive would take whatever action was necessary to maintain the Republic against British aggression, but would take no offensive action against Free State forces. The minister of defense at once replied that responsibility for dealing with the situation must be left to the coalition government.

Any lingering hope of reunification vanished with publication of the Constitution. In response to a demand by militants in the Four Courts for immediate war against British troops in Dublin, the Executive appointed a committee to consider the question. The committee assessed the military resources of the IRA and its opponents, recommended certain organizational changes, and suggested attacking British troops throughout Ireland in hope of provoking armed conflict between Britain and the Free State. It also urged that operations in England be resumed. Maximum military activity should be undertaken in the Six Counties, but reinforcements should not be sent north because IRA strength did not permit this.

At an IRA convention on June 18, Lynch and his followers supported Mulcahy's compromise proposals for reunification, but they encountered vehement opposition. To end debate, Tom Barry moved that the IRA give the British seventy-two hours to evacuate Ireland and that it carry out the military committee's suggestions on war measures. Brugha, Lynch, and almost all the delegates from Lynch's division opposed Barry's motion, feeling it was neither the time nor the place to discuss such a proposal. While O'Connor and Mellows probably privately agreed with this objection, they wanted an end to compromise and supported the motion. When it was narrowly defeated, 118 to 103, its supporters retired to the Four Courts in protest, closing the gates against their opponents and deposing Lynch as chief of staff. What remained of the convention adjourned without bothering to vote on Mulcahy's plan, which had served only to divide the IRA more deeply.[17]

The IRA's desperate desire to wreck the Treaty was almost achieved by the assassination of Sir Henry Wilson on June 22. Wilson was shot to death outside his London home by two members of the local IRA, who were caught as they fled the scene. Tried and found guilty of murder, both men were hanged on August 10.

Wilson was murdered because of his fanatic hostility to Irish nationalism, but the question of who ordered his death will probably never be answered satisfactorily. According to his killers, the decision to shoot Wilson was their own. A story with much wider currency is that Collins ordered the assassination before the truce and confirmed the order during the Treaty negotiations—making clear, however, that it was to be carried out only if the negotiations failed. Some persons maintain that the order was never canceled and was therefore executed in June 1922. But this contention ignores the fact that acceptance of the Treaty should have canceled the order automatically. It is not difficult to understand why Collins could have ordered Wilson's death before the Treaty. He had other men killed who were less hated and less dangerous, but it is not easy to see why Collins would have had Wilson killed in 1922, when such action would have endangered a peace settlement on which he had staked everything. However, Collins was tormented by the sufferings of Belfast Catholics and probably blamed Wilson for the Orange pogrom. In his anguish, he might well have ordered Wilson's killing as a long-overdue act of retribution, without stopping to assess the damage this could do. Yet, in the last analysis, there is no conclusive proof that Collins ordered the assassination, and the only verdict that can be returned on the available evidence is "not proven."[18]

British opinion was shocked and outraged by Wilson's murder.[19] The prime minister at once met with Churchill and a few other colleagues to decide what action was called for. After approving security measures to protect other possible victims, the conference agreed that British troops in Dublin should be confined to barracks in view of possible danger. One of the documents found on the assassins was a printed plan of IRA organization; another was a typed and annotated letter discussing IRA problems in Britain. The conference concluded that these documents provided sufficient evidence to justify the arrest of suspected subversives in London. Convinced that the Four Courts was the main source of IRA conspiracies, the conference considered methods of clearing out the building, in particular the question of using British troops. It was felt that the Provisional Government was unwilling or unable to attack the Four Courts and, though naturally bound to protest a British assault, would probably be very glad to have this difficult situation cleared up. The conference decided to ask Macready's advice about a British attack. In the meantime, Churchill was to draft a letter expressing the government's attitude, which the prime minister would send to Collins.[20]

Lloyd George's letter went to Dublin by special messenger on the night of the 22d. It stated that documents found on Wilson's murderers con-

nected them with the IRA and revealed the existence of a definite conspiracy against Great Britain. Other information received by the government showed that the IRA was preparing to resume its attacks in
England and Northern Ireland. The government could no longer ignore the IRA's ambiguous position. Still less could Rory O'Connor and
his followers be allowed to remain in open rebellion in the heart of
Dublin, occupying the courts of justice and organizing murderous conspiracies. British aid had been given to Dominion governments in the
past when rebels challenged their authority, and it was available to the
Provisional Government in the form of artillery or other assistance. The
Irish government was now supported by the declared will of the people,
and it should therefore take immediate action to end a situation which
the British government deemed incompatible with faithful execution of
the Treaty.[21]

News of Wilson's murder produced various reactions in Dublin. The
IRA Executive disclaimed all responsibility for the crime. So did de
Valera, but he also called attention to the sufferings of Belfast Catholics
and said of the assassination: "I do not approve, but I must not pretend
to misunderstand."[22] Ernest Blythe reported that the murder upset and
enraged Griffith. Collins was also disturbed, but he seemed to know
more about the shooting than Griffith, although Blythe never believed
Collins had ordered it. Griffith's statement, which Collins helped to
draft, condemned the assassination as an "anarchic deed," which could
neither be justified nor condoned.[23]

When Lloyd George's letter arrived, Collins was in Cork, and Diarmuid O'Hegarty, the Cabinet's secretary, replied on behalf of Griffith
and the Provisional Government. He expressed the government's belief
that internal disruption would destroy the Four Courts IRA, making it
unnecessary to use force, a move which might win the rebels "misplaced
sympathy." Having sidestepped the demand for action, O'Hegarty as-
tutely requested the information about IRA conspiracies, claiming it
would enable the government to ask the new Parliament to support
adequate measures against the Republicans.[24]

Churchill refused to disclose the information, on the grounds it was
highly confidential, and declared the British still awaited a reply to the
prime minister's letter.[25] Of course, the real reason why the British refused to divulge the contents of the documents that were found on the
assassins was that they offered no proof of any connection between the
Four Courts and the murder. Such a revelation was bound to weaken
British demands for action against the Republicans.

On the evening of June 23 British ministers discussed the Four Courts
with Macready, who explained that a plan for a surprise assault had been
prepared and could be put into action at short notice. While confident it
would succeed, he pointed out that it might enable the Republicans to

rally considerable popular support. The conference decided that Sunday or Monday, June 25 or 26, would be the best time for the operation. Macready was to return to Dublin and prepare for the attack. If it were approved, he would receive orders by telephone. The prime minister impressed on him the importance of giving civilians ample time to clear the target area. Macready promised he would give sufficient warning—perhaps thirty minutes.[26]

On June 24 two more conferences considered the proposed operation. The ministers discussed reports that British troops had been fired on from the Four Courts, as well as a secret-service report that indicated imminent renewal of IRA hostilities against Britain. The decision was made that Macready should attack the Four Courts the next day, and Lord Cavan sent him the order, "Proceed Sunday." The British expected a strong protest from the Provisional Government, but they did not believe the attack would cause Griffith and Collins to sever relations.[27]

Macready received the order to attack but failed to carry it out, ostensibly because he had not had time to ensure the safety of British personnel in Dublin. However, other considerations weighed heavily against proceeding with the operation, and Macready sent a senior staff officer, Colonel Brind, to London with a letter summarizing his objections. In this missive, Macready pointed out that most Irishmen accepted O'Connor's denial of complicity in Wilson's murder, however little value it might have. Moreover, an attack on the Four Courts would probably not capture the IRA leaders, and it would enable them to win the support of most of Collins' followers, who would claim that the British had broken the year-old truce. Finally, Macready argued that civilian casualties and damage to the Four Courts would be blamed on the British.[28]

On the morning of the 25th, Brind met with the prime minister and a few of his colleagues and presented his chief's letter, supplementing it with his own explanation. He discounted reports of Republican sniping and plans to attack British troops. Warning the prime minister that an ultimatum would lose the good effect of the election, Brind urged that the Irish government be given a chance to expel the Republicans on its own. Lord Cavan then read a General Staff memorandum which concurred with Macready's views. Impressed by this strong protest, especially the argument that a surprise attack would violate the truce, the ministers called off the attack for the time being. Churchill was to tell the House of Commons the following day only that the government would not proceed with the Treaty's implementation until the Four Courts problem was resolved. By timely inaction, coupled with a tardy but effective protest, Macready had saved his superiors from a step which might very well have reopened the Anglo-Irish war.[29]

When Churchill rose to speak on the afternoon of Monday, June 26, the House of Commons was in an angry mood.[30] He began with a review of events since the Treaty, referring to the deep divisions it had produced in Southern Ireland and the Provisional Government's efforts to overcome them. After discussing the Ulster situation and paying a handsome tribute to the murdered Wilson, Churchill reminded both Irish governments of their duty. The North must protect its Catholic minority; the South must carry out the terms of the Treaty. Republican occupation of the Four Courts was a clear violation of the Treaty, and the time had come when Britain had a right to demand that it be ended. If the Provisional Government did not assume the initiative very soon, the British government must regard the Treaty as formally violated and resume full liberty of action to safeguard its rights and interests.[31]

Although ultra-Unionists savaged the government, Bonar Law's sober remarks were much more disturbing. Law was not prepared to say that Britain should scrap the Treaty, but he doubted he would have voted for it had he been able to foresee the results. His pessimism was not the product of Irish anarchy or Wilson's murder (such things were inevitable in the existing situation), but he had been deceived on two vital points. He had assumed that the Treaty's Irish signatories would not try to coerce Ulster and that they meant to honor their agreement and run all risks in carrying it out. Instead, they favored coercion of Ulster and had entered into pacts with the Treaty's foes, who instigated the murders which were the root of the trouble in the North. This must be stopped. If the Provisional Government failed to restore peace and order, Britain must do so. Law believed the government meant to see the problem through; but if it failed to do so, he would oppose it, and he hoped the House of Commons would oppose it too.[32]

Winding up the debate for the government, the prime minister contended that the Treaty had been justified because the public would not agree to reconquest unless it were shown that no other policy was possible. Even if the Treaty proved a failure, it gave Britain advantages it did not possess in 1921. The British would not have to govern Ireland, but only reconquer those areas they chose to occupy. Furthermore, if Ireland broke faith now, the British government could count on united opinion at home and abroad in support of stern measures, something that was not true a year before. However, Lloyd George was not ready to admit that the Treaty was a failure. Disorder was inevitable in a period of transition to self-government, especially in a country with an inherited popular antagonism to government and without experienced leaders. He confessed disappointment that the Provisional Government had not done more to protect life and property, and certainly there was no excuse for Republican occupation of the Four Courts. Such flagrant defiance of the Irish government's authority was intolerable and must be ended quickly. However, he would prefer that the Irish take action on their own initiative rather than with the appearance of British compulsion. The new Irish Parliament was to meet within a week. What it did or failed to do would be the real test of its fitness to govern, and by that test the Treaty must stand or fall. For the moment, Britain must remain calm. The world was watching, and Britain must not be stampeded into violence by panic. He did not ask the House to let things drift indefinitely. The government was pressing the North to deal impartially with Catholics and Protestants, while insisting that the South fulfill the Treaty in every detail. If the government failed, the House must replace it with men who could do the job.[33]

Although the government won a large majority in the division on its Irish policy, the speeches of some supporters showed their patience was wearing very thin. After the debate, Bonar Law told Lloyd George and Churchill with intense feeling: "You have disarmed us today. If you act up to your words, well and good, but if not—!!" At this point, with obvious effort, he stopped speaking and stalked off.[34] The Cabinet did not want to force Collins' hand, but Law's attitude made painfully clear that it could not wait indefinitely for him to act.

During the last week of June, events in Dublin moved rapidly toward a showdown. Collins knew he must assert his authority or abdicate. What would be done, and when, depended to a large extent on the IRA. Its position, like that of the British government, was more sharply defined in the week that followed Wilson's assassination.

On June 25 a policy discussion was held in the Four Courts. Some of the participants argued that reunification with Lynch and his supporters was the first order of business. Others claimed that the surest way to restore army unity would be to attack the British, or argued that men and guns should be sent to the North to help protect Catholics from reprisals for Wilson's murder. Eventually, the meeting decided that part of the IRA should move north without delay. No further decisions were made, but early in the week conversations with Lynch took place and friendly relations were reestablished between the two factions of the anti-Treaty IRA.[35]

A series of incidents on June 26 formed the immediate prelude to civil war. First, the IRA demanded money from two firms to help support the Belfast boycott. When the government was informed of this, it decided to arrest any Republicans who engaged in similar tactics. Unaware of this decision, the IRA raided a garage to commandeer cars that had been imported in defiance of the boycott and to use them to transport men and supplies to Ulster. The raiders made off with sixteen cars, but Free State troops captured their leader, Leo Henderson. Although the IRA's raid was a violation of the May truce, officers complained to Free State GHQ about Henderson's arrest. They were told he would receive proper treatment and be released on parole, but that night they learned he was being held as an ordinary prisoner in Mountjoy jail. In retaliation, the

IRA kidnaped the popular Free State deputy chief of staff, General J. J. "Ginger" O'Connell, and held him at the Four Courts pending Henderson's release.[36]

On the afternoon of the 26th, the Provisional and Dail Governments discussed the garage raid and the IRA's threat to attack the British. Although they deferred a final decision until the next morning, Griffith and Mulcahy claimed later that the decision to attack the Four Courts was "practically taken" at the afternoon meeting. Mulcahy also recalled Collins' remarking as the meeting broke up: "I think we'll have to fight these fellows." Mulcahy replied he was sure of this, but said the decision should be left until the following day.[37]

Next morning there was much activity in the Four Courts as part of the garrison prepared to go north. Meanwhile, Free State political and military leaders pondered their course of action. Several new developments had taken place since the previous afternoon. The threat of an attack on the Six Counties had become more immediate and the IRA had shown its complete contempt for the government by kidnaping O'Connell, which strengthened the case for prompt and forceful action. On the other hand, news of Churchill's speech demanding just such action had reached Dublin. This caused resentment and made some ministers reluctant to order an attack on the IRA. "Let Churchill come over and do his own dirty work," was Collins' initial reaction.[38] However, this was only a last protest against the inevitable; Collins knew a show of force must be made. The Cabinet decided to order the evacuation of the Four Courts and the surrender of its garrison. If this ultimatum were rejected, military action would be taken at once. Griffith was to draft a press release explaining that the government's action was the result of a series of criminal acts that culminated in O'Connell's kidnaping.[39] Before adjourning, the Free State leaders agreed to ask the British for the loan of artillery, and Collins warned his fellow ministers not to sleep anyplace that night where they might be taken as hostages by the IRA.[40]

Brigadier General Patrick Daly was put in charge of the Four Courts operation. A veteran of Collins' Squad, Daly commanded the Dublin Guards, the Free State army's best unit. Major General Emmet Dalton, director of military operations, was to obtain the necessary artillery. Having seen service with the British army in France, Dalton knew something about field guns, and it was he who urged their use against the Four Courts. He was aware they could not do much damage to the massive structure, but he hoped a bombardment would demoralize the garrison. Macready at first refused Dalton's request for guns and shells but Cope quickly contacted Churchill, who ordered Macready to comply. After dark on the night of the 27th, Dalton got two 18 pounders and a small supply of ammunition. The next day, two more 18 pounders and two armored cars were obtained. Dalton could have obtained bigger guns but heavy artillery would have required British gun crews, and the government would not use British troops.[41]

While the Free Staters proceeded with their plans, life in the Four Courts continued undisturbed. The garrison had been warned that an attack was imminent but was later informed the order had been canceled. Most IRA leaders did not believe Collins would use force against them, but Oscar Traynor, commander of the Dublin Brigade, disagreed. He had already tried to persuade the garrison commanders to evacuate the Four Courts because he opposed concentrating a large number of men in a fixed position. O'Connor and Mellows, on the other hand, shared the 1916 leaders' belief in the symbolic value of occupying an important building as Republican headquarters. They refused to occupy surrounding buildings, however, since this could be considered offensive action. If there was to be civil war, the Free State must strike the first blow so that it could be branded the aggressor.

On the evening of the 27th, Mellows, Lynch, and other high-ranking officers conferred about reunification of the Executive forces. Their meeting ended cordially but inconclusively about 10 p.m. and Lynch returned to his hotel. At about this time, two government couriers arrived at the Four Courts with an ultimatum, demanding the garrison's evacuation and surrender by midnight. The headquarters staff made no reply and debated a course of action. No one wanted to surrender, but a proposal was made that staff officers should evacuate Dublin and organize resistance in the provinces. However, GHQ decided to remain in the Four Courts and conferred with Traynor, who at once began to mobilize the Dublin Brigade.

By 11 p.m. there was considerable Free State military activity in the area around the Four Courts, but a minor mutiny of government troops and the tardy return of the couriers prevented a midnight assault. In the early hours of Wednesday, June 28, government forces surrounded the Four Courts, blocked its gates, and brought their artillery into position on the opposite side of the Liffey River. At 3:40 a.m., another ultimatum was delivered, setting a 4 a.m. deadline for evacuation and surrender. No reply was forthcoming, and when General Daly telephoned the Four Courts at 4 a.m. he was told there was no reply. He therefore passed the order to open fire. A burst of rifle and machine-gun fire, followed by the explosion of artillery shells, marked the beginning of the Irish civil war.[42]

Inevitably, any consideration of the causes of the civil war starts with the Treaty, for it precipitated the split that led to armed conflict. However, controversy over the Treaty revealed a more fundamental division of opinion, over a principle which Collins rightly maintained transcended all others: "It is the right of the people to govern themselves. It is the principle of government by consent of the governed."[43] In considering whether the Treaty were worth civil war, O'Higgins expressed the same idea. The agreement conferred very great benefits and opportunities on the Irish people, and he would not declare offhand that it was not worth civil war.

> But if civil war occurs in Ireland it will not be for the Treaty. It will not be for a Free State versus anything else. It will be for a vital fundamental, democratic principle—for the right of the people of Ireland to decide any issue, great or small, that arises in the politics of this country. Never before in Ireland by Irishmen has that right been challenged. That right is sacred. That right, in my opinion, is worth defending by those who have a mandate to defend it.[44]

Foes of the Treaty faced this issue head on. They would have preferred to have popular support, but lack of it did not deter them. The revolution had begun in 1916 without the people's support; only after the execution of its leaders had public opinion begun to change. Exhaustion and fear of renewed war might tempt the people to abandon the Republic, but if its guardians remained faithful in the time of trial, the country would soon rally again to the Republican standard. Those who held this view stated it in various ways. They asserted that the people's will was only the expression of one generation and had no power over the people's sovereignty, which was the expression of the life of the race from beginning to end.[45] De Valera put it more simply: "The majority have no right to do wrong."[46] Perhaps the idea was best expressed by Childers, shortly before his death in the civil war: "For we hold that a nation has no right to surrender its declared and established independence, and that even a minority has a right to resist that surrender in arms."[47]

Whatever the words, this argument was an unqualified denial of the people's right to govern themselves, a right proclaimed as the primary goal of the revolution from its beginning. Yet the idea of a self-ordained elite was embedded in Ireland's history as deeply as that of national and individual freedom. The elitest mentality was present to some degree in every nationalist movement—constitutional as well as revolutionary—but it was strongest among the leaders of 1916 and some of their successors. The issue of Free State versus Republic overlay that of democracy versus dictatorship, but in the latter may be found the true origins of the civil war.

The immediate causes of the war are more difficult to summarize. Republican apologists have generally claimed that the decision to attack the Four Courts was the result of British dictation—like everything else since the Treaty.[48] Mounting pressure from London played a part in

determining the Irish government's course of action, but it was not decisive. The Free State leaders were very sensitive to the danger of being
labeled British puppets. They refused to bow to Lloyd George's ultimatum of June 22, and when they decided to fight, Churchill's public
demand that they do so produced anger and momentary hesitation.
Griffith claimed it was "pure coincidence" that the assault occurred so
soon after Churchill's speech.

> When the garage was occupied, we nearly decided to move; but when
> O'Connell was kidnapped we did decide to move, and the order was given.
> Then came Churchill's speech, and we wavered again. Some of us wanted
> to cancel it. But we said that we had either to go on or to abdicate, and
> finally we went on.[49]

Griffith's chronology may not be exact, but his description of the government's reaction to British pressure is supported by other ministers.[50]

In considering the question of British dictation, it must be remembered that Griffith himself, as well as other members of the government,
had been urging a showdown with the Republicans for months. Furthermore, it should be noted that neither Lloyd George nor Churchill
delivered an ultimatum on June 26. Churchill used some bellicose
phrases, but neither he nor the prime minister set any time limit for
action against the Four Courts. Indeed, the prime minister assumed that
Griffith and Collins would lay the whole problem before the new Parliament when it met on July 1. Had the British been assured this would
be done, they would certainly have refrained from direct intervention.

In the last analysis, it was Collins, rather than Griffith or the British,
who decided the issue in this crisis, as in previous ones. And he decided
to fight because the IRA's refusal to obey the government or the electorate left him no other choice. Taking the problem to Parliament would
not have resolved it, because the Dail would almost certainly have urged
another attempt at compromise, and experience had taught Collins the
futility of compromise with the IRA. Now that the government had a
mandate and the guns to carry out that mandate, its duty was clear.[51]

All that was lacking by the last week of June was an incident that would
justify a showdown. The Republicans supplied this by their garage raid
and their kidnaping of O'Connell. "Ginger" O'Connell was one of the
most popular officers in the government army, and a much more appealing cause for its IRA veterans than the Treaty, the Constitution, or
majority rule.[52] The division in the anti-Treaty IRA bolstered arguments
for prompt action. Collins and Mulcahy knew about the split at the June
18 convention, but they were probably unaware of reconciliation attempts after June 25. In all likelihood, they hoped that if they struck at
once, fighting might be largely confined to Dublin. If Lynch and his

followers stood aside, opposition outside the capital could be overcome in a short time. In fact, the fighting might be ended in a week or so, as Gearoid O'Sullivan predicted to the Cabinet on June 27.[53]

By all odds, the time was ripe for action, and—to paraphrase Shakespeare—they had to take the current when it served, or lose their ventures.

Chapter 16
From Dublin to
Beal na mBlath

As its troops blazed away at the Four Courts, the Provisional Government declared its determination to end Republican outrages and restore law and order under free institutions. All citizens were urged to cooperate actively with the government's efforts.[1] Angry IRA leaders were quick to reply. The Free State attack closed the breach between the forces of Lynch and O'Connor, with the result that Lynch and other senior officers outside the Four Courts issued a defiant proclamation on June 28. Addressed to "Fellow Citizens of the Irish Republic," the manifesto denounced the government's treachery and appealed to all patriotic citizens to support the fight against British oppression.[2]

De Valera at first refused to believe that the Free Staters were attacking the Four Courts. However, by the time he arrived in the city center (from his home), he realized the news must be true. Brugha and Stack confirmed it, but when de Valera appealed for their help to stop the fighting, both men said it was too late. De Valera issued a statement blaming England for the civil war and calling on the IRA and the people to support the men in the Four Courts, "the best and bravest of our nation." Feeling he had no choice but to stand with the men who embodied "the unbought indomitable soul of Ireland," de Valera rejoined his old battalion. However, he refused to assume any position of command, seeking instead to end the war by political compromise.[3]

On the evening of the 28th, the Free Staters ran out of high-explosive shells, and Macready refused to supply more, claiming his stock had been reduced to the minimum required for his troops' security. While frantic efforts were made to expedite British ammunition shipments to Dublin, Dalton informed Macready that his men would give up the fight if the artillery fire ceased. Macready thereupon gave him fifty rounds of shrapnel to maintain a noisy if ineffective bombardment through the night.[4]

News of the fighting in Dublin caused a great stir in Whitehall, and four high-level conferences were held on June 28–29 to discuss the situation. At 11:30 a.m. on the 28th, the prime minister met with Churchill, the war secretary, and General Lord Cavan and was assured that Macready had been told to give the Irish government whatever support it requested, including troops. The progress of the fighting was discussed at the other conferences that night, and it was agreed that the attack must not be allowed to fail, even if this necessitated British intervention.[5]

On June 29 the military subcommittee on Irish affairs approved a large-scale transfer of arms and ammunition to the Provisional Government. Churchill told the subcommittee that Britain must be prepared to intervene militarily, if this were necessary to defeat the IRA in Dublin. He asked Lord Cavan to prepare a plan for such action, and Cavan assured him that one was ready.[6] Next day, Churchill reviewed the latest developments for the Cabinet, emphasizing that the Irish government had acted on its own initiative in attacking the IRA. Shortly before the conclusion of this meeting, news was received of the partial destruction of the Four Courts.[7]

Any possibility of British intervention faded rapidly as it became apparent that the Free Staters would capture the Four Courts. Fresh supplies of high-explosive ammunition reached Dalton on the 29th, and by that night continuous shelling had opened a breach in the wall of the building's west wing. Government troops mounted a massive assault at about 11 p.m., and by midnight a large part of the Four Courts was in their hands. Early next morning a temporary truce was arranged to evacuate wounded IRA from the battle area. Shortly after fighting resumed, the Four Courts caught fire, probably as a result of repeated shelling. Within an hour, a tremendous explosion destroyed a large part of the building's interior. This blast was probably caused by flames igniting the ammunition dump. Three more explosions completed destruction of the building's interior on the afternoon of the 30th.[8]

The garrison's surviving members were trapped; if they remained where they were, they would be killed by flames or explosions. While officers debated whether to surrender or try to fight their way out, a message from Traynor arrived, ordering immediate surrender. He could not fight his way through to the Four Courts, and as senior officer outside the Four Courts he had the right to order a move that would strengthen his military position. At 3:30 p.m. the garrison asked for terms and was informed that surrender must be unconditional. Shortly afterward, O'Connor and Mellows led out about 150 survivors of the original force of just under 200 men, along with "Ginger" O'Connell, the ostensible cause of the attack. The government at first refused to treat the Republicans as prisoners of war, but gave way in the face of their determination to accept nothing less.[9]

Whatever the government's expectations, Republican resistance did not end with the fall of the Four Courts. Instead, the Dublin fighting began a bitterly contested conflict that lasted almost a year. Its continuance was not due to any lack of peacemaking efforts, however, for these began almost as soon as the fighting itself.

Some prominent women were the first to try their hand at mediation. Their first effort failed because Traynor refused to accept the government's demand for arms surrender. The ladies thereupon called on the government to summon the Dail, whose meeting it had postponed, before undertaking further military operations. Griffith replied that the Dail would meet only when the armed challenge to its authority had been suppressed. Undeterred, the women persuaded the Labor Party to join with the lord mayor and the archbishop of Dublin in another mediation effort, but this also failed when Griffith and Collins reiterated that there would be no truce unless Republicans surrendered their arms. Labor leaders tried twice more to end the fighting, but both sides remained adamant.[10]

An attempt by the Free State's chief of staff to promote peace proved a costly mistake. Shortly after their arrest on June 28, Eoin O'Duffy released Liam Lynch and two other high-ranking IRA officers, inferring from some ambiguous remarks by Lynch that he would take no part in the fighting. Unaware that Lynch had just helped draft a call to arms, O'Duffy hoped that he would serve as a neutralizing influence on the IRA in the South. However, Lynch and his companions at once left Dublin to organize Republican resistance in Munster, and the government paid dearly for misinterpreting his attitude.[11]

After the fall of the Four Courts, the Free State army prepared for an assault on the remaining Republican positions in Dublin. On July 2 government forces began to apply pressure on the IRA's major stronghold, a block of buildings on the east side of O'Connell Street. By evening of the next day, Traynor ordered evacuation of this position. With de Valera, Stack, and others, he slipped through the Free State cordon around the area, leaving Brugha in command of a small rearguard. On July 4 the government tightened its noose around the enemy-occupied buildings, which had caught fire. Traynor twice ordered Brugha to surrender but his messages did not get through. By early evening on the 5th, Brugha realized that further resistance was impossible and ordered his command into the street to surrender. Once this was done, he rushed from the burning buildings, a pistol in each hand. Ignoring demands to surrender, he began firing and was cut down by machine guns. The fallen warrior was taken to a hospital, where he died two days later, the first prominent victim of a war he had no wish to survive.[12]

The battle of O'Connell Street ended heavy fighting in Dublin, leaving 65 killed and 281 wounded. To offset its soldiers' inexperience, the Provisional Government made maximum use of artillery to reduce enemy positions, and this caused considerable destruction. When the battle was over, the Four Courts and the east side of O'Connell Street were in ruins and the west side had suffered heavy damage. Total property destruction was estimated at between £3 million and £4 million.[13]

Fighting brought the city's life to a standstill. Most citizens kept to their homes, shops were closed, and communications with the rest of the country were almost cut off. Had the battle continued much longer, provisioning the capital would have become a serious problem. Once the shooting tapered off, however, things returned almost to normal very quickly. Newspapers resumed publication even before the battle ended, although they were subject to strict military censorship. The streets were soon filled with people going about their business, despite the inconvenience of roadblocks and arms searches.

The British government was quick to applaud the Free Staters' forceful action. Churchill wrote Collins on July 7, voicing sympathy for his "terrible ordeal" but maintaining that strong measures were essential. Had the Provisional Government not acted firmly, he said, neither the British government nor the Treaty could have survived another parliamentary debate on Ireland.[14]

Although the civil war lasted almost a year, the IRA's initial errors determined its outcome. The Republicans' most serious mistake was adoption of a defensive strategy. The Four Courts leaders should not have concentrated their forces in a position where they were vulnerable to siege and bombardment. Since Traynor apparently understood the weakness of a static defense, it is strange that he repeated O'Connor's mistake. He would have done better to harass the enemy with ambushes and sniping, while calling on the IRA outside Dublin to rush in troops before the government could overcome the local opposition. The Provisional Government probably had about 10,000 men under arms, 2,500 of whom were in Dublin. Although outnumbered in the capital, the IRA was much larger than the Free State army, and its supply of 3,000 rifles could have been rapidly augmented by the capture of isolated government posts in the provinces.[15]

Once fighting broke out in Dublin, IRA leaders elsewhere should have mobilized as many men and guns as possible and moved on the city. If the IRA won there, there was no need to worry about the rest of the country; but if it lost there, it lost the war. However, irregular leaders in the country were no more aggressive than those in the capital. Lynch assumed a defensive position in the "Republic of Munster," allowing the government to gain control of Dublin and the west before turning its full power against the south.

Inexperience in conventional warfare and a shortage of equipment made effective planning difficult for the IRA, but divided authority made it impossible. When the Four Courts was attacked, IRA leaders who were on the outside decided that each division should act on its own. Lynch resumed the position of chief of staff, but he was never able to exert effective control over all units.[16] Unified command would probably not have prevented the IRA's defeat, but without it, defeat was certain.

While Free State leaders also had neglected to do serious planning for war, they lost no time in devising and implementing a coherent strategy once the fighting started. The Provisional Government recruited soldiers as quickly as Britain supplied money and equipment for them. Utilizing unity of command, Collins and his associates first crushed organized resistance in Dublin and then turned to the provinces. Once field operations were completed, the government applied increasing pressure against IRA guerrilla bands. This phase of the war was the longest and hardest, but unrelenting use of superior force eventually broke the IRA.

As soon as the Provisional Government had secured control of Dublin, it issued a call to arms. The army grew so rapidly that many recruits could not be provided with uniforms and adequate training. By November it contained almost 30,000 men, and by the end of the civil war its total strength was 50,000.[17] In most cases, the rush to the colors was not prompted by devotion to the Treaty or the idea of democratic government, but by personal loyalties, unemployment, or anger at the Irregulars. While initial preference was given to IRA veterans, recruiting was opened to other volunteers once the war began. A large number of Irish veterans of the British army, as well as some British and American soldiers, joined the new army, and this influx gave it badly needed discipline and professional expertise.[18]

On July 8 Dalton briefed Macready on the military situation. The government planned to organize recent volunteers into a force of 10,000 men, with some 1,600 support troops. To equip this force, it needed a third battery of 18 pounders, plus 240 machine guns and 10,000 rifles with ample supplies of ammunition. According to Dalton, almost all of Leinster had been cleared of major opposition, but the IRA controlled the area west of the Shannon and of the Cork-Limerick line, although the people there supported the Free State. The government was preparing to move against Limerick, where about 1,000 Irregulars were concentrated. If this force could be broken up, the trouble in the west could be ended in about a month.[19]

As Dalton spoke with Macready, the Free Staters had just completed an operation that destroyed a possible threat to Dublin. While fighting for the capital was still in progress, Traynor appealed for aid from IRA units south of the city, and these units began to concentrate around the town of Blessington. Free State GHQ ordered a force of over 1,000 troops to encircle them. Faced with entrapment and aware of Traynor's defeat, the IRA carried out a rapid withdrawal. When the Free State advance guard entered Blessington on the morning of July 8, they found their birds had flown. Nevertheless, the operation secured the safety of Dublin and its communications with the Free State base at the Curragh of Kildare, as well as netting more than 100 prisoners.[20]

The Republican retreat from Blessington made Limerick the first major confrontation outside Dublin. If the IRA controlled the city, the western flank of its Limerick-Waterford defense line would be safe. Moreover, its possession would enable Lynch to help Irregulars west of the Shannon hold Connaught. On the other hand, loss of Limerick would divide Republican forces in Munster and Connaught and give the Free Staters a base for operations against Cork, Kerry, and Tipperary.

The Republicans controlled four barracks in the city of Limerick. Government troops, under the command of Generals Hannigan and Brennan, occupied several other positions. Although the two Free State commanders were willing to fight, they were very short of guns and ammunition and decided to play for time. On July 4 they made a truce with Lynch, but when news of this reached Dublin, O'Duffy thought they had betrayed the government. Further parleys with Lynch, against O'Duffy's orders, made GHQ even more suspicious of Brennan and Hannigan. It now appeared doubtful that they would get the guns they needed to break off negotiations and to fight, simply because they had parleyed in order to hold their ground until those guns arrived. An arms convoy was on its way, but the officer in charge had been ordered to make sure Brennan was loyal before transferring the weapons to him. Fortunately, this officer knew Brennan well and was quickly convinced of his loyalty when they met on July 11. He turned over the guns and ammunition and reported favorably to GHQ on Brennan's conduct. Brennan at once ended the truce, and that evening his troops opened fire on the IRA. Fighting lasted a week, with neither side winning a decisive advantage.

On July 18, Free State reinforcements arrived from Dublin, and the next day government forces began a bombardment which probably turned the scale in a hard-fought battle. In the early hours of the 21st, the IRA evacuated the city, blocking roads and destroying bridges to hold up the enemy advance. When they entrenched some miles south of the city, Lynch was not among them. He had left Limerick before the fighting started and set up new headquarters at Clonmel, in Tipperary.[21]

On July 12 the government created a War Council, composed of Collins, who was named commander in chief; Mulcahy, minister of defense and chief of staff; and O'Duffy, assistant chief of staff and general officer commanding, Southwestern Division. Cosgrave became chairman of the Provisional Government and minister of finance for the duration of Collins' military service.[22]

On the same day, the government again postponed the opening of the Dail and further postponements deferred its assembly until September 9.[23] Although this arbitrary action aroused widespread criticism, circumstances justified it. The Treaty had both legislative and popular approval, but it could not be carried out until armed resistance was crushed. Only when victory was assured could the government afford the restraints of parliamentary rule. Even if the government had wanted to convene the Dail, practical considerations argued against it. Communications were badly disrupted, and some deputies found it very hard to attend, while others, including several ministers, were on active military service.

During July the government took another step that provoked strong objections. It suspended the sittings of the Supreme Court of the Republic, declaring that the Republican court system was largely irregular and illegal and that the government preferred to use the former British courts, now under its control, pending reorganization of the judicial system. This explanation, however, did not give the real reasons for the government's action. Ministers knew that the British wanted the Republican courts suppressed without delay. More important, the government was aware that Republicans intended to use these courts to challenge its imprisonment of rebels and refusal to convene the Dail, thereby hindering prosecution of the war. When the Republicans persisted in this effort, the government abolished the entire system of Republican courts.[24]

In protest against this attack on the judicial system, Gavan Duffy resigned from the government in August. Although he had a case on the court question, Duffy's resignation may well have owed more to other causes. He had been nervous since the start of the war and may well have been looking for a "way out," which he found on the court issue. Duffy later claimed that objections to the Constitution had led him to offer his resignation to Griffith in June, but Griffith had persuaded him to withdraw it, at least until the new Dail met.[25]

Despite political problems, military matters remained the government's chief concern. One of the most perplexing was Frank Aiken and the 4th Northern Division. Unwilling to engage in a conflict they held to be tragic and futile, many members of the IRA took no part in the civil war. But though individuals might remain neutral, an entire division could not, as was demonstrated by the experience of Aiken and his command. The 4th Northern Division was financed by Free State GHQ, but Aiken had retained freedom of action and worked hard to restore army unity in the months prior to the civil war. On July 4 he wrote Mulcahy that he would not take part in the fighting because it would ruin Ireland without advancing the Republican cause, but he asked if the government were prepared to wage war to enforce an abhorrent oath while it had the chance to unite the country against England. Apparently, this letter led Mulcahy to take action against Aiken. While Aiken was in Limerick, a pro-Treaty officer was placed in charge of his divisional headquarters in Dundalk; when Aiken returned, he was informed his troops were under orders to attack Republicans. On July 14, he and his officers agreed that if the government did not give its opponents a constitutional way to carry on the struggle for the Republic, they would give the government no support. Next day, Aiken presented his views to Mulcahy, with the result that he and 200 of his men awoke on July 16 to find themselves Free State prisoners. This was not the end of the story, however. On July 27, 200 of Aiken's men who had evaded capture rescued their commander and 100 comrades in a daring raid on Dundalk. Soon after his escape, Aiken recaptured Dundalk, freed the remaining prisoners, and locked up the Free State garrison. To avoid entrapment, the Republicans evacuated the town three days later, and some of them were captured in the withdrawal. But Aiken and the others who got away continued to wage guerrilla operations in the area.[26]

By the time the 4th Northern pulled out of Dundalk, the war in the field was over. After capturing Galway City on July 7, government troops cleared Sligo, Mayo, and Donegal in a series of minor engagements.[27] By the end of the month, the west was under government control and organized resistance in the south was crumbling.

When Free State commanders turned their attention to the Limerick-Waterford defense line in mid-July, they found it was not a line at all in a military sense. It marked the northern boundary of the "Republic of Munster," and roughly followed a river and road line, but the IRA lacked the resources to hold a front of seventy-five miles, even if it had been able to plan an adequate defense. After hurriedly fortifying some important positions along their perimeter, the Irregulars settled back to await attack, which was not long in coming. While fighting continued in Limerick, the Free Staters struck at the opposite end of the front. Some 400 troops under Major General Prout advanced on Waterford from their base in Kilkenny. Unopposed, they occupied the commanding heights of Mount Misery, across the River Suir from the city. The two sides exchanged fire on July 18, and next day, government forces shelled Waterford. That night, some of Prout's troops crossed the river east of Waterford and won a foothold in the city. On July 20, Prout was able to lower the bridge across the Suir and bring his main body into Waterford. The defenders had already begun their evacuation, and after offering some resistance, the remainder of the garrison surrendered on July 21. The fighting produced few casualties, but property damage was extensive because of the bombardment and the IRA's barracks-burning.[28]

While the Free Staters were engaged at Waterford, the IRA in Tipperary planned to attack their right flank, but the plan misfired and the Irregulars withdrew to Carrick-on-Suir, twenty miles northwest of Waterford. The Republicans were now in a bad way, with their front turned at both ends. On July 29–30, the Free Staters captured Tipperary town, driving a wedge in the Republican center, forcing the evacuation of Cashel, and isolating the strongpoint of Clonmel.[29]

Government troops followed their seizure of Tipperary town with an assault on the 500-man garrison at Carrick-on-Suir, a necessary preliminary to attacking Clonmel. While Prout's main body advanced northwest from Waterford toward Carrick, another Free State column moved south from Kilkenny and Callan and pushed through the IRA's outer defenses north of the town. Prout's advance party made contact with the IRA on July 31 and his main body came up the next day. On August 2, a shrapnel bombardment forced a Republican retreat to a defense line along the Lingaun River. The Free Staters attacked that line and turned back a desperate counterattack with shrapnel and machine-gun fire. This repulse ended the main IRA resistance, and the Carrick garrison withdrew to Clonmel under cover of darkness, after burning their barracks and the courthouse and wrecking the town's bridges. On August 3, Prout's advance guard entered Carrick, and five days later he moved against Clonmel. In two days his troops fought their way to the town, and at their approach, the Irregulars burned the barracks and retreated.[30]

While Free State troops were fighting in Tipperary, O'Duffy's forces began to push south from Limerick toward Cork. The retreating Irregulars took up positions at the town of Kilmallock and the villages of Bruff and Bruree. These positions formed a rough triangle, with Bruff at the apex, about fifteen miles south of Limerick. The IRA intended to use Bruff and Bruree to protect Kilmallock, an important road center which lay very close to the main Dublin-Cork railway line. On July 23, the Free Staters' pursuit of the Republicans was checked near Kilmallock in a confused night battle, and next day an IRA counterattack recaptured Bruff. The struggle in the triangle continued for a week, with both sides digging in, in conventional military style. Although the Free Staters retook Bruff, neither side gained a decisive advantage. On July 30, O'Duffy's troops launched a two-sided attack on Bruree and captured it after a stiff five-hour fight. Three days later the Irregulars counterattacked in force, but Bruree's defenders held out until the approach of reinforcements from Limerick caused the attackers to retire. On August 4 the Free Staters advanced on Kilmallock and fought their way into the town early the following morning. However, most of the garrison had left before the final attack and were heading home for Kerry, where the Free Staters had launched an attack from the sea on August 2.[31] Although it was the longest and hardest-fought battle of the civil war, Kilmallock was more a clash between armed mobs than a conventional engagement between regular armies. Not only were many of the soldiers untrained for combat, very few of the officers could direct more than 100 men in any kind of firefight.

Eager to avoid a difficult overland advance in Kerry, the government decided, on General Dalton's advice, to attack by sea as well as land. Part of the Dublin Guards sailed from Limerick to the village of Fenit in Kerry, seven miles from Tralee. With most of the local IRA engaged at Kilmallock, there were few Irregulars to contest the Guards' advance, but spirited resistance enabled IRA officers to burn the barracks before the Free State invaders captured Tralee on the night of August 2. Simultaneously with the landing at Fenit, government troops advanced from Clare and Limerick, and the Free Staters soon controlled the fertile plains of north Kerry. The mountainous region of south Kerry was a much harder nut to crack, and it became a center of last-ditch IRA resistance in the civil war.[32]

With the Limerick-Waterford line broken and operations in north Kerry successful, Free State GHQ turned its attention to County Cork, concentrating on the capture of Cork City, whose inhabitants eagerly awaited liberation. The Irregulars censored the city's press, commandeered goods and transport, tried to levy an income tax, and seized large sums to help pay their expenses. Unemployment was alarmingly high, business almost at a standstill, food in short supply, and water rationed by the beginning of August. Civic leaders did what they could to ease the situation, setting up an administration which helped maintain order and protect citizens from IRA demands. They also tried their hand at peacemaking, but both the government and the IRA rejected mediation. Collins was anxious to take Cork, realizing its capture would greatly strengthen the government's hand.[33]

When the question of attacking the city was discussed, Dalton advised against a land offensive from the north. The IRA's destruction of roads, railway lines, and bridges would make the transport problem almost insuperable. Furthermore, the Irregulars would expect such an attack, and they had large numbers of men ready to resist it. Dalton pressed for a surprise attack from the sea, as in Kerry. Collins and Mulcahy agreed, and Dalton was put in command of the operation. Though Dalton's advice was sound, there were risks in his plan. The IRA had not mined the harbor of Queenstown, but it had mined the narrow inlet between the island of Cobh and the mainland town of Passage West (seven miles from the harbor mouth and Cork City) and had blocked the River Lee beyond Passage West. However, these defense measures gave the Republicans a false sense of security, and this was the most obvious advantage of Dalton's plan.

Some 500 government troops were loaded onto two cross-Channel steamers at Dublin's North Wall on August 7, and the expedition sailed south. It reached Cork harbor late the same night and picked up a pilot for the trip through the harbor and upriver to the city. When the pilot told Dalton that the river was blocked and its shipping berths mined, Dalton ordered him at gunpoint to take the ships as far upriver as he safely could. IRA sentries spied the ships but could neither identify nor make contact with them as they moved through the harbor and anchored at Passage West, picking the only safe landing on the river. However, the Free Staters had been forced to land some miles below the city, and a rapid advance was essential if they were to exploit their advantage of surprise.

When the ships anchored at 2 a.m., Dalton sent a small reconnaissance party ashore. This movement was reported to IRA headquarters, which alerted posts around the city that a hostile landing had been made. The Free State advance, which began shortly after daybreak, met stiff resistance, and the government troops took three days to clear the way to the city. IRA leaders knew they could not hold Cork once a landing had been made; if they tried, their forces would soon be attacked on all sides. They therefore followed their usual tactics and attempted to delay the enemy advance long enough to burn the city's barracks and demolish its bridges. On August 10, with the barracks on fire but the bridges only slightly damaged, the Irregulars streamed westward from the city, completing their evacuation only a short time before Dalton's troops entered Cork that night. Government soldiers received a warm welcome, and within a few days a measure of normality was restored to the city's life.[34]

Immediately following their occupation of Cork, Dalton's troops cleared the River Lee and the area around Queenstown to ensure the port's smooth functioning. Then they pushed west and south into the market towns and smaller ports of west Cork—Macroom, Bandon, Clonakilty, Skibbereen, Kinsale, and Bantry. On August 11 the Republicans evacuated the last two towns they controlled, and the war in the field was over.[35]

After the fall of Cork, the IRA's position seemed hopeless. It had failed to win a major battle or provoke British intervention. More important, its destructive tactics had intensified public hostility toward the Republican cause. When the Four Courts fell, Mellows admitted: "The workers weren't with us." In Limerick, citizens were jubilant when the IRA was driven from the city, and in Cork, people looked at the Irregulars sullenly, as if they belonged to an invading army. Early in August, when the aged nationalist William O'Brien told him of popular anger at IRA destruction of the railway bridge over the Blackwater River at Mallow, de Valera sadly admitted that if these tactics continued much longer, "the people will begin to treat us as bandits."[36]

Concluding that defeat was inevitable, de Valera appealed to the IRA's leaders to make peace after the loss of Cork,[37] but Lynch had other ideas. He felt that the IRA, having been freed from the necessity of defending fixed points, could revert to familiar guerrilla tactics. Under Lynch's direction, small flying columns were formed to carry on the war through raids and ambushes. The chief of staff believed that prolonged resistance would prevent the government from functioning and force it to unite with Republicans to demand better terms from Britain. He refused to see that lack of popular support crippled the IRA's morale and effectiveness. Nor did he realize that guerrilla warfare could not be waged successfully against men who knew the mentality and methods of the guerrillas.[38]

On the other hand, though most people had no use for the Irregulars and hoped for a Free State victory, the government could not count on their active support. When the Dail met in September, ministers complained that people were not giving the army enough information and were not helping to restore order.[39] Macready noted this apathy and the press deplored it,[40] but it is not hard to understand. Centuries of alien rule had made the Irish indifferent or hostile to government. When Ireland finally won independence, the definition of patriotism had to be changed, but it took time to develop a sense of civic responsibility. Some people displayed great moral courage during the civil war, but many were still under the spell of a history that put a curse on informers or felt that restoring order was "the government's business." This lack of energetic popular support made the government's work much more difficult.

Protests were another problem. At its annual convention in August, the Labor Party condemned the Republicans for their political pretensions and destructive tactics, but it also attacked the government for waging war without the Dail's approval. Strongly objecting to this arbitrary exercise of power, the convention unanimously resolved that if the Dail did not meet by August 26, its Labor members would resign their seats.[41]

British observers also were none too happy with the Provisional Government; they believed it was neither pressing the war effort hard enough nor planning a civil policy to consolidate public support. Claiming that everything waited upon Collins, they believed he was too emotional, and not tough enough, to use drastic measures against former comrades. British agents had no more confidence in the army, reporting that its troops lacked discipline and proper leadership. Despite this pessimism, none of the observers advised intervention, although Macready warned it might become necessary.[42]

The British Cabinet did not enjoy hearing these gloomy reports. It had problems enough with the Provisional Government over Northern Ireland. Craig strongly resisted British pressure for an impartial inquiry into local disorders, and in the end he had his way.[43] The outbreak of civil war in the South brought a marked decline in violence in the North. IRA militants in Ulster either joined the fighting in the Free State or simply abandoned action in the Six Counties, glad to end a campaign that had already proved a dismal failure.[44] Craig's government now had a better chance to assert its authority and Protestant extremists less excuse to defy it. Order was soon restored throughout Northern Ireland, and the British dropped demands for an inquiry.

The decline in anti-Catholic violence in the North did not pacify Collins, however, and he complained bitterly about the Ulster government's policy. He asked Churchill to disavow Craig's repudiation of the Boundary Commission, and he denounced Craig's intention to abolish proportional representation in local elections. Such a step would destroy a very important safeguard for the minority, intensify nationalist discontent throughout Ireland, and weaken the Provisional Government's hold on its supporters.[45] Churchill's assurance that the British were firmly committed to the Boundary Commission, coupled with his admonitions to Craig and the Provisional Government's preoccupation with more immediate problems, ended discussion on that subject in 1922. But the proposed abolition of proportional representation continued to cause friction, and the British delayed approval of the measure in order to study its possible effects. Craig claimed that his government had the power to abolish proportional representation, that every local authority had requested its abolition, and that the old simple-plurality voting system was superior in every respect, including protection of minorities. Churchill relayed these arguments to Collins, but Collins maintained that abolition of proportional representation would deprive Catholics of their fair share of local administration and was designed to prevent the transfer of Tyrone and Fermanagh to the Free State. He also contended that approval of the proposal would violate Britain's Treaty obligations. Although British legal experts largely rejected Collins' arguments, they agreed that nationalists regarded proportional representation as a good safeguard for the minority. Its abolition would prejudice prospects for peace and cooperation both within Northern Ireland and between North and South. The royal assent to the bill could therefore be postponed.[46]

Faced with compelling arguments from both Irish governments, Churchill laid the question before a meeting of his fellow Treaty signatories, to which he invited Craig. Lloyd George appealed for a suspension of the Abolition Bill until the Dail passed the Free State Constitution, with its minority safeguards intact. Craig refused to do this, but he agreed to postpone the local elections that were scheduled for that autumn. On this understanding, the British approved the Abolition Bill.[47]

It was most unfortunate that the British government did not display as much concern for the Catholic minority in Ulster as it did for the Protestant minority in the Free State. Despite Craig's assertion that abolition of proportional representation in local elections was not designed to discriminate against Catholics, it proved to be part of a deliberate policy to deny them their rights as British subjects.[48] Continued indifference to systematic discrimination in Northern Ireland would confront Britain with an even more serious problem in the 1970s than it faced in 1922.

In the midst of its struggle for survival, the Free State suffered a traumatic loss through the death of its two founders. Although Arthur Griffith was only fifty-one, he was worn out and prematurely aged. He was also very bitter toward his foes, especially Childers and de Valera. To him, Childers was a meddling English fanatic, and he held de Valera to blame for the civil war, telling a friend "de Valera is responsible for this—for all of it. There would have been no trouble but for him."[49] Expecting the assassination of Collins and himself, plagued with worry and insomnia, the brooding president lost all trace of humor in the last weeks of his life. He left most of his work to associates, especially Cosgrave, and he signaled his intention to retire by saying that he would propose Collins for president of the Dail when it met.[50] When his friend and physician, Oliver St. John Gogarty, examined Griffith early in August, he found the president had suffered a slight stroke, had tonsillitis, and was badly in need of rest and care. He therefore placed Griffith in a private nursing home—where Griffith continued to work, despite Gogarty's orders. On the morning of August 12 he had a cerebral hemorrhage and died immediately.[51]

Arthur Griffith died a poor man, having sacrificed the prospect of material success as a journalist to devote his life to Ireland. His trenchantly expressed ideas helped inspire a dramatic struggle for independence, in which he played a leading part and secured great gains for his country. Had Griffith lived, his experience and resolution would have helped guide the work of national reconstruction. On the other hand, his real work was done, and his hatred for foes of the Treaty might have made post-civil-war politics even more rancorous than they were. For if Griffith's career testified to his dedication and integrity, it also showed that he could be dogmatic and intolerant of opposition.[52] Events from 1916 to 1921 brought out the best in him, but his survival might have tarnished the outstanding accomplishments that gained him lasting eminence.

Because of his integrity and moderation, Griffith was much admired
by British leaders who dealt with him, and they were truly saddened by
his death. So was de Valera, who did not reciprocate Griffith's hatred,
and privately paid tribute to his patriotism.[53] Collins received word of
the president's death during an inspection tour of the southwest and
returned to Dublin for the funeral. Prophetically, he observed that a
malignant fate seemed to dog Ireland: at every critical period in the
nation's history, the man whom Ireland trusted and followed was taken
from it.[54]

While the civil war drained Griffith's last reserves of strength, Collins
recovered his old determination and energy once the decision to fight
had been taken. Intent on effective prosecution of the war, he battled
constantly against apathy and slackness.[55] But even though a multitude
of problems engaged his attention, Collins never ceased to feel keenly
the tragedy of fratricidal strife. He mourned the death of Brugha as well
as that of Griffith,[56] and the death of Harry Boland moved him deeply.
Working side by side in 1917–18, the two men had become like brothers
and their friendship survived Boland's long absence in America, his
growing devotion to de Valera, and his opposition to the Treaty. When
Boland joined the Republicans in the civil war, Collins implored him to
desist before it was too late. But Boland would not yield to a man he now
regarded as a dictator, bent on destroying Republicans with his "Green
and Tans." On July 31 Boland was fatally wounded by government
troops who were arresting him. When he died two days later, Collins
wept in anguish, but he insisted that the soldier who shot Boland must
admit his action. They were a government now, he declared, and there
must be no more anonymous killings.[57]

After Griffith's funeral, Collins decided to resume his inspection tour,
reassuring friends, and perhaps himself as well, that he would be safe
among his own people in Cork.[58] On August 20 he drove from Dublin to
Limerick, then on to Cork, arriving in the city that night. Next day, he
joined Dalton in an inspection tour of local posts, discussed financial
matters with bank managers, and traveled west to inspect the garrison at
Macroom.[59] After spending the night in Cork City, Collins made a tour
of posts in his native country of west Cork on August 22. As he was
returning to Cork that evening, his party ran into an ambush on a
backroad between Bandon and Macroom. In the ensuing skirmish, Collins was shot and killed.

On his tour of west Cork, Collins' convoy had to travel over secondary
roads because of roadblocks and demolished bridges on the main routes.
Leaving Macroom on its way to Bandon, the convoy passed through a
small valley known as Beal na mBlath (Pass of Flowers), an ideal ambush
site. By coincidence, a high-level IRA meeting was being held close to
this spot at the time; about twenty-five Cork officers had assembled to

determine military policy and consider the possibility of peace. When it was reported that Collins' party had passed through the valley, the officers decided there was a good chance Collins would return to Cork by the same route and they laid an ambush. However, after lying in wait all day, the Irregulars decided the convoy had taken another way back to the city, and most of the ambush party withdrew, leaving a few men behind to remove the barricade that had been placed on the road. Around 7:15 p.m., while part of the rearguard was clearing the road, lookouts on the hillside sighted the convoy and fired at it to alert the main party and the men at the barricade.

Had the convoy—motorcyclist, Crossley tender, touring car, and armored car—pushed through the barricade, there would have been no skirmish. This was the course urged by Dalton, who shouted "Drive like hell!" but he was overruled by his pugnacious chief, who had remarked earlier that if they were ambushed, they would stand and fight.

The exchange of fire lasted about half an hour, with the Free Staters doing most of the shooting. The main ambush party heard the firing and began to work its way back to the east side of the road, where its members could join the rearguard on the west slope in a crossfire. But the main party made slow progress and did little shooting before the engagement was broken off. During the fighting, Collins changed position at least twice to get a better view of scarcely visible targets. He had moved a short distance down the road from the convoy when he was killed by a bullet that struck the back of his head. Dalton and two doctors who examined the gaping wound concluded it had been caused by a ricochet. The fatal shot was probably fired from the west slope and deflected by the armored-car turret or another hard surface near Collins' position. It is possible, however, that Collins was killed by the main IRA party on the east side of the road or by an accidental shot from one of his own men. Death by treachery has been suggested but seems most unlikely by all accounts.

The Irregulars did not know that Collins had been killed, and other members of his party kept up a covering fire while they got the corpse to shelter. The shooting subsided as daylight began to fade (about 8 p.m., 9 p.m. summer time), and after placing the body in the touring car and clearing the road, the convoy moved off. A series of mishaps forced abandonment of the armored car and the touring car, but the party reached Cork City about midnight, and Dalton sent word of Collins' death to Mulcahy in Dublin.[60]

Although it is known that Collins intended to meet with IRA leaders in the south in an attempt to end the war, it is unlikely he would have been successful. Having spelled out his terms repeatedly and won the war in the field, Collins would not have compromised on essentials. The Republicans could have amnesty and freedom to oppose the Treaty, but only on condition that they surrendered their arms and accepted the government's authority. Since Republican leaders were unwilling to agree to these terms, peace negotiations could hardly have been fruitful.[61]

The dead leader's body was brought from Cork to Dublin by sea. Thousands filed past his bier in City Hall and tens of thousands lined the streets on August 28 to watch silently as the funeral procession made its way to Glasnevin Cemetery. There, where Griffith, O'Connell, and Parnell were buried, Collins was laid to rest.

He died two months short of his thirty-second birthday, after a meteoric career that had made his name known around the world. An almost universal expression of sorrow greeted his death. Many of those who had known him and many more who had known only the legend wept openly. For Mulcahy, Collins was "the greatest reaper" Ireland had ever known. O'Higgins called him "the greatest man that ever served this Nation's cause." And Cosgrave hailed him as "the greatest Irishman since Brian Boru."[62] Lynch, Stack, and Childers all praised his services in the war against England, while de Valera grieved for the man who had once been his comrade.[63]

News of his death produced shocked silence among Republican prisoners in Kilmainham jail, which was followed by mass recitation of the rosary for the repose of the dead man's soul.[64] From Belfast, Craig wired his sympathy to the Provisional Government, and the leading Unionist newspaper declared that Southern Ireland had suffered a great loss. Lloyd George was depressed by the "terrible loss," while Birkenhead expressed shock at the passing of a complex and very remarkable man. Churchill later wrote of Collins: "Regard will be paid by widening circles to his life and to his death."[65] Although there were a few, isolated reprisals, most Free State soldiers heeded Mulcahy's appeal not to dishonor themselves or their fallen commander's memory by acts of revenge.[66]

Collins' untimely death was an irreparable loss to his country. In some ways he was naive about politics and society, he was often emotional and impulsive, and he had much to learn. But in five short years he had lived a lifetime, coupling a remarkable record of achievement with an equally remarkable capacity for growth. His magnanimity, open-mindedness, intelligence, energy, and popular appeal would have been invaluable assets to Ireland after the civil war. He could have been a tremendous force for reconciliation and progress in the years ahead. When the Big Fellow died, much of the color, excitement, and hope that marked the national revival died with him.

Chapter 17
The Ordeal of Birth:
September-December 1922

Upon the deaths of Griffith and Collins, William T. Cosgrave became head of the government. He had become acting chairman of the Provisional Government when Collins was appointed commander in chief, and acting president of the Dail when Griffith died. There was no formal opposition to his succession within the Cabinet, and he was undoubtedly the best man for the job. At forty-two, Cosgrave's long career in local government had given him a fund of administrative experience none of his colleagues could match, and his participation in the Easter Rising provided him with unimpeachable nationalist credentials. Finally, the fact that he had no connection with the army showed the government's eagerness to avoid any appearance of military dictatorship.

But although Cosgrave's elevation was a logical move, he accepted the leadership reluctantly, as a duty he could not avoid. At his first meeting with Craig he protested: "You know, I've been pushed into this. I'm not a leader of men!"[1] And he was not, of course—in the sense that de Valera or Collins was—because he lacked their personal magnetism and drive for power. Yet Cosgrave's self-assessment was too modest, for in his quiet, commonsensical way he made an effective leader. He delegated authority wisely, handled ministerial disputes even-handedly, and was, on the whole, an ideal chairman. His colleagues valued his advice and steadiness, and long before he left office his competence and wit had made him personally very popular with voters.[2]

Although Cosgrave and his colleagues remained firmly committed to the Treaty, the deaths of Griffith and Collins seem to have momentarily weakened their resolve to crush armed opposition. On September 2 Cosgrave and Mulcahy assured Tom Johnson and William O'Brien, the Labor Party's parliamentary leaders, that if the Irregulars disbanded, they could keep their arms and the government would not molest them. O'Brien conveyed this offer to the Irregulars but it was rejected. Although the government subsequently denied making such a proposal, O'Brien could hardly have misunderstood so important a concession. The IRA's refusal of the offer and the government's renewed determination to achieve a clear-cut victory probably explain the denial that it had been made.[3]

Shortly after this incident, at the request of a clerical intermediary,

Mulcahy met de Valera to discuss peace. De Valera appealed for unity and another effort to win external association. Mulcahy said the Republicans could have peace when they surrendered their arms and that de Valera should try to bring this about. The ex-president replied that he was a man of reason but the IRA leaders were men of faith. When they said they would carry on the struggle, he could only follow as a humble soldier. On this note the interview ended.[4] When Mulcahy's fellow ministers learned of this meeting, they became angry, especially O'Higgins. Only the day before it took place, the Cabinet had decided that no member should engage in peace negotiations without Cabinet approval. Despite Mulcahy's good intentions, he had violated the principle of collective responsibility, and his colleagues' indignation was justified.[5]

On September 9 the Dail finally met. The only anti-Treaty deputy to attend its opening at Leinster House was Lawrence Ginnell, recently returned from a long diplomatic mission abroad. He demanded to know whether the assembly was the Dail Eireann or the "Partition Parliament," but his queries were brushed aside and he was quickly expelled by order of the House.[6] After Ginnell's expulsion, Cosgrave was nominated to be president of the Dail. The Labor Party voted against him but he won easily. With the Republicans absent, the Treaty party had an absolute majority and could usually count on the support of the Farmers and Independents. After the vote, Cosgrave announced his intention formally to merge the Dail and the Provisional Governments, thereby ending the executive dualism which had existed since the previous January.[7]

In opposing Cosgrave's election, the Labor deputies assumed the indispensable role of constitutional opposition. To them (and a few Independents) fell the task of offering responsible criticism of the government's policies and making it justify them. Without such opposition, parliamentary government would have been reduced to a sham. The Executive Council was well aware of this, and although its members frequently expressed impatience with Labor's criticisms, they also paid tribute to the "loyal opposition."

In nominating his Cabinet, Cosgrave retained the Finance Ministry for himself. He proposed O'Higgins for minister of home affairs, Mulcahy for defense, Desmond Fitzgerald for external affairs, Ernest Blythe for local government, Eoin MacNeill for education, Patrick Hogan for agriculture, Joseph McGrath for industry and commerce (which absorbed the Ministry of Labor and Economics), J. J. Walsh for postmaster general, and as ministers without portfolio, Eamonn Duggan and Finian Lynch.[8]

On September 11 President Cosgrave reviewed the events which had led to civil war, denounced the IRA's tactics, and reaffirmed the government's determination to suppress armed resistance to the popular will. The outspoken Labor deputy, Cathal O'Shannon, at once attacked the president, criticizing his failure to justify the government's war policy or to discuss pressing social questions. The government, he claimed, cared more for property than human life. Labor was not interested in the history of the past six months but in getting rid of humbug and sentimentalities and in getting down to realities. O'Higgins responded that he too wanted to get down to realities—one of which was that basic principles were under challenge, and until they were vindicated there could be no democratic state in Ireland. The government had attacked the Irregulars to prevent them from attacking the British and to save the Dail. Its action deserved emphatic endorsement; if the Dail disapproved, let it say so and relieve ministers of the burden of office. In trying to build a true democratic state, the government had every right to count upon the Labor Party's support rather than suffer carping criticism.[9]

At this time, de Valera was also seeking understanding and support. Unburdening himself in a letter to Joe McGarrity, he blamed the Treaty party for precipitating civil war but admitted a majority of people supported the Treaty—and that was the crux of his dilemma. If the Republicans let the agreement be carried out, they surrendered their ideals; but if they continued their resistance, they repudiated what they recognized as the basis of political order and democracy: majority rule. Was it any wonder, then, that there was civil war in the minds of most Republicans as well as in the country at large? He had no hope of any agreement with the government. Its members were very weak men, who had "burned their boats," and Cosgrave was a "ninny," who would "be egged on by the Church" against the Republicans.[10]

After conferring with some associates, de Valera decided that Republicans should boycott the Provisional Parliament. Attendance at an illegal assembly would be wrong in principle, and in any case, the Republicans' presence would only unite other groups against them and retard peace. Since they lacked the force to prohibit the assembly, they should abstain from attendance and say nothing.[11]

Abstention from Parliament, however, did nothing to clarify relations with the IRA. De Valera was convinced that this question must be resolved but uncertain how to proceed. Lynch's refusal of de Valera's request for a policy meeting with the IRA's executive brought matters to a head. The chief of staff claimed that he considered a meeting unnecessary in view of the improved military situation, adding that he would be pleased to consider de Valera's views on the general situation at any time.[12] Angry at this dismissal, de Valera at once wrote another Republican: "This is too good a thing, and won't do." The political party's position must be clarified. If its policy was to leave everything to the IRA, party members should resign as public representatives. "The present position is that *we* have all the public responsibility, and no voice and no authority." If he could not get the position made "quite clear," he would resign publicly.[13]

As de Valera saw the situation, there were three possible solutions. The IRA executive could control both political and military policy; the Republican party could take control and act as the Third Dail; or a joint committee of the party and the executive could decide policy for both. Constitutionally, in his opinion, the second course would be the correct one. Yet he opposed it because the political leaders could not obtain the IRA's unconditional allegiance, and without it a Republican government would be a farce. De Valera admitted he was partly to blame for this: "Rory O'Connor's unfortunate repudiation of the Dail, which I was so foolish as to defend even to a straining of my own views in order to avoid the appearance of a split, is now the greatest barrier that we have."

Even if a Republican government could get the IRA's allegiance, Republicans did not have the military strength to make their will effective, "and we cannot, as in the time of the war with the British, point to authority derived from the vote of the majority of the people. We will be turned down definitely by the electorate in a few months' time in any case."

Finally, a Republican government could not refuse to let the people choose between Free State and Republic, and popular rejection of the Republic would be the worst possible result. As things stood, de Valera preferred army control of policy because this was most in accord with reality. Joint control of policy by the party and the army would not work because each body had different functions.[14]

On October 16–17, the IRA executive held its first meeting since July, gathering at Lynch's headquarters in southwest Tipperary. Lynch called the meeting because he felt a review of the military situation was desirable and because of de Valera's demand for clarification of army–party relations. Twelve members appeared and four more were coopted to replace those in prison. During the meeting the executive appointed a five-man army council to discharge its functions when it was not in session, with Lynch heading this body as well as the executive. After deciding they could not accept peace terms which brought Ireland into the British Empire, the IRA leaders turned to the question raised by de Valera. Lynch read a letter from the ex-president which revealed he had changed his mind since September. He now argued that all sides of the movement supported the establishment of a Republican government. A government was necessary to provide a rallying point, coordinate efforts to preserve the Republic, maintain continuity, and prevent the Free State from establishing itself as the legal successor of the Second Dail. Since army allegiance was essential for a Republican government, the executive must take the initiative in establishing it. The only public policy necessary for the moment was to maintain the Republic, but the army and the government must agree on three vital matters: majority rule, peace terms with the Free State, and, if the IRA won the civil war, peace terms with Britain. The executive voted to form a civil government, but it stipulated that this government could accept no peace terms which made Ireland part of the Empire and it reserved final approval of any peace agreement to itself.[15]

On receipt of this news, de Valera and other available Republican deputies from the Second Dail met secretly in Dublin on October 25. They decided that only anti-Treaty deputies constituted the Second Dail, which remained the *de jure* government. The assembly unanimously chose de Valera as president of the Republic and approved a council of state which included Stack and Barton. The next day, these decisions were publicized, and on October 28 the IRA executive pledged allegiance to the new government.[16] However, all this really changed nothing. What power there was in the Republican movement was still held by the IRA; effective authority over most of the country remained with the Free State regime.

The formation of a Republican government made no impression on the Catholic bishops, whose pastoral letter of October 10 had roundly condemned the anti-Treaty forces for waging a war of wanton destruction, of murder and assassination against the people and the people's government. This defiance of legitimate authority could not be justified: "A Republic without popular recognition behind it is a contradiction in terms."[17] The Republicans vigorously protested the bishops' action, charging them with trying to use their spiritual authority to impose anti-national views on patriots.[18]

In defense of the bishops, it can be argued that the rebels were fighting a native government, not an alien one, and that senseless violence seriously threatened morality as well as social order. On the other hand, the hierarchy should have realized that its threat of excommunication could not end the resistance of dedicated Republicans, but it could make them as hostile to the Church as they were to the Treaty. De Valera and rebels like him may have been more saddened than angered by episcopal denunciations, but others were alienated from the Church for years (or even permanently) by such attacks. However well intentioned their attitude, the bishops might have better served the Church and the cause of peace had they been less vehemently anti-Republican during the civil war.

However, episcopal sanctions against the rebels proved far less drastic and controversial than those employed by the government. In September, General Mulcahy proposed that the army be granted authority to try and punish a wide range of offenses. After a lengthy discussion, the Cabinet unanimously agreed and submitted the proposal to the Dail on

September 27.[19] Under the terms of the special-powers resolution, military courts were empowered to try cases involving attacks on the national forces, specified offenses against property, unauthorized possession of lethal weapons, ammunition, or explosives, or breaches of any general regulation made by the military authorities. These courts could impose the death penalty if they chose.[20]

The Labor Party opposed the resolution, claiming it would sanction a military dictatorship and make martyrs of the rebels.[21] In rejoinder, Mulcahy argued that without extraordinary powers the army could not complete pacification of the country, and there was no other force to do this. All the army wanted was the power to impose sentences that civil administration would impose if it existed. This power would not be used in any spirit of revenge, but as a preventive measure against destruction, and its employment would improve army discipline and morale. Cosgrave assured the Dail that it could reject any general order issued under the authority of the resolution and that the government was prepared to review every sentence handed down by the military courts. After making minor amendments, the Dail approved the resolution, 47 to 15.[22]

Although the Labor Party maintained its opposition to special military powers, its leader left no doubt that he supported the government on the fundamental issue. Peace, said Tom Johnson, could only be achieved through recognition that the Treaty must be accepted and worked, and armed resistance to it must end. Johnson felt, however, that the government should give the Irregulars a chance to quit fighting before it put the new military powers into operation. He suggested a truce to discuss the possibility of Republican surrender.[23] The government refused to commit itself to a cease-fire, but President Cosgrave announced an amnesty on October 3, to give rebels a chance to surrender before the military courts went into action. This move failed to secure decisive results and the special-powers regulations were put into effect on October 15, the day the amnesty offer expired.[24]

The first executions took place a month later. Four youths were arrested in Dublin, found guilty of carrying guns without authorization, and shot by a firing squad on November 17.[25] Johnson at once demanded a fuller explanation of the case. He did not believe the victims were shot simply because of unauthorized possession of arms, and the country would support his demand for more information. Mulcahy replied that the four men had been executed because they had been found in the streets at night, carrying loaded revolvers and waiting to take the lives of other men. He realized the executions would shock and sadden people; but people had to be shocked and stern measures taken, or assassins, wreckers, and looters would destroy the country. Johnson was satisfied. He assumed that the executed men had been preparing an ambush, and only stringent measures could stop such detestable crimes.

But he believed it essential to provide full information on future executions to justify them to the public.[26]

Within a week of the first executions, the firing squad claimed a much more eminent victim. During the early months of the civil war, Erskine Childers had directed Republican propaganda, but dissatisfaction with this work led him to resign and make his way toward Dublin.[27] On November 11, Free State troops captured Childers at his cousin's home in County Wicklow. At the time, Childers had in his possession a small automatic pistol given him by Collins. On November 17, he was tried by a military court for unlawful possession of this weapon, found guilty and sentenced to death, and the sentence was confirmed by the Army Council. However, before sentence was passed, Childers alleged probable prejudice in the verdict. A speech by O'Higgins on the day of his trial, accusing him of "wicked activities," seemed to Childers an order to the court to convict and execute him. Childers also mentioned a recent address by Churchill, branding it slander and an appeal for his death. While affirming his belief that the executions policy was wrong and disastrous, Childers declared he was not trying to escape any penalty, but felt he must protest slander and ignominy.[28]

Even though he had no desire to seek a reprieve and refused to recognize the authority of the court which tried him, Childers was persuaded to apply for a writ of *habeas corpus* on behalf of eight other condemned prisoners. No application could be made in their names, because the government refused to divulge them, but a successful application for the writ in Childers' name would surely bring their reprieve.[29] The master of the rolls rejected the application for *habeas corpus* on the grounds that a state of war existed, and the military's authority was not subject to judicial control. This decision was somewhat embarrassing to the government in that, technically, it made Childers a prisoner of war rather than a captured rebel. But neither this fact nor an appeal by Childers' counsel against the adverse decision stayed the execution. At 8 a.m. on November 24, he was shot.[30]

De Valera and other Republicans mourned Childers' death[31] and news of his execution raised an outcry in the Dail. Gavan Duffy paid tribute to the dead man and denounced the vile personal attacks on him. Claiming that many people believed this propaganda, Duffy maintained that the government had a paramount duty to make sure it would not be influenced by anything that had not been proved against Childers in court. Yet he had been tried in secret, with no public statement of the charge against him, and condemned to death. His application for *habeas corpus* had been rejected because of the existence of a state of war, but he had not been treated as a prisoner of war. Instead, he had been executed for possession of a pistol in what was virtually his own home, while other men had only been imprisoned for similar crimes. Turning to the previous executions, Duffy asserted that the four prisoners had been charged only with possession of arms, but according to the minister of defense they had been condemned and shot for intent to kill other men, something which was very hard to prove. The army had no business charging a man with one thing, then condemning and executing him for something more serious. Either Childers had been executed for a minor offense, which did not justify capital punishment, or other factors had influenced those who confirmed his execution. Duffy believed the latter supposition was correct and that an awful injustice had been done.[32]

President Cosgrave heatedly declared the government had no defense to make for Childers' execution because none was necessary. Those who inspired acts of violence would receive the same punishment as those who committed them. The government simply wanted to restore order. The purpose of the executions was to save lives, and the government would not be terrorized from doing its duty, as Duffy had been.[33]

The following day, O'Higgins delivered a stinging attack on Childers and the Irregulars. Childers had come into the Irish struggle "on the last emotional wave," without any understanding of it. Ireland was not a stage where "certain neurotic women and a certain megalomaniac kind of men may cut their capers." Anyone who came to Ireland for adventure would get it, if he menaced the life of the nation. Use of force might not settle the issues in dispute, but it might cause people to conclude that reason rather than road mines should be the deciding factor in political affairs.[34]

Dr. Patrick McCartan, a reluctant supporter of the Treaty, accused the government of murdering prisoners of war. Ministers talked of majority rule, but they had no popular mandate for waging civil war or executing their opponents. Whether the Republicans' tactics were right or wrong, they were men who were fighting for a noble ideal, and Childers was a great man who had tried to do his best for Ireland. The Irregulars had done much to kill the Republican ideal, but the government's mistaken policy was reviving it, and as a Republican, he was glad.[35]

Eoin MacNeill admitted that there was a "deep, public prejudice" against Childers, which he had never shared. But the Republicans were responsible for horrible propaganda that was creating deep feelings of hatred and vengeance among Irishmen. They were committing acts of violence which could destroy the nation's material life. The government had a duty to prevent that, and this meant that whatever amount of force was necessary to suppress armed violence, as quickly as possible, must be used. It was not enough to criticize the government's actions; critics must produce an alternative to what the government felt it had to do.[36]

Debate resumed next day, when it was announced that three more prisoners had been shot for unauthorized possession of revolvers and bombs.[37] Tom Johnson denounced such action as anarchy. He demanded that military trials be made public and warned that the government could not expect the people's support unless it informed them about such vital matters. Darrell Figgis supported Johnson, claiming that secrecy only encouraged the people to refuse any responsibility for what the government did in their name.[38]

Mulcahy asked how much more the people of Cork, Kerry, Tipperary, and Mayo needed to know about the executions, when they saw with their own eyes the destruction done by the Irregulars. The army did not like the work it was doing, but there was no one else to do it. Military courts met in secret only because of the weakness of the government and the people. Perhaps, when the situation improved, there could be more publicity, or civil courts could try rebel offenses. The three men who had just been executed had been captured near the headquarters of the Criminal Investigation Department, immediately after an attempt to blow up the building. The attempt had failed but damage had been done, and many persons could have been killed but for the terrorists' inexperience. That was the kind of thing the army had to deal with, and it had to act as it did to save the country.[39]

Before we adjourn discussion of the executions, a brief comment is in order. Unquestionably, the intense personal hostility which some Free State leaders felt toward Erskine Childers, coupled with an exaggerated estimate of his influence in the Republican movement, played a part in his execution. But there is another side to the question. Childers was technically guilty of a capital offense. Much more important, he was an avowed enemy of democratic government. Shortly before his death, he stated his position succinctly:

> The slow growth of moral and intellectual conviction had brought me where I stood, and it was and is impossible and unthinkable to go back. I was bound by honour, conscience and principle to oppose the Treaty by speech, writing and action, both in peace and, when it came to the disastrous point, in war. For we hold that a nation has no right to surrender its declared and established independence, and that even a minority has a right to resist that surrender in arms.[40]

It did not matter that Childers was mistaken in his assessment of the Treaty or that he differed from the great majority of his countrymen in this view. It mattered very much that he refused to allow the people to decide their own political future. Neither their will nor that of the Dail counted when they opposed his convictions. Ministers saw this plainly enough, however prejudiced some of them might have been toward Childers. And they held it unjust that this man should live while others died because of actions he helped inspire. So Erskine Childers was executed, dying—as he had lived—magnanimous but irreconcilable;

perhaps knowing the only peace he would ever find was the peace of the grave.

One word more. Whatever criticism may be made of the executions, they achieved their end. In the words of the leading Republican apologist:

> The Provisional Government had devised a war-measure better calculated than any used by the British Government to break down the resistance of those opposed to them.[41]

When the civil war began, Lynch intended that the IRA should not violate the rules of war.[42] By the end of November, however, he felt it could no longer tolerate the government's war measures. On November 27, Lynch addressed a letter to the Speaker of the Dail, pointing out that Republican troops had consistently adhered to recognized rules of war (with the important exception of not wearing uniforms). But the government and its army had shown no such concern for these rules and had treated prisoners cruelly—torturing, wounding, even murdering them. Every member of the Dail who had voted for the special-powers resolution shared guilt with its sponsors, and unless the Free State obeyed the laws of war, the IRA would adopt "very drastic measures" to protect itself.[43]

Three days later, Lynch issued orders that persons in fourteen categories were to be shot on sight and their homes and offices burned. The categories included all Dail deputies who had voted for the "Murder Bill" that gave the army power to execute prisoners; certain senators who were soon to take office; High Court judges; hostile newspaper publishers and writers; and "aggressive Free State supporters." Also on the death list were Free State officers who approved the "Murder Bill" and British army veterans who had joined the Free State army.[44]

De Valera was not consulted in advance about the reprisals policy. He wrote Lynch that he doubted its efficacy but admitted he saw no other way to protect Republicans and could not disapprove. Torn between a desire for Republican unity and misgivings about terrorism, de Valera did nothing except warn Lynch that due notice should be given before action was taken.[45] As far as Lynch was concerned, such notice had already been given.

Before the IRA could strike, however, the Free State was finally inaugurated, its Constitution having been formally enacted and approved. On September 18, President Cosgrave introduced the Constitution in the Dail, explaining it was divided into three categories—those articles vital to the Treaty, those implementing the agreement with Southern Unionists, and those recommended by the government but not essential.[46] The Cabinet gave the task of steering the Constitution through Parliament to O'Higgins because of his incisive mind and debating skills. After brisk debate, the Constitution Bill passed its second reading, 47 to 16, on September 21.[47]

During the bill's committee stage, Gavan Duffy, with Labor's support, made an unsuccessful attempt to make the Treaty oath voluntary for members of Parliament.[48] Proposed amendments of other essential articles were likewise defeated, but some provisions were altered. One change made it possible to amend the Constitution by ordinary legislative enactment for eight years without need for a popular referendum. This was designed to facilitate removal of any defects which became apparent in the initial period of the Constitution's operation.[49]

On October 25 the Dail completed the debate on the bill, with O'Higgins predicting it would take the Irish people some time fully to realize how much freedom the Constitution gave them, but they would learn that by working with it. Johnson was not completely satisfied with either the Treaty or the Constitution but he conceded that both documents gave a very high level of individual liberty and national autonomy. It was up to the people to secure complete political freedom and use it to end capitalistic exploitation. Duffy thought the Constitution gave England more than the Treaty entitled it to and contained provisions offensive to the national dignity. Nonetheless, in the big things, the Constitution secured Ireland's rights under the Treaty, and there was enough good in it to enable the country to develop as it chose, without outside interference. After a few more minor amendments, the Dail gave final approval to the Constitution Bill.[50]

Despite a few arresting exchanges, the debate on the Constitution resembled a low-key replay of the one on the Treaty. Unlike the Republicans, however, the Labor Party and its allies did not allow objectionable symbols to blind them to political realities. The formalities insisted on by Britain were accepted as the price of "freedom to achieve freedom." Cosgrave expressed the spirit in which the Dail approved the Constitution when he declared the government intended "to get the last ounce out of the Treaty."[51]

As the Dail neared the end of its debate, a Conservative revolt in Britain toppled the coalition. Many Tories had long been restive under Lloyd George's leadership, and by September 1922, party managers and MPs were on the verge of revolt. Within the Cabinet, Stanley Baldwin, president of the Board of Trade, was deeply disturbed by what he regarded as the prime minister's political opportunism and lack of principle. With many other Conservatives, Baldwin felt that continuance of the coalition threatened to destroy not only party unity but the standards of honesty and responsibility which were the foundations of British political life.

Despite Lloyd George's towering achievements, there was much in his record to inspire distrust. The coalition's blatant sale of honors provoked anger and charges of corruption. The prime minister's unconventional methods, his failure to solve Britain's grave economic problems, his conciliatory Russian policy, and his strong support of Greece (which brought Britain to the brink of war with Turkey in the autumn of 1922) upset many Conservatives. Ireland stood high on the list of complaints. Lloyd George had led Britain into a sordid conflict with Sinn Fein, which he ended only by repealing the Union and awarding the rebels Dominion status. Ultra-Unionists would never forgive this "surrender to murder," while more moderate Conservatives undoubtedly felt some resentment against Lloyd George and their own leaders for mishandling the Irish problem so badly. Disenchantment over the Treaty increased this resentment.

In September 1922, Chamberlain, Birkenhead, and Balfour agreed with Lloyd George and Churchill to continue the coalition and seek a new electoral mandate as soon as possible, but this could not be done until the Tory leaders quelled the incipient mutiny in their party. Chamberlain therefore called a meeting of Conservative MPs for October 19 to gain a vote of confidence for the party leaders' decision. At this gathering, Baldwin spoke strongly against continuing the coalition; Bonar Law also came out against it, and his intervention was decisive. The MPs voted 187 to 87 to end the coalition, with most Cabinet ministers voting in the minority. Chamberlain and his colleagues thereupon resigned office and Lloyd George at once submitted the government's resignation to the king. After succeeding Chamberlain as party leader, Bonar Law took office as prime minister and formed an all-Conservative government.

Law's government was much less talented than its predecessor because he lacked the services of the ablest Tory leaders, who remained loyal to Lloyd George and the coalition idea. Nonetheless, the split in the Liberal Party and the Labor Party's inexperience gave the Conservatives an overall majority of seventy-five seats in the general election which followed formation of the new government.[52]

Shortly after he took office, Bonar Law announced that his government was fully prepared to honor the coalition's commitments to Ireland. The Cabinet approved the Constitution without amendment and Parliament was called into session to ratify it—and with it the Treaty.[53]

Urging passage of the Constitution Bill, Law conceded that the Irish Constitution contained expressions of the meaning of Dominion status which many MPs did not like, but any attempt legally to define that status as a consequence of the Constitution would involve not only Southern Ireland but the other Dominions. The Dominions' increased stature, which resulted from their part in the war, made it more necessary than ever that nothing be done to derogate from the powers they enjoyed. The prime minister did not believe the bill required prolonged discussion. Britain wanted peace in Ireland and good relations with it, but the Irish people must work out their own problems. All that Britain could do was to stand by the Treaty and ratify the Constitution.[54]

After a brief debate, which included the inevitable diehard criticism of the Constitution and the Irish government, the bill passed the Commons and was sent to the Lords, which passed it on December 4. The next day, the royal assent was given and the king approved the appointment of T. M. Healy as governor general of the Free State. On December 6, 1922, just within the time limit set by the Treaty for completion of the ratification process, the king signed the proclamation announcing adoption of the Constitution, and the Irish Free State came officially into existence.[55]

Timothy Michael Healy might seem a strange choice for governor general. Although he possessed great gifts, his scathing tongue and inability to work with others had made him "a brilliant disaster" in prewar nationalist politics. However, British and Sinn Fein leaders alike respected Healy; the former for his wit, ability and experience, the latter because he had never shown the hostility of Redmond and Dillon toward them and their cause. His appointment was not widely popular in Ireland, but he made a good governor general.[56] Healy's designation was significant not only for Ireland but also for other members of the Commonwealth. He was the first Dominion citizen to be named a governor general. More important, his appointment was made in accordance with the express wishes of the government concerned; indeed, it was made on Irish initiative.[57] In honoring the pledge they made to Griffith and Collins on this point, the British set a precedent with far-reaching implications.

In late November the Imperial General Staff recommended evacuation of British troops from Dublin and the government decided to carry out this recommendation as soon as the Free State was officially established. The first units of the garrison sailed for Britain on December 14 and the last detachments departed three days later.[58]

Even before Macready's troops left Dublin, Northern Ireland excluded itself from the Free State. On December 7, in accordance with the Treaty, the Northern Parliament voted an address to the king, petitioning that the powers of the Free State should not extend to Northern Ireland.[59] Despite an expression of willingness to cooperate with the Free State, Craig's attitude toward the Council of Ireland, like that he displayed toward the Boundary Commission, did not augur well for harmony. The Provisional Government offered to delay establishment of the council until both parts of Ireland agreed to alteration of its constitution, suggesting a maximum postponement of five years. Craig liked the proposal but not the time limit, since he did not want the council set up. However, under British pressure, he gave way and agreed to the five-year limit.[60] In the end, Northern Ireland's opposition prevented establishment of the council, thereby reinforcing partition.

Chapter 18
Ending the Civil War:
December 1922-May 1923

The Irish people took the Free State's inauguration quietly. When the Dail assembled on December 6, there were only a few spectators outside Leinster House.[1] The popular mood seemed much the same as when the Treaty was signed—a mixture of relief, resignation, and satisfaction. Most Irishmen and -women wanted the Free State, but they were not inclined to celebrate a triumph so overshadowed by tragedy.

The Speaker opened the first meeting of the Free State Parliament by administering the oath to the deputies. Immediately afterward, Tom Johnson declared the oath would not restrict the Labor Party if and when the people chose to denounce the Treaty or amend the Constitution.[2] When Johnson had finished speaking, Cosgrave was elected president of the Executive Council without opposition. Again keeping the Finance Ministry for himself, Cosgrave nominated an Executive Council composed of O'Higgins as vice-president, Mulcahy, MacNeill, Blythe, McGrath, and Fitzgerald, with each minister retaining the office he had held in the Provisional Government. After approving these nominations, the Dail agreed to establish a committee which would appoint external ministers for Agriculture, Fisheries, and the Post Office.[3]

At the close of the first day's session, President Cosgrave read his list of thirty Senate nominations. Among his selections were Dr. Oliver St. John Gogarty, an eminent surgeon as well as a close friend of Griffith and Collins; John Bagwell, a distinguished historian; Andrew Jameson, head of a large Dublin distillery; Sir Bryan Mahon, a retired British general; Sir Horace Plunkett, founder of the Irish Cooperative movement and the Irish Dominion League; and William Butler Yeats. The president's choices were elected automatically; half would serve a full twelve-year term, and half six years. The remaining thirty senators, half of whom would serve nine years and half three, were elected by the Dail on December 7. Among those chosen were Alice Stopford Green, another well-known historian; Colonel Maurice Moore, brother of the novelist and a former commander of the famed Connaught Rangers; and James Douglas, of the Constitution Committee. The fact that a sizable number of senators were Protestants and former Unionists demonstrated the government's desire to reconcile the old ascendancy to the new order.[4]

When the Senate met on December 11, Lord Glenavy, a prominent jurist, was elected chairman with only two dissenting votes. The strong support he received from nationalist senators signified that the government's conciliatory attitude was widely shared. As one former loyalist declared: "The past is dead, not only for us but for this country. We are assembled here no longer in a Nationalist or Unionist sense, but merely as members of the Senate."[5]

The next day, Governor General Healy outlined the government's program to Parliament. Its first priority was suppression of disorder, so that urgent social and economic problems could be dealt with. Healy also pledged that the government would take steps to set up the Boundary Commission, enact full adult suffrage, establish a judicial system, organize a police force and a regular army, and complete the land-purchase program.[6]

No sooner had the Free State come into existence than the Dail and the country were shocked by a new kind of outrage and by the government's savage reaction. On December 7, gunmen shot down two Dail deputies in the streets of Dublin and escaped, leaving one of their victims dead and the other wounded. The slain deputy was General Sean Hales, a hero of the war for independence and a staunch Treaty supporter, whose brother Tom was an Irregular leader in Cork. His wounded companion was Padraic O'Maille, deputy speaker of the Dail. Both men had voted for the Special Powers Bill. Coming on the heels of Lynch's November 27 warning, the ambush seemed to prove that the IRA had begun reprisals. Intelligence agents had warned that the Irregulars planned to test the government's reaction before trying large-scale reprisals. Reporting this to the Cabinet, the Army Council contended that if the attack on Hales and O'Maille were not met with drastic measures, an assassination campaign might begin.[7]

In an emergency Cabinet meeting, Mulcahy submitted the Army Council's proposal for the immediate execution of four imprisoned IRA leaders: Rory O'Connor, Liam Mellows, Dick Barrett, and Joe McKelvey. All but Barrett had been members of the IRA's executive, and McKelvey had also been a member of the IRB's Supreme Council. After a discussion of the proposal, Cosgrave polled the Cabinet. Of the ministers present, only O'Higgins hesitated, asking if there were not some alternative. He was told there was not, and if the Cabinet did not act swiftly, ruthlessly, and unanimously, there would be more assassinations, and Dail members would start to resign. If it were left without an effective Parliament, the Executive Council would become a dictatorship. O'Higgins soon yielded and helped convince Joe McGrath, who arrived late to the meeting. The fact that O'Connor had been best man at his wedding only a year before intensified O'Higgins' anguish.[8]

On the morning of December 8 the four Republicans were executed in Mountjoy jail. At the same time, an Army Council proclamation announced the existence of an assassination conspiracy and extended the military's power of summary execution.[9] News of the four executions appeared in the evening papers, together with the government's explanation that they were a reprisal and a solemn warning to those in the conspiracy against public representatives.

The news roused a storm in the Dail. While denouncing the killing of Hales, Tom Johnson branded the government's response as murder. The four victims had been in jail for months and had no connection with Hales's death. The executions were nothing but an act of vengeance, carried out with no pretense of legality. Neither the security nor the honor of the state could be served by such an act. Gavan Duffy demanded to know where this "Corsican vendetta" was to end, asserting that the men who sanctioned the executions were not fit to have the country's destiny in their hands. Cathal O'Shannon condemned the whole executions policy as horrible and self-defeating, and called on the Dail to throw out the government. Gerald Fitzgibbon, an Independent, appealed to the government not to allow a repetition of that morning's event. He believed the Dail would support a request for drastic measures against the rebels, but arbitrary reprisals could not be condoned.

Mulcahy defended the government by citing Lynch's threat against Dail members. The four executions were a deterrent intended to prevent destruction of the government and the country by an armed minority bent on the systematic murder of the people's representatives. O'Higgins refuted allegations that blind anger was responsible for the executions. The decision was made coldly and deliberately; the action was at once punitive and deterrent. It was no use talking of rules of war because there were no real rules. The only law which held good when the life of the nation was threatened was *salus populi suprema lex*. The four executions were not an ordinary act of government to which ordinary standards could be applied; they were an act of war, and all that war implied. The ministers had a duty to protect the state and its people and they would do it, regardless of personal consequences and with no effort to evade responsibility. But they had never acted in hot blood or a desire for revenge. "Personal spite, great heavens! Vindictiveness! One of these men was a friend of mine," O'Higgins protested. At this point, he broke down and was unable to continue.

Summing up, President Cosgrave contended it had been impossible for the Cabinet to consult the Dail before acting, but elementary law justified its action. Those who challenged society put themselves outside the law. There was only one way to deal with their diabolical conspiracy: to crush it and strike terror into them. In the division that followed, the Dail upheld the government's summary action by a vote of 39 to 14.[10]

Sean Hales's family expressed "horror and disgust" at the government's reprisal, and even the strongly pro-Treaty *Irish Independent* voiced the hope that there would be no more such executions. On the other hand, Ernest Blythe claimed that the government received many messages of approval after the four executions, proving that people were glad to see firm action taken to suppress terrorism.[11] Over forty years later, an Irish writer delivered as fair a verdict on the reprisal as we are ever likely to get: "It made no pretence to be a legal act; it was an attempt to meet terror with terror. In this it was successful. No more deputies were shot."[12]

But if the IRA shot no more deputies, it tried other forms of intimidation. Irregulars killed O'Higgins' father, burned Cosgrave's home, threatened senators, and put a number of their homes to the torch.[13] At the same time, using the railways as its main target, the IRA engaged in an orgy of destruction designed to bring the government to its knees.[14]

While the IRA waged war with petrol and land mines, the Free State tightened the screws. In December, the military authorities in Kerry announced that four IRA officers had been sentenced to death. The sentence had been suspended, but it would be carried out if there were any more Republican attacks in the area. This tactic became standard in the final stages of the civil war, and the threat of execution was also used to force captured Irregulars to divulge information.[15] In January 1923, the Army Council proposed a further extension of the army's powers to execute or imprison civilians. The Dail approved the request and the new powers went into operation in February. By that time, fifty-five Republicans had been executed and a number of others were under sentence of death.[16]

In response, Lynch again threatened reprisals if the execution of prisoners continued. He also indicted the Free State army for general mistreatment of prisoners, and these charges were repeated in a Republican complaint to the International Red Cross.[17]

While the prisoners' lot was far from pleasant, it was by no means as bad as the Republicans claimed. Under the strain of civil war, Irishmen proved themselves no worse (and probably better) than men in similar circumstances in other civilized countries. In Southern Ireland in 1922–23 there was nothing approaching the barbarous treatment of prisoners during the French Revolution's Reign of Terror or the suppression of the Paris Commune in 1871, and nothing like the cruelty inflicted on prisoners during the Russian and Spanish civil wars of this century. Nor was there anything remotely like the horrors of some prison camps during the American Civil War.

Overcrowding was the major cause of trouble. By April 1923, some 13,000 prisoners were confined in jails and camps that were never meant to hold such large numbers.[18] The authorities did the best they could, but congestion made hardship inevitable. The inmates aggravated the problem by acts of defiance and destruction calculated to embarrass their captors. Having done all they could to make their lot worse than it need have been, they blamed the government for mistreatment. These tactics made some impression on the public, but not on men who had played the same game against the British. Given the problems caused by overcrowding, it is not surprising that the authorities were impatient with recalcitrant prisoners. Warders and guards hit back hard at rioters and men who attempted to escape. Sometimes they went too far and prisoners were humiliated, beaten, and even tortured by guards.[19]

Discouragement of independent inquiries was the weakest point in the government's defense of its prison operations, but it eventually permitted an inspection by a Red Cross committee, whose report generally vindicated the authorities. The inspectors noted that although inmates were denied the status of prisoners of war, they were treated as such in practice. The committee found grounds for complaints about overcrowding but concluded that other complaints were unfounded. The fact that the Red Cross team was not authorized to question prisoners weakened the authority of its report, but in other respects the investigation was thorough, and it was made by persons who knew their jobs.[20]

Like the British, the Free State had to deal with hunger strikes as well as riots and escape efforts. A women's hunger strike in the spring of 1923 extorted some concessions but the government then took a hard line, and the Dail resolved that the question of detention or release should not be affected by hunger strikes.[21] This settled the matter for the time being, but it came up again in autumn. Although the civil war ended in May, most Irregulars remained in custody because they refused to sign a statement that they would not take up arms in the future. Fearing a new uprising if it released thousands of Republicans without their written parole, the government obtained legislation to hold them in confinement. In October, the prisoners tried to force unconditional release by staging a mass hunger strike. But the government stood firm and most strikers gave in after a few weeks. However, some refused nourishment until their leaders called off the strike on November 23, after two men died from the long fast.[22]

Although the government generally handled the problem of prisoners as well as could be expected, some excesses occurred, especially in Kerry. South Kerry was the Irregulars' last stronghold and they remained active there until the end of the war. In some cases they would ambush government troops, fire a volley or two, then surrender and demand to be treated as prisoners of war. It was hard to stop soldiers from killing men who shot at them from ambush one moment and the next moment threw up their hands and invoked the rules of war. It was equally hard to prevent troops from exacting vengeance in areas where IRA land mines killed or maimed their comrades.

Major General Daly, late of the siege of the Four Courts, was the Free State commander in Kerry. "No one told me to bring kid gloves, so I didn't," summed up his attitude toward this assignment.[23] Daly's troops killed a few prisoners in the fall of 1922, but the situation got out of hand the next spring. In reprisal for the killing of five Free Staters by a trap mine, nine Republican prisoners were taken from Tralee jail on March 7 and tied together over a land mine, which was then exploded. Eight were killed, but one was blown clear and escaped to tell what had happened. In a similar occurrence near Killarney the same day, four prisoners were murdered but a fifth survived to describe the crime. Five more men were killed by their captors at Cahirciveen on March 12, and this time it was an outraged Free State officer who revealed the truth.

However, military inquiries officially cleared the soldiers involved in the killings and Mulcahy defended them in the Dail. He pointed out that the troops in Kerry had had to fight "every ugly form of warfare which the Irregulars could think of"and had endured heavy casualties. Soldiers of their outstanding record could not possibly be guilty of the alleged atrocities. Admittedly, prisoners were used to clear roads in Kerry because of the IRA's indiscriminate minelaying, but that was not murder. However, while he professed satisfaction with the results of the army inquiries, Mulcahy refused to produce evidence from them.[24]

Despite the defense minister's assertions, murder had been done in Kerry. At first, the government did not know all the facts—perhaps because it did not want to know. Eventually, however, public pressure forced a new inquiry and Daly was removed from his command. More important, the murder of prisoners was stopped, but only after several more had been killed.[25] The atrocities committed in Kerry and a few other places can be attributed to the army's inexperience and the strain imposed by guerrilla war, but no explanation can excuse what was done. Only seven men were executed in Kerry under the army's special powers, which were partly intended to prevent reprisals. Had Daly and his officers used military courts more often, their troops would have been less tempted to resort to lynch law.

Military excesses inevitably caused friction in the Cabinet. Angered by the army's indiscipline and its delay in restoring order, O'Higgins challenged Mulcahy's apparent assumption that the military was entitled to special status and treatment. He also opposed the Army Council's attempts to revive the IRB, a move Mulcahy supported. Mulcahy, for his part, resented O'Higgins' acid-tongued criticism, feeling he understood neither the army's mentality nor the problems confronting it. A crisis threatened in March 1923 when Mulcahy submitted the Army Council's resignation in response to ministerial criticism. Cosgrave refused to accept the resignation, but the Cabinet tried to exercise greater supervision over the army after this incident. The antipathy between O'Higgins and

Mulcahy grew worse, however, and Cosgrave was hard pressed to maintain peace within the Executive Council. The problem was not resolved until the government secured the army's complete subordination after an attempted mutiny by disaffected officers in 1924.[26]

As the civil war dragged on, peacemaking efforts revived. The most promising initiative came from Liam Deasy, the IRA's deputy chief of staff and commander in Munster, who had become convinced by the end of 1922 that further armed resistance was futile and that the war should be ended without delay. Before he had a chance to communicate his views to other members of the executive, however, Deasy was captured, tried, and sentenced to death. In return for a stay of execution, he agreed to aid in the immediate and unconditional surrender of all Irregulars and their arms. Having made this pledge, Deasy was taken to Dublin, where he was told he must sign an appeal for unconditional surrender. He agreed to this demand, on condition that he be allowed to accompany the appeal with a confidential letter to Republican leaders explaining his position.

In his peace appeal of January 29, Deasy repeated his endorsement of unconditional surrender. He asked other leaders to follow suit, order an immediate surrender, and give themselves up. In his covering letter, Deasy blamed the Free State for continuation of the war, but expressed his conviction that a cease-fire was best for the nation.

There was no response to the appeal, and further communications between Deasy and his comrades were no more productive. On February 9 the government published Deasy's appeal, together with a similar statement made by prisoners in Limerick. It supported these entreaties with an offer of amnesty to all rebels who surrendered with their arms on or before February 18. The government also announced it was suspending executions until it knew whether there would be an answer to Deasy's appeal.[27]

Publication of the peace appeal brought a response from Lynch, in which he declared the proposal for surrender could not be considered.[28] At the same time, Lynch called on the IRA to stand fast and not be seduced by enemy intrigue; victory was assured if the army remained united.[29] Privately, he counseled that the peace appeal represented only a temporary setback and should not be taken too seriously. The general situation was satisfactory and improving, but whatever sacrifices might be required, there could be no compromise on the Republic.[30] De Valera took the same line. While Deasy's appeal was "the biggest blow we have got since we started," there could be no turning back.

> One big effort from our friends everywhere and I think we would finally smash the Free State. Our people have a hard time of suffering before them, and we have of course to face the possibility of the British forces

coming back and taking up the fight where the others lay it down—But God is good![31]

Unsuccessful as it was, Deasy's appeal spurred other peace efforts. In February, neutral veterans of the pre-truce IRA formed a mediation association with 20,000 members. On February 16 it asked both sides for a month's cease-fire to make possible an exchange of peace proposals. When Cosgrave and de Valera rejected a truce, the association announced it would not offer any further suggestions pending the outcome of a mediation effort by the archbishop of Cashel. The archbishop made no more headway than the neutral IRA, however, and both withdrew from the field.[32] An attempt at peacemaking by a papal envoy, Monsignor Luzio, in March and April likewise failed to win the belligerents' cooperation, and he left Ireland as he found it.[33] To rebels clinging stubbornly to their arms and the Republic, O'Higgins proclaimed that the war was "not going to be a draw, with a replay in the autumn."[34]

Early in 1923, Lynch decided to carry the fight to England, a move the executive had favored since the start of the civil war. De Valera agreed with the decision and advised a big first strike, followed by a rapid succession of other blows.[35] However, the Free State government alerted the British, who arrested over 100 suspected subversives in March and deported them to Ireland, where they were locked up. (British courts later ruled the deportations illegal, but by that time the civil war was over.)[36]

The abortive plan to terrorize England was a measure of the IRA's desperation. In February, its attacks on army posts dropped steeply. By March, over 10,000 Republicans were in internment camps, and the 8,000 still at large were opposed by 40,000 troops.[37] The size of the government army indicated that military success did not come cheaply. The Free State entered its first full fiscal year (1923–24) with a deficit of £2.3 million. The estimated deficit for 1923–24 was £20 million, half of it chargeable to the cost of the army. The deficits were made good by borrowing, but war debt was a heavy burden to the new state.[38]

With the IRA's capacity for resistance steadily deteriorating, a number of officers had reached the same conclusion as Deasy and they demanded that Lynch convene the executive to discuss peace. On February 6, Tom Barry urged a meeting and two other members of the executive supported him, but Lynch refused. Although he claimed that a meeting would be too difficult and dangerous, Lynch almost certainly feared that his associates would opt for peace negotiations, if given the chance. However, he decided to discuss the situation with local commanders in Cork and Kerry. As he prepared to leave Dublin, officers of the 1st Southern Division concluded that they could not carry on a summer campaign and that the executive should meet at once to review the situation. Barry and three other members of the executive therefore wrote Lynch, repeating the request for a meeting, but he had already left the capital for the south.[39]

After interviewing officers in the southwest, Lynch met with the 1st Southern Division's Council on February 26. While conceding that things were very bad in the south, Lynch claimed that the general situation was good, and he held great hopes for the future. The assembled officers felt differently, and the division's commander summed up their views by declaring: "We are fought to a standstill and at present we are flattened out." Although this gloomy assessment in no way weakened Lynch's determination, he realized that he must convene the executive.[40]

Hearing nothing from Lynch after he left Dublin, de Valera became anxious. Viewing continuation of armed resistance as a questionable and, perhaps, futile policy, de Valera sought desperately for some way to make peace without abandoning the Republic. He got no help in this matter from Lynch, however. On February 28 the chief of staff rebuked him for publicly proposing external association as a basis for peace, claiming such a compromise offer had an adverse effect on army morale. De Valera replied a week later, defending his action and contending that the isolated Republic could not be won by continuing the war. He even doubted whether he could secure external association from the British.[41] Although Lynch had written de Valera, his silence about the military situation seemed ominous. De Valera was afraid that Lynch might refuse to summon the executive and that the IRA in the south might surrender before he had a chance to lay his peace proposals before the executive. It was with considerable relief, therefore, that de Valera received Lynch's invitation to attend an executive meeting on March 23. In disguise, he made his way south with Stack and Aiken.[42]

Eleven members of the executive were able to attend the meeting, held in Bliantas and Glenanore, County Waterford, from March 23 to 27. Lynch urged carrying on resistance until the Free Staters were forced to negotiate. De Valera expressed the hope that peace might be made if both sides accepted three principles: the Irish people's right to complete independence, their supreme authority to decide national questions, and the right of anyone who subscribed to these principles to take part in politics without any oath or test. While admitting that this would involve a limited acceptance of the Treaty position, he claimed it would leave the Republicans free to win the Republic honorably. Lynch disagreed, and Stack held that if they had to stop fighting, they should simply quit without offering terms. Aiken, now deputy chief of staff, supported de Valera's proposals, but he asked that they be published as a declaration of war aims and that fighting be continued until the enemy was willing to parley. He hoped that this would rally opinion to the Republican cause and force the Free State to accept de Valera's terms. Others said further fighting was useless and urged arms surrender.

On March 26 the executive considered two resolutions. The first proposed that the Republican government be empowered to negotiate on the basis of de Valera's terms. The vote on this was 5 to 5, with Lynch abstaining, and the tie defeated the motion. Tom Barry then moved that further armed resistance would not advance the cause of independence. Lynch, Stack, Aiken, and three other officers opposed this motion and it was defeated, 6 to 5. Unable to reconcile their differences, the officers adjourned for two weeks, having asked de Valera to work out specific peace proposals for their consideration.[43]

De Valera left Glenanore convinced that the executive would have to agree to peace at its next meeting, and events proved him correct. The breakup of the IRA's command structure continued in early April as more high-ranking officers were captured. On April 10 Lynch was killed, and his death took the heart out of Republican resistance.

When General Prout learned that IRA leaders were in the Waterford–South Tipperary area, he ordered over 1,000 troops to comb it. News of the proposed operation led Lynch to decide against proceeding to the planned executive rendezvous. Instead, he remained near the town of Newcastle in South Tipperary, just north of the Knockmealdown mountains. However, the Free State sweep also threatened this location, and to avoid encirclement, Lynch and his party began a hasty retreat south toward the mountain passes. They were on their way up the slope when they were sighted by a small Free State force which opened fire at several hundred yards. Lynch was badly hit and ordered his comrades to leave him, knowing he was dying and that they could escape no other way. Reluctantly, they agreed and left him to the pursuing troops. Lynch identified himself to his captors, who bandaged his painful wound and bore him down the mountain. He died that night in Clonmel hospital, lamenting the tragedy of civil war.[44]

Foes as well as friends mourned Liam Lynch's death. Like Childers, a gentle manner veiled his political rigidity, and all who knew him attested to his high ideals. Lynch's insistence on waging a hopeless fight almost wrecked his country, but his devotion to a "deathless dream" nourished the Republican legend and embellished the myth of the heroic gunman. Inspired by martyrs, he became one himself and helped create others.

On April 14 the Republicans suffered another serious blow. Austin Stack was captured while carrying a memorandum proposing an immediate end to resistance, which the government at once published. Dan Breen was caught at almost the same time. With IRA resistance rapidly disintegrating, the end of the war was near.[45]

Meeting in southeast Tipperary on April 20, the executive elected Aiken to succeed Lynch as chief of staff and appointed him head of a

three-man army council. After some discussion, the executive resolved
that the Republican government and the army council should make
peace on the following basis:

1. The sovereignty of the Irish Nation and the integrity of its territory
   are inalienable and
2. That any instrument purporting to the contrary is, to the extent of its
   violation of the above principle, null and void.

Members of the army council took this news to Dublin and a joint meeting of the council and the Republican Cabinet on the night of April 26
decided unanimously in favor of a formal peace initiative. On April 27,
de Valera issued a proclamation to this effect on behalf of his government, while Aiken ordered the IRA to suspend all aggressive action
from noon of April 30.[46]

In his proclamation, de Valera announced willingness to negotiate
peace on certain conditions, which included national and popular sovereignty. No one who subscribed to these principles could justly be
excluded from political life by any oath or test. The government must
also agree to freedom of speech, assembly, and the press. Finally, the
army was the nation's servant and, subject to the principles stated, it
would obey the national assembly freely chosen by the people.[47]

These terms were a strange assortment. Exempting Republicans from
the oath to the Crown meant scrapping the Treaty, while the other
proposals were accepted by everyone but the Republicans. For instance,
de Valera declared that majority vote should decide all national questions and that everyone should accept this verdict, "not because the
decision is necessarily right or just or permanent, but because acceptance
of this rule makes for peace, order, and unity in national action, and is
the democratic alternative to arbitrament by force." Since supporters of
the Treaty had repeatedly endorsed this principle, one might ask what
the civil war was all about. In fact, de Valera's proposals were more an
attempt to convert his side than the opposition.

Most newspapers found de Valera's terms unacceptable, pointing out
their incompatibility with the Treaty and their omission of any offer of
arms surrender. The government made no response of any kind and
continued to round up Republicans. On May 2, two more prisoners were
executed, the last of seventy-seven shot in the civil war.[48]

In hope of securing positive results, de Valera wrote to Senators Andrew Jameson and James Douglas on April 30, asking them to discuss
steps toward an immediate peace settlement. The two senators agreed to
act as intermediaries and presented de Valera's request for a peace conference to the Executive Council on May 2. It rejected the request and
gave Jameson a statement of peace terms requiring that Parliament de-

cide all political issues and that the government control all lethal weapons. Acceptance of these terms, with arms surrender, were the preconditions for a cease-fire and the release of prisoners, who must subscribe individually to the terms. The government promised that the Republicans could contest the next election without hindrance, if they adhered strictly to constitutional methods, but it made plain that the oath would remain in the Constitution. Cosgrave asked that de Valera give the names of Republican leaders for whom he could speak and estimate what proportion of the rank and file would abide by his decision, if he accepted the government's terms.

After examining the terms, de Valera submitted an alternative draft, stating he would sign the proposals on behalf of all Republican forces and would make sure of their acceptability before he signed. De Valera's terms were largely those he had offered on April 27, although he added that the government should control all lethal weapons. To give practical effect to his proposals, de Valera made a number of suggestions designed to ensure political fair play for his followers. Among other things, he suggested that, pending the election, Republican weapons should be stored under Republican guard. Once this was done, all prisoners should be released under a general amnesty. After the election, the stored arms should be reissued to their owners or disposed of in some other way acceptable to the new government.

On May 8, the Executive Council received and rejected these proposals. President Cosgrave informed Jameson that de Valera's response was not an acceptance of the government's terms but "a long and wordy document inviting debate where none is possible." His proposals for national and popular sovereignty and freedom of expression were guaranteed by the Constitution and had no place in a statement of peace terms, and the government could not consider exempting Republicans from the oath. Once the government's preliminary terms were accepted and rebel arms placed under Free State control, prisoners who subscribed to the agreement would be released and Republicans given a free field for electioneering. No further communication could be received from de Valera except his written acceptance of these terms. Disappointed with this reply, de Valera thanked the two senators for their good offices.[49]

Rejection of de Valera's proposals was inevitable. They neither secured government control of rebel arms nor provided any guarantee of good behavior by the rebels, especially the prisoners. Quite apart from the question of the oath, agreement to these terms would have meant that the civil war settled nothing.

On the night of May 13 the Republican cabinet and army council met. De Valera told them that the Free State government wanted pure and simple submission, being motivated more by a desire to prevent political rivalry than to secure an honorable and lasting peace. The rebel leadership therefore decided to end the war without accepting the government's terms.[50] Republicans would simply quit fighting, thereby admitting defeat but refusing to surrender their principles. On May 24 Aiken ordered the IRA to cease fire and hide its arms. The guns would be kept until the Republicans could find an honorable way to reach their objective without using them.[51] Also, de Valera issued a stirring message to the IRA on May 24, hailing the "Legion of the Rearguard," whose courage and sacrifice had saved the nation's honor and kept open the road to independence.[52] Taking what consolation they could from this tribute, the weary but still defiant Republicans hid their arms and went home.

Although the shooting stopped, the government could not be sure the civil war was over; with rebel arms caches scattered all over Ireland, fighting might resume at any time. But it did not. Despite the hopes and fears of many Irishmen in May 1923, the revolution initiated by the Easter Rising ended as it began, "in the springing of the year."

Reliable casualty figures for the civil war do not exist. Exact records of Republican and civilian casualties were not kept, and the Free State government never made public its own casualty figures. General Mulcahy stated that approximately 540 government troops were killed from the signing of the Treaty to the end of the civil war, and it is safe to assume that almost all these deaths occurred between June 1922 and May 1923. A rough guess, based on available estimates, puts the total number of military casualties during the civil war at about 5,000. How many civilians were killed or wounded will never be known.[53]

Material damage caused by the fighting exceeded £30 million and the cost of prosecuting the war came to another £17 million.[54] The destruction in the struggle with Britain was repeated on a larger scale in 1922–23, while the massive damage to the railways found no parallel in the earlier conflict. Although the repair of this damage placed a heavy burden on the new state's limited resources, it was completed in a remarkably short time.

Other injuries proved more lasting. The tragic deaths of such leaders as Collins and Boland, as well as hundreds of other young men, robbed Ireland of badly needed talent. Even worse, the civil war's heritage of hatred divided Irishmen deeply for many years, subjecting the country more than ever to the tyranny of the dead.

Epilogue
and Conclusion

In the election of 1923, the Treaty party was returned to office and remained in power until 1932. During its tenure, Cosgrave's government laid the foundations of the state, with institutions closely modeled on those of Britain; established the national credit; and completed land purchase. While generally conservative in its economic policies, the government made a bold departure when it harnessed the Shannon River to supply large-scale hydroelectric power. In connection with this enterprise, it also founded the first of the state-sponsored companies which played such a prominent role in Ireland's later economic development. Having used the army to restore public order, the government brought it firmly under control in 1924 by purging rival military factions that were contending for political influence.

Abroad, the Free State entered the League of Nations. It appointed its own representatives to foreign countries and worked with other Dominions to secure full national sovereignty. This goal was reached with enactment of the Statute of Westminster in 1931, vindicating those who maintained that the Treaty gave Ireland the freedom to achieve freedom.

The worse setbacks the government suffered in its decade of rule were the Boundary Commission fiasco in 1925 and the assassination of Kevin O'Higgins in 1927. The former resulted from changes in Britain's political climate, Ulster's implacable hostility, the government's mistakes, and the ambiguities of the Treaty's Boundary Commission clause. But although the Free State failed to acquire the nationalist districts in Northern Ireland to which it laid claim (Tyrone, Fermanagh, south Armagh, south Down, and west Derry), it escaped liability for a share of Britain's national debt in an agreement that legitimized the existing boundary. And as tragic as O'Higgins' death was, it produced a positive result of lasting significance. Following the assassination, the government secured passage of a bill that required every parliamentary candidate to swear, upon nomination, that if elected he would take the prescribed parliamentary oath and his seat within two months of his election. Refusal to take this pledge and keep it would disqualify the candidate. This measure ended the abstentionist policy of de Valera and his followers, who took the oath and entered the Dail, making their party a constitutional opposition and thereby buttressing the foundations of democratic government.

When de Valera came to power in 1932, he was able to repudiate the Treaty with relative ease, thanks to advances made by the Free State in the previous decade. To reach his goal of external association, he had to wage an economic war with Britain and to counter threats from quasi-Fascists and diehard Republicans. But by 1938, Southern Ireland had ended the economic war, recovered control of the Treaty ports, severed almost every political link with Britain, and become a Republic in all but name. It had also begun industrial development and had moved toward greater economic self-sufficiency. By a remarkable combination of political agility and tenacity, de Valera had made his party nationally dominant and had reversed the verdict of the civil war. Only partition remained an outstanding problem in Anglo-Irish relations when World War II began in 1939.

Despite intense Anglo-American pressure, Southern Ireland remained neutral throughout the war, although its neutrality was certainly benevolent as far as the Allies were concerned. The government's policy was supported by all parties and conclusively demonstrated Irish sovereignty. However, the wartime emergency imposed considerable hardship on the people and intensified Irish isolation, as well as reinforced partition. When the war ended in 1945, Ireland's future seemed bleak.

In 1948, the postwar election ended de Valera's long rule and the coalition which took power cut the last formal tie with Britain and declared Southern Ireland a Republic. This made no difference in Anglo-Irish relations, except to evoke from Britain a reaffirmation of Northern Ireland's status in the United Kingdom.

The next decade was a period of political and economic stagnation, but this began to change when the government launched a program for industrial development, which produced rapid economic growth in the early 1960s. Less dramatic but still impressive gains followed, and in 1973 Ireland joined the European Common Market. Whatever the Republic's response to this economic challenge, the era of isolation was over, its end marked in the 1960s by the impact of the Vatican Council and television, and the inflow of foreign capital.

As events in Northern Ireland have recently reminded the world, an important part of the Irish Question remains unresolved. The outcome of the present crisis cannot be predicted, but one thing is certain. When the troubles began in the North, a new era opened in Irish history—one as full of promise and peril as that which began with the birth of the Irish Free State.

Looking back on the events of half a century ago, it seems clear that the Dail's approval of the Treaty marked the culmination of the Irish Revolution, for this action formally dissolved the Union with Britain. Wiser policies might have prolonged the Union or ended it more harmoniously, but British concessions were always too little or too late. Still, those that were made, coupled with the obvious futility of insurrection, had rendered extremism moribund by the turn of the century.

All this changed when Redmond failed to deliver Home Rule. The Irish Parliamentary Party played the game by British rules, but the Unionists' stubborn refusal to concede defeat did a good deal to discredit constitutionalism, and World War I finished the job. Supporting Britain, with nothing to show in return, compounded Redmond's problems at home, while the terrible slaughter in Europe cheapened life and intensified the struggle of oppressed nationalities for freedom. The war which helped precipitate the Easter Rising might also have vindicated the militant nationalism of that "blood sacrifice," even without Britain's obtuse reaction. As it was, executions, deception, repression and, finally, the threat of conscription demoralized the Old Party, leaving it to be crushed between rival extremes in the postwar election.

Ensuing events amply demonstrated the dangers of extremism, but the struggle for independence cannot be dismissed as an unfortunate aberration engineered by a band of fanatics. Ireland's demand for freedom was part of a worldwide chorus inspired by the war; indeed, Irish aspirations were quite modest compared with those of other nationalities. Sinn Fein demanded no fundamental change in Ireland's social and economic structure; it was prepared to make substantial concessions to the loyalist minority and had, at most, a limited commitment to the restoration of Gaelic culture. The rebels' overriding aim was simply to expel the British from Ireland, and British blunders did as much as the rebels' efforts to win their cause popular support. Although many Irishmen were alarmed or dismayed by IRA terrorism, this was no help to a government that rejected their claim to self-determination, partitioned their country, and loosed the Black and Tans on them. So long as Britain offered only a Home Rule carrot and swung a sizable stick, moderation had little appeal for most nationalists.

In the end, Irish resistance and an aroused British public forced the Cabinet to negotiate with Sinn Fein. Despite important differences, these negotiations produced a settlement, partly because both sides wanted one very much but also because partition had removed a major obstacle to agreement. Since Northern Ireland really "saved itself," however, the British gave up much more than they kept in the Treaty of 1921. Southern Ireland was to remain in the Empire, at least for the time being, but it was to enjoy almost complete self-government, with the prospect of full freedom and perhaps even national unity in the not too distant future. An exhausted people were understandably satisfied with this achievement, but most separatists were not. Led by President de Valera, they demanded another round of negotiations—or war—to win the Republic and safeguard Ireland's honor and sovereignty. With the aid of their more moderate and realistic associates, Griffith and Collins secured the Dail's endorsement of the Treaty. But their margin of victory was narrow, the IRA unreconciled, and the future perilous. While the revolution had scored an impressive success, the full price had yet to be paid.

That price, of course, was civil war, but the roots of that conflict went much deeper than the Treaty and its reviled oath. Only British pressure made possible a united nationalist front after 1916. Once that pressure was relaxed, the division between moderates and extremists inevitably reappeared, aggravated by the tensions and animosities arising from the struggle for independence. In reopening this split, the Treaty revealed a more fundamental difference than that of Crown versus Republic. Whether the state was to be ruled by the people or by a revolutionary junta was the most important question confronting Ireland in 1922 and the underlying cause of the civil war.

Although de Valera did not face this question squarely, his actions showed which side he had chosen. Opposition to the Treaty led him to become first the champion and then the prisoner of diehard Republicans. Had he accepted the peace settlement or bowed to the Dail's decision and unequivocally condemned armed resistance to its will, there might have been no civil war. Certainly, the clash would not have assumed the proportions it did had he denied the IRA his prestige and support. His conduct may be ascribed to miscalculation, vanity, or the influence of Childers, but a tenacious belief in external association was almost certainly his principal motivation. De Valera would not repeat his disastrous performance of 1922–23, but he clung to his brainchild for twenty-five years, making it the basis for his foreign policy in the 1930s, even though the Statute of Westminster had made it obsolete.

As de Valera abdicated his position as national leader, Collins did his best to assume the role. Although an extremist in the struggle against England, Collins was also a supreme realist who wanted no more "blood sacrifices" after 1916. He pursued the goal of complete independence ruthlessly, forcing the pace with his own people as well as the British, but only so long as such methods seemed productive. By 1921 he sensed that armed resistance could not continue much longer and that the time had come to consolidate the revolution's hard-won gains, even at the cost of temporarily abandoning the Republic. By all odds, his decision to sign and support the Treaty was right, although it cost him his life. Whatever his shortcomings, Collins' concern for the Irish people and his vision of what the Treaty could mean to them vindicated his claim to national leadership, and his death was a terrible loss.

Collins' death helped embitter and perhaps prolong a conflict that blighted the hopes of his generation. Yet costly as it was, the civil war safeguarded the solid gains embodied in the Treaty, and it firmly established democratic rule. Even with its promise dimmed at birth, the Irish Free State remained a remarkable achievement for the revolution begun in Easter Week, 1916. If it seems paradoxical that the forces unleashed by that revolution almost destroyed what they had created, the explanation must be sought in the inevitable clash between fanatical idealism and stubborn reality, and, ultimately, in the contradictions of human nature itself.

Appendix I
Proclamation of the
Irish Republic
April 24, 1916

Poblacht na h-Eireann
The Provisional Government
of the
IRISH REPUBLIC
To the people of Ireland

Irishmen and Irishwomen: In the name of God and of the dead generations from which she receives her old tradition of nationhood, Ireland, through us, summons her children to her flag and strikes for her freedom.

Having organised and trained her manhood through her secret revolutionary organisation, the Irish Republican Brotherhood, and through her open military organisations, the Irish Volunteers and the Irish Citizen Army, having patiently perfected her discipline, having resolutely waited for the right moment to reveal itself, she now seizes that moment, and, supported by her exiled children in America and by gallant allies in Europe, but relying in the first on her own strength, she strikes in full confidence of victory.

We declare the right of the people of Ireland to the ownership of Ireland, and to the unfettered control of Irish destinies, to be sovereign and indefeasible. The long usurpation of that right by a foreign people and government has not extinguished the right, nor can it ever be extinguished except by the destruction of the Irish people. In every generation the Irish people have asserted their right to national freedom and sovereignty; six times during the past three hundred years they have asserted it in arms. Standing on that fundamental right and again asserting it in arms in the face of the world, we hereby proclaim the Irish Republic as a Sovereign Independent State, and we pledge our lives and the lives of our comrades-in-arms to the cause of its freedom, of its welfare, and of its exaltation among the nations.

The Irish Republic is entitled to, and hereby claims, the allegiance of every Irishman and Irishwoman. The Republic guarantees religious and civil liberty, equal rights and equal opportunities to all its citizens, and declares its resolve to pursue the happiness and prosperity of the whole nation and of all its parts, cherishing all the children of the nation equally, and oblivious of the differences carefully fostered by an alien government, which have divided a minority from the majority in the past.

Until our arms have brought the opportune moment for the establishment of a permanent National Government, representative of the whole people of Ireland and elected by the suffrages of all her men and women, the Provisional Government, hereby constituted, will administer the civil and military affairs of the Republic in trust for the people.

We place the cause of the Irish Republic under the protection of the Most High God, Whose blessing we invoke upon our arms, and we pray that no one who serves that cause will dishonour it by cowardice, inhumanity, or rapine. In this supreme hour the Irish nation must, by its valour and discipline and by the readiness of its children to sacrifice themselves for the common good, prove itself worthy of the august destiny to which it is called.

Signed on behalf of the Provisional Government

THOMAS J. CLARKE

SEAN MAC DIARMADA	THOMAS MACDONAGH
P. H. PEARSE	EAMONN CEANNT
JAMES CONNOLLY	JOSEPH PLUNKETT

Appendix II
Articles of Agreement
for a Treaty between
Great Britain and Ireland

1. Ireland shall have the same constitutional status in the Community of Nations known as the British Empire as the Dominion of Canada, the Commonwealth of Australia, the Dominion of New Zealand, and the Union of South Africa, with a Parliament having powers to make laws for the peace, order and good government of Ireland and an Executive responsible to that Parliament, and shall be styled and known as the Irish Free State.

2. Subject to the provisions hereinafter set out the position of the Irish Free State in relation to the Imperial Parliament and Government and otherwise shall be that of the Dominion of Canada, and the law, practice and constitutional usage governing the relationship of the Crown or the representative of the Crown and of the Imperial Parliament to the Dominion of Canada shall govern their relationship to the Irish Free State.

3. The representative of the Crown in Ireland shall be appointed in like manner as the Governor-General of Canada and in accordance with the practice observed in the making of such appointments.

4. The oath to be taken by Members of the Parliament of the Irish Free State shall be in the following form:—

I................do solemnly swear true faith and allegiance to the Constitution of the Irish Free State as by law established and that I will be faithful to H. M. King George V., his heirs and successors by law, in virtue of the common citizenship of Ireland with Great Britain and her adherence to and membership of the group of nations forming the British Commonwealth of Nations.

5. The Irish Free State shall assume liability for the service of the Public Debt of the United Kingdom as existing at the date hereof and towards the payment of war pensions as existing at that date in such proportion as may be fair and equitable, having regard to any just claims on the part of Ireland by way of set off or counter-claim, the amount of such sums being determined in default of agreement by the arbitration of one or more independent persons being citizens of the British Empire.

6. Until an arrangement has been made between the British and Irish Governments whereby the Irish Free State undertakes her own coastal defence, the defence by sea of Great Britain and Ireland shall be undertaken by His Majesty's Imperial Forces, but this shall not prevent the construction or maintenance by the Government of the Irish Free State of such vessels as are necessary for the protection of the Revenue or the Fisheries.

The foregoing provisions of this article shall be reviewed at a conference of Representatives of the British and Irish Governments to be held at the expiration of five years from the date hereof with a view to the undertaking by Ireland of a share in her own coastal defence.

7. The Government of the Irish Free State shall afford to His Majesty's Imperial Forces:—

(a) In time of peace such harbour and other facilities as are indicated in the Annex hereto, or such other facilities as may from time to time be agreed between the British Government and the Government of the Irish Free State; and

(b) In time of war or of strained relations with a Foreign Power such harbour and other facilities as the British Government may require for the purposes of such defence as aforesaid.

8. With a view to securing the observance of the principle of international limitation of armaments, if the Government of the Irish Free State establishes and maintains a military defence force, the establishments thereof shall not exceed in size such proportion of the military establishments maintained in Great Britain as that which the population of Ireland bears to the population of Great Britain.

9. The ports of Great Britain and the Irish Free State shall be freely open to the ships of the other country on payment of the customary port and other dues.

10. The Government of the Irish Free State agrees to pay fair compensation on terms not less favourable than those accorded by the Act of 1920 to judges, officials, members of Police Forces and other Public Servants who are discharged by it or who retire in consequence of the change of Government effected in pursuance hereof.

Provided that this agreement shall not apply to members of the Auxiliary Police Force or to persons recruited in Great Britain for the Royal Irish Constabulary during the two years next preceding the date hereof. The British Government will assume responsibility for such compensation or pensions as may be payable to any of these excepted persons.

11. Until the expiration of one month from the passing of the Act of Parliament for the ratification of this instrument, the powers of the Parliament and the Government of the Irish Free State shall not be exercisable as respects Northern Ireland, and the provisions of the Government of Ireland Act, 1920, shall, so far as they relate to Northern Ireland, remain of full force and effect, and no election shall be held for the return of members to serve in the Parliament of the Irish Free State for constituencies in Northern Ireland, unless a resolution is passed by both Houses of the Parliament of Northern Ireland in favour of the holding of such elections before the end of the said month.

12. If before the expiration of the said month, an address is presented to His Majesty by both Houses of the Parliament of Northern Ireland to that effect, the powers of the Parliament and Government of the Irish Free State shall no longer extend to Northern Ireland, and the provisions of the Government of Ireland Act, 1920 (including those relating to the Council of Ireland) shall so far as they relate to Northern Ireland, continue to be of full force and effect, and this instrument shall have effect subject to the necessary modifications.

Provided that if such an address is so presented a Commission consisting of three persons, one to be appointed by the Government of the Irish Free State, one to be appointed by the Government of Northern Ireland, and one who shall be Chairman to be appointed by the British Government, shall determine in accordance with the wishes of the inhabitants, so far as may be compatible with economic and geographic conditions, the boundaries between Northern Ireland and the rest of Ireland, and for the purposes of the Government of Ireland Act, 1920, and of this instrument, the boundary of Northern Ireland shall be such as may be determined by such Commission.

13. For the purpose of the last foregoing article, the powers of the Parliament of Southern Ireland under the Government of Ireland Act, 1920, to elect members of the Council of Ireland shall after the Parliament of the Irish Free State is constituted be exercised by that Parliament.

14. After the expiration of the said month, if no such address as is mentioned in Article 12 hereof is presented, the Parliament and Government of Northern Ireland shall continue to exercise as respects Northern Ireland the powers conferred on them by the Government of Ireland Act, 1920, but the Parliament and Government of the Irish Free State shall in Northern Ireland have in relation to matters in respect of which the Parliament of Northern Ireland has not power to make laws under that Act (including matters which under the said Act are within the jurisdiction of the Council of Ireland) the same powers as in the rest of Ireland, subject to such other provisions as may be agreed in manner hereinafter appearing.

15. At any time after the date hereof the Government of Northern Ireland and the provisional Government of Southern Ireland hereinafter constituted may meet for the purpose of discussing the provisions subject to which the last foregoing Article is to operate in the event of no such address as is therein mentioned being presented and those provisions may include:—

(a) Safeguards with regard to patronage in Northern Ireland.
(b) Safeguards with regard to the collection of revenue in Northern Ireland.
(c) Safeguards with regard to import and export duties affecting the trade or industry of Northern Ireland.
(d) Safeguards for minorities in Northern Ireland.
(e) The settlement of the financial relations between Northern Ireland and the Irish Free State.
(f) The establishment and powers of a local militia in Northern Ireland and the relation of the Defence Forces of the Irish Free State and of Northern Ireland respectively.

and if at any such meeting provisions are agreed to, the same shall have effect as if they were included amongst the provisions subject to which the powers of the Parliament and Government of the Irish Free State are to be exercisable in Northern Ireland under Article 14 hereof.

16. Neither the Parliament of the Irish Free State nor the Parliament of Northern Ireland shall make any law so as either directly or indirectly to endow any religion or prohibit or restrict the free exercise thereof or give any preference or impose any disability on account of religious belief or religious status or affect prejudicially the right of any child to attend a school receiving public

money without attending the religious instruction at the school or make any discrimination as respects State aid between schools under the management of different religious denominations or divert from any religious denomination or any educational institution any of its property except for public utility purposes and on payment of compensation.

17. By way of provisional arrangement for the administration of Southern Ireland during the interval which must elapse between the date hereof and the constitution of a Parliament and Government of the Irish Free State in accordance therewith, steps shall be taken forthwith for summoning a meeting of members of Parliament elected for constituencies in Southern Ireland since the passing of the Government of Ireland Act, 1920, and for constituting a provisional Government, and the British Government shall take the steps necessary to transfer to such provisional Government the powers and machinery requisite for the discharge of its duties, provided that every member of such provisional Government shall have signified in writing his or her acceptance of this instrument. But this arrangement shall not continue in force beyond the expiration of twelve months from the date hereof.

18. This instrument shall be submitted forthwith by His Majesty's Government for the approval of Parliament and by the Irish signatories to a meeting summoned for the purpose of the members elected to sit in the House of Commons of Southern Ireland, and if approved shall be ratified by the necessary legislation.

(Signed),

On behalf of the British Delegation.

On behalf of the Irish Delegation.

D. LLOYD GEORGE.
AUSTEN CHAMBERLAIN.
BIRKENHEAD.
WINSTON S. CHURCHILL.
L. WORTHINGTON-EVANS.
HAMAR GREENWOOD.
GORDON HEWART.

ART Ó GRÍOBHTHA.
MÍCHEÁL Ó COILEÁIN.
RIOBÁRD BARTÚN.
E. S. Ó DUGÁIN.
SEÓRSA GHABHÁIN UÍ DHUBHTHAIGH.

6th December, 1921.

Annex

1. The following are the specific facilities required:—

Dockyard Port at Berehaven

(a) Admiralty property and rights to be retained as at the date hereof. Harbour defences to remain in charge of British care and maintenance parties.

Queenstown

(b) Harbour defences to remain in charge of British care and maintenance parties. Certain mooring buoys to be retained for use of His Majesty's ships.

Belfast Lough

(c) Harbour defences to remain in charge of British care and maintenance parties.

Lough Swilly

(d) Harbour defences to remain in charge of British care and maintenance parties.

Aviation

(e) Facilities in the neighbourhood of the above ports for coastal defence by air.

Oil Fuel Storage

(f) Haulbowline   To be offered for sale to commercial companies under
                     guarantee that purchasers shall maintain a certain
    Rathmullen   minimum stock for Admiralty purposes.

2. A Convention shall be made between the British Government and the Government of the Irish Free State to give effect to the following conditions:

(a) That submarine cables shall not be landed or wireless stations for communication with places outside Ireland be established except by agreement with the British Government; that the existing cable landing rights and wireless concessions shall not be withdrawn except by agreement with the British Government; and that the British Government shall be entitled to land additional submarine cables or establish additional wireless stations for communication with places outside Ireland.

(b) That lighthouses, buoys, beacons and any navigational marks or navigational aids shall be maintained by the Government of the Irish Free State as at the date hereof and shall not be removed or added to except by agreement with the British Government.

(c) That war signal stations shall be closed down and left in charge of care and maintenance parties, the Government of the Irish Free State being offered the option of taking them over and working them for commercial purposes subject to Admiralty inspection and guaranteeing the upkeep of existing telegraphic communication therewith.

3. A Convention shall be made between the same Governments for the regulation of Civil Communication by Air.

Appendix III
Document No. 2
(revised version)

The following Motion will be proposed by the President at the present Session of Dáil Éireann:

"That inasmuch as the 'Articles of Agreement for a Treaty between Great Britain and Ireland', signed in London on December 6th, 1921, do not reconcile Irish National aspirations and the Association of Ireland with the Community of Nations known as the British Commonwealth, and can not be the basis of an enduring peace between the Irish and the British **peoples, DÁIL ÉIREANN**, in the name of the Sovereign Irish Nation, makes to the Government of Great Britain, to the Governments of the other States of the British Commonwealth, and to the peoples of Great Britain and of these several States, the following Proposal for a Treaty of Amity and Association which **DÁIL ÉIREANN** is convinced could be entered into by the Irish people with the sincerity of goodwill":—

PROPOSED TREATY OF ASSOCIATION BETWEEN IRELAND AND THE BRITISH COMMONWEALTH

In order to bring to an end the long and ruinous conflict between Great Britain and Ireland by a sure and lasting peace honourable to both nations, it is agreed

Status of Ireland

1. That the legislative, executive, and judicial authority of Ireland shall be derived solely from the people of Ireland.

Terms of Association

2. That, for purposes of common concern, Ireland shall be associated with the States of the British Commonwealth, viz: the Kingdom of Great Britain, the Dominion of Canada, the Commonwealth of Australia, the Dominion of New Zealand, and the Union of South Africa.

3. That when acting as an associate the rights, status, and privileges of Ireland shall be in no respect less than those enjoyed by any of the component States of the British Commonwealth.

4. That the matters of "common concern" shall include Defence, Peace and War, Political Treaties, and all matters now treated as of common concern amongst the States of the British Commonwealth, and that in these matters there shall be between Ireland and the States of the British Commonwealth "such

concerted action founded on consultation as the several Governments may determine."

5. That in virtue of this association of Ireland with the States of the British Commonwealth citizens of Ireland in any of these States shall not be subject to any disabilities which a citizen of one of the component States of the British Commonwealth would not be subject to, and reciprocally for citizens of these States in Ireland.

6. That, for purposes of the Association, Ireland shall recognise His Britannic Majesty as head of the Association.

Defence

7. That, so far as her resources permit, Ireland shall provide for her own defence by sea, land and air, and shall repel by force any attempt by a foreign power to violate the integrity of her soil and territorial waters, or to use them for any purpose hostile to Great Britain and the other associated States.

8. That for five years, pending the establishment of Irish coastal defence forces, or for such other period as the Governments of the two countries may later agree upon, facilities for the coastal defence of Ireland shall be given to the British Government as follows:

(a) In time of peace such harbour and other facilities as are indicated in the Annex hereto, or such other facilities as may from time to time be agreed upon between the British Government and the Government of Ireland.

(b) In time of war such harbour and other Naval facilities as the British Government may reasonably require for the purposes of such defence as aforesaid.

9. That within five years from the date of exchange of ratifications of this treaty a conference between the British and Irish Governments shall be held in order to hand over the coastal defence of Ireland to the Irish Government, unless some other arrangement for naval defence be agreed by both Governments to be desirable in the common interest of Ireland, Great Britain, and the other associated States.

10. That, in order to co-operate in furthering the principle of international limitation of armaments, the Government of Ireland shall not

(a) Build submarines unless by agreement with Great Britain and the other States of the Commonwealth.

(b) Maintain a military defence force, the establishments whereof exceed in size such proportion of the military establishments maintained in Great Britain as that which the population of Ireland bears to the population of Great Britain.

Miscellaneous

11. That the Governments of Great Britain and of Ireland shall make a convention for the regulation of civil communication by air.

12. That the ports of Great Britain and of Ireland shall be freely open to the ships of each country on payment of the customary port and other dues.

13. That Ireland shall assume liability for such share of the present public debt of Great Britain and Ireland and of the payment of war pensions as existing at this date as may be fair and equitable, having regard to any just claims on the part of Ireland by way of set off or counter claim, the amount of such sums being determined, in default of agreement, by the arbitration of one or more independent persons being citizens of Ireland or of the British Commonwealth.

14. That the Government of Ireland agrees to pay compensation on terms not less favourable than those proposed by the British Government of Ireland Act of 1920 to that Government's judges, officials, members of Police Forces and other Public Servants who are discharged by the Government of Ireland or who retire in consequence of the change of government effected in pursuance hereof.

Provided that this agreement shall not apply to members of the Auxiliary Police Force or to persons recruited in Great Britain for the Royal Irish Constabulary during the two years next preceding the date hereof. The British Government will assume responsibility for such compensation or pensions as may be payable to any of these excepted persons.

15. That neither the Parliament of Ireland nor any subordinate legislature in Ireland shall make any law so as either directly or indirectly to endow any religion or prohibit or restrict the free exercise thereof or give any preference or impose any disability on account of religious belief or religious status or affect prejudicially the right of any child to attend a school receiving public money without attending the religious instruction at the school or make any discrimination as respects State aid between schools under the management of different religious denominations or divert from any religious denomination or any educational institution any of its property except for public utility purposes and on payment of compensation.

Transitional

16. That by way of transitional arrangement for the Administration of Ireland during the interval which must elapse between the date hereof and the setting up of a Parliament and Government of Ireland in accordance herewith, the members elected for constituencies in Ireland since the passing of the British Government of Ireland Act in 1920 shall at a meeting summoned for the purpose elect a transitional government to which the British Government and Dáil Éireann shall transfer the authority, powers and machinery requisite for the discharge of its duties, provided that every member of such transitional government shall have signified in writing his or her acceptance of this instrument. But this arrangement shall not continue in force beyond the expiration of twelve months from the date hereof.

Ratification

17. That this instrument shall be submitted for ratification forthwith by His Britannic Majesty's Government to the Parliament at Westminster, and by the Cabinet of Dáil Éireann to a meeting of the members elected for the constituencies in Ireland set forth in the British Government of Ireland Act 1920, and when ratifications have been exchanged shall take immediate effect.

ANNEX

1. The following are the specific facilities referred to in Article 8 (a):—

Dockyard Port at Berehaven

(a) British Admiralty property and rights to be retained as at the date hereof. Harbour defences to remain in charge of British care and maintenance parties.

Queenstown

(b) Harbour defences to remain in charge of British care and maintenance parties. Certain mooring buoys to be retained for use of His Britannic Majesty's ships.

Belfast Lough

(c) Harbour defences to remain in charge of British care and maintenance parties.

Lough Swilly

(d) Harbour defences to remain in charge of British care and maintenance parties.

Aviation

(e) Facilities in the neighbourhood of the above ports for coastal defence by air.

Oil Fuel Storage

(f) Haulbowline   To be offered for sale to commercial companies under
    Rathmullen   guarantee that purchases shall maintain a certain minimum stock for Admiralty purposes.

2. A Convention covering a period of five years shall be made between the British and Irish Governments to give effect to the following conditions:

(a) That submarine cables shall not be landed or wireless stations for communication with places outside Ireland be established except by agreement with the British Government; that the existing cable landing rights and wireless concessions shall not be withdrawn except by agreement with the British Government; and that the British Government shall be entitled to land additional submarine cables or establish additional wireless stations for communication with places outside Ireland.

(b) That lighthouses, buoys, beacons, and any navigational marks or navigational aids shall be maintained by the Government of Ireland as at the date hereof and shall not be removed or added to except by agreement with the British Government.

(c) That war signal stations shall be closed down and left in charge of care and maintenance parties, the Government of Ireland being offered the option of taking them over and working them for commercial purposes subject to British Admiralty inspection and guaranteeing the upkeep of existing telegraphic communication therewith.

ADDENDUM

North East Ulster

RESOLVED:

That whilst refusing to admit the right of any part of Ireland to be excluded from the supreme authority of the Parliament of Ireland, or that the relations between the Parliament of Ireland and any subordinate legislature in Ireland can be a matter for treaty with a Government outside Ireland, nevertheless, in sincere regard for internal peace, and in order to make manifest our desire not to bring force or coercion to bear upon any substantial part of the province of Ulster, whose inhabitants may now be unwilling to accept the national authority, we are prepared to grant to that portion of Ulster which is defined as Northern Ireland in the British Government of Ireland Act of 1920, privileges and safeguards not less substantial than those provided for in the "Articles of Agreement for a Treaty" between Great Britain and Ireland signed in London on December 6th, 1921.

Appendix IV
Possible British Sanctions Against Southern Ireland in 1922

A subcommittee of the Cabinet's Irish Committee studied economic sanctions from February through June. It is unlikely that Britain would have imposed a general blockade on Southern Ireland in the event of war or severed relations, as the investigation concluded that this would pose too many problems. A limited blockade was a distinct possibility, however. By cutting off imports of vital fuel supplies, the British could put considerable pressure on the Republicans with minimum risk and inconvenience to themselves. Such a blockade would be enforced by occupation of Dublin, Queenstown, and Limerick, which would also deny the bulk of Irish revenues to the enemy.[1]

The question of military sanctions was investigated by a subcommittee of the Committee of Imperial Defense. Headed by Churchill and including the chiefs of the armed services, the subcommittee met eight times between April 6 and June 2, holding its most crucial sessions on June 1 and 2 during the crisis over the Constitution. According to the subcommittee's plan, a break with Southern Ireland would probably have caused the British to occupy the waterline of rivers and lakes from County Donegal to County Louth (Letterkenny–Donegal–Bally-shannon–Belleek–Clones–Dundalk) to defend Ulster from invasion. At the same time, reinforcements would be sent to the South (as well as the North) to hold Dublin and take control of the customs there and at Queenstown and Limerick.[2]

The Provisional Government's surrender on the Constitution removed the danger of hostilities and the need for sanctions. Within a few weeks, the economic and military subcommittees were disbanded.

Notes

Chapter 1

1. On the labor movement and the Citizen Army, see Lawrence J. McCaffrey, *The Irish Question, 1800-1922* (Lexington: University of Kentucky Press, 1968), 143-45; J. W. Boyle, "Connolly, the Citizen Army and the Rising," in *The Making of 1916: Studies in the History of the Rising,* ed. Kevin D. Nowlan (Dublin: The Stationery Office, 1969), 51-68; Donal Nevin, "The Irish Citizen Army," in *1916: The Easter Rising,* ed. Owen Dudley Edwards and Fergus Pyle (London: MacGibbon and Kee, 1968), 119-31.

2. On Griffith and Sinn Fein, see Padraic Colum, *Arthur Griffith* (Dublin: Browne and Nolan, 1959), pt. I, chs. 6-15; P. S. O'Hegarty, *A History of Ireland under the Union, 1801-1922* (London: Methuen, 1952), chs. 60-63, and *The Victory of Sinn Fein* (Dublin: Talbot Press, 1924), 30-31, 130-34; Robert Brennan, *Allegiance* (Dublin: Browne and Nolan, 1950), 216-17; and Donal McCartney, "The Sinn Fein Movement," in *The Making of 1916,* 31-48.

3. The IRB was organized in Circles, Counties or Districts, and Divisions; an elected Center headed each unit and served as the link with other units. The Brotherhood's ruling body was the Supreme Council in Dublin, which included Division Centers and four members coopted by them. The Council's Executive consisted of a president, secretary, and treasurer elected by Council members. Under its constitution, the IRB was "the sole government of the Irish Republic," and its president or head center was president of the Republic. Every member owed unquestioning obedience to the Supreme Council, whose policy and decisions were regularly reported to the leadership of the Clan na Gael. On the IRB, see O'Hegarty, *History of Ireland,* chs. 32-36 and pp. 595-96, 633-34, 656. F. S. L. Lyons, *Ireland since the Famine* (London: Weidenfeld and Nicolson, 1971), 114-23, 151-56, 313-17; Robert Kee, *The Green Flag* (New York, Delacorte Press, 1972), 308-10; Diarmuid Lynch, *The I.R.B. and the 1916 Insurrection* (Cork: Mercier Press, 1957), ed. Florence O'Donoghue, 22, 33; Bulmer Hobson, *Ireland Yesterday and Tomorrow* (Tralee: Anvil Books, 1968), 31-39, 103-7.

4. On Unionists and Home Rule, see Patrick Buckland, *Irish Unionism: One: The Anglo-Irish and the New Ireland, 1885-1922* (Dublin: Gill and Macmillan, 1972), introduction and ch. 1, and *Irish Unionism: Two: Ulster Unionism and the Origins of Northern Ireland, 1886-1922* (Dublin: Gill and Macmillan, 1973), introduction and chs. 1-4; Robert Blake, *The Unknown Prime Minister: The Life and Times of Andrew Bonar Law, 1858-1923* (London: Eyre and Spottiswoode, 1955), chs. 7-14; Denis Gwynn, *The History of Partition (1912-1925)* (Dublin: Browne and Nolan, 1950), 42-43; Nicholas Mansergh, "The Unionist Party and the Union, 1886-1916," in *1916: The Easter Rising,* 79-89; J. C. Beckett, "Carson— Unionist and Rebel," in *Leaders and Men of the Easter Rising, Dublin 1916,* ed. F. X. Martin (Ithaca, N.Y.: Cornell University Press, 1967), 81-93.

5. Blake, 130.

6.   Ireland's population in 1911 was 4,390,319. Ulster accounted for roughly one-third of this total with 1,581,696 people, of whom 890,880 were Protestant and 690,816 Catholic. There were 711, 767 Protestants and 293, 483 Catholics in Antrim, Down, Armagh and Derry, and 820,370 Protestants and 430,161 Catholics in these four counties plus Tyrone and Fermanagh. While not every Protestant was a Unionist or every Catholic a nationalist, there was and is a very close correlation between religious and political affiliation in Northern Ireland. Gwynn, 122; Dorothy Macardle, *The Irish Republic* (1st American ed.; New York: Farrar, Straus and Giroux, 1965), 75-76.

Chapter 2

1.   For the background of the rising, see especially Maureen Wall, "The Background to the Rising, from 1914 until the Issue of the Countermanding Order on Easter Saturday, 1916," and "The Plans and the Countermand: The Country and Dublin," in *The Making of 1916*, 155-251. These essays are excellent and well-documented syntheses of printed sources through 1968.
2.   The most fully documented account of the military events of Easter Week is G. A. Hayes-McCoy, "A Military History of the 1916 Rising," in *The Making of 1916*, 255-338.
3.   On the state of Irish opinion at this time, see O'Hegarty, *Sinn Fein*, 3, and *History of Ireland*, 703; Colum, 152; Edgar Holt, *Protest in Arms* (London: Putnam, 1960), 103, 112, 117; Sir James O'Connor, *History of Ireland, 1798-1924* (London: Arnold, 1926), II, 277-79; Darrell Figgis, *Recollections of the Irish War* (London: Benn, 1927), 149-50; Earl of Longford and Thomas P. O'Neill, *Eamon de Valera* (London: Hutchinson, 1970), 45-47; Ernie O'Malley, *Army without Banners* (London: Four Square Books, 1967; 1st pub. 1936 as *On Another Man's Wound*), 23-35; Sean O'Faolain, *Vive Moi!* (Boston: Little, Brown, 1964), 130-31; John Dillon's speech in the House of Commons, May 11, 1916, in *1916: The Easter Rising*, 74-75; and esp. James Stephens, *The Insurrection in Dublin* (Dublin: Scepter Books, 1966; 1st pub. 1916).
4.   O'Hegarty, *History of Ireland*, 704-8; O'Connor, 278.
5.   John H. Whyte, "1916—Revolution and Religion," in *Leaders and Men of the Easter Rising*, 215-26; Roger McHugh, "The Catholic Church and the Rising," in *1916: The Easter Rising*, 196-201; Lyons, 9-10, 123.
6.   F. S. L. Lyons, "Dillon, Redmond, and the Irish Home Rulers," in *Leaders and Men of the Easter Rising*, 32-33.
7.   Lyons, 374-75; Macardle, 188-89.
8.   Lyons, in *Leaders and Men of the Easter Rising*, 34-35.
9.   Leon O'Broin, *Dublin Castle and the 1916 Rising* (Dublin: Helicon, 1966), 130-34.
10.   Colum, 157.
11.   Proinsias MacAonghusa and Liam O'Reagain, eds., *The Best of Pearse* (Cork: Mercier Press, 1967), 189-90.
12.   O'Broin, 142; Macardle, 185-90; O'Malley, 35-38; Figgis, 150-51.
13.   O'Broin, 141-43.

14.   Owen Dudley Edwards, "American Aspects of the Rising," in *1916: The Easter Rising*, 153-80; Alan J. Ward, *Ireland and Anglo-American Relations, 1899-1921* (London: Weidenfeld and Nicolson, 1969), 111-13, 126-28.

15.   Buckland, I, 54-82, and II, 105-7.

16.   Figgis, 168-69; Macardle, 201-3; Brennan, 72-151; Rex Taylor, *Michael Collins* (London: Hutchinson, 1958), 69-81.

17.   Macardle, 208-9; Colum,173-74.

18.   Colum, 174; Macardle, 213-15.

19.   Lyons, 384-85; Macardle, 216-19.

20.   Most of this minority remained opposed to any compromise, however. Their stubborn attitude led Lord Midleton and other prominent Southern loyalists to withdraw from the Irish Unionist Alliance in January 1919 and form the Unionist Anti-Partition League, which aimed at securing effective safeguards for the minority in a self-governed Ireland. Buckland, I, 129-85.

21.   On the convention, see R. B. McDowell, *The Irish Convention* (Toronto: University of Toronto Press, 1970); see also Gwynn, 158-75, and Buckland, I, 83-128, and II, 107-13.

22.   Edwards, in *1916: The Easter Rising*, 162; Lyons, 376.

23.   Piaras Beaslai, *Michael Collins and the Making of a New Ireland* (New York: Harper, 1926), I, 158, 174; Mary C. Bromage, *De Valera and the March of a Nation* (London: Hutchinson, 1956), 60, 65.

24.   On the Sinn Fein convention, see Macardle, 231-34; Beaslai, 169-74; Colum, 169; Longford and O'Neill, 67-69; O'Hegarty, *History of Ireland*, 716-17.

25.   Beaslai, I, 175; Brennan, 154-55; Macardle, 231; Taylor, 87-88.

26.   Beaslai, I, 174-75.

27.   On the conscription issue, see Alan J. Ward, "Lloyd George and the 1918 Irish Conscription Crisis," in *The Historical Journal*, XVII, (1974), 107-29; Macardle, 248-57; Holt, 153-64; Beaslai, I, 231; Donal O'Sullivan, *The Irish Free State and Its Senate* (London: Faber and Faber, 1940), 42; Dan Breen, *My Fight for Irish Freedom* (rev. ed.; Tralee: Anvil Books, 1964), 31.

28.   W. Alison Phillips, *The Revolution in Ireland, 1906-1923* (2d ed.; London: Longmans, 1926), 150.

29.   Figgis, 216-21, 225-26; O'Hegarty, *Sinn Fein*, 75-76; Frank O'Connor, *The Big Fellow: Michael Collins and the Irish Revolution* (rev. ed.; Springfield, Ill.: Templegate, 1965), 38-39.

30.   Brian Farrell, *The Founding of Dail Eireann: Parliament and Nation-Building* (Dublin: Gill and Macmillan, 1971), 29-47; Holt, 166-67; Macardle, 262-65; David W. Miller, *Church, State and Nation in Ireland, 1898-1921* (Pittsburgh: University of Pittsburgh Press, 1973), 422-25.

31.   Macardle, 919, 921, 264-65.

32.   The Irish electorate in 1918 numbered just over 1.9 million persons. In the contested constituencies, slightly more than 1 million out of 1.5 million voters cast ballots. Sinn Fein got 484,000 of these votes, the Unionists 297,000, and the Home Rulers 233,000.

33.   David Butler and Jennie Freeman, *British Political Facts, 1900-1960* (New York, St. Martin's, 1963), 122.

34.   O'Hegarty, *Sinn Fein*, 31-32.

35.   On the 1918 election, see Farrell, 45–50; Labor Party (British), *Report of the Commission of Inquiry into the Present Conditions in Ireland* (London: Labor Party, 1920), 5–6; J. L. McCracken, *Representative Government in Ireland, 1919–1948* (London: Oxford University Press, 1958), 20–21; Macardle, 266–67; Lyons, 396–97; O'Hegarty, *History of Ireland,* 725, 728; Beaslai, I, 250–51; J. O'Connor, 293–94, 309; F. S. L. Lyons, "The Two Faces of Home Rule," in *The Making of 1916,* 122–23.

Chapter 3

1.   Dail Eireann (Official Record), *Minutes of Proceedings of the First Parliament of the Republic of Ireland, 1919–1921* (Dublin: The Stationery Office), January 21, 1919, 15–16 (cited hereafter as *Dail Debates*); Macardle, 272.

2.   *Dail Debates,* January 21, 1919, 22–23; Farrell, 57–61; O'Hegarty, *History of Ireland,* 726–27. This Dail and its successor were made up largely of members of the urban lower-middle class, leaving workers and farmers very much underrepresented (McCracken, 30–34).

3.   Macardle, 274; Holt, 173–74. See also O'Hegarty, *History of Ireland,* 727–30; Figgis, 228–37; Colum, 185–86; F. O'Connor, 40–41.

4.   *Dail Debates,* January 22, 1919, 26–27; Macardle, 276–77.

5.   On the RIC, see O'Hegarty, *History of Ireland,* 401–4; Holt, 26–27; David Neligan, *The Spy in the Castle* (London: MacGibbon and Kee, 1968), 75; G. C. Duggan, "The Royal Irish Constabulary," in *1916: The Easter Rising,* 91–99; and esp. Richard Hawkins, "Dublin Castle and the Royal Irish Constabulary (1916–1922)," in *The Irish Struggle, 1916–1926,* ed. Desmond Williams (Toronto: University of Toronto Press, 1966), 167–81.

6.   Beaslai, I, 273–78; Tom Barry, *Guerrilla Days in Ireland* (Dublin: Irish Press, 1949), 8–9, 185–86; Breen, 102–3; O'Malley, 98; Florence O'Donoghue, *No Other Law* (Dublin: Irish Press, 1954), 44–45, 54–55, 69–70, 85–86, 107, 127; G. A. Hayes-McCoy, "The Conduct of the Anglo-Irish War (January 1919 to the Truce in July 1921)," in *The Irish Struggle,* 55–56; Desmond Ryan, *Remembering Sion* (London: Barker, 1934), 235; Brennan, 211–12; F. O'Connor, 41–44; O'Hegarty, *Sinn Fein,* 44–48.

7.   *Dail Debates,* August 20, 1919, 151–53; F. O'Connor, 76; Macardle, 304–5; David Hogan, *Four Glorious Years* (Dublin: Irish Press, 1953), 245–47; *Irish Press,* February 13, 1964. On the relations of Dail Eireann and the Volunteers, see Kevin B. Nowlan, "Dail Eireann and the Army: Unity and Division (1919–1921)," in *The Irish Struggle,* 67–77; O'Malley, 130; Breen, 96; Beaslai, I, 277–78; O'Donoghue, 42–43; Macardle, 289–91, 436–38; Dail Eireann (Official Report), *August, 1921 and February–June, 1922* (Dublin: The Stationery Office), April 27–28, 1922, 323, 327–29 (cited hereafter as *Dail Debates*).

8.   Longford and O'Neill, 92–96; Bromage, 84–85; Macardle, 283–84.

9.   Macardle, 285, 445; D. G. Boyce, *Englishmen and Irish Troubles: British Public Opinion and the Making of Irish Policy, 1918–1922* (Cambridge, Mass: MIT Press, 1972), 86.

10.   *Dail Debates,* April 4, June 18, August 19–20, 1919, 41, 121–23, 140–41, 146–48, 150; Macardle, 302–3, 986; Rex Taylor, 295–96.

11.   *Dail Debates*, April 10, 1919, 67–69; Beaslai, I, 338, 444–45; Figgis, 262–63; "Periscope" (G. C. Duggan), "The Last Days of Dublin Castle," *Blackwood's Magazine* (London), CCXII (August 1922), 141–42; Neligan, 80–81.

12.   Beaslai, I, 338; O'Donoghue, 48–54; Holt, 187–88.

13.   Macardle, 308, 315–17; Winston S. Churchill, *The World Crisis, 1918–1928: The Aftermath* (New York: Scribner's, 1929), 297.

14.   The fullest and best-documented study of the goverment's Irish policy, particularly its military policy, is in Charles Townshend, *The British Campaign in Ireland, 1919–1921: The Development of Political and Military Policies* (London: Oxford University Press, 1975).

15.   Cabinet Paper (C.P.) 56, First Report of the Cabinet Committee on the Irish Question, November 4, 1919 (Cab 27/68).

16.   Cabinet Conclusions 5(19), 2, November 11, 1919 (Cab 23/18).

17.   Cab 10(19), 4, December 3, 1919; Cab 12(19), 10 and 12, December 10, 1919; Cab 14(19), 2, December 15, 1919; Cab 16(19), 5–6, December 19, 1919 (Cab 23/18); Cab 12(20), 1, February 24, 1920 (Cab 23/20).

18.   C.P. 190, Third Report of the Committee on Ireland, November 24, 1919; CI 15th Minutes, February 17, 1920 (Cab 27/68); CI 83, 84, 87, September 10, 16, 29, 1920 (Cab 27/70); Boyce, 121; Cab 59(20), 7c (Appendix III), November 3, 1920: Conclusions of a Conference of Ministers, October 13, 1920 (Cab 23/23).

19.   Cab 59(20), 7c (App. III), November 3, 1920: Conclusions of a Conference of Ministers, October 13, 1920 (Cab 23/23).

20.   Government of Ireland Act, 10 and 11, Geo. 5 (H. M. Stationery Office, London, 1920).

21.   On initial Irish reaction to the Government of Ireland Bill, especially that of Ulster Unionists, see Buckland, I, 224–32, II, 115–21; Macardle, 402; Ian Colvin, *The Life of Lord Carson* (London: Gollancz, 1936), III, 382–85; Maureen Wall, "Partition: The Ulster Question (1916–1926)," in *The Irish Struggle,* 83.

22.   Churchill, 299–300; Boyce, 110–17.

23.   Labor Party, *Report on Ireland* (1920), 11; Boyce, 111–12, 118–25; Memorandum to the Prime Minister by Tom Jones, July 24, 1920; General Sir Nevil Macready to Frances Stevenson (Lloyd George's private secretary and mistress), with Memorandum attached, May 25, 1920, F/24/3/3 and F/36/2/14, Lloyd George Papers.

24.   Cab 16(19), 9, December 19, 1919 (Cab 23/18); see also C.I. 87, Memorandum by Walter Long, chairman of Cabinet's Irish Committee, September 29, 1920 (Cab 27/70). Macardle, 401–2; *Parliamentary Debates* (Official Report), *Fifth Series.* House of Commons (London: H. M. Stationery Office), vol. 127, March 30, 1920, 1125–26 (cited hereafter as H.C. (or H.L.) Deb. 5s.); Boyce 65n., 126–28; *The Political Diaries of C. P. Scott, 1911–1928,* ed. Trevor Wilson (Ithaca, N.Y.: Cornell University Press, 1970), 342–43.

25.   Hugh Martin, *Ireland in Insurrection* (London: O'Connor, 1921), 212–18; Macardle, 325–27, 351–52; McCracken, 27.

26.   *Dail Debates,* June 29 and September 17, 1920, 185, 219–22; idem, January 25 and March 11, 1921, 253–55, 268–71; Phillips, 179–80; Sir Henry Robinson, *Memories: Wise and Otherwise* (London: Cassell, 1923), 307–9; W. K. Hancock, *Survey of British Commonwealth Affairs,* I: *Problems of Nationality, 1918–*

1936 (London: Oxford University Press, 1937), 114–15; Macardle, 327–28, 352; "Periscope," 160–61, 173.

27. *Dail Debates,* June 29, 1920, 178–80; Dail Eireann, *Private Sessions of [the] Second Dail, 1921–1922* (Dublin: The Stationery Office), August 14, 1921, 20–26 (cited hereafter as *Dail Debates* [P.S.]); Macardle, 348–51, 375–77; Phillips, 180–82; Hancock, 115–19; Hogan, 72–82; Figgis, 292–300; Lyons, 406; Farrell, 74–78; Thomas Jones, *Whitehall Diary,* III: *Ireland, 1918–1925,* ed. Keith Middlemas (London: Oxford University Press, 1971), 24–25.

28. Macardle, 328, 330, 333, 344, 353 n.5; Neligan, 90; Hogan, 160–61; Beaslai, I, 435, 441; II, 30.

29. Macardle, 344–45; Holt, 206–7; Frank Gallagher, *Days of Fear* (Cork: Mercier Press, 1967).

30. General Sir Nevil Macready, *Annals of an Active Life* (London: Hutchinson, 1924), II, 472; Boyce, 67–71; Macardle, 347; Richard Bennett, *The Black and Tans* (London: Four Square Books, 1961), 125.

31. Lynch, 32; Beaslai, I, 109–10.

32. F. O'Connor, 22.

33. Lynch, 32; Beaslai, I, 135, 160.

34. Neligan, 137; Douglas V. Duff, *May the Winds Blow* (London: Hollis and Carter, 1948), 79–81.

35. On Collins' life and work, see the volumes already cited: Beaslai, Taylor, and Frank O'Connor; see also Margery Forester, *Michael Collins—The Lost Leader* (London: Sidgwick and Jackson, 1971). Beaslai's work is the most detailed study; Taylor offers important material from Collins' diaries and letters on the 1921 Treaty negotiations; and Forester is good on Collins' personal life. O'Connor's book is the best character study. The finest short sketch of Collins is in Ryan, *Remembering Sion,* 229–38.

36. Brennan, 151–53, 321; F. O'Connor, 36.

37. Taylor, 117–20, 136; F. O'Connor, 47, 89–92; Colum, 223–24; Barry, 187–88; Brennan, 266; Frank Pakenham, *Peace by Ordeal* (3d ed.; London: Chapman, 1962), 92–96.

38. Brennan, 211–12; Colum, 179–80.

39. Ryan, 241–42; Taylor, 116–17; O'Malley, 271–73; F. O'Connor, 51, 108; Longford and O'Neill, 116, 148; Interview with Ernest Blythe, January 1959.

40. On the sorry state of the Irish Executive, see Sir Warren Fisher, Confidential Reports to the Prime Minister, Bonar Law, and Austen Chamberlain, May 12 and 15, 1920, and Sir John Anderson to Chief Secretary Sir Hamar Greenwood, July 20, 1920, F/31/1/32–33 and F/19/2/14, LGP; Macready, 456–57; Lord Riddell, *Intimate Diary of the Peace Conference and After, 1918–1923* (London: Gollancz, 1933), 146–47.

41. "Periscope," 155–56, Holt, 204–5; Robinson, 295–96; Labor Party, *Report of the Labour Commission to Ireland* (London: Labor Party, 1921), 52–53; Charles Loch Mowat, *Britain between the Wars, 1918–1940* (Chicago: University of Chicago Press, 1955), 64.

42. "Periscope," 150–52; Macready, 492–93; Holt, 204.

43. Sir Ormonde Winter, *Winter's Tale* (London: Richards Press, 1955), 291–305, 337–38; Townshend, 50–51.

44. Macready, 425.

45. Cab 23A (20), Ireland: Note of a Conversation of Ministers, April 30, 1920; Cab 29(20), May 19, 1920, appendix II: Conclusions of a Conference of Ministers, May 11, 1920; Cab 31(20), 4, June 2, 1920; Cab 33(20), 2, June 7, 1920, and app. III: Conclusions of a Conf. of Ministers, May 31, 1920 (Cab 23/21); Lloyd George to Bonar Law, May 10, 1920, 103/4/2, Bonar Law Papers; Macready, 439, 453–54, 468, 479; Townshend, 40–41. Jones's account of the Cabinet's discussions of May 31 and July 23, 1920, offers a revealing picture of individual ministers' attitudes on Ireland (16–23, 25–31).

46. Hawkins, in *The Irish Struggle,* 172–81; Townshend, 41–46; Hogan, 70–71; Neligan, 84–85. Statistics on RIC strength are given in the Irish Office's Weekly Surveys, Cabinet Papers, C.P. series (Cab 24).

47. Provisional Government of Ireland Committee, PGI 4, Memorandum of the Chief Secretary, December 21, 1921 (Cab 27/154); Hawkins, in *The Irish Struggle,* 178–79.

48. On the Black and Tans, and the Auxies, see Bennett; Martin; Duff (chs. 6 and 7); Pakenham (Ch. 3); Labor Party *Report* (1921); Frank P. Crozier, *Ireland Forever* (London: Cape, 1932); Douglas Goldring, *Odd Man Out* (London: Chapman and Hall, 1935), Chs. 4 and 5; Macready, 455, 470–71, 481–83; Phillips, 186–88; Hogan, 102–3; Winter, 335–36, 344–45; O'Donoghue, 67–69; Jones, 52–53; Duggan, in *1916: The Easter Rising,* 95–99; Hawkins, in *The Irish Struggle,* 178–81; Neligan, 87; F. O'Connor, 81; "Periscope," 177–78; Townshend, 95–96 and *passim.* For a list of reprisals, January–September 1920, see Martin, 178–85.

49. Macready, 486–87, 498, 500–502.

50. Major General Sir C. E. Callwell, *Field Marshal Sir Henry Wilson: His Life and Diaries* (London: Cassell, 1927), II, 252–54, 263–65; Martin Gilbert, *Winston S. Churchill,* IV: *1917–1922* (London: Heinemann, 1975), 463–64.

51. Cab 79A (20), 1, December 29, 1920 (Cab 23/23).

52. Prime Minister to Greenwood, February 25, 1921, F/19/3/4, LGP.

53. Pakenham, 56–61.

54. An official report gives the IRA's strength at the truce as 72,363 officers and men (GHQ Memorandum, Director of Organization to the Chief of Staff, November 23, 1921, P7/C/69/26/14, Richard Mulcahy Papers). Its armament in June 1921 consisted of 3,295 rifles, 49 Thompson submachine guns, and 12 machine guns, plus some 15,000 shotguns and about 6,000 pistols (P7/D/64/22/93, Mulcahy Papers). On the IRA and its tactics, see Macready, 499, 506–7; O'Donoghue, 72, 97–98; 111; Barry, 19–22; Beaslai, II, 96–97; Breen, 124–25; Macardle, 341–44; Labor Party *Report* (1921), 8.

55. Barry, 36–51, 122–32; Kee, 694–95; Holt, 242–43.

56. Townshend, 50–51, 90–92; Hogan, 155; Macready, 462–63; "Periscope," 159, 171.

57. Taylor, 130–33; Bennett, 97–106; Neligan, 91, 122–23; Crozier, 90, 102, 147–49; Hogan, 242–43; F. O'Connor, 98–100; Townshend, 129–31. The fullest account of the day's events is in Philip Gleeson, *Bloody Sunday* (London: Four Square Books, 1965).

58. Bennett, 106–7; Labor Party *Report* (1921), 40–43.

59. On McSwiney and Barry, see Macardle, 382–83, 391–94; Holt, 221–23; Bennett, 68, 89–91.

60. Holt, 214; Bennett, 44–45; "Periscope," 165–70; O'Faolain, 174–81.

61. J. O'Connor, 311–12; Phillips, 177–79; Holt, 233; Neligan, 95–96; Miller, 431–34, 450–84.

62. C.P. 3130, Weekly Survey of the State of Ireland (Irish Office), 4 n.3, July 11, 1921 (Cab 24/126); Macardle, 356–57, 730; Holt, 218–19; Bennett, 49, 57–60; Martin, 87–88, 167–76; St. John Ervine, *Craigavon: Ulsterman* (London: Allen and Unwin, 1949), 397–99.

63. Cab 53(20), September 30, 1920, apps. IV–V: Conclusions of Conferences of Ministers, 3, September 2; and 3, September 8, 1920 (Cab 23/22).

64. On the Belfast boycott, see *Dail Debates,* August 6 and September 17, 1920, January 25 and August 17, 1921, and March 1–2, 1922; O'Hegarty, *Sinn Fein,* 49–53; Macardle, 387.

65. Macardle, 412–15; Frank Gallagher, *The Anglo-Irish Treaty* (London: Hutchinson, 1965), 19–24; Colum, 239–42; Bennett, 115; Prime Minister to Greenwood, December 2, 1920, and Greenwood's Minute on Clune's Interview with Collins and Mulcahy, n.d., F/19/2/26 and F/19/2/31, LGP; Cab 66(20), 2, December 6, 1920; Cab 68(20), 2, December 9, 1920, and apps. I–IV; Cab 70(20), 2, December 13, 1920; Cab 77(20), 6, December 24, 1920 (Cab 23/23).

66. Cab 79A(20), December 29, 1920 (Cab 23/23).

67. Cab 81(20), 1–2, December 30, 1920 (Cab 23/23); Gallagher, 25–33; Jones, 52.

68. This proposal foreshadowed de Valera's plan of external association, which formed the basis for Sinn Fein's peace proposals in 1921.

69. F. O'Connor, 75–76; O'Hegarty, *History of Ireland,* 764; Sean Cronin, *The McGarrity Papers* (Tralee: Anvil Books, 1972), 83–85, 93–101.

70. On de Valera in America, see Cronin, 73–92; Ward, esp. ch. 10; Longford and O'Neill, chs. 8 and 9; Macardle, 309–14, 366–71, 409–11.

Chapter 4

1. Longford and O'Neill, 119; Beaslai, II, 146; F. O'Connor, 109.

2. *Dail Debates,* January 25, 1921, 240–49; Longford and O'Neill, 121; O'Malley, 271–73; Barry, 188–91; Interview with Richard Mulcahy, January 1959.

3. *Dail Debates,* March 11, 1921, 264, 278–79; Macardle, 436–38.

4. Macardle, 931; C. J. C. Street, *Ireland in 1921* (London: Allan, 1922), 85–86.

5. Beaslai, II, 221; Street, 22–23; Macardle, 462–63; Bennett, 172–76.

6. Macardle, 429; Holt, 241–42; Townshend, 214.

7. Macardle, 403–4, 443; Bennett, 163–64; Holt, 243.

8. O'Donoghue, 154–57, 163.

9. According to its chief of staff, the IRA in June 1921 had only 43 rounds per rifle, 13 or 14 per pistol, and 500 for each of its automatic weapons. P7/D/64/22/93, Mulcahy Papers.

10. On the military situation in 1921, see Townshend, chs. V–VI, *passim;* Macready, chs. XVII–XVIII, *passim;* Beaslai, 182–84, 233–34; 248–51; Barry, 60, 154, 159–63, 172–73, 180, 227; O'Malley, 199, 279, 284–85, 292–93, 308–9, 314–17; O'Donoghue, 135, 146, 150–51, 166–67, 173–77; Macardle, 460–63, 983–84; F. O'Connor, 121–23; Forester, 193; Bennett, 159; Street, 76–78.

11. C. L. Mowat, "The Irish Question in British Politics (1916–1922)," in *The Irish Struggle*, 147.

12. Lord Beaverbrook, *The Decline and Fall of Lloyd George* (New York: Duell, Sloan and Pearce, 1963), 82, 281–82; Boyce, 63–66; Bennett, 141–45, 149; Holt, 224–25, 237; Macardle, 358, 391; Mowat, 81–83.

13. On the role of the press in the Irish debate, see J. L. Hammond, *C. P. Scott* (London: Bell, 1934), ch. XV; *The History of the Times*, IV: *1912–1948* (New York: Macmillan, 1952), ii, 553–78; Martin, *passim;* Mowat, in *The Irish Struggle*, 147–50; and esp. Boyce, chs. 2–4, 6, *passim*.

14. Bennett, 141.

15. Ward, 237–46.

16. Harold Nicolson, *King George the Fifth* (London: Constable, 1952), 347.

17. Street, 33–43.

18. Ibid., 43–45.

19. Cab 27(21), 2, April 21, 1921 (Cab 23/25); Jones, 55–63.

20. Bennett, 169; Macardle, 453–54, 472–73.

21. Bennett, 170; Street, 67–68; Buckland, II, 130–31; Macardle, 454.

22. O'Hegarty, *History of Ireland*, 745–46.

23. Cab 39(21), 2, May 12, 1921 (Cab 23/25).

24. Jones, 63–70; Boyce, 132–33; Beaverbrook, 262; Forester, 184–85.

25. C.P. 2964, Ireland and the General Military Situation, Memorandum by S/S for War, May 24, 1921; C.P. 2965, Memoranda by C.I.G.S., May 24, 1921, and C.-in-C., Ireland (A and B), May 23, 1921 (Cab 24/123).

26. Churchill, 307–8; Cab 41(21), 3 and app., May 24, 1921 (Cab 23/25).

27. Cab 42(21), 2, May 25, 1921 (Cab 23/25).

28. The reinforcements were to consist of 16–18 infantry battalions of 400–600 men each and 2 or 3 cavalry regiments, a total force of 10,000–15,000 men. S.I.C., 8th Conclusions, 1 and 2, May 26, 1921 (Cab 27/107); C.P. 2983, Report by the S.I.C. Committee, May 27, 1921 (Cab 24/123); Cab 47(21), 2, June 2, 1921 (Cab 23/26); Jones, 72–74.

29. Macready, 563–65.

30. S.I.C., 9th Concls., 4, June 15, 1921 (Cab 27/107); Jones, 76–77. Wilson endorsed Macready's views emphatically, and they were also shared by Macready's senior officers and an independent military observer. Callwell, 291–92, 295–96; Macready to Miss Stevenson, June 20, 1921, F/36/2/19, LGP; C.P. 3075, Memorandum on the Military Situation in Ireland by Colonel Sir Hugh Elles (Cab 24/125).

31. Macready to Miss Stevenson, June 20, 1921, F/36/2/19, LGP. Anderson strongly agreed with Macready in this matter. Anderson to Greenwood, June 18, 1921, 31/2/3, Austen Chamberlain Papers.

32. Churchill, 304–5; Beaverbrook, 262–63; Winter, 340; Riddell, 289–90; Pakenham, 73; Jones, 63–70, 85. Churchill would have preferred to beat the rebels and then offer Ireland a generous measure of autonomy, but he realized further coercion was impossible unless the government first tried to make peace. Churchill, 305; Colum, 285; Pakenham, 127 n.1.

33. Riddell, 288.

34. Gallagher, 25–37; Pakenham, 74–76; Macardle, 446–51; Longford and O'Neill, 122; Jones, 52; Ervine, 404–13.

35. Sir W. K. Hancock, *Smuts*, II: *The Fields of Force 1919–1950* (London: Cambridge University Press, 1968), 51–54; Nicolson, 350.

36. Nicolson, 351; Hancock, *Smuts*, II, 54; S.I.C., 10th Concls., 1–2, June 16, 1921, and 11th Concls., 1, June 17, 1921 (Cab 27/107); Frances Stevenson, *Lloyd George, a Diary* (London: Hutchinson, 1971), ed. A. J. P. Taylor, 221.

37. Nicolson, 351–54.

38. Ibid., 352.

39. Pakenham, 77–78; Austen Chamberlain, *Down the Years* (London, Cassell, 1935), 144–45; Chamberlain to Hilda Chamberlain, June 26, 1921, 5/1/202, ACP; Lord Stamfordham to the Prime Minister, June 24, 1921 F/29/4/55, LGP.

40. Cab 60(21), 7, July 20, 1921, app. I: Conclusions of a Conference of Ministers, 3, June 24, 1921 (Cab 23/26); Jones, 79.

41. Cab 53(21), 1, June 24, 1921 (Cab 23/26); Jones 79–81.

42. Longford and O'Neill, 124–28; Jones, 81.

43. Dail Eireann, *Official Correspondence relating to the Peace Negotiations, June–September, 1921* (Dublin, October 1921), 3.

44. Churchill, 303. As late as June 21, Birkenhead had proclaimed the government's determination to suppress the Irish rebellion. 45 H.L. 5s., June 21, 1921, 679–96.

45. Jones, 81.

46. Colvin, 403.

47. Longford and O'Neill, 136; Boyce, 139–140; Michael Collins, *The Path to Freedom* (Dublin: Talbot Press, 1922), 100–104.

48. Dail Eireann, *Official Correspondence*, de Valera to Lloyd George, June 28, 1921, 3; Macardle, 473; Earl of Midleton, *Records and Reactions, 1856–1939* (London: Murray, 1939), 258–60.

49. Midleton, 260–61; Buckland, I, 240. It seems obvious that de Valera wanted a truce (without arms surrender) as a precondition of negotiations, although he could not press this point too hard lest it be interpreted as a sign of weakness.

50. Hancock, *Smuts*, II, 55–58; Longford and O'Neill, 130–31; *Dail Debates* (P.S.), August 22, 1921, 27–28; Jones, 82–84; Stevenson, 226.

51. This was untrue. Cab 53(21), 1, June 24, 1921 (Cab 23/26).

52. Midleton, 261–62; Midleton to the Prime Minister, July 7, 1921, F/38/1/19, LGP; Jones 84–85; Street, 138.

53. Macready, 571–81; Midleton, 262–63; Macardle, 474–76. Both sides assumed that negotiations would last only a few weeks, and the truce terms were not precisely drafted. Differences of interpretation arose at once, causing considerable friction during the protracted negotiations.

54. Dail Eireann, *Official Correspondence*, 5; Macready, 577.

55. Macready, 577–78; *Irish Independent* (Dublin), July 12–13, 1921.

56. C.P. 3151, Weekly Survey (I.O.), July 18, 1921 (Cab 24/126); Dail Eireann (Official Report), *Parliamentary Debates* (Dublin: The Stationery Office), III, June 6 and 23, 1923, 1515–16, 1815 (cited hereafter as *Dail Debates*); Macardle, 461 n. 3.

57. According to Macready, the reinforcements that were allocated for the Irish garrison would have raised its strength to 80,000 troops (Macready, 561–62), but this figure seems much too high. At the end of March 1921, his com-

mand numbered just under 40,000 men (Townshend, 175), and its size was increased to only about 55,000 by the time of the truce. Even so, Macready would have enjoyed a 10 to 1 advantage over the IRA's flying columns, if all his infantry battalions could be freed for offensive operations.

58.   Taylor, 168; Gallagher, 46; Longford and O'Neill, 136; L. S. Amery, *My Political Life*, II: *War and Peace, 1914–1929* (London: Hutchinson, 1953), 230.

59.   *Irish Independent*, July 12, 1921; Macardle, 477; Brennan, 314; O'Hegarty, *History of Ireland*, 742–43.

60.   Taylor, 139, 142.

Chapter 5

1.   Stevenson, 227–28; Longford and O'Neill, 131–34; Pakenham, 82–84; Jones, 89; Prime Minister to the King, July 14, 1921, F/29/4/57, LGP.

2.   Prime Minister to the King, July 15, 1921, F/29/4/58; Stevenson, 228–29.

3.   Stevenson, 228–29; Cab 60(21), 1, July 20, 1921 (Cab 23/26).

4.   Cab 60(21), 1–3, July 20, 1921 (Cab 23/26).

5.   Dail Eireann, *Official Correspondence,* Proposals of the British Government for an Irish Settlement, July 20, 1921, 6–8.

6.   Prime Minister to the King, July 21, 1921, F/29/4/60, LGP; Stevenson, 230–31; Pakenham, 85; Longford and O'Neill, 136–37.

7.   Prime Minister to the King, July 21, 1921, and Stamfordham to the Prime Minister, July 21, 1921, F/29/4/60–61, LGP; Austen Chamberlain to Ivy, Lady Chamberlain, August 14, 1921, 6/1/408, ACP.

8.   Beaverbrook, 89; Geoffrey Shakespeare, *Let Candles Be Brought In* (London: Macdonald, 1949), 76. For a brief summary of the Lloyd George–de Valera meetings, see Tom Jones's letter to Bonar Law, July 22, 1921, in Jones, 90–91.

9.   Stevenson, 231; Callwell, 300–301; T. M. Healy, *Letters and Leaders of My Day* (New York: Stokes, 1929), II, 640, 643.

10.   Pakenham, 86; Colum, 266–67; Longford and O'Neill, 138–40.

11.   Hancock, *Smuts,* II, 59–60; Macardle, 488–89; Pakenham, 86–87.

12.   Dail Eireann, *Official Correspondence,* Reply of the Ministry, August 10, 1921, 10–11.

13.   Cab 66(21), 1, August 13, 1921 (Cab 23/26).

14.   Dail Eireann, *Official Correspondence,* Prime Minister to President de Valera, August 13, 1921, 11–12.

15.   Boyce, 145–50.

16.   Ibid., 149; Macardle, 498–99.

17.   *Dail Debates,* August 16, 1921, 8–11.

18.   Ibid., August 17, 1921, 12–16.

19.   Ibid. (P.S.), August 22, 1921, 29–35.

20.   Ibid., August 23, 1921, 42–43; Dail Eireann, *Official Correspondence,* Reply of the Ministry, August 24, 1921, 12–13.

21.   *Dail Debates* (P.S.), August 23, 1921, 57–59.

22.   Ibid., August 22 and 23, 1921, 29–30, 57; O'Hegarty, *History of Ireland,* 765–66.

23.   *Dail Debates,* August 26, 1921, 77–82.

24.   Ibid., 82–83.

25. Terence de Vere White, *Kevin O'Higgins* (London: Methuen, 1948), 54.

26. Cab 72(21), 1, August 25, 1921 (Cab 23/26); Jones, 102; Cab 73(21), 1–2, August 26, 1921 (Cab 23/26).

27. Dail Eireann, *Official Correspondence*, Prime Minister to President de Valera, August 26, 1921, 13–15.

28. Ibid., Reply of the Ministry, August 30, 1921, 15–17.

29. Nicolson, 359.

30. Cab 74(21), 1, September 7, 1921 (Cab 23/27); Jones, 106–13.

31. Dail Eireann, *Official Correspondence*, British Cabinet's Reply, September 7, 1921, 17–18.

32. Ibid., Reply of the Ministry, September 12, 1921, 18–19.

33. Brennan, 314–19; Longford and O'Neill, 141–42; *Dail Debates* (P.S.), September 14, 1921, 87–98; C.P. 3316, Prime Minister's Interview with Irish Representatives at Gairloch, September 13, 1921 (Cab 24/128).

34. Dail Eireann, *Official Correspondence*, Prime Minister to President de Valera, September 15, 1921, 19–20.

35. Ibid., President de Valera to Prime Minister, September 16, 1921; P.M. to de Valera, September 17, 1921; de Valera to P.M., September 17, 1921, 20–21.

36. The King to the Prime Minister, September 18, 1921, F/29/4/80, LGP; Jones, 114–16.

37. Dail Eireann, *Official Correspondence*, Prime Minister to President de Valera, September 18, 1921; de Valera to P.M., September 19, 1921, 21–22.

38. Cab 76(21), October 6, 1921, app. III: Conclusions of a Conference of Ministers at Gairloch, 1, September 21, 1921 (Cab 23/27); see also Lloyd George to Chamberlain, September 21, 1921, 31/2/32, ACP.

39. Dail Eireann, *Official Correspondence*, Prime Minister to President de Valera, September 29, 1921; de Valera to P.M., September 30, 1921, 22–23.

40. Committee on Ireland, CIP 2, 6, August 19, 1921 (Cab 27/130); Street, 145–52.

41. F. O'Connor, 130.

42. Macardle, 539.

43. Taylor, 165; see also Forester, 264–65.

44. On the condition of the IRA during the truce, see Macardle, 477, 539; Beaslai, II, 248–53, 270–72; F. O'Connor, 129–30; Street, 145–57; O'Malley, 294–95, 299–300; O'Donoghue, 180–85; Breen, 160–61; O'Hegarty, *Sinn Fein*, 68–69; *History of Ireland*, 760–62. On the general state of Ireland, see Macready's Weekly Reports (Cab 24/126–31).

45. Pakenham, 96–98; Longford and O'Neill, 145; Beaslai, II, 274–75; *Dail Debates* (P.S.), September 14 and December 15, 1921, 95–98, 171.

46. *Dail Debates* (P.S.), September 14, 1921, 97; Pakenham, 97–98; de Valera to Joseph McGarrity, December 27, 1921, Ms. 17,440, McGarrity Papers.

47. Colum, 246–47, 266–67; Pakenham, 98–102.

48. Pakenham, 120–21; Colum, 246–47; F. O'Connor, 16.

49. Beaslai, II, 275, 292; Colum, 276; Pakenham, 97; Taylor, 145; Healy, 644; O'Hegarty, *History of Ireland*, 752; Batt O'Connor, *With Michael Collins in the Fight for Irish Independence* (London: Davies, 1929), 178–79.

50. *Dail Debates* (P.S.), September 14, 1921, 95; Longford and O'Neill, 145–46; Pakenham, 96–97; Macardle, 526–27; Gallagher, 73–76; de Valera to McGarrity, December 27, 1921, Ms. 17,440, McGarrity Papers.

51. De Valera to McGarrity, December 27, 1921, Ms. 17,440, McGarrity Papers.

52. Brennan, 311–12; Longford and O'Neill, 138–40; de Valera to McGarrity, December 27, 1921, Ms. 17,440, McGarrity Papers.

53. Macardle, 937–42.

54. Brennan, 311–12; O'Hegarty, *Sinn Fein*, 86–87; Pakenham, 115–19; F. O'Connor, 132–33, 135–37.

55. *Dail Debates* (P.S.), September 14, 1921, 91.

56. Pakenham, 89–91; Brennan, 314; Longford and O'Neill, 143–44; Boyce, 153–54; Forester, 208–9; Hancock, *Survey,* 135–39; Miller, 486; *Irish Times* (Dublin), October 1, 1921; *Cork Examiner,* October 8, 1921.

57. *Dail Debates* (P.S.), app. 5, 289.

58. Dail Eireann (Official Report), *Debate on the Treaty between Great Britain and Ireland* (Dublin: The Stationery Office) December 14, 1921, 14 (cited hereafter as *Treaty Debate*); Jones, 188–89.

59. *Dail Debates* (P.S.), app. 5, 289.

60. O'Hegarty, *History of Ireland,* 751 52; Colum, 278–79.

61. Taylor, 152–53, 157–58, 171; Colum, 276–77; Pakenham, 132–35; *Dail Debates* (P.S.), August 18, 1921, 13–14; Macardle, 529–30 (and n.3), 937–39; Note by Robert Barton on Draft Treaty A, n.d., Dail Eireann Files, DE 2/304: Records of the Treaty Negotiations, 1921 (cited hereafter as DE 2/304).

62. Cab 76(21), 6, October 6, 1921 (Cab 23/27); Beaverbrook, 93.

63. Pakenham, 124–27; Jones, 157; Beaverbrook, 30–38, 55–56, 58, 67–68, 73–74, 90, 93–95, 99–102, 115; Churchill, 316–18; Stanley Salvidge, *Salvidge of Liverpool* (London: Hodder and Stoughton, 1934), 193.

64. Pakenham, 136–37. The third volume of Jones's *Whitehall Diaries* is an invaluable account of the peace negotiations and his role in them.

Chapter 6

1. Jones, 119; Pakenham, 121–22; Macardle, 532.

2. (List of) Subconferences of the Plenary Conference, DE 2/304; Taylor, 161.

3. Oliver St. John Gogarty, *As I Was Going Down Sackville Street* (New York: Reynal and Hitchcock, 1937), 277; Chamberlain, 146–47; Winston S. Churchill, *Thoughts and Adventures* (London: Butterworth, 1932), 188–89; David Lloyd George, *Is It Peace?* (London: Hodder and Stoughton, 1923), 271; Pakenham, 136–37, 150; Shakespeare, 83.

4. Chamberlain, 145–46; Taylor, 153–56; Churchill, *Aftermath,* 320, 355; idem, *Thoughts,* 191; F. O'Connor, 159; Riddell, 328–30; Lloyd George, 272–73; Crozier, 220; Earl of Birkenhead, *"F.E.": The Life of F. E. Smith, First Earl of Birkenhead* (London: Eyre and Spottiswoode, 1960), 374.

5. Taylor, 154; Jones, 173; Lloyd George, 273–74; Chamberlain, 147–48; Churchill, *Aftermath,* 320.

6.   First Conference, October 11, 1921, DE 2/304; Tom Jones's Notes of the
Sinn Fein Conference, October 11–24, 1921, First Session, October 11, 1921
(Cab 21/253) (3).

7.   At this committee's only meeting, on October 19, Collins and the British
representatives agreed to exchange memoranda on the 22d. The British set
Southern Ireland's liability for debt and pension charges at £153 million. The
Irish counterclaim, based on alleged overtaxation since the Union and con-
sequent retardation of Ireland's capital development, came to over £3 billion.
SFC 15, 19, 20 (Cab 43/3).

8.   127 H.C. Deb. 5s., March 30, 1920, 1125–26.

9.   Second Conference, October 11, 1921, DE 2/304; Jones's Notes, Second
Session (Cab 21/253) (3); SFC 2, Aide Memoire on first two sessions, October 11,
1921 (Cab 43/3).

10.   Griffith to de Valera, October 11, 1921; de Valera to Griffith, October
12, 1921, DE 2/304.

11.   Third Conference, October 13, 1921, DE 2/304; Jones's Notes, Third
Session (Cab 21/253) (3).

12.   Griffith to de Valera, October 13, 1921, DE 2/304.

13.   Griffith wrote de Valera that the British were "remarkably ignorant of
the facts—this is not play-acting though they tried this also. Their knowledge
geographically and statistically of the province is very poor." October 14, 1921,
DE 2/304; Jones's Notes, Fourth Session (Cab 21/253) (3).

14.   Jones's Notes, Fourth and Fifth Sessions (Cab 21/253) (3).

15.   Griffith to de Valera, October 14, 1921, DE 2/304. On this point, see also
Wilson, 404–5.

16.   Riddell, 328–29.

17.   Griffith to de Valera, October 14, 1921, DE 2/304.

18.   De Valera to Griffith, October 14, 1921, and Northeast Ulster Draft
Clause, DE 2/304.

19.   Jones's Notes, Fifth Session, October 17, 1921 (Cab 21/253) (3); Fifth
Conference, DE 2/304.

20.   Pakenham, 165–66; Longford and O'Neill, 152.

21.   SFB 6th Conclusions of British Representatives to the Sinn Fein Conference, October 21, 1921 (Cab 43/1).

22.   Gallagher, 90; Colum, 291; Taylor, 162.

23.   Sixth Conference, October 21, 1921, DE 2/304; Jones's Notes, Sixth Session (Cab 21/253) (3).

24.   Taylor, 165, 168–69; F. O'Connor, 138–39; Forester, 236–37.

25.   SFC 18, Irish Memorandum of October 24, 1921 (Cab 43/3); see also
Macardle, 940–42. Sinn Fein's claim now fell short of formal neutrality. A "free"
Ireland would not be compelled to aid Britain in war, but would not be prohib-
ited from doing so, as a "neutral" Ireland would. This change was consistent with
Collins' view that Britain could expect greater cooperation in defense matters if
Ireland were not bound to provide it. Pakenham, 174 n.1.

26.   Sir Edward Grigg's Notes of a Meeting of British Representatives, October 24, 1921, 3:30 p.m. (Cab 21/253) (2).

27.   Seventh Conference, October 24, 1921, DE 2/304; Jones's Notes, Seventh
Session (Cab 21/253) (3).

28. Jones's Notes of British Representatives' Meeting after Seventh Session, (Cab 21/253) (3).

29. Pakenham, 176–77; Gallagher, 94–95; Wilson, 405; Shakespeare, 82; Chamberlain to Ivy, Lady Chamberlain, October 23, 1921, 6/1/427, ACP.

30. Griffith to de Valera, October 24, 1921, DE 2/304.

31. Grigg's Notes of a Meeting of British Representatives, October 24, 1921, 7:30 p.m. (Cab 21/253) (2).

32. Ibid.

33. De Valera to Griffith, October 25, 1921, DE 2/304.

34. Pakenham, 182; Gallagher, 97–98; Taylor, 165, 171; F. O'Connor, 136.

35. Delegation to de Valera, October 26, 1921, DE 2/304; Gallagher, 98.

36. De Valera to Griffith, October 27, 1921; Griffith to de Valera, October 27, 1921, DE 2/304.

37. Chartres to Griffith, October 14, 1921; Notes on the Crown, October 20, 1921, DE 2/304; Pakenham, 178 n.1, 193; Longford and O'Neill, 154–55.

38. Griffith to de Valera, October 25, 1921, DE 2/304.

39. De Valera to Griffith, October 26, 1921, DE 2/304.

40. Grigg's Notes of a Meeting of British Representatives, October 25, 1921, 6:45 p.m. (Cab 21/253) (2); Jones, 146–48.

41. SFB 11th Conclusions, 5, October 27, 1921 (Cab 43/1); SFC 21, Memorandum by the British Government, October 27, 1921 (Cab 43/3).

42. Pakenham, 191–92, n.1.

43. Griffith to de Valera, October 27, 1921, DE 2/304.

44. SFC 21A, Further Memorandum by Irish Delegates, October 29, 1921 (Cab 43/3).

45. De Valera to Griffith, October 29, 1921, DE 2/304.

46. Jones, 149–51; Churchill, *Thoughts,* 191; Shakespeare, 83; Wilson, 402; Stevenson, 233–34.

47. Memorandum of a Meeting at Churchill's House at 10 p.m., Sunday, October 30, 1921; Griffith to de Valera, October 31, 1921, DE 2/304.

48. Riddell, 330. Chamberlain was sure they would not; partition, "like all compromises, is illogical and indefensible," and unlike Crown and Empire, it would not mobilize English support. Chamberlain to Ivy, Lady Chamberlain, October 29 and 31, 1921, 6/1/439 and 6/1/441, ACP.

49. Shakespeare, 83; Riddell, 332. See also Wilson, 402–3.

50. 147 H.C. Deb. 5s., October 31, 1921, 1367–1480; Jones, 152.

51. Macardle, 548–49; Bromage, 134–35; Longford and O'Neill, 155.

52. O'Donoghue, 197–200; F. O'Connor, 138; Macardle, 549.

53. Preliminary Draft of a Letter from Griffith to Lloyd George, November 1, 1921; Duffy to Griffith, November 2, 1921, DE 2/304; Pakenham, 195–96.

54. Pakenham, 234–35; Longford and O'Neill, 158; Macardle, 556–57.

55. Revised Letter, Griffith to Lloyd George, November 2, 1921, DE 2/304.

56. Griffith to de Valera, November 3, 1921, DE 2/304.

57. Ibid.; Final Draft of Griffith's Letter to Lloyd George, November 2, 1921, DE 2/304; Macardle, 555–56; Gallagher, 109.

58. Griffith to de Valera, November 3, 1921, DE 2/304; Pakenham, 199; Jones, 153.

59. Pakenham, 199–200; Gallagher, 108.

60. Minutes of Subconference, November 3, 1921; Griffith to de Valera, November 3, 1921, DE 2/304.

Chapter 7

1. Ervine, 444–46; Beaverbrook, 109–18, 286; Blake, 430–31; Wilson, 403; Jones, 91–92, 154–55, 160–64, 166–68; Chamberlain to Ivy, Lady Chamberlain, November 8, 9, 10, 1921, 6/1/457–60, ACP.
2. Bonar Law to J. P. Croal (editor of *The Scotsman*), November 12, 1921, 107/1/83, Bonar Law Papers.
3. Chamberlain to Sir George Younger and Leslie Wilson, November 8, 1921, 31/3/40a; Wilson and Younger to Chamberlain, November 9, 1921, 31/3/41–42, ACP.
4. Chamberlain had already expressed this view to his wife on October 29 and 31 (6/1/439 and 441, ACP).
5. Jones, 154–56; Stevenson, 234–35; Riddell, 332; Ervine, 445–46; Balfour to Prime Minister, November 2, 1921; Churchill to Prime Minister, November 9, 1921, F/3/5/17 and F/10/1/60, LGP.
6. Stevenson, 235–37; Ervine 445–46; Chamberlain to Ivy, Lady Chamberlain, November 4, 1921, 6/1/449, ACP.
7. Jones, 160–62; Cab 87(21), November 10, 1921 (Cab 23/27).
8. SFB 22, Prime Minister to Craig, November 10, 1921 (Cab 43/2).
9. SFB 24, Craig to Prime Minister, November 11, 1921 (Cab 43/2).
10. Jones, 163–64.
11. Ibid., 164; Stevenson, 237; SFB 15th Conclusions, 1, November 14, 1921 (Cab 43/1).
12. SFB 27, Prime Minister to Craig, November 14, 1921 (Cab 43/2).
13. SFB 29, Craig to Prime Minister, November 17, 1921 (Cab 43/2); Pakenham, 211, 245.
14. Boyce, 160–63; Macardle, 574–75.
15. Jones, 154–55.
16. Ibid., 155–56; Stevenson, 235; Griffith to de Valera, November 8, 1921, DE 2/304.
17. To what extent Jones was responsible for this impression is impossible to say, but it is most probable that he encouraged Griffith and Collins to expect large-scale gains from boundary revision.
18. Griffith to de Valera, November 8, 1921, DE 2/304.
19. De Valera to Griffith, November 9, 1921, DE 2/304.
20. Stevenson, 235; Jones, 156.
21. Griffith to de Valera, November 9, 1921, DE 2/304; Jones, 156–57.
22. Stevenson, 235–36, 238; Jones, 157–59, 161, 163.
23. Bonar Law to J. P. Croal, November 12, 1921, 107/1/83, BLP.
24. Griffith to de Valera, November 12 and 15, 1921, DE 2/304.
25. Chamberlain to the Prime Minister, November 11, 1921, F/7/4/31, LGP.
26. Griffith to de Valera, November 11, 1921, DE 2/304.
27. Jones, 162–63.

28. Such an Act would presumably include both the right of exclusion for the northeast and provision for boundary revision if that right were exercised.

29. Griffith to de Valera, November 12, 1921, DE 2/304.

30. Pakenham, 216–18; Stevenson, 237.

31. Pakenham, 218.

32. The fullest account of the events of November 12–13 is in Pakenham, 210–24. This is corroborated by Stevenson (237), by Chamberlain's letter to his wife, November 13, 1921 (6/1/463, ACP), and by the exchange between Lloyd George and Griffith during the subconference of December 5. Jones notes only that he showed Griffith the Ulster proposals on November 13 (173).

33. Birkenhead, 378; Salvidge, 194–200.

34. Salvidge, 200–5.

35. Ibid., 205–14; Sir Charles Petrie, *The Life and Letters of the Right Hon. Austen Chamberlain* (London: Cassell, 1940), II, 164–68; Chamberlain to Ivy, Lady Chamberlain, November 19, 1921, 6/1/466, ACP.

36. Jones, 168; Salvidge, 215–19; Beaverbrook, 119–21; Lord Derby to the Prime Minister, November 18, 1921, F/14/5/33, LGP; Sir George Younger to Bonar Law, November 19, 1921, 107/1/72, BLP.

37. Chamberlain to Ivy, Lady Chamberlain, November 23, 1921, 6/1/470; Memorandum, November 23, 1921, 31/2/38, ACP; Salvidge, 219. Needless to say, Law felt boundary revision would be only a matter of minor rectification.

38. Griffith to de Valera, November 15 and 16, 1921; British Treaty Proposals, November 16, 1921, DE 2/304.

39. De Valera to Griffith, November 17, 1921, DE 2/304.

40. The safeguards designed to secure Ulster's assent to unity were omitted by mistake. The British therefore told the Irish that the proposals were incomplete but that they indicated the government's position on certain vital points. Pakenham, 228–29; Jones, 166.

41. Griffith to de Valera, November 18, 1921, DE 2/304.

42. Pakenham, 232.

43. Memorandum by the Irish Representatives, November 22, 1921, DE 2/304.

44. Pakenham, 233–36.

45. Taylor, 155–56, 165–67; F. O'Connor, 134.

46. 22/N/143, Notes of British Representatives' Meeting, November 22, 1921 (Cab 43/4); Jones, 169–70; Pakenham, 237; Stevenson, 238.

47. In fact, as Jones soon realized, Lloyd George was upset not about the lack of specific safeguards but about Sinn Fein's failure to recognize Ulster's right of exclusion. Jones, 170.

48. Jones, 171–72; Griffith to de Valera, November 22, 1921, DE 2/304.

49. Jones, 172; Stevenson, 238.

50. Griffith to de Valera, November 23, 1921, DE 2/304.

51. Ibid.; 22/N/143, Chamberlain's Notes of the November 23 Meeting (Cab 43/4); Pakenham, 240; Jones, 173.

52. Further Note on the Crown by Chartres, November 22, 1921, DE 2/304.

53. Meeting of Subcommittee on the Crown, November 24, 1921, Draft Note by Chartres, DE 2/304. See also Pakenham, 376–77; Gallagher, 129–30; Jones, 174–76; Stevenson, 238.

54. Meeting of the Irish Cabinet, November 25, 1921, DE 2/304.

55. Memorandum of the Irish Delegates on Their Proposal for the Association of Ireland with the Commonwealth, November 28, 1921, DE 2/304.

56. Ibid.

57. Jones, 176.

58. Chamberlain to Lloyd George, November 28, 1921, F/7/4/34, LGP.

59. Griffith to de Valera, November 29, 1921, DE 2/304; Jones, 177.

60. Griffith to de Valera, November 29, 1921, DE 2/304; 22/N/143, Chamberlain's Notes of the Meeting, November 29, 1921 (Cab 43/4); Jones, 177–78.

Chapter 8

1. SFC 28, Proposed Articles of Agreement, November 30, 1921 (Cab 43/3).

2. Collins' Notes on Proposed Articles of Agreement, DE 2/304. SFB 20th Conclusions, 1–8 and Note, December 1, 1921 (Cab 43/1); SFC 29, Proposed Articles of Agreement, December 1, 1921 (revise of SFC 28) (Cab 43/3).

3. Longford and O'Neill, 160; de Valera to McGarrity, December 27, 1921, Ms. 17,440, McGarrity Papers.

4. Customarily, the Cabinet's secretary recorded only its decisions. But the regular secretary, Diarmuid O'Hegarty, was in London, and his assistant, Colm O'Murchadha, took notes of the six-hour meeting. While these notes are very brief, they were the only ones made at the time. Pakenham, 378–79; Gallagher, 137–38.

5. Longford and O'Neill, 160–61.

6. De Valera later explained that he felt his going to London would make the British think he had come to prevent a breakdown, which might lead them to harden their demands. De Valera to McGarrity, December 27, 1921, Ms. 17,440, McGarrity Papers.

7. Copy of Secretary's Notes of the Meeting of the Cabinet and the Delegation, December 3, 1921, DE 2/304; Pakenham, 255–62; Gallagher, 137–43; Longford and O'Neill, 160–63; *Dail Debates* (P.S.), December 14 and 16, 1921, 103–6, 118, 185–91; de Valera to McGarrity, December 27, 1921, Ms. 17,440, McGarrity Papers.

8. De Valera to McGarrity, December 27, 1921, Ms. 17,440, McGarrity Papers.

9. Taylor, 176.

10. The clause failed to specify an electoral unit for local option. Colum 295–96.

11. Taylor, 165.

12. F. O'Connor, 140.

13. Amendments by Irish Representatives to Proposed Articles of Agreement, December 4, 1921, DE 2/304; Cab 89(21), 1, December 5, 1921 (Cab 23/27); Pakenham, 264–66.

14. Barton may have been right on this point. O'Hegarty, *History of Ireland,* 753.

15. Pakenham, 261 n.1.

16. Ibid., 266–67.

17. Collins' Minute of His Interview with Lloyd George, December 5, 1921, DE 2/304; *Irish Independent,* April 25, 1922.

18. Griffith to de Valera, December 4, 1921, DE 2/304; 22/N/143, Chamberlain's Notes of the Meeting of December 4 (Cab 43/4).

19. Pakenham, 270; 22/N/143, Record of Negotiations, December 4, 1921 (Cab 43/4).

20. Jones to the Prime Minister, December 5, 1921, F/25/2/51, LGP.

21. Taylor, 184. Jones had evidently found that Lloyd George considered further talks with Craig a waste of time, and he therefore emphasized the advantages of boundary revision to Collins.

22. Pakenham, 273-74.

23. Collins' Minute of His Interview with Lloyd George, December 5, 1921, DE 2/304; Cab 89(21), 1, December 5, 1921 (Cab 23/27).

24. Cab 89(21), 1, December 5, 1921 (Cab 23/27).

25. Collins' Memorandum on the International Aspects of the Anglo-Irish Settlement, November 23, 1921, DE 2/304.

26. **SFB 3 (revise), Memorandum on Dominion Status (Lionel Curtis),** October 17, 1921 (Cab 43/2).

27. Taylor, 162-63, 167, 176-78; *Treaty Debate,* December 19, 1921, 33.

28. Pakenham, 383; Jones, 182.

29. Cab 89(21), 1, December 5, 1921 (Cab 23/27).

30. *Treaty Debate,* December 19, 1921, 49.

31. Churchill, *Aftermath,* 321.

32. Chamberlain, 150.

33. Churchill, *Aftermath,* 321. This account of the subconference is based primarily on those of Barton and Chamberlain (Barton's Notes of Two Subconferences, December 5-6, 1921, No. 1-3 p.m., DE 2/304; and 22/N/143, Chamberlain's Notes of the Subconference, 3-7:15 p.m., December 5, 1921 [Cab 43/4]). Griffith's sketch of the proceedings was of help in reconstructing events (Griffith's Notes ... 5-6 December, 1921, December 6, 1921, DE 2/304). Churchill lends highly dramatic detail to the meeting in *The Aftermath,* while Chamberlain's description in *Down the Years* follows his notes. Lloyd George says little about the subconference in *Is It Peace?* but see the brief, distorted version he gave C. P. Scott the next day (Wilson, 411-12). Tom Jones provides a useful timetable of events for December 5 (182), but nothing more. Frank Pakenham generally follows Barton's account, but his sequence of events on Ulster differs from that of Barton and Chamberlain, whom I chose to follow. Lloyd George's ultimatum as well as his remarks to Griffith about the latter's pledge on Ulster are quoted from Chamberlain's notes of the subconference.

34. Churchill, *Aftermath,* 321; Salvidge, 224; Shakespeare, 88-89.

35. Pakenham, 300.

36. Taylor, 177-78; Collins, 31-32; Batt O'Connor, 181; Churchill, *Thoughts,* 189-90; *Treaty Debate,* December 19, 1921, 34.

37. Pakenham, 300-2; Shakespeare, 87-88. Collins later claimed that none of the Irish team on that fateful night even raised the question of a promise to refer to the Cabinet any document giving allegiance to the King. *Irish Independent,* April 25, 1922.

38. Pakenham, 298-99, 303-5.

39. Chamberlain, 150; Churchill, *Aftermath,* 321–22.

40. Barton's Notes . . . , No. II—11:30 p.m. to 2 a.m., December 5–6, 1921, DE 2/304; 22/N/143, Chamberlain's Notes . . . , 11:15 p.m. to 2:10 a.m., December 5–6, 1921 (Cab 43/4).

41. The five delegates who were not present signed later; they were Duffy, Duggan, Greenwood, Worthington-Evans, and Hewart.

42. Churchill, *Aftermath,* 322; Chamberlain, 150.

43. Shakespeare, 89–90.

44. Colum, xv.

45. Taylor, 189.

Chapter 9

1. For a brief but searching analysis of the Treaty, see Hancock, *Survey,* 146–50.

2. For an excellent discussion of the oath, see Leo Kohn, *The Constitution of the Irish Free State* (London: Allen and Unwin, 1932), 53–58, 71–73.

3. Pakenham, parts 3 and 4 and app. 8; Colum, 296; Brennan, 330–31; Macardle, 567, 583, 659–60; O'Hegarty, *History of Ireland,* 754.

4. On British assurances, see Pakenham, 204–7; Taylor, 184; O'Hegarty, *History of Ireland,* 754; William O'Brien, "The Irish Free State: [The] Secret History of its Foundation," chs. I, 14–28, and IV, 21–29, Ms. 4210, O'Brien Papers, National Library of Ireland; William O'Brien, *The Irish Revolution and How It Came About* (London: Allen and Unwin, 1923), 441–42.

5. Jones, 161; The *Times* (London), December 7, 1921; 149 H.C. Deb. 5s., December 14, 1921, 40–41, 150; February 16, 1922, 1271–72.

6. Birkenhead's private assurance to Balfour that drastic reduction of Northern Ireland's area was out of the question seems to have been unavoidable. It was sought after Collins had publicly laid claim to a large part of the Six Counties, at a time when Republican opposition had produced growing British dissatisfaction with the Treaty. Birkenhead to Balfour, March 3, 1922, 30/1/27, ACP.

7. Of 338 pages of Dail Eireann's public debate on the Treaty, only nine deal with partition, and six of them consist of remarks made by three deputies who were Ulstermen (Wall, in *The Irish Struggle,* 87). Except for some brief remarks by de Valera, the private debates are even less enlightening, as fewer than five of 182 pages deal with Ulster.

8. *Dail Debates* (P.S.), December 14, 15, 17, 1921, 137, 153, 272; apps. 17–18, 317–24.

9. *Dail Debates* (P.S.), August 22, 1921, 29; Dail Eireann, *Official Correspondence,* de Valera to Lloyd George, August 10, 1921.

10. Nicholas Mansergh, "Ireland and the British Commonwealth of Nations: The Dominion Settlement," in *The Irish Struggle,* 137–38.

11. Wilson, 407, 410–11; Shakespeare, 88; The *Times,* November 26, 28, 1921; Salvidge, 224.

12. SFB 39, Draft Reply to the Irish Memorandum on the Proposed Articles of Agreement (Cab 43/2); Jones, 181.

13. Committee on Ireland, CIP 2, "Belligerency," 1–6, August 19, 1921 (Cab 27/130); Jones, 99–100; Copy of Macready to S/S for War, August 24, 1921, F/16/3/32, LGP.

14. SFB 14, Memorandum by S/S for War, October 22, 1921, and app. B., September 13, 1921 (Cab 43/2).

15. Pakenham, 272.

16. SFB 37, Memorandum from Macready to S/S for War, December 1, 1921 (Cab 43/2).

17. Cab 90(21), December 6, 1921; Cab 91(21), 1, December 7, 1921 (Cab 23/27).

18. Nicolson, 470; Pakenham, 326–27; *Irish Independent,* December 8, 1921.

19. SFB 43, Letter from Secretary, Admiralty to Secretary, Cabinet, December 8, 1921, a–b (Cab 43/2).

20. Callwell, 315.

21. *Belfast Telegraph,* December 7–8, 1921; Street, 277–78; SFB 42, Craig to the Prime Minister, December 14, 1921 (Cab 43/2); Craig to Chamberlain, December 15, 1921, 31/2/48, ACP.

22. Macardle, 592–93; O'Sullivan, 76.

23. SFB 21st Conclusions, December 7, 1921 (Cab 43/1); Street, 268; *Irish Times,* December 7, 1921.

24. 149 H.C. Deb. 5s., December 14, 1921, 25–43.

25. Ibid., 50–59, December 15, 1921, 144–51.

26. Ibid., December 15, 1921, 198–209.

27. 48 H.L. Deb. 5s., December 14, 1921, 36–53.

28. Ibid., December 16, 1921, 196–212; Birkenhead, 390, 392.

29. *Irish Independent, Freeman's Journal* (Dublin), *Irish News* (Belfast), *Cork Examiner,* December 7, 1921.

30. Miller, 490; O'Sullivan, 49; Street, 267–69; Phillips, 247.

31. Sir J. O'Connor, 345; Street, 266; Phillips, 247; Brennan, 314; *Irish Independent,* December 7, 1921; C.P. 3562, Macready's Report, December 10, 1921 (Cab 24/131).

32. De Valera to McGarrity, Dec. 27, 1921, Ms. 17,440, McGarrity Papers.

33. Longford and O'Neill, 159.

34. Ibid., 159–60, 163–66; Macardle, 593.

35. Longford and O'Neill, 166–67; Pakenham, 329–30; de Valera to McGarrity, Dec. 27, 1921, Ms. 17,440, McGarrity Papers.

36. De Valera to McGarrity, December 27, 1921, Ms. 17,440, McGarrity Papers.

37. Longford and O'Neill, 168; Pakenham, 330–31.

38. Pakenham, 331–32; Longford and O'Neill, 169.

39. *Irish Independent,* December 9, 1921.

40. Pakenham, 332; Longford and O'Neill, 170.

41. Holt, 278; O'Hegarty, *Sinn Fein,* 103.

42. Cronin, 114–15, 178.

43. Street, 265–66.

44. *Treaty Debate,* December 19, 1921, 21–22; Jones, 187–88.

45. Colum, 309–10; Brennan, 330–31.

46. Batt O'Connor, 180–82

47. *Dail Debates* (P.S.), app. 17, 317-20; Longford and O'Neill, 171-72; Gallagher, 175-77.

48. Taylor, 176-77; F. O'Connor, 143; Forester, 259-260.

49. Two-thirds of the headquarters staff supported the Treaty, including Collins himself, director of intelligence; Mulcahy, chief of staff; Eoin O'Duffy and J. J. O'Connell, assistant chiefs of staff; Gearoid O'Sullivan, adjutant general; Sean MacMahon, quartermaster general; Emmet Dalton, director of training; Eamonn Price, director of organization; and Piaras Beaslai, director of publicity. Those opposed to the Treaty were Rory O'Connor, director of engineering; Liam Mellows, director of purchases; Sean Russell, director of munitions; and Seamus O'Donovan, director of chemicals.

50. P7/D/64/22/95, Mulcahy Papers.

51. De Valera to McGarrity, December 27, 1921, Ms. 17,440, McGarrity Papers.

52. Street, 264-65.

53. Breen, 161-63.

54. *Dail Debates* (P.S.), December 14, 16, 1921, 128-34, 181-82.

55. Peadar O'Donnell, *There Will Be Another Day* (Dublin: Dolmen Press, 1963), 82.

56. O'Donoghue, 190.

57. De Valera to McGarrity, Dec. 27, 1921, Ms. 17,440, McGP.; *Dail Debates*, May 19, 1922, 467; Cronin, 112; Pakenham, 280; Macardle, 624-25.

58. Harry Boland, Joe McKelvey, and Charlie Daly joined Lynch on this issue. The other Irish members of the council, aside from Collins, were Mulcahy, Gearoid O'Sullivan, Diarmuid O'Hegarty, Sean O'Muirthile, Martin Conlan, Joseph Vize, and a man called Steve, whom I am unable to identify. P7/D/53/14/19, Mulcahy Papers.

59. On this subject, see Joseph M. Curran, "The Decline and Fall of the IRB," in *Eire-Ireland* (Spring 1975), X, 1, 14-23.

Chapter 10

1. C.P. 3575, Weekly Survey (I.O.), December 19, 1921 (Cab 24/131); O'Hegarty, *Sinn Fein*, 75-78; McCracken, 29-30, 33-34.

2. In private, de Valera was much angrier about this matter than he appeared to be in the Dail. Longford and O'Neill, 171-72.

3. *Treaty Debate*, December 14, 1921, 7-16.

4. *Dail Debates* (P.S.), December 14-17, 1921, 101-272.

5. *Treaty Debate*, December 19, 1921, 19-20.

6. Ibid., 20-23, 24-27, 27-28.

7. Ibid., 30-36.

8. Ibid., 36-42, 42-48, 49.

9. Ibid., December 20, 1921, 53.

10. Beaslai, II, 328. No record was made of this discussion.

11. *Treaty Debate*, December 20, 1921, 68-74. Next day, the *Freeman's Journal* published the Cabinet and Treaty oaths, referring to them as "Tweedledum and Tweedledee."

12. *Treaty Debate*, December 21, 1921, 85-88, 96-99.

13. Ibid., 102-8, 108-27.

14. Ibid., December 22, 1921, 141-44.

15. Ibid., 166-71; Forester, 271; Longford and O'Neill, 175; Macardle, 623-24; de Valera to McGarrity, Dec. 27, 1921, Ms. 17,440, McGarrity Papers.

16. *Irish Independent,* December 23, 1921, January 4, 7, 1922; C. Desmond Greaves, *Liam Mellows and the Irish Revolution* (London: Lawrence and Wishart, 1971), 275.

17. Macardle, 623-24; *Irish News,* December 29, 1921.

18. De Valera to McGarrity, December 27, 1921, Ms. 17,440, McGP.

19. Ernie O'Malley, *The Singing Flame* (Dublin: Anvil Books, 1978), 43-46.

20. *Republic of Ireland,* January 3, 5, 1922; Greaves, 275.

21. *Irish Independent,* December 16, 17, 24, 1921.

22. *Treaty Debate,* January 3, 1922, 176-80.

23. Ibid., 202-3.

24. Ibid., January 4, 1922, 227-34.

25. Ibid., 217, 258-59.

26. *Dail Debates* (P.S.), December 17, 1921, 272. For the original Document No. 2, see app. 17, 317-20, of the above; for the revised version, see app. III of this work.

27. *Treaty Debate,* January 5, 1922, 261, 269-70.

28. *Freeman's Journal,* January 5, 1922; *Treaty Debate,* January 5, 1922, 262-66.

29. *Treaty Debate,* January 5, 1922, 266-68.

30. Ibid., January 6, 7, 1922, 277, 318-19, 343-44; Beaslai, II, 330-33; *Dail Debates* (P.S.), January 6, 1922, 273-83.

31. *Treaty Debate,* January 6, 1922, 274, 271-75.

32. Ibid., 281.

33. Ibid.

34. Ibid., 281-82.

35. Ibid., 288-92.

36. Ibid., January 7, 1922, 301-4.

37. Ibid., 325-34; O'Hegarty, *Sinn Fein,* 88; Holt, 281; Taylor, 236.

38. *Treaty Debate,* January 7, 1922, 335-44.

39. Ibid., 344.

40. Ibid., 344-46. One deputy had resigned his seat rather than follow his constituents' wishes and vote for the Treaty; this left 124 members of Dail Eireann. Of these, 118 sat for constituencies in Southern Ireland, one represented a Northern Ireland constituency, and the remaining five held seats in both Irish Parliaments. Three of the 124 deputies did not vote on the Treaty. One was ill; one was abroad on a government mission; and the third was the Speaker, who could vote only in case of a tie. If all deputies had voted, the result would have been 66 to 58 for the Treaty.

41. Ibid., 346-47.

42. Gallagher, 187-88.

43. On this point, see Colum, 312-13, 316-17, 321.

44. Ibid., 311, 319-21; Ryan, 279; F. O'Connor, 150. See also Padraig de Burca and John F. Boyle, *Free State or Republic?* (Dublin: Talbot Press, 1922), a journalistic account of the debate.

45. *Treaty Debate,* January 9, 1922, 349–79. De Valera and two pro-Treaty deputies abstained, while Barton and another member who voted for the Treaty switched sides.

46. Ibid., 379–80.

47. Ibid., 381–89.

48. Ibid., January 10, 1922, 392–410.

49. Ibid., 410.

50. Ibid., 410–11. Five non-Cabinet ministers were appointed after January 10: Patrick Hogan, agriculture; Joseph McGrath, labor; Michael Hayes, education; Ernest Blythe, trade and commerce; and Desmond Fitzgerald, publicity. Macardle, 652; *Dail Debates,* February 28, 1922, 91–102.

51. *Treaty Debate,* January 10, 1922, 411–14.

52. Ibid., 414–16, 423–24.

53. Taylor, 219; O'Hegarty, *History of Ireland,* 780.

54. O'Donoghue, 202–3.

Chapter 11

1. Provisional Government of Ireland Committee, PGI 1 and 2, December 21, 1921 (Cab 27/154).

2. Macardle, 651–52.

3. White, 83.

4. C.P. 3648, PGI Heads of Working Arrangements, January 24, 1922 (Cab 24/132).

5. Churchill, *Aftermath,* 330–31; Callwell, 320, 324; Macready, 618.

6. C.P. 3743, Macready's Report, February 11, 1922 (Cab 24/133); C.P. 3638, 3658, 3803, Weekly Surveys (I.O.), January 16, 23, and February 27, 1922 (Cab 24/132 and 134).

7. Macready, 620, 622; Callwell, 320; C.P. 3769, Macready's Report, February 18, 1922 (Cab 24/133).

8. O'Donoghue, 203–4.

9. PGI 5, Memorandum, December 21, 1921 (Cab 27/154); O'Donoghue, 225; 150 H.C. Deb. 5s., February 9, 10, 13, 1922, 273–75, 559, 589 (Statements by Churchill), and February 13, 1922, 639 (Statement by Worthington-Evans).

10. Macardle, 649; Greaves, 272, 285.

11. O'Donoghue, 208; Macardle, 649–50; O'Malley, *Singing Flame,* 50–52; *Dail Debates,* April 26, 1922, 253.

12. *Dail Debates,* April 26, 1922, 253–55; O'Donoghue, 210–11; O'Malley, *Singing Flame,* 52–53.

13. Macardle, 654–56; O'Donoghue, 205; Beaslai, II, 155, 371–72; Eoin Neeson, *The Civil War in Ireland* (Cork: Mercier Press, 1966), 51; Mulcahy Interview; C.P. 3879, Macready's Report, March 18, 1922, app. I: Military Forces of the IFS (Cab 24/134).

14. Macardle, 654; *Dail Debates,* I, September 12, 1922, 205; T.P. Coogan, *Ireland since the Rising* (New York: Praeger, 1966), 47–48.

15. O'Donoghue, 193–95, 231–32; Greaves, 285.

16. *Irish Independent,* January 13, 1922.

17. Greaves, 288–89, 291; *Irish Independent,* January–February 1922.

18. *Irish Independent,* February 22, 1922.

19. Ibid., January 23, 1922; Churchill, *Aftermath,* 333.

20. *Irish Independent,* January 23, 28, 1922; *Irish News,* January 24, 27, and February 2, 1922; Macardle, 659; F. O'Connor, 171; Letter from Collins to Louis Walsh (a Derry nationalist), February 7, 1922, Ms. 3486, N.L.I.

21. *Irish Independent,* February 4, 1922.

22. Ibid.

23. 22/N/60 (3–5), Conferences on Ireland with Irish Ministers, February 5–6, 1922 (Cab 43/6); Note on [an] interview with Irish representatives by Lionel Curtis, February 7, 1922 (Cab 21/252).

24. The three condemned men had already been reprieved, but the IRA did not know this.

25. Macready, 621; Macardle, 660–61; C.P. 3747, Weekly Survey (I.O.), February 13, 1922 (Cab 24/133).

26. Macready, 621; PGI 13th Conclusions, February 14, 1922, annexes I and II (Cab 27/153).

27. C.P. 3747 and 3769, Weekly Survey (I.O.) and Macready's Report, February 13 and 18, 1922 (Cab 24/133); Cab 10(22), 3, February 16, 1922 (Cab 23/29); Macready, 623; Churchill, *Aftermath,* 342.

28. Beaslai, II, 373–74; Greaves, 290–91; Longford and O'Neill, 184.

29. *Irish Independent,* February 22–23, 1922; Macardle, 666; Beaslai, II, 374.

30. Longford and O'Neill, 184–85; O'Hegarty, *History of Ireland,* 786–87.

31. C.P. 3803, Weekly Survey (I.O.), February 27, 1922 (Cab 24/134); *Republic of Ireland,* February 28, 1922; *Irish Independent,* February 23, 1922; Longford and O'Neill, 184.

32. PGI 15th Conclusions, 1 and app., February 23, 1922 (Cab 27/153); 22/N/60 (6), Conference with Irish Ministers, February 26, 1922 (Cab 43/6).

33. 151 H.C. Deb. 5s., February 27, 1922, 21–22.

34. 150 H.C., February 16, 1922, 1261–82.

35. 151 H.C., March 2, 1922, 687–88.

36. Macardle, 689.

Chapter 12

1. O'Malley, *Singing Flame,* 53–54; O'Donoghue, 205; Macardle, 673; C.P. 3803 and 3828, Weekly Surveys (I.O.), February 27 and March 6, 1922 (Cab 24/134).

2. Cab 16(22), 1, March 8, 1922 (Cab 23/29).

3. 153 H.C. Deb. 5s., April 12, 1922, 400–401.

4. *Dail Debates,* April 28, 1922, 347–48.

5. Churchill, *Aftermath,* 338.

6. *Irish Independent,* March 10, 1922; de Valera to Mulcahy, March 6, 1922, P7/B/33/8/25, Mulcahy Papers.

7. Blythe and Mulcahy Interviews, January 1959; White, 88–89; F. O'Connor, 157, 167–68; Taylor, 215–16; Colum, 337; Interview between Griffith and Mayor O'Mara of Limerick, March 9, 1922, P7/B/33/8/25, Mulcahy Papers.

8. O'Donoghue, 205–7; Macardle, 673–75; O'Malley, *Singing Flame,* 55–62; Calton Younger, *Ireland's Civil War* (London: Muller, 1968), 233–35; *Irish Independent,* March 13, 1922; *Dail Debates,* April 26, 1922, 255.

9. Churchill, *Aftermath,* 340.

10. *Dail Debates,* April 26, 1922, 249–55; O'Donoghue, 214–15.

11. O'Donoghue, 216–19.

12. *Irish Independent,* March 23, 1922.

13. Macardle, 679; O'Donoghue, 219–21, 335; *Freeman's Journal,* March 29, 1922; *Dail Debates,* I, September 11, 1922, 67.

14. Macardle, 679; O'Donoghue, 221, 335–38.

15. O'Donoghue, 221–23, 334; Memorandum on the Strength of the IRA, Dir/Org to Chief of Staff, November 23, 1921, P7/C/69/26/14, Mulcahy Papers; *Irish Independent,* March 23–24, April 3 and 7, 1922; C.P. 3933, Macready's Report, April 1, 1922, app. III; C.P. 3938, Macready's Report, April 8, 1922, apps. A and B; C.P. 3943, Macready's Report, April 15, 1922 (Cab 24/136).

16. Macardle, 679; Younger, 244–45.

17. 152 H.C. Deb. 5s., April 5, 1922, 2235; Beaslai, II, 383–84; Younger, 253–54; Neeson, 56–59; PGI 71, Conference of Churchill with British Military and Naval Authorities, March 31, 1922 (Cab 27/154).

18. Brennan, 337; Longford and O'Neill, 187; Dail Eireann, Parliamentary Paper 1, *Correspondence of Mr. Eamon de Valera and Others* (Dublin, 1922), (20), de Valera to Cathal O'Murchadha, September 13, 1922.

19. Longford and O'Neill, 184.

20. *Irish Independent,* March 17, 1922.

21. Ibid., March 18, 1922.

22. Ibid.

23. Ibid., March 20, 1922.

24. Ibid.; O'Hegarty, *History of Ireland,* 782–83; Rex Taylor, 221; O'Sullivan, 57–58.

25. O'Sullivan, 58.

26. *Irish Independent,* March 27, 1922.

27. Ibid., March 23, 1922; *Republic of Ireland,* March 22, 1922.

28. Bromage, 164.

29. Longford and O'Neill, 185–86.

30. *Treaty Debate,* January 9, 1922, 379.

31. *Irish Independent,* April 7, 1922.

32. Ibid., March 20, 1922; *Republic of Ireland,* April 20, 1922.

33. *Irish Independent,* March 6, 1922.

34. Ibid., March 13, 1922.

35. F. O'Connor, 169–70.

36. Cab 30(22), 3, May 30, 1922 (Cab 23/30).

37. For a more sympathetic view of the Specials, see Buckland, II, 161–68.

38. PGI 19 and 20th (1) Conclusions, 4:30 and 5:30 p.m., March 24, 1922 (Cab 27/153); PGI 66, Macready to S/S for War, March 27, 1922 (Cab 27/154); Macardle, 680–81.

39. Macardle, 704; Buckland, II, 158–59, 168.

40. C.P. 3884, Collins to Churchill, March 21, 1922 (Cab 24/134).

41. Rex Taylor, *Assassination* (London: Hutchinson, 1961), 62–63; Macready, 629; Callwell, 332–33, 341.

42. *Irish News,* March 31, 1922. For an account of the negotiations, see Conferences of the Irish Committee with Representatives of Northern and Southern Ireland, March 29–30, 1922 (Cab 43/5).

43. *Belfast Telegraph,* March 31, 1922; *Irish News,* April 1, 1922; C.P. 3932, Craig to Collins, April 4, 1922 (Cab 24/136).

44. Macardle, 731–32, 971; F. O'Connor, 171–72; O'Donoghue, 249–54; Interview with Frank Aiken, September 1960; 152 H.C. Deb. 5s., March 23, 1922, 712; *Dail Debates,* April 28, 1922, 335; Greaves, 326–27.

45. C.P. 3909 and 3955, Macready's Reports, March 25 and April 29, 1922 (Cab 24/136); Cab 30(22), 3, May 30, 1922 (Cab 23/30).

46. O'Donoghue, 251–53; Memorandum to GHQ from O/C, 3d No. Div., IRA, July 27, 1922, P7/B/11/2/104, Mulcahy Papers; Macardle, 731–32.

47. *Dail Debates,* April 28, 1922, 335; Letter from Liam Lynch to the *Irish Independent,* April 27, 1922.

Chapter 13

1. O'Donoghue, 223–24, 227–28, 338–41; Macardle, 693.

2. Macardle, 695.

3. C.P. 3943, Macready's Report, April 15, 1922 (Cab 24/136).

4. Macardle, 694–98; *Irish Independent,* April 20, May 3 and 6, 1922; Younger, 275–79; *Dail Debates,* April 26, 1922, 249–50.

5. *Dail Debates,* April 26, 1922, 255–57, and April 28, 1922, 340; Macardle, 696–97.

6. *Dail Debates,* May 10, 1922, 393–95; Younger, 387–88; Phillips, 259–60; *Irish Times,* May 9, 15, 18, 1922.

7. *Irish Independent,* April 4, 25, 1922; Younger, 260–65; F. O'Connor, 163.

8. Cab 23(22), April 5, 1922, app.: Committee of Imperial Defense, Subcommittee on Ireland, Note on Irish Situation (Summary of Note by Churchill), April 10, 1922 (Cab 23/30).

9. Cab 23(22), 1, April 5, 1922, and app. II: Instructions from Army Council to Macready, April 6, 1922 (Cab 23/30); Cab 24(22), 1a, April 10, 1922 (Cab 23/30).

10. Churchill, *Aftermath,* 341–43.

11. Ibid., 343–46.

12. O'Donoghue, 232–37.

13. *Irish Independent,* April 27, 1922.

14. Macardle, 701; *Republic of Ireland,* April 27, 1922.

15. *Irish Independent,* April 12, 20, 21, 25, 1922.

16. Ibid., May 1, 1922. De Valera had grounds for complaint about the electoral register. It had been prepared improperly in some places in 1921 and listed many people who were dead or had left the country, while omitting others who were entitled to vote. On the other hand, no previous register had been compiled in three months, the time Republicans claimed would be adequate to

prepare a new one, and the agreement to add 400,000 women to the electorate was sure to complicate revision. When a new register was compiled in 1922-23, the task took more than six months. Although de Valera expected to gain support from the young voters who would be added to a new register, he knew the Republicans had no hope of winning an election on the Treaty, even if the register were updated. Collins and Griffith also realized this and rightly concluded that the real purpose of Republican protests was to postpone and, if possible, prevent an election which would repudiate the Republic.

17. *Irish Independent,* May 2, 1922; Macardle, 707-8.

18. Macardle, 969; *Irish Independent,* May 1, 1922.

19. *Dail Debates,* February 28-March 2, 1922, 89-228.

20. Ibid., April 26, 1922, 235-36.

21. Ibid., April 27, 1922, 293-310.

22. Ibid., May 3, 1922, 357-58, 363; Younger, 266-67; O'Donoghue, 236-37; F. O'Connor, 165.

23. O'Donoghue, 237-38.

24. *Dail Debates,* May 3, 1922, 357-68; O'Donoghue, 238-39.

25. *Dail Debates,* May 10, 11, 17, 1922, 379, 398-406, 409-15.

26. Ibid., May 17, 1922, 426-28, 432-40.

27. Macardle, 711.

28. *Dail Debates,* May 19, 1922, 459-63, 473-78.

29. Ibid., May 20, 1922, 479-80.

30. Ibid., 479.

31. Blythe interview, January 1959; Colum, 343.

32. Collins, 17-18.

33. Bromage, 170; de Valera to McGarrity, September 10, 1922, Ms. 17,440, McGP.

34. De Valera to McGarrity, September 10, 1922, Ms. 17,440, McGP.; O'Malley, *Singing Flame,* 152.

35. *Republic of Ireland,* May 25, 1922; *Irish Independent,* May 24, 1922.

36. *Irish Independent,* May 24, 1922.

37. Jones, 199-200; Churchill, *Aftermath,* 348-49.

38. Cab 27(22), 3, May 16, 1922 (Cab 23/30).

39. C.P. 3993, Macready's Report, May 20, 1922 (Cab 24/136).

40. 154 H.C. Deb. 5s., May 22, 1922, 800.

41. 22/N/148 (1), Secretary's Notes of Conference of British Representatives, May 23, 1922 (Cab 43/1); SFB 22d Conclusions, May 23, 1922 (Cab 43/1).

42. Colum, 351; PG 25, Minutes of Meeting of Provisional Government, May 25, 1922, P7/B/6/2/2, Mulcahy Papers.

43. 22/N/60 (7), Conference with Irish Ministers, May 26, 1922 (Cab 43/6).

44. 22/N/148 (2), Secretary's Notes of Conference of British Representatives, May 26, 1922 (Cab 43/1).

45. Jones, 202; 22/N/148 (3), Conference of British Representatives, May 27, 1922 (Cab 43/1); 22/N/163, Chamberlain's Notes of an Interview of British Signatories with Griffith and Collins, May 27, 1922 (Cab 43/7).

46. 22/N/60 (8), Conference with Irish Ministers, May 27, 1922 (Cab 43/6); SFC 38, Conference Aide Memoire, May 27, 1922 (Cab 43/3). Although problems arising from the Constitution inevitably became entangled with those pro-

duced by the pact and Ulster, negotiations on the Constitution are treated separately for the sake of clarity.

47.   C.P. 3993, 4022, 4056, 4072, Macready's Reports, May 20, June 3, 17, 24, 1922 (Cab 24/136–37); Macardle, 728–30.

48.   Cab 30(22), 3, May 30, 1922, and Cab 31(22), June 1, 1922 (Cab 23/30).

49.   On this point, see also Jones, 203.

50.   Cab 30(22), 3, May 30, 1922 (Cab 23/30).

51.   154 H.C. Deb. 5s., May 31, 1922, 2125–41, 2166.

52.   Churchill, *Aftermath,* 355.

53.   C.P. 4022 and 4031, Macready's Reports, June 3 and 10, 1922 (Cab 24/137); *Irish News,* June 1, 1922; 22/N/153, Invasion of Northern Ireland by Republican Forces (Cab 43/7); C.P. 4017, Exchange of Telegrams between Collins/Cope and Churchill, June 5–6, 1922 (Cab 24/137); PGI 22d Conclusions, 1, 6, and 7, June 6, 1922 (Cab 27/153); PGI 79–80, Operations in the Pettigo Area, June 7 and 9, 1922 (Cab 27/154); SS(IC), Conference, June 7, 1922 (Cab 16/42).

54.   Macready, 645; Report of British GHQ (Dublin) to Director of Military Operations and Intelligence (London), June 2, 1922 (Cab 21/254).

55.   Early in May, Collins had decided on a policy of peaceful obstruction of the Belfast government, and in approving this policy on June 3, the Irish Cabinet ordered that no troops—Free State or Irregular—be permitted to invade the Six County area. PG 12, 17, 27 (Minutes), May 3, 15, and June 3, 1922, P7/B/6/2/2, Mulcahy Papers.

56.   Prime Minister to Churchill, June 8, 1922, F/10/3/3, LGP; Jones, 210–12; 22/N/163, Diary of Negotiations on Draft Irish Constitution, June 7, 1922, 1:15 p.m. entry and Churchill to the Prime Minister (Cab 43/7).

57.   Churchill, *Aftermath,* 357–58.

58.   *Morning Post* (London), June 9, 1922.

59.   Jones, 212.

Chapter 14

1.   Unless otherwise indicated, information on the Constitution Committee and its work is taken from D. H. Akenson and J. F. Fallin, "The Irish Civil War and the Drafting of the Free State Constitution," parts I and II, in *Eire-Ireland* (St. Paul, Minn.), V, nos. 1 and 2 (Spring–Summer 1970), 10–26, 42–93.

2.   Colum, 356.

3.   Akenson and Fallin, part I, 23.

4.   O'Hegarty, *History of Ireland,* 786–87.

5.   Collins and O'Shiel were too busy to give full attention to the committee's work and did not sign any of the drafts.

6.   Akenson and Fallin, part II, 42–93.

7.   The complete texts of Drafts A and B and part of Draft C appear in Akenson and Fallin, part II.

8.   Akenson and Fallin, part III, *Eire-Ireland,* V, no. 4 (Winter 1970), 29–30; Longford and O'Neill, 184–85; Cronin, 117.

9.   PG Minutes of Meetings, April 10–May 25, 1922, P7/B/6/2/1–2, Mulcahy Papers; Akenson and Fallin, part III, 53–55; Macardle, 724–25.

10. Although Collins did not want the Constitution to deal with external affairs, the committee felt that certain aspects of Anglo-Irish relations must be clarified. Akenson and Fallin, part I, 24.

11. SFC 34, Draft Irish Constitution Presented to the British Government (Cab 43/3).

12. *Dail Debates*, I, September 20, 21, 1922, 498–99, 536.

13. Ibid., September 18, 1922, 383.

14. Ibid., 358–59, and September 29, 1922, 1008–9.

15. 22/N/163, Chamberlain's Notes of an Interview of British and Irish Signatories, May 27, 1922, 3:45 p.m. (Cab 43/7).

16. SFB 24th Conclusions, May 27, 1922, 4:15 p.m. (Cab 43/1).

17. 22/N/60 (8), Conference with Irish Ministers, May 27, 1922, 6 p.m. (Cab 43/6).

18. SFB 25–27th Conclusions, 10 a.m., 1 and 3:30 p.m., May 29, 1922 (Cab 43/1); SFB 56, 57, 59, Memoranda on the Draft Constitution, May 28–29, 1922; SFB 58, Midleton's Objections to the Draft Constitution, May 29, 1922 (Cab 43/2).

19. SFC 35, Memorandum on the Draft Constitution, May 29, 1922 (Cab 43/3).

20. SFB 60, Draft Constitution, Note on Negotiations and Appendix: Observations on the Criticism of the British Government on the Draft Constitution (Cab 43/2).

21. 22/N/163, Diary of Negotiations on the Draft Constitution, Meeting at 7 p.m., May 31, 1922 (Cab 43/7); Jones, 203.

22. Jones, 203; 22/N/163, Diary of Negotiations, Interview between Jones, Griffith, and Collins, May 31, 1922, 8:40–10 p.m. (Cab 43/7).

23. Cab 31(22), June 1, 1922 (Cab 23/30).

24. SFC 40, I: Letter from the Prime Minister to Griffith, June 1, 1922 (Cab 43/3).

25. Cab 32(22), 1, June 2, 1922, 11 a.m. (Cab 23/30); Jones, 205–6.

26. 22/N/163, Curtis' Record of an Interview between the Prime Minister, Griffith, and Collins, June 1, 1922, 6:30 p.m. (Cab 43/7); Cab 32(22), 1, June 2, 1922, 11 a.m. (Cab 23/30).

27. Jones, 206.

28. Cab 32(22), 1–3, 5, June 2, 1922 (Cab 23/30); Jones, 207–9.

29. Jones, 208.

30. SFC 40, II: Letter from Griffith to the Prime Minister, June 2, 1922 (Cab 43/3).

31. Cab 33(22), June 2, 1922, 8:15 p.m. (Cab 23/30).

32. PG 26–29 (Minutes), June 2–6, 1922, P7/B/6/2/2, Mulcahy Papers.

33. 22/N/163, Diary of Negotiations, June 7, 1922 (Cab 43/7).

34. However, this was not the general right of appeal as in Canada but the limited right of appeal as in South Africa, which was not exercised in cases dealing with domestic matters. *Dail Debates*, I, October 10, 1922, 1401–4.

35. SFB 63, IFS Draft Constitution, First Revision (Cab 43/2); SFB 28th Conclusions, 2–8, June 9, 1922 (Cab 43/1).

36. SFB 28th Conclusions, 2–8, June 9, 1922 (Cab 43/1).

37. SFB 64, IFS Draft Constitution, Second Revision (Cab 43/2); SFB 29th Conclusions, 5, June 10, 1922 (Cab 43/1).

38. 22/N/60 (9), Conference with Irish Ministers, 1-3, 9, June 10, 1922 (Cab 43/6).

39. PG 33 (Minutes), June 12, 1922, P7/B/6/2/2, Mulcahy Papers; 22/N/163, Diary of Negotiations, June 14, 1922 (Cab 43/7).

40. SFB 28th Conclusions, 7, June 9, 1922 (Cab 43/1); SFB 58, Midleton's Objections to the Draft Constitution, May 29, 1922 (Cab 43/2); 22/N/163, Chamberlain's Notes of a Conference, June 10, 1922 (Cab 43/7); 22/N/4, Agreement of Irish Representatives and Southern Unionists, June 13, 1922, 8:30 p.m. (Cab 43/7); O'Sullivan, 78-80.

41. SFB 30th Conclusions, 2, June 15, 1922, 11:30 a.m. (Cab 43/1); SFB 65 (Revise), Position of Southern Unionists, June 15, 1922 (Cab 43/2).

42. O'Sullivan, 81-82; Phillips, 278 n. 1.

43. SFB 30th Conclusions, 1a and 4, June 15, 1922 (Cab 43/1); 22/N/60 (10), Conference with Irish Ministers, June 15, 1922 (Cab 43/6); Cab 35(22), 2, June 16, 1922 (Cab 23/30); C.P. 4042, Draft Constitution of the IFS (Cab 24/137).

44. Macardle, 724; *Irish Independent,* June 16-17, 22, 1922; *Republic of Ireland,* June 22, 1922; *Dail Debates,* I, September 18, 1922, 358-60.

45. Kohn, 81.

46. Hancock, *Survey,* 158.

47. The *Times* (London), June 19, 1922; Hancock, *Survey,* 165 n.1.

Chapter 15

1. *Irish Independent,* June 3, 1922.

2. Ibid., June 6, 1922.

3. Ibid., June 6 and 15, 1922.

4. *Republic of Ireland,* June 1 and 15, 1922; Breen, 168; *Irish Independent,* June 7, 8, 13, 1922; *Dail Debates,* I, September 9, 1922, 26.

5. *Irish Independent,* June 7, 1922.

6. Ibid., June 15, 1922.

7. Ibid., June 16, 1922.

8. Macardle, 721; Macready, 642; *Republic of Ireland,* June 22, 29, 1922; Bromage, 172.

9. *Dail Debates,* I, October 20, 1922, 1844-59; McCracken, 74-75; *Irish Independent,* June 17-26, 1922.

10. Dan Breen, a candidate on both sides of the panel, won 3,000 votes.

11. *Irish Independent,* June 26, 1922.

12. Ibid.

13. Macardle, 722-23.

14. *Irish News,* June 22, 1922; *Republic of Ireland,* June 22, 29, 1922.

15. *Irish Independent,* June 21, 1922.

16. F. O'Connor, 175; *Irish News,* June 23, 1922.

17. Macardle, 732-35, 971; O'Donoghue, 238-46; Brennan, 338; *Dail Debates,* I, September 12, 1922, 167-73; Sean McBride's Report of the IRA Convention, June 18, 1922, P7/B/58/19/3, Mulcahy Papers.

18. Taylor, *Assassination,* esp. 203-19; F. O'Connor, 173-75; O'Donoghue, 255. Collins' attempts to free the assassins prove nothing more than that he felt men who had killed an enemy of Ireland should not be abandoned to the hangman.

19. Boyce, 178-79; Churchill, *Aftermath,* 359.

20. Cab 36(22), June 30, 1922, app. III: Conclusions of a Conference of Ministers, June 22, 1922, 5 p.m. (Cab 23/30), and Supplement (Cab 21/255).

21. Cab 36(22), June 30, 1922, app. III: Prime Minister to Collins, June 22, 1922 (app. III) (Cab 23/30).

22. Macardle, 736-37.

23. Blythe Interview, July 1967; Taylor, *Assassination,* 76-77, 126-27; *Irish Independent,* June 23, 1922.

24. Longford and O'Neill, 191-92; PG 35 (Minutes), June 23, 1922, P7/B/ 6/2/3, Mulcahy Papers.

25. Supplement to Conclusions of a Conference of Ministers, June 23, 1922, 6:30 p.m. (Cab 21/255).

26. Supplement to Conclusions of a Conference of Ministers, June 23, 1922, 6:30 p.m. (Cab 21/255). Macready gives a somewhat different version of this conference in his memoirs, claiming he strongly opposed the assault. However, his doubts about the wisdom of the operation really crystallized only after his return to Dublin. Macready, 652-54.

27. Conclusions of Conferences of Ministers, June 24, 1922, 11 a.m. and 5:30 p.m. (Cab 21/255).

28. Macready, 653.

29. Ibid., 654; Conclusions of a Conference of Ministers, June 25, 1922, 11:30 a.m. (Cab 21/255).

30. Churchill, *Aftermath,* 360; Macardle, 740.

31. 155 H.C. Deb. 5s., June 26, 1922, 1695-1712.

32. Ibid., 1744-49.

33. Ibid., 1792-1804.

34. Churchill, *Aftermath,* 363.

35. Macardle, 740; O'Donoghue, 258.

36. Macardle, 742-43; *Irish Independent,* June 29, 1922; O'Malley, *Singing Flame,* 88-90.

37. O'Hegarty, *Sinn Fein,* 123; *Dail Debates,* I, September 12, 1922, 173; Colum, 366; Mulcahy Interview.

38. F. O'Connor, 177; O'Hegarty, *Sinn Fein,* 123.

39. PG 37 (Minutes), June 27, 1922, P7/B/6/2/3, Mulcahy Papers.

40. Colum, 366-67.

41. Macready, 655; Younger, 312-13; Conference of Ministers No. 133, June 23, 1922, appendix: Conclusions of Conferences of Ministers, June 28, 1922, 9:50 p.m., and June 29, 1922, 12:15 a.m. (Cab 23/39).

42. Macardle, 743-44; Younger, 311-14, 322; O'Donoghue, 258; Greaves, 340-44; O'Malley, *Singing Flame,* 91-97.

43. *Dail Debates,* May 17, 1922, 437.

44. Ibid., May 19, 1922, 464.

45. *Republic of Ireland,* April 5, 1922.

46. O'Sullivan, 59.

47. Macardle, 813.
48. Ibid., 742, 745–47; Neeson, 66–67; O'Donoghue, 256.
49. O'Hegarty, *Sinn Fein,* 123.
50. Mulcahy Interview; Blythe interview, July 1967; Younger, 308–9; White, 101; Beaslai, 402–3.
51. By June 26 the Provisional Government had received from the British 11,900 rifles, 79 Lewis guns, 1.7 million rounds of rifle ammunition, 6 armored cars, and a large number of trucks. At this time the IRA had 3,000 rifles with 120 rounds apiece, and correspondingly small supplies of other war materiel. Gov. 41, C.-in-C. to Acting Chairman, PG, August 5, 1922, P7/B/7/2/24; Report of (IRA) Executive Subcommittee, June, 1922, P7/B/58/19/1, Mulcahy Papers.
52. F. O'Connor, 177; Younger, 313.
53. Colum, 367; O'Donoghue, 256; Younger, 396.

Chapter 16

1. *Irish Independent,* June 28, 1922.
2. Macardle, 745–46.
3. Brennan, 343; Longford and O'Neill, 195–96.
4. Macrcady, 655–57; Churchill, *Aftermath,* 364; Conference 133, app.: Conclusions of Conferences of Ministers, June 28, 1922, 7:45 and 9:50 p.m., and June 29, 1922, 12:15 a.m. (Cab 23/39).
5. Conference 133, App: Conclusions of Conferences of Ministers, June 28, 1922, 11:30 a.m., 7:45 and 9:50 p.m., and June 29, 1922, 12:15 a.m. (Cab 23/39).
6. SS(IC), 8th Minutes, 1–2, 5, June 29, 1922 (Cab 16/42).
7. Cab 36(22), 1, June 30, 1922 (Cab 23/30).
8. Younger, 318–21, 323–24; Neeson, 72–76; O'Malley, *Singing Flame,* 97–115, 123.
9. Younger, 321–22; Macardle, 751–52; Greaves, 349–51; O'Malley, *Singing Flame,* 98, 115–27.
10. Macardle, 750; Neeson, 78; Younger, 326; Bromage, 176–77; Taylor, *Collins,* 236–37; Greaves, 351; Irish Labor Party and Trades Union Congress, *Report of the Annual Meeting, August, 1922:* "Peace Efforts." (Dublin: Irish Labor Party, n.d.)
11. O'Donoghue, 259–60; Younger, 327–28; Mulcahy and O'Donoghue Interviews.
12. Younger, 328–32; Macardle, 753–54.
13. *Irish Independent,* July 6 and 10, 1922; Younger, 329, 333; Macready, 658–60.
14. Forester, 323; Macardle, 757; Churchill, *Aftermath,* 365–67.
15. On the size of the two armies, see PGI 23d Conclusions, 2, July 14, 1922 (Cab 27/153); C.P. 4085, Macready's Report, July 1, 1922 (Cab 24/137); Neeson, 72; Beaslai, II, 404.
16. O'Donoghue, 260, 272.
17. *Irish Independent,* July 6, 1922; *Dail Debates,* I, November 29, 1922, 2436; III, June 7, 1923, 1637–38.
18. On the Free State army, see Younger, 395, 414; O'Donoghue, 261; Beaslai, II, 404, 407, 418–19; F. O'Connor, 180; Neeson, 81–82; C.P. 4101, Mac-

ready's Report, July 8, 1922 (Cab 24/138); C.P. 4227, Report by Major Whittaker, September 19, 1922 (Cab 24/139); *Dail Debates,* I, November 29, 1922, 2435–38.

19.   SS(IC) 16, July 10, 1922 (Cab 16/42).

20.   Younger, 335–38; Neeson, 83–86; O'Malley, *Singing Flame,* 129–30.

21.   Younger, 362–74; Neeson, 87–94; O'Donoghue, 261–65.

22.   PG 57, 58 (Minutes), July 12, 1922, P7/B/6/2/3, Mulcahy Papers; Younger, 370.

23.   PG 57 (Minutes), July 12, 1922, P7/B/6/2/3, Mulcahy Papers; Macardle, 769, 771, 773.

24.   Macardle, 767–71.

25.   Ibid., 769–70; Blythe Interview, July, 1967; *Dail Debates,* I, September 21, 1922, 531–32.

26.   Younger, 374–76; Neeson, 128–32; Macardle, 761–64; Aiken to Mulcahy, July 15–16, 1922, P7/B/7/2/27, Mulcahy Papers.

27.   On military action in the west, see Younger, 346–61; Neeson, 119–23.

28.   Younger, 381–85; Neeson, 96–103.

29.   Neeson, 100–101, 104–7; Younger, 379–81, 386–88.

30.   Younger, 389–93; Neeson, 108–16.

31.   Neeson, 133–39; Younger, 393–96.

32.   Younger, 396–98; Neeson, 140–43.

33.   Neeson, 144–49; Younger, 399–400; Brennan, 352; C.P. 4158, Macready's Report, August 5, 1922 (Cab 34/138); Macardle, 772–73; F. O'Connor, 180.

34.   Younger, 399–413; Neeson, 149–55; C.P. 4165, Macready's Report, August 12, 1922 (Cab 24/138).

35.   C.P. 4165, August 12, 1922 (Cab 24/138); Younger, 415, 418; Macardle, 775–76.

36.   Greaves, 349–50; Brennan, 352; O'Duffy to Collins, July 23, 1922, P7/B/9/2/61, Mulcahy Papers; O'Brien, *Irish Free State, Secret History of Its Foundation,* ch. X, 9, Ms. 4210, N.L.I.

37.   Neeson, 155; Macardle, 776.

38.   O'Donoghue, 267–68; O'Malley, *Singing Flame,* 144–45; C.P. 4172, Macready's Report, August 19, 1922 (Cab 24/138); C.P. 4227, Report by Major Whittaker, September 19, 1922 (Cab 24/139); Sean Moylan to Lynch, September 14, 1922, File 78, Florence O'Donoghue Papers.

39.   *Dail Debates,* I, September 22 and 29, 1922, 598–99, 618–19, 627, 959–61.

40.   C.P. 4174, Macready's Report, August 26, 1922 (Cab 24/138); *Irish Independent,* July 31–August 2 and September 30, 1922; *Irish Times,* July 29, 1922.

41.   Irish Labor Party and TUC, *Report.* Despite this threat, Labor deputies did not resign when the Dail's opening was again postponed. The deaths of Griffith and Collins changed the political situation in a way the convention had not anticipated. *Irish Independent,* September 1, 1922.

42.   C.P. 4134, 4174, 4187, Macready's Reports, July 22, August 26, and September 2, 1922 (Cab 24/138); C.P. 4138, Memorandum on the Irish Situation (probably by Cope), July 31, 1922 (Cab 24/138); C.P. 4226, Position of Irish PG, Report by Sir Samuel Hoare, September 21, 1922; C.P. 4227, Major Whittaker's Report, September 19, 1922 (Cab 24/139); PGI 25th Conclusions, 2, August 1, 1922 (Cab 27/153).

43. SFB 31st Conclusions, June 16, 1922 (Cab 43/1).

44. On the IRA in the northeast at this time, see the reports of the O/C 3d Northern Division (IRA) to Chief of Staff (Free State), July 7 and 20, 1922, P7/B/11/2/104, Mulcahy Papers.

45. PGI Committee, Memoranda: ITC 53, Collins to Churchill, June 28, 1922 (Cab 27/160).

46. SFB 67 and 68, Local Government (N.I.) Bill for Abolition of Proportional Representation in Local Government Elections (Correspondence) (Cab 43/2).

47. SFB 32d Conclusions, 3, September 7, 1922 (Cab 43/1).

48. Buckland, II, 157.

49. O'Hegarty, *Sinn Fein*, 123.

50. W. T. Cosgrave, "Arthur Griffith," *Dictionary of National Biography, 1922–1930* (London: Oxford University Press, 1937), 368.

51. Colum, 373–74; Gogarty, 173–78.

52. Hobson, 4; Lyons, 244.

53. Chamberlain to Ivy, Lady Chamberlain, August 12, 1922, 6/1/497, ACP; Cab 45(22), 1, August 12, 1922 (Cab 23/30); Longford and O'Neill, 198.

54. *Irish Independent*, August 14, 1922.

55. Beaslai, II, 418–19; Younger, 414; F. O'Connor, 180; Taylor, *Collins*, 237.

56. Taylor, 236.

57. Ibid., 238–39; Brennan, 337; Cronin, 121–22; Macardle, 776–77; F. O'Connor, 180; Forester, 329; Blythe Interview, January 1959; Boland to McGarrity, July 13 and 25, 1922, Ms. 17,424 (2), McGP.

58. F. O'Connor, 181.

59. Younger, 420–21.

60. This account of the ambush is based on those by Younger and Taylor, and by Neeson in *The Civil War in Ireland* and *The Life and Death of Michael Collins* (Cork: Mercier Press, 1968); see also Coogan, 46.

61. Beaslai, II, 411–13; Younger, 417–18, 421–22; F. O'Connor, 182; Taylor, *Collins*, 240; Cronin, 123.

62. *Dail Debates*, I, September 9, 1922, 18; White, 104; Cosgrave Interview.

63. Lynch to Deasy, O/C 1st Southern Division, August 28, 1922, P7/B/58/19/3, Mulcahy Papers; Stack to McGarrity, August 27, 1922, Ms. 17,489, McGP; Bromage, 183–84; Forester, 342.

64. Barry, 183.

65. *Irish Independent*, August 24, 1922; *Belfast Telegraph*, August 23, 1922; Jones, 215; Taylor, *Collins*, 254; Churchill, *Aftermath*, 355–56.

66. Younger, 430.

Chapter 17

1. Ervine, 480.

2. Coogan, 53–54; Brian Farrell, *Chairman or Chief, The Role of the Taoiseach in Irish Government* (Dublin: Gill and MacMillan, 1971), 18–25.

3. William O'Brien, *Forth the Banners Go* (Dublin: Three Candles, 1969), 225–26; "Corrections and Notes on Macardle's *Irish Republic*," Ms. 13,972, William O'Brien Papers, N.L.I.

4. Mulcahy Interview; Mulcahy's account of the meeting, P7/D/65/22/20, Mulcahy Papers; de Valera to McGarrity, September 10, 1922, Ms. 17,440, McGP.

5. PG 108 (Minutes), September 5, 1922, P7/B/6/2/4, Mulcahy Papers; Mulcahy Interview; White, 120–21.

6. *Dail Debates*, I, September 9, 1922, 7–13; Macardle, 781–82.

7. *Dail Debates*, I, September 9, 1922, 17–30, 56.

8. Ibid., 29–58.

9. Ibid., September 11, 1922, 65–88, 94–99.

10. De Valera to McGarrity, September 10, 1922, Ms. 17,440, McGP.

11. Dail Eireann, P.P. 1, *Correspondence of Mr. Eamon de Valera and Others* (13), Letter of de Valera, September 7, 1922.

12. Ibid. (8), Lynch to de Valera, August 30, 1922.

13. Ibid. (18), de Valera to Cathal O'Murchadha, September 12, 1922.

14. Ibid. (20), de Valera to O'Murchadha, September 13, 1922.

15. O'Donoghue, 270–72, 274–77; Cronin, 193–96.

16. Macardle, 807–8; O'Donoghue, 342–43.

17. *Irish Independent*, October 11, 1922.

18. O'Sullivan, 67; Longford and O'Neill, 203–4; Stack to McGarrity, October 18, 1922, Ms. 17,489, McGP.

19. Younger, 469–70.

20. *Dail Debates*, I, September 26 and 27, 1922, 790–91, 801–4.

21. Ibid., September 27, 1922, 811–18, 830.

22. Ibid., 840–50, 874–82, September 28, 1922, 931.

23. Ibid., 940–41.

24. *Irish Independent*, October 5 and 12, 1922.

25. Macardle, 811.

26. *Dail Debates*, I, November 17, 1922, 2262–65, 2275–78.

27. Macardle, 811; Younger, 479–81; Longford and O'Neill, 205.

28. Statement by Childers, November 19, 1922, P7/B/58/19/2, Mulcahy Papers. Churchill called Childers a "mischief-making renegade," who hated England and had done great harm to Ireland (*Irish Independent*, November 13, 1922). Inaccurate reporting distorted O'Higgins' remarks of November 17 and exaggerated the extent to which they applied to Childers. However, O'Higgins' animosity is clearly revealed in an earlier speech. *Dail Debates*, I, September 27 and November 17, 1922, 859, 2267; White, 126–27 and note.

29. In the end, the condemned prisoners were sentenced to penal servitude.

30. Macardle, 811–14; Younger, 478–82.

31. Longford and O'Neill, 206.

32. *Dail Debates*, I, November 28, 1922, 2356–62.

33. Ibid., 2362–66.

34. Ibid., November 29, 1922, 2404–9.

35. Ibid., 2410–11.

36. Ibid., 2412–16.

37. Macardle, 816.

38. *Dail Debates,* I, November 30, 1922, 2529-35.

39. Ibid., 2537-44.

40. Macardle, 813.

41. Ibid., 817.

42. O'Donoghue, 291.

43. Ibid., 279.

44. O'Sullivan, 100; Neeson, *Civil War,* 189.

45. Longford and O'Neill, 207.

46. *Dail Debates,* I, September 18, 1922, 354-57.

47. Ibid., September 21, 1922, 579.

48. Ibid., October 3, 1922, 1038-67.

49. Ibid., October 5, 1922, 1235-39.

50. Ibid., October 25, 1922, 1909-14, 1947.

51. Ibid., October 11, 1922, 1500.

52. On the fall of the coalition and the subsequent election, see Mowat, 132-45, and A. J. P. Taylor, *English History, 1914-1945* (Oxford: Clarendon Press, 1965), 187-98. On the Conservative Party and the Irish Settlement, see Churchill, *Aftermath,* 322; Blake, 436; Beaverbrook, 287; Birkenhead, 435; Petrie, 190-91; Keith Middlemas and John Barnes, *Baldwin: A Biography* (New York: Macmillan, 1970), 101-2, 107, 123.

53. Macardle, 799; Cab 68(22), November 29, 1922, app. II: Conclusions of a Conference of Ministers, 1b and 1d, November 22, 1922 (Cab 23/32); Irish Free State Constitution Act (session 2) (13 Geo. 5, ch. 1).

54. 159 H.C. Deb. 5s., November 27, 1922, 327-32.

55. Macardle, 820.

56. Ibid.; White, 139.

57. Jones, 218.

58. C.P. 4315, Memorandum by S/S for War, November 21, 1922 (Cab 24/140); Cab 68(22), November 29, 1922, app. II: Conclusions of a Conference of Ministers, 2a-b, November 22, 1922 (Cab 23/32); Macready, 671-75.

59. *Irish Independent,* December 8, 1922.

60. CIL, 2d Meeting, 2, and 3d Meeting, 1, November 21-22, 1922 (Cab 27/157); Cab 68(22), November 29, 1922, app. II: Conclusions of a Conference of Ministers, 1f, November 22, 1922 (Cab 23/32).

Chapter 18

1. Macready, 670-71; *Irish Independent,* December 7, 1922.

2. *Dail Debates,* II, December 6, 1922, 1-4.

3. Ibid., 4-18, 22-27.

4. O'Sullivan, 90-95.

5. Ibid., 117.

6. *Dail Debates,* II, December 12, 1922, 97-102.

7. White, 132.

8. Blythe Interview, July 1967; White, 128-29.

9. *Irish Independent,* December 8, 1922.

10. *Dail Debates,* II, December 8, 1922, 48-73, 93-96; White, 131.

11. Greaves, 391–92; *Irish Independent,* December 9, 1922; Blythe Interview, July 1967; *Dail Debates,* II, December 8, 1922, 88–89.

12. Coogan, 44.

13. O'Sullivan, 100–108.

14. For examples, see *Irish Independent,* January 6, 12, 17, February 5, and March 1, 1923; Phillips, 287–91; *Dail Debates,* II, January 17, 1923, 892–94.

15. Macardle, 823; O'Donoghue, 289; Blythe Interview, January 1959.

16. *Dail Debates,* II, January 17, 1923, 876–934; Macardle, 832, 984–85.

17. O'Donoghue, 292–93.

18. Younger, 494; Macardle, 838.

19. *Dail Debates,* I, October 4, November 16 and 28, 1922, 1193–1202, 2187–91, 2319–34; *Irish Independent,* October 18, 1922; Macardle, 774–75, 838–39; Phillips, 299–300; Neeson, *Civil War,* 187–88; Greaves, 356–57; Younger, 438–41. For two very informative accounts of prison life during the civil war, see Peader O'Donnell, *The Gates Flew Open* (London: Cape, 1932; Cork: Mercier Press, 1965), and O'Malley, *Singing Flame,* 202–90.

20. *Dail Debates,* IV, July 3 and 12, 1923, 101–5, 668, 673–75.

21. Ibid., III, May 2, 1923, 540.

22. Macardle, 867; *Annual Register, 1923* (London: Longmans), 157. The last Republican prisoners were not released until July 1924.

23. Younger, 488.

24. Macardle, 839–40; *Dail Debates,* III, April 17, 1923, 133–38, 185–90.

25. Younger, 488; Blythe Interview, January 1959. For a Republican account of the atrocities, see Dorothy Macardle, *Tragedies of Kerry* (Dublin: Irish Book Bureau, 1924).

26. White, 119–20, 154–67; No. Cl/75, 81, and 85, Minutes of the Executive Council, March 27, April 9 and 23, 1923, P7/B/48/13/1; and Mulcahy to Cosgrave, March 28, 1923, P7/C/69/26/14, Mulcahy Papers.

27. *Irish Independent,* February 9, 1923; *Dail Debates,* II, February 9, 1923, 1469–74; O'Donoghue, 289–90; Macardle, 832–34; Younger, 491–92.

28. De Valera drafted this reply. O'Donoghue, 290; Longford and O'Neill, 213; *Irish Independent,* February 10, 1923.

29. O'Donoghue, 293.

30. CS/4, Lynch to Sean Moylan, February 6, 1923, Ms. 17,466 (2), McGP; Lynch to Deasy (February 1923), P7/B/33/8/34, Mulcahy Papers.

31. De Valera to McGarrity, February 5, 1923, Ms. 17,440, McGP.

32. O'Donoghue, 288, 298–99; *Irish Independent,* February 5, 17 and March 8–9, 1923.

33. Macardle, 840–42; Longford and O'Neill, 218–22; *Irish Independent,* March 20 and April 7, 21, 23, 1923.

34. *Irish Independent,* March 12, 1923.

35. O'Donoghue, 281; Longford and O'Neill, 213.

36. *Annual Register, 1923,* 154–55; Macardle, 839.

37. *Irish Independent,* March 6 and 12, 1923; Younger, 494; O'Donoghue, 297.

38. *Irish Independent,* April 14, 1923.

39. O'Donoghue, 294; *Irish Independent,* April 9, 1923 (captured Republican documents).

40. *Irish Independent,* April 9, 1923 (captured Republican documents); O'Donoghue, 296–97.

41. Longford and O'Neill, 206–16; *Irish Independent,* April 11, 1923 (captured Republican documents).

42. *Irish Independent,* April 11, 1923 (captured Republican documents); Younger, 493–94.

43. O'Donoghue, 299–301; Macardle, 843–44; Longford and O'Neill, 217–18; *Irish Independent,* April 9, 1923 (captured Republican documents).

44. O'Donoghue, 301–7; Younger, 494–97.

45. *Irish Independent,* April 16, 1923; Breen, 179.

46. O'Donoghue, 308–10.

47. *Irish Independent,* April 28, 1923.

48. Ibid., April 30, 1923; Macardle, 985.

49. For an account of these negotiations, see *Seanad Debates,* I (May 9, 1923), 1018–26; *Dail Debates,* III (May 9, 1923), 676–83.

50. Republican Government and Army Council, Minutes of Meeting, night of May 13–14, 1923, File 74, Florence O'Donoghue Papers.

51. *Irish Independent,* May 29, 1923; Macardle, 857.

52. Ibid., 858.

53. *Dail Debates,* III (June 6 and 13, 1923), 1515–16, 1815; O'Donoghue, 272, 274; Coogan, 47; C.P. 4266, Macready's Report, September 30, 1922 (Cab 24/139).

54. O'Sullivan, 115; Macardle, 861.

Appendix IV

1. PGI (A), 1–9, Reports and Memoranda of the Economic Subcommittee of the PGI Committee, February 27–June 9, 1922 (Cab 27/161); PGI 21st Conclusions, 2–5, June 1, 1922, 4:30 p.m. (Cab 27/153); Committee of Imperial Defense, Subcommittee on Ireland, SS(IC) 12, Restriction of Supplies to Southern Ireland, June 14, 1922 (Cab 16/42).

2. SS(IC) Conference, 1–8, June 1, 1922, 5 p.m.; SS(IC), 7th Minutes, 1–9, June 2, 1922 (Cab 16/42).

Select Bibliography

Official Records

Cabinet Office Records, Public Record Office, London
  Cab 23 Conclusions of Cabinet Meetings, 1919–22
  Cab 24 Cabinet Papers, 1921–22
  Cab 27 Cabinet Committees on Ireland, 1919–22
  Cab 43 Records of Anglo-Irish Negotiations, 1921–22
  Cab 21 Cabinet Registered Files, 1921–22
  Cab 16/42 Committee of Imperial Defense, Subcommittee on Ireland, 1922

Dail Eireann Files, DE 2/304, State Paper Office, Dublin Castle, Records of the Treaty Negotiations, 1921

Private Papers

Lloyd George Papers, Series F, Prime Minister, 1916–22, Beaverbrook Library, London
Bonar Law Papers, 103, 107, Correspondence, 1920–21, Beaverbrook Library, London
Austen Chamberlain Papers, AC 5–6, 30–31, Correspondence, 1921–22, University of Birmingham Library
Richard Mulcahy Papers, University College Archives, Dublin
Joseph McGarrity Papers, National Library of Ireland, Dublin
Florence O'Donoghue Papers, National Library of Ireland, Dublin
Michael Collins Assorted Papers, National Library of Ireland, Dublin
Michael Collins Assorted Papers, Liam Collins, Clonakilty, County Cork
William O'Brien Papers, National Library of Ireland, Dublin

Official Publications

Dail Eireann (Dublin: The Stationery Office)
(Official Record) *Minutes of Proceedings of the First Parliament of the Republic of Ireland, 1919–1921*
(Official Report) *August, 1921 and February–June, 1922*
Private Sessions of [the] Second Dail, 1921–1922 (August–September 1921 and December 1921–January 1922)
(Official Report) *Debate on the Treaty between Great Britain and Ireland* (December 1921–January 1922)
(Official Report) *Parliamentary Debates*, vols. I–III (September 1922–July 1923)
Official Correspondence relating to the Peace Negotiations, June–September, 1921

P.P. 1 (Parliamentary Paper), 1922, *Correspondence of Mr. Eamon de Valera and Others*
Draft Constitution of the Irish Free State
Constitution of the Free State of Ireland

British Parliament (London: H.M. Stationery Office)
Parliamentary Debates (Official Report), *Fifth Series.* Vols. 147–59 (House of Commons) and vols. 45–52 (House of Lords), 1921–22
Government of Ireland Act, 1920 (10 & 11 Geo. 5, ch. 67)
Articles of Agreement for a Treaty between Great Britain and Ireland, 1921 (Cmd. 1560)
Irish Free State (Agreement) Act, 1922 (12 Geo. 5, ch. 4)
Irish Free State Constitution Act, 1922 (session 2) (13 Geo. 5, ch. 1)

Irish Labor Party and Trades Union Congress, *Report of the Annual Meeting, August, 1922* (Dublin: Irish Labor Party, n.d.)

Labor Party, *Report of the Commission of Inquiry into the Present Conditions in Ireland* (London: Labor Party, 1920)
Labor Party, *Report of the Labour Commission to Ireland* (London: Labor Party, 1921)

Interviews

January 1959: Ernest Blythe, William T. Cosgrave, Sean MacEoin, and Richard Mulcahy (Dublin)
February 1959: Eamon de Valera (Dublin)
September 1960: Frank Aiken (New York City)
June 1967: Florence O'Donoghue (Cork)
July 1967: Ernest Blythe (Dublin)

Newspapers and Periodicals

Belfast Telegraph, 1921–22
Cork Examiner, 1921–22
Free State (Dublin), 1922
Freeman's Journal (Dublin), 1921–22
Irish Independent (Dublin), 1921–23
Irish News (Belfast), 1921–22
Irish Times (Dublin), 1921–22
Republic of Ireland (Dublin), 1922
The Times (London), 1921–22
Annual Register (London), vols. CLXIII–CLXV (1921–23)

Books and Articles

Akenson, D. H., and J. F. Fallin. "The Irish Civil War and the Drafting of the Free State Constitution," parts I–III, *Eire–Ireland* (St. Paul, Minn.), V, nos. 1, 2, 4, pp. 10–26, 42–93, 28–70 (Spring, Summer, Winter, 1970).

Barry, Tom. *Guerilla Days in Ireland*. Dublin: Irish Press, 1949.

Beaslai, Piaras. *Michael Collins and the Making of a New Ireland*. 2 vols, New York: Harper, 1926.

Beaverbrook, Lord. *The Decline and Fall of Lloyd George*. New York: Duell, Sloan and Pearce, 1963.

Beckett, J. C. *The Making of Modern Ireland, 1603–1923*. London: Faber and Faber, 1966.

Bennett, Richard. *The Black and Tans*. London: Four Square Books, 1961.

Birkenhead, Second Earl of. *"F. E.": The Life of F. E. Smith, First Earl of Birkenhead*. London: Eyre and Spottiswoode, 1960.

Blake, Robert. *The Unknown Prime Minister: The Life and Times of Andrew Bonar Law, 1858–1923*. London: Eyre and Spottiswoode, 1955.

Boyce, D. G. *Englishmen and Irish Troubles: British Public Opinion and the Making of Irish Policy, 1918–1922*. Cambridge, Mass.: MIT Press, 1972.

Breen, Dan. *My Fight for Irish Freedom*. rev. ed. Tralee: Anvil Books, 1964.

Brennan, Robert. *Allegiance*. Dublin: Browne and Nolan, 1950.

Bromage, Mary C. *De Valera and the March of a Nation*. London: Hutchinson, 1956.

Buckland, Patrick. *Irish Unionism*, vol. 1: *The Anglo-Irish and the New Ireland, 1885 to 1922*. Dublin: Gill and Macmillan, 1972.

———. *Irish Unionism*, vol. 2: *Ulster Unionism and the Origins of Northern Ireland, 1886 to 1922*. Dublin: Gill and Macmillan, 1973.

Callwell, Major General Sir C. E. *Field Marshal Sir Henry Wilson: His Life and Diaries*. Vol. II. London: Cassell, 1927.

Chamberlain, Austen. *Down the Years*. London: Cassell, 1935.

Churchill, Winston S. *The World Crisis, 1918–1928: The Aftermath*. New York: Scribner's, 1929.

———. *Thoughts and Adventures*. London: Butterworth, 1932.

Collins, Michael. *Arguments for the Treaty*. Dublin: Lester, 1922.

———. *The Path to Freedom*. Dublin: Talbot Press, 1922.

Colum, Padraic. *Arthur Griffith*. Dublin: Browne and Nolan, 1959.

Colvin, Ian. *The Life of Lord Carson*. Vols. II and III. London: Gollancz, 1934–1936.

Coogan, Timothy Patrick. *Ireland since the Rising*. New York: Praeger, 1966.

Costigan, Giovanni. "The Anglo-Irish Conflict, 1919–1922: A War of Independence or Systematized Murder," *University Review* (Dublin), V, no. 1, 64–86 (Spring, 1968).

Cronin, Sean, *The McGarrity Papers*. Tralee: Anvil Books, 1972.

Crozier, Frank P. *Ireland Forever*. London: Cape, 1932.

Curran, Joseph M. "Lloyd George and the Irish Settlement, 1921–1922," *Eire–Ireland*, VII, no 2, 14–46 (Summer, 1972).

———. "The Decline and Fall of the IRB," *Eire–Ireland*, X, no. 1, 14–23 (Spring, 1975).

De Burca, Padraig, and John F. Boyle. *Free State or Republic?* Dublin: Talbot Press, 1922.

Dublin's Fighting Story. Tralee: Kerryman Press, 1949.

Duff, Douglas V. *May the Winds Blow*. London: Hollis and Carter, 1948.

Edwards, Owen Dudley and Fergus Pyle (eds.). *1916: The Easter Rising*. London: MacGibbon and Kee, 1968.

Ervine, St. John. *Craigavon Ulsterman*. London: Allen and Unwin, 1949.

Farrell, Brian. *The Founding of Dail Eireann, Parliament and Nation-Building*. Dublin: Gill and Macmillan, 1971.

Figgis, Darrell. *Recollections of the Irish War*. London: Benn, 1927.

Fitzgerald, Desmond. "Mr. Pakenham on the Anglo-Irish Treaty," *Studies* (Dublin), XXIV, pp. 406–14 (September, 1935).

Forester, Margery. *Michael Collins—The Lost Leader*. London: Sidgwick and Jackson, 1971.

Gallagher, Frank. *The Anglo-Irish Treaty*. Ed. Thomas P. O'Neill. London: Hutchinson, 1965.

————. *The Indivisible Island*. London: Gollancz, 1957.

Gleeson, James. *Bloody Sunday*. London: Four Square Books, 1965.

Gogarty, Oliver St. John. *As I Was Going Down Sackville Street*. New York: Reynal and Hitchcock, 1937.

Goldring, Douglas. *Odd Man Out*. London: Chapman and Hall, 1935.

Greaves, C. Desmond. *Liam Mellows and the Irish Revolution*. London: Lawrence and Wishart, 1971.

Gwynn, Denis. *The History of Partition (1912–1925)*. Dublin: Browne and Nolan, 1950.

Hammond, J. L. *C. P. Scott*. London: Bell, 1934.

Hancock, W. K. *Smuts*. vol. II, *The Fields of Force, 1919–1950*. London: Cambridge University Press, 1968.

————. *Survey of British Commonwealth Affairs*. vol. I, *Problems of Nationality, 1918–1936*. London: Oxford University Press, 1937.

Harkness, D. W. *The Restless Dominion: The Irish Free State and the British Commonwealth of Nations, 1921–31*. London: Macmillan, 1969.

Healy, T. M. *Letters and Leaders of My Day*. Vol. II. New York: Stokes, 1929.

The History of the Times. vol. IV: *1912–1948*, pt. II. New York: Macmillan, 1952.

Hobson, Bulmer. *Ireland Yesterday and Tomorrow*. Tralee: Anvil Books, 1968.

Hogan, David (Frank Gallagher). *The Four Glorious Years*. Dublin: Irish Press, 1953.

Holt, Edgar. *Protest in Arms*. London: Putnam, 1960.

Hyde, H. Montgomery. *Carson*. London: Heinemann, 1953.

Jenkins, Roy. *Asquith*. London: Collins, 1965.

Jones, Thomas. *Whitehall Diary*, vol. III: *Ireland, 1918–1925*. Ed. Keith Middlemas. London: Oxford University Press, 1971.

Kee, Robert. *The Green Flag*. New York: Delacorte Press, 1972.

Kohn, Leo. *The Constitution of the Irish Free State*. London: Allen and Unwin, 1932.

Larkin, Emmet. *James Larkin, Irish Labour Leader, 1876–1947*. London: New English Library, 1965.

Lloyd George, David. *Is It Peace?* London: Hodder and Stoughton, 1923.

Longford, Earl of (Frank Pakenham) and Thomas P. O'Neill. *Eamon de Valera*. London: Hutchinson, 1970.

Lynch, Diarmuid. *The I.R.B. and the 1916 Insurrection*. Ed. Florence O'Donoghue. Cork: Mercier Press, 1957.

Lyons, F. S. L. *Ireland Since the Famine*. London: Weidenfeld and Nicolson, 1971.

MacAonghusa, Proinsias and Liam O'Reagain (eds.). *The Best of Pearse*. Cork: Mercier Press, 1967.

Macardle, Dorothy. *The Irish Republic*. 1st American ed. New York: Farrar, Straus and Giroux, 1965.

McCaffrey, Lawrence J. *The Irish Question, 1800–1922*. Lexington: University of Kentucky Press, 1968.

McCracken, J. L. *Representative Government in Ireland, 1919–1948*. London: Oxford University Press, 1958.

MacDonagh, Oliver. *Ireland*. Englewood Cliffs, N.J.: Prentice-Hall, 1968.

MacManus, Francis. *The Years of the Great Test, 1926–1939*. Cork: Mercier Press, 1967.

Macready, General Sir Nevil. *Annals of an Active Life*. Vol. II. London: Hutchinson, 1924.

Mansergh, Nicholas. *The Irish Question, 1840–1921*. Rev. ed. London: Allen and Unwin, 1965.

Martin, F. X. (ed.). *Leaders and Men of the Easter Rising: Dublin 1916*. Ithaca, N.Y.: Cornell University Press, 1967.

Martin, Hugh. *Ireland in Insurrection*. London: O'Connor, 1921.

Middlemas, Keith and John Barnes. *Baldwin, A Biography*. New York: Macmillan, 1970.

Midleton, Earl of. *Records and Reactions, 1856–1939*. London: Murray, 1939.

Miller, David W. *Church, State and Nation in Ireland, 1898–1921*. Pittsburgh: University of Pittsburgh Press, 1973.

Mowat, Charles Loch. *Britain between the Wars, 1918–1940*. Chicago: University of Chicago Press, 1955.

Neeson, Eoin. *The Civil War in Ireland*. Cork: Mercier Press, 1966.

———. *The Life and Death of Michael Collins*. Cork: Mercier Press, 1968.

Neligan, David. *The Spy in the Castle*. London: MacGibbon & Kee, 1968.

Nevinson, H. W. *Last Changes, Last Chances*. London: Nisbet, 1928.

Nicolson, Harold. *King George V: His Life and Reign*. London: Constable, 1952.

Nowlan, Kevin B. (ed.). *The Making of 1916: Studies in the History of the Rising*. Dublin: The Stationery Office, 1969.

O'Brien, Conor Cruise (ed.). *The Shaping of Modern Ireland*. Toronto: University of Toronto Press, 1960.

O'Brien, William. *Forth the Banners Go: Reminiscences as Told to Edward MacLysaght*. Dublin: Three Candles, 1969.

O'Brien, William. "The Irish Free State: [The] Secret History of Its Foundation." Ms. 4,210, National Library of Ireland (Dublin).

———. *The Irish Revolution and How It Came About*. London: Allen and Unwin, 1923.

O'Broin, Leon. *Dublin Castle and the 1916 Rising*, Dublin: Helicon, 1966.

———. *Revolutionary Underground: The Story of the Irish Republican Brotherhood, 1858–1924*. Dublin: Gill and Macmillan, 1976.

O'Connor, Batt. *With Michael Collins in the Fight for Irish Independence*. London: Davies, 1929.

O'Connor, Frank (Michael O'Donovan). *The Big Fellow: Michael Collins and the Irish Revolution*. Rev. ed. Springfield, Ill.: Templegate, 1965.

O'Connor, Sir James. *History of Ireland, 1798–1924.* Vol. II. London: Arnold, 1926.

O'Donnell, Peadar. *The Gates Flew Open.* Cork: Mercier Press, 1965.

———. *There Will Be Another Day.* Dublin: Dolmen Press, 1963.

O'Donoghue, Florence. *No Other Law.* Dublin: Irish Press, 1954.

O'Faolain, Sean. *Vive Moi!* Boston: Little, Brown, 1964.

O'Hegarty, P. S. *A History of Ireland under the Union, 1801–1922.* London: Methuen, 1952.

———. *The Victory of Sinn Fein.* Dublin: Talbot Press, 1924.

O'Higgins, Kevin. *Civil War and the Events Which Led to It.* Dublin: Talbot Press, 1922.

O'Leary, Cornelius. *The Irish Republic.* Notre Dame, Ind.: University of Notre Dame Press, 1961.

O'Malley, Ernie. *Army without Banners* (formerly *On Another Man's Wound*). London: Four Square Books, 1967.

———. *The Singing Flame.* Dublin: Anvil Books, 1978.

O'Sullivan, Donal. *The Irish Free State and Its Senate.* London: Faber and Faber, 1940.

Owen, Frank. *Tempestuous Journey: Lloyd George, His Life and Times.* London: Hutchinson, 1954.

Pakenham, Frank (Lord Longford). *Peace by Ordeal.* 3d ed. London: Chapman, 1962.

"Periscope" (G. C. Duggan). "The Last Days of Dublin Castle," *Blackwood's Magazine* (Edinburgh and London), CCXII, no. 1,282, 137–90 (August, 1922).

Petrie, Sir Charles. *The Life and Letters of the Right Hon. Sir Austen Chamberlain.* Vol. II. London: Cassell, 1940.

Phillips, W. Alison, *The Revolution in Ireland, 1906–1923.* 2d ed. London: Longmans, 1926.

Riddell, Lord. *Intimate Diary of the Peace Conference and After, 1918–1923.* London: Gollancz, 1933.

Robinson, Sir Henry. *Memories: Wise and Otherwise.* London: Cassell, 1923.

Ryan, Desmond. *Remembering Sion.* London: Barker, 1934.

———. *The Rising.* 3d ed. Dublin: Golden Eagle Books, 1957.

———. *Unique Dictator: A Study of Eamon de Valera.* London: Barker, 1936.

Salvidge, Stanley. *Salvidge of Liverpool.* London: Hodder & Stoughton, 1934.

Shakespeare, Sir Geoffrey. *Let Candles Be Brought In.* London: Macdonald, 1949.

Stephens, James. *The Insurrection in Dublin.* 3d ed. Dublin: Scepter Books, 1966.

Stevenson, Frances. *Lloyd George: A Diary.* Ed. A. J. P. Taylor. London: Hutchinson, 1971.

Strauss, Eric. *Irish Nationalism and British Democracy.* New York: Columbia University Press, 1951.

Street, C. J. C. *Ireland in 1921.* London: Allan, 1922.

Taylor, A. J. P. *English History, 1914–1945.* Oxford: Clarendon Press, 1965.

Taylor, Rex. *Assassination.* London: Hutchinson, 1961.

———. *Michael Collins.* London: Hutchinson, 1958.

Thomson, Malcolm. *David Lloyd George.* London: Hutchinson, 1948.

Townshend, Charles. *The British Campaign in Ireland, 1919–1921: The Development of Political and Military Policies.* London: Oxford University Press, 1975.

Wallace, Martin. *Northern Ireland: 50 Years of Self-Government.* Newton Abbot, England: David & Charles, 1971.

Ward, Alan J. *Ireland and Anglo-American Relations, 1899–1921.* London: Weidenfeld and Nicolson, 1969.

Wheeler-Bennett, John W. *John Anderson, Viscount Waverly.* New York: St. Martin's, 1962.

White, Terence de Vere. *Kevin O'Higgins.* London: Methuen, 1948.

Williams, Desmond (ed.). *The Irish Struggle, 1916–1926.* Toronto: University of Toronto Press, 1966.

Wilson, Trevor (ed.). *The Political Diaries of C. P. Scott, 1911–1928.* Ithaca, N.Y.: Cornell University Press, 1970.

Winter, Sir Ormonde. *Winter's Tale.* London: Richards Press, 1955.

Younger, Calton. *Ireland's Civil War.* London: Muller, 1968.

Index